Leadership - Advancing Great Leaders and Leadership

Edited by Joseph Crawford

Published in London, United Kingdom

Leadership - Advancing Great Leaders and Leadership
http://dx.doi.org/10.5772/intechopen.104266
Edited by Joseph Crawford

Contributors
Winsome Mashele, Imhotep Paul Alagidede, Aboubacar Garba Konte, Kumars Ahmadi, Nguyen Thanh Hung, Tom Karp, Hanan AlMazrouei, Majda I. Ayoub/Al-Salim, Marcela Fang, Alberto Abadia, Doris M. Dickerson, Maryam Memar Zadeh, Joseph Crawford, James Williams, Julie Wilson, Lee Ann Avery, Vânia Bessi, Paula Schmitz, Caren Rinker

First published in London, United Kingdom, 2023 by IntechOpen
IntechOpen is the global imprint of INTECHOPEN LIMITED, registered in England and Wales, registration number: 11086078, 5 Princes Gate Court, London, SW7 2QJ, United Kingdom
Printed in Croatia

British Library Cataloguing-in-Publication Data
A catalogue record for this book is available from the British Library

Additional hard and PDF copies can be obtained from orders@intechopen.com

Leadership - Advancing Great Leaders and Leadership
Edited by Joseph Crawford
p. cm.

This title is part of the Business, Management and Economics Book Series, Volume 5
Topic: Business and Management
Series Editor: Taufiq Choudhry
Topic Editor: Vito Bobek and Tatjana Horvat

Print ISBN 978-1-83768-307-9
Online ISBN 978-1-83768-308-6
eBook (PDF) ISBN 978-1-83768-309-3
ISSN 2753-894X

For EU product safety concerns:
IN TECH d.o.o., Prolaz Marije Krucifikse Kozulić 3, 51000 Rijeka, Croatia,
info@intechopen.com or visit our website at intechopen.com.

IntechOpen Book Series

Business, Management and Economics

Volume 5

Aims and Scope of the Series

This series will provide a comprehensive overview of recent research trends in business and management, economics, and marketing. Topics will include asset liability management, financial consequences of the financial crisis and covid-19, financial accounting, mergers and acquisitions, management accounting, SMEs, financial markets, corporate finance and governance, managerial technology and innovation, resource management and sustainable development, social entrepreneurship, corporate responsibility, ethics and accountability, microeconomics, labour economics, macroeconomics, public economics, financial economics, econometrics, direct marketing, creative marketing, internet marketing, market planning and forecasting, brand management, market segmentation and targeting and other topics under business and management. This book series will focus on various aspects of business and management whose in-depth understanding is critical for business and company management to function effectively during this uncertain time of financial crisis, Covid-19 pandemic, and military activity in Europe.

Meet the Series Editor

Prof. Choudhry holds a BSc degree in Economics from the University of Iowa, as well as a Masters and Ph.D. in Applied Economics from Clemson University, USA. In January 2006, he became a Professor of Finance at the University of Southampton Business School. He was previously a Professor of Finance at the University of Bradford Management School. He has over 80 articles published in international finance and economics journals. His research interests and specialties include financial econometrics, financial economics, international economics and finance, housing markets, financial markets, among others.

Meet the Volume Editor

Dr. Joseph Crawford is an award-winning leadership and higher education scholar based at the University of Tasmania, Australia. He is passionate about leaders and how they shape the world around them. He has a Ph.D. in Leadership Psychometrics and works on applying leadership and organizational behavior theory to understanding how students and teachers interact and learn together. He is editor-in-chief of the *Journal of University Teaching and Learning Practice*. Dr. Crawford received the 2021 Vice Chancellor's Award for Innovation for his work in learning and teaching. He has also won national awards for his social entrepreneurship with the sustainable men's grooming products business Fifth Estate Co. and the carbon-negative gin distillery Negative Distillery.

Contents

Preface XIII

Section 1
Introduction 1

Chapter 1 3
Introductory Chapter: Leadership Roles Do Not Exist – The Case of Leaders and Managers
by Joseph Crawford

Section 2
Theoretical Positions 11

Chapter 2 13
Leadership is a Practice Shaped by Everyday Actions in Messy Organisational Realities
by Tom Karp

Chapter 3 29
Leadership Styles during Disruption: A Multi-Case Study
by Alberto Abadia

Chapter 4 49
Emotional Intelligence: Constraints and Possibilities in Leadership Practices
by Doris M. Dickerson

Section 3
Leadership Styles 65

Chapter 5 67
Shepherd Leadership: A Review and Future Research Directions
by Majda I. Ayoub/Al-Salim

Chapter 6 83
Dyadic Relationship Quality (DRQ) – Describing the Development of Leader-Follower Relationship Quality: A Qualitative, Longitudinal Study
by Julie Wilson

Chapter 7 107
An Introduction to High-Reliability Leadership Style in Healthcare
by Maryam Memar Zadeh

Chapter 8 125
Chameleon Leadership and Traits to Serve on a Global Scale
by James Williams

Section 4
Developing Leadership Practices 135

Chapter 9 137
Leadership Coaching to Drive Transformation in the Experience Economy
by Marcela Fang

Chapter 10 157
What Offshore Sailing Captains Teach Us about Leadership
by Lee Ann Avery

Chapter 11 179
When Spotting the Glass Cliff Matters for Women: A Qualitative Study Focusing on Gender Inequalities in Corporate South Africa
by Winsome Mashele and Imhotep Paul Alagidede

Chapter 12 195
Mindfulness in Organizations: The Concept of Mindful Leadership
by Aboubacar Garba Konte

Section 5
Leadership Context 227

Chapter 13 229
Leveraging Leader Relations to Cultivate Brain-Friendly Workplaces
by Kumars Ahmadi

Chapter 14 255
Impact of Human Resource Management Practice on Organizational Performance: The Case of Food Processing Enterprises in Vietnam
by Nguyen Thanh Hung

Chapter 15 275
Authentic Leadership: Supporting Employees' Performance, Creativity, Involvement in Decision-Making and Outcomes
by Hanan AlMazrouei

Chapter 16 293
Perspective Chapter: Creativity in the Work Environment – Reflections on the Role of Management for Creative Individuals Work
by Vânia Bessi, Paula Schmitz and Caren Rinker

Preface

This book aims to bring leadership scholars and those studying leadership-adjacent topics together to consider how we might better cultivate great leadership practices and good leaders.

The first section is the Introduction.

Section 2 provides three theoretical positions on leadership, beginning with Chapter 2 by Tom Karp. Karp discusses how practice-oriented perspectives of leadership often consist of certain patterns of action that are argued to be underdeveloped in leadership research to date. In this chapter, Karp recommends leaders build and develop their own bespoke leadership practice based on the messy and complex organizational reality within which they operate. In Chapter 3, Alberto Abadia examines how the leadership style of nine organizational leaders can be examined using secondary data sources. While a promising approach, Abadia does tend to focus more on positive elements of leadership styles, noting considerable commentary on these leaders is from perspectives of narcissism, unethical behavior, and corporate psychopathy. In Chapter 4, Doris M. Dickerson adopts a similar positive approach to leadership in considering how principals can be inclusive in their leadership approaches to support diversity, equity, and inclusion in their staff and students using emotional intelligence.

The third section introduces four novel leadership styles and considers them across specific contexts. In Chapter 5, Majda I. Ayoub/Al-Salim presents the first leadership approach, perhaps akin to stories in the Alchemist by Paulo Coelho. In shepherd leadership, leaders consider care and compassion in the vision to build intrinsically motivated followers. In Chapter 6, Julie Wilson goes on to expand on the leader–member exchange theory by considering the dyadic relationship quality as a concept. Using longitudinal qualitative research in high-tech start-up companies, the author finds relationship quality to be a key component to the development of relationships rather than purely an outcome. In Chapter 7, Maryam Memar Zadeh highlights the unique challenges hospital and healthcare leaders face in the provision of patient care and introduces the style of high-reliability leadership. This style, while not new, remains in its infancy and this chapter considers the opportunities it may afford in higher quality and more reliable patient care. In Chapter 8, James Williams examines another leadership theory in its infancy, chameleon leadership, and discusses how leaders move through complex environments with adaptability. Interestingly, this theory may act in opposition to some approaches to authentic leadership and may need to be considered more deeply. These approaches, while tending to draw on some empirical data, would benefit from considering approaches to measuring and conceptualizing style dimensions in order to examine their utility and begin developing their nomological networks.

The fourth section focuses on key mechanisms by which leaders might be developed. In Chapter 9, Marcela Fang discusses leadership coaching and leaders-as-coaches within hospitality and tourism enterprises. Using Vietnam as a case study, the author discusses a six-week leadership program and evaluates the efficacy of the development initiative. In Chapter 10, Lee Ann Avery considers an unconventional leadership environment – offshore sailing captains – to consider how these leaders engaged with extreme events during their tenure. The qualitative analysis presents interesting findings about leaders acting in crisis conditions. In Chapter 11, Winsome Mashele and Imhotep Paul Alagidede consider the effect that the glass cliff, and its identification, is having on gender imbalances in leadership across South African organizations. In Chapter 12, Aboubacar Garba Konte presents an analysis of the histories of mindfulness and the organizational research on mindful leaders. The chapter also considers the developmental applications of the mindful leader proposition.

The final section focuses on the application of leadership theory and practice in specific contextual environments. A more recent development in the leadership discipline is a greater focus and emphasis on how context influences the way we lead. In Chapter 13, Kumars Ahmadi explores contemporary neuroscience and organizational behavior literature to consider how seven elements of a leader's context influence their ability to lead teams. These elements include communication, happiness and mobility, ability by self-awareness, respect, purposefulness and focus, security and relaxation, and sleep and rest. In Chapter 14, Nguyen Thanh Hung presents a quantitative study on human resource practices in Vietnam. While not directly a leadership study, the chapter speaks to the role that leaders have in creating organizational commitment and contributing to the corporate social responsibility of an organization. In Chapter 15, Hanan AlMazrouei discusses how authentic leadership can be leveraged to support inclusive participation in decision-making and overall organizational performance. Finally, in Chapter 16, Vania Bessi et al. examine how managers can support employees to engage in effective individual creative projects as part of an organization's mission.

This book aims to create opportunities for scholars to break down current leadership and leaders and conceptualize new ways of being a leader and doing it well. Through constructing and exploring novel approaches to leadership, scholars consider what it means to lead in contexts not always commonly discussed in the leadership literature.

I hope this book supports a thought-provoking journey for its readers.

Dr. Joseph Crawford
University of Tasmania,
Launceston, Australia

Section 1

Introduction

Chapter 1

Introductory Chapter: Leadership Roles Do Not Exist – The Case of Leaders and Managers

Joseph Crawford

1. Introduction

The concept of leadership roles occupies much of the day-to-day organizational dialog. We speak of leadership teams, of the organizational leadership, of the leadership, and of the lack of leadership with great frequency. In practical contexts, these terms are often used as synonymous with what we call managers who can exercise positional power to manage others. When we discuss the 'leadership' of the organization, we often do so without reference to individual character or enactment of leadership. Many refer to 'leadership' indiscriminately, and in reference to those who hold senior positions. Those with *authority*, not those who always have *influence.*

The emphasis on positions of leadership, as I go on to discuss, offers masquerade to individuals whose leader behaviors are uncultivated, and leadership practices not enacted. Allow me to pose a few questions to orient: are all U.S. Presidents leaders? How about all Australian Prime Ministers, Chief Executive Officers, Vice Chancellors, Chairpersons, and Senior Managers? Or are these people whose role affords them authority and social power. The differences between positional power and other forms of power and influence are not new concepts, with French and Raven [1] conceptualizing social power in the 1950s. And these differences remain important in contemporary work and life.

To provide a couple of simple contemporary examples of the conceptual ambiguity, I offer a brief viewing of my Google News feed (on 27 June 2022). In one article, the Pacific Island Forum highlights three Micronesian leaders will join talks with the Fiji Prime Minister. In another, the BBC [2] comments on the European Union leadership being "noticeably lacking". Were either of the articles discussing individuals enacting leadership practices, or people with positions and authority based on that position? In this, those members occupying national management roles (e.g., Prime Ministers and Presidents) may be leaders, they may be enacting leadership. Equal too, they may only be leveraging their own position, and never cultivating or practicing great leadership.

The concept of this book was inspired by early work on the domains of leadership (comprising leader, follower, and relationship: [3, 4]) and on the importance of clear specification in research (e.g., levels of analysis: [5]; construct clarity: [6]). In work on authentic followership [7], colleagues and I extended this conversation to argue that the relationship is best understood as two directional relationships of leadership (leader to follower) and followership (follower to leader). This is important, as it allows researchers to begin to understand how leaders enact influence, and how followers respond.

The importance of this text is in beginning to challenge existing practical and theoretical attitudes towards the nature of leadership. That is, no one inherits a title of leader by meeting the selection criteria at interview for a senior management role. Instead, individuals are appointed to management roles that afford opportunities to enact leadership using their own leader behaviors and self. This distinction may seem theoretical on face value, but there are key differences from a practical perspective. It explains moments when individuals are promoted because of their technical competency and struggle to achieve as managers. Their leader behaviors were underdeveloped, and their leadership enactment under-practiced. It also allows practitioners and scholars to identify those in positions of authority who are good leaders.

Wilson and Newstead [8] use a virtue-based leader behavior analysis on female heads of state and their enactment of leadership during the COVID-19 crisis. This study highlights that while individuals hold positions of power, their effectiveness is based in-part on how their values, behaviors, and character as leaders are leveraged. Granted, positions of power offer opportunities to magnify leadership potency... but they do not guarantee it.

This book seeks to allow opportunities for scholars to highlight research that focuses on enabling good leaders and/or great leadership. Scholars writing this text have been asked to avoid conflating the use of position as synonymous with leader or leadership. In doing so, each seeks to extend their current understanding and advance a scholarly position in opposition to positional leadership. To further strengthen and clarify this position, the remainder of this introduction seeks to provide conceptual clarity across three related domains. First, I discuss the difference between influence, power, and authority as key foundations that leading has been defined from. Second, I discuss the conceptual and practical differences between leaders and managers and highlight their convergence and independence. Third, I discuss the differences between good leaders and great leadership. I conclude this chapter with a lens by which to view this book as readers progress through either chronologically or in self-selected sequence.

2. Influence, power, and authority

There are many scholars who before me have sought to define differences in influence, power, manipulation, authority, coercion, among others.

Kellerman [9] argues that power is the capacity of one individual to get another individual to do what they want, regardless of means. Machiavelli Niccolò [10] would perhaps agree, with his text *The Prince* articulating individuals whose primary role it was to obtain and keep power, without regard for consequence. Authority is the likelihood of commands being obeyed by the target individual [11]. The key difference between power and authority seems to be that power is without consent or against someone's will, and authority relates to position [11].

Leadership, however, is directed towards informal influence leveraged in communication processes to achieve a desired outcome (or work towards it). Yukl [12] broadly defined leadership as:

> *The process of influencing others to understand and agree about what needs to be done and how to do it, and the process of facilitating individual and collective efforts to accomplish shared objectives.*

More recently, colleagues and I defined informal influence in the context of authentic leader behaviors:

> *Informal influence is the ability to inspire and motivate individuals to accomplish goals of their own volition, regardless of rank or position [13].*

This book focuses less on the practices of Princes, and the exertion of power over others, and instead on individuals and their practices of influence. As I go on to discuss further, the chapters featured share a pursuit of these individuals being good, and their practices great.

3. The difference between leaders and managers

As has been highlighted briefly, the managerial and leadership differences are not always easy to distinguish. The core difference is often self-referential, and more tangible as an individual enacting leadership (the process of influencing) when stepping into management roles. An individual can also enact management skills (the process of authority) when moving into those management roles. It is worth considering from a practical perspective.

> *John is a high performing barista in a fast-paced café business with five individual cafés across the city. He, because of his coffee-making competency is promoted to store manager[1]. Because he is not trained to be an effective leader he emulates the previous manager's style; to use the new position to require his subordinates to meet their team objectives. In this model, the organization receives a less capable manager and loses a high performing front-line staff member. John uses managerial practices to ensure staff meet their objectives, but often requires changes in salary or extrinsic motivators to cultivate continued performance gains.*
>
> *Sam is an acceptable barista, in a different store, but not the best. People gravitate to her, and she cultivates high quality relationships with those around her. When staff feel uncomfortable speaking to their manager about issues, they reach out to her. She informally mentors some team members to make better coffee, and recognizes that many of her colleagues are far more effective at making coffee than her. She is promoted based on her ability to influence informally, even without a position, and she continues to deploy informal influence in her formal management role. This leads to far greater creativity, job satisfaction, and productivity as Sam supports staff to develop their intrinsic motivation for making great coffee.*

In these cases, the key difference is in how they influence their staff to achieve, and how they cultivate team performance. Another difference might include how they build and communicate a vision for the future, and how they bring subordinates into this vision. However, management outcomes tend to be shorter in time frame and often emulate activities described in transactional leadership [15]. Or put simply, using resource deployment – like wages – and to encourage action. Managerialism is often the practice of enumerating these 'motivators' into the bureaucracy's policies and procedures [16], whereas an outcome of effective leadership can often be a lesser need for heavy deontological frameworks applied in organizations. Instead, leaders

[1] see a later chapter on this 'technical promotion': [14]

might spend more time building capability in individuals as a key antecedent to organizational performance.

4. Good leaders and great leadership

Good leaders are individuals who enact leadership, and much of the study of leaders has focused on effective leadership styles and personality. I borrow the term good leaders from Toby Newstead and colleagues where they highlights some key differences in good leaders and leadership:

> *When it comes to leader and leadership development, we argue that it is not simply influence that we should aim to develop. Rather, we suggest that we should seek to connect leaders to the best versions of themselves, to enable leaders to foster meaningful relationships with their counterparts, and to engage effectively and ethically with their organizations, communities, society, and the environment. In other words, we should seek to develop good leaders who engage in good leadership practices [17].*

Interestingly, at its core, leadership does not typically have judgment of 'good' or 'bad attached. Instead practices of influence can be cultivated in the context of achieving normatively unethical or ethical outcomes. And, in many cases, it may not always be clear what the ethical orientation of an action is, given its ethicality may be viewed quite differently by the actor, and those around them.

Styles of unethical leadership include concepts such as corporate psychopaths [18], dark leadership [19], Machiavellian leadership [20], toxic leadership [21], among others. These styles, while not good leadership, explain how leaders act in negative contexts. I argue that these styles are often 'low' performance on a positive leadership style rather than inherently new practices of leadership. Rego et al. [20] discuss the authenticity-Machiavellian grid whereby Machiavellian leadership is considered to exist when authentic leadership is low.

In the study of good leaders and great leadership, taking a positive organizational scholarship (see [22]) does not diminish the importance of understanding conditions when leadership performance is low. Instead, leadership scholars have a critical opportunity to develop solutions to unethical leadership by cultivating good leaders and great leadership. This book focuses on the latter two.

5. Close

Across this book there are stories of leaders across the globe seeking to do, and be, good. The pursuit of this book is to provide a readable tome that supports scholars to upskill in leadership, and likewise practitioners to develop a stronger understanding of leaders and managers. Across the book there will unique leadership contexts drawn upon with diverse methods of data collection, analysis, and synthesis. However, each will be pursuing the expansion of a common theme. That common theme is to support the emergence and understanding of the good leader and of their practices towards great leadership. This may involve using manager-subordinate samples, as is commonplace in leadership research, however they are not the only way to study leaders in context. This text and its comprised chapters offer a thought-provoking curation of possible directions in leadership, and seeks to extend the current knowledge on the nature of leaders *and* leadership.

Conflict of interest

The author declares no conflict of interest.

Author details

Joseph Crawford
University of Tasmania, Launceston, Australia

*Address all correspondence to: joseph.crawford@utas.edu.au

References

[1] French J, Raven B. The bases of social power. In: Cartwright D, editor. Studies in Social Power. Ann Arbor, MI: Institute for Social Research; 1959. pp. 150-167

[2] BBC. Ukraine war: Where's Europe's leadership in crisis with Russia? BBC News. Viewed 27 June 2022. 2022. Available from: https://www.bbc.com/news/world-europe-61904360

[3] Day D, Fleenor J, Atwater L, Sturm R, McKee R. Advances in leader and leadership development: A review of 25 years of research and theory. The Leadership Quarterly. 2014;**25**(1):63-82

[4] Graen G, Uhl-Bien M. Relationship-based approach to leadership: Development of leader-member exchange (LMX) theory of leadership over 25 years: Applying a multi-level multi-domain perspective. The Leadership Quarterly. 1995;**6**(2):219-247

[5] Klein K, Dansereau F, Hall R. Levels issues in theory development, data collection and analysis. Academy of Management Review. 1994;**19**(2):195-229

[6] Suddaby R, editor. Editor's comments: Construct clarity in theories of management and organization. Academy of Management Review. 2010;**35**(3):346-357

[7] Crawford J, Dawkins S, Martin A, LewisG.Conceptualisingauthenticfollowers and developing a future research agenda. In: Cotter-Lockard D, editor. Authentic Leadership and Followership. Cham: Palgrave Macmillan; 2018. pp. 271-293

[8] Wilson S, Newstead T. The virtues of effective crisis leadership: What managers can learn from how women heads of state led in the first wave of COVID-19. Organizational Dynamics. 2022 Advanced Online Publication

[9] Kellerman B. The End of Leadership. New York: HarperCollins; 2012

[10] Machiavelli N. The Prince. England: Harmondsworth; 1981. 1469-1527

[11] Grimes AJ. Authority, power, influence and social control: A theoretical synthesis. Academy of Management Review. 1978;**3**(4):724-735

[12] Yukl G. Leadership in Organisations. Albany, NY: Prentice Hall; State University of New York; 2013

[13] Crawford JA, Dawkins S, Martin A, Lewis G. Putting the leader back into authentic leadership: Reconceptualising and rethinking leaders. Australian Journal of Management. 2020;**45**(1):114-133

[14] Crawford J. On technical promotion: Is it time to promote based on leadership potency. In: Crawford J, editor. Leadership – Advancing Great Leadership Practices and Good Leaders. London: InTech Open; 2023

[15] Bass BM, Avolio BJ, Jung DI, Berson Y. Predicting unit performance by assessing transformational and transactional leadership. Journal of Applied Psychology. 2003;**88**(2):207

[16] Maor M. The paradox of managerialism. Public Administration Review. 1999;**59**(1):5-18

[17] Newstead T, Dawkins S, Macklin R, Martin A. We don't need more leaders– We need more good leaders. Advancing a virtues-based approach to leader (ship) development. The Leadership Quarterly. 2021;**32**(5):101312

[18] Mathieu C, Neumann C, Hare R, Babiak P. A dark side of leadership: Corporate psychopathy and its influence on employee well-being and job satisfaction. Personality and Individual Differences. 2014;**59**:83-88

[19] Conger JA. The dark side of leadership. Organizational Dynamics. 1990;**19**(2):44-55

[20] Rego P, Lopes M, Simpson A. The authentic-Machiavellian leadership grid: A typology of leadership styles. Journal of Leadership Studies. 2017;**11**(2):48-51

[21] Mehta S, Maheshwari G. Consequence of toxic leadership on employee job satisfaction and organizational commitment. Journal of Contemporary Management Research. 2013;**8**(2):1-23

[22] Cameron K, Dutton J, editors. Positive organizational scholarship: Foundations of a new discipline. San Francisco, California: Berrett-Koehler Publishers; 2003

Section 2

Theoretical Positions

Chapter 2

Leadership is a Practice Shaped by Everyday Actions in Messy Organisational Realities

Tom Karp

Abstract

Practice-oriented perspectives of leadership suggest that we should relate more to organisational realities as they are 'in practice'. This entails studying patterns of actions with a certain form, direction, purpose or objective. Leadership researchers have not often focused on conducting empirical studies of everyday life and challenges within organisations, which may have contributed to a possible gap between theory and leadership practice. Thus, there is a need for other perspectives, both for researchers and leaders. Rather than presenting idealised notions of what leaders should do, the premise of practice perspectives is that leadership is shaped through leaders' actions in their everyday environments. The sum of such actions over time constitutes a practice that takes place within a community of collective practice. This entails leadership is understood as a function, a process and an action. Accordingly, research into practice is not so much concerned with identifying normative models and characteristics of the individual but rather shifts the focus from the individual to processes and actions. For leaders, this means that they must develop their own leadership practice regarding how to deal with organisational realities, their messiness and complexity.

Keywords: leadership, practice, everyday interactions, power, processes

1. Introduction

A leader in an MBA course recently explained that he spent most of his day reacting to events, dealing with ad-hoc problems, finding resources and prioritising tasks without knowing whether his actions contributed to the overall objectives set by the organisation. He had not found much help in textbooks or from the many leadership development courses he had taken. He had learned, at least in theory, about how to be transformational, authentic, inspire trust, serve others and exhibit empathic understanding and emotional intelligence. He, therefore, asked me why there is such a gap between the normative ideals and the realities often experienced by leaders in everyday organisational life. Frustrated, he asked, *'Is it only me who experiences this, or is it a structural or systemic problem?'* He is not alone, and this is a common challenge for many leaders. They often discover that leadership theories and abstract models do not help them in dealing with everyday organisational challenges and are left with little support from leadership research and leadership development programmes.

Some, therefore, question whether the best available evidence-based knowledge is used when theorising and practicing leadership [1].

Practice-oriented perspectives on leadership are premised on other perspectives, both in theory and in practice, suggesting that researchers and leaders should pay more attention to real-life organisational realities. In this chapter, I, therefore, examine which practice-oriented perspectives can contribute to the field of leadership and which implications this would have for research into, as well as the exercise of leadership within organisations. Within a range of disciplines, the growing interest in studying practice as a social phenomenon reflects a desire to move away from the restrictions imposed by dualisms, such as subject/object, structure/actor, head/body, thinking/doing, individual/social structure, leader/follower, leader/manager and explicit/implicit. The objective is to contribute new perspectives of what constitutes and creates social systems and thus practice with all its movement, dynamics, relationships, reflections, learning, development and knowledge. To the extent that there is an underlying premise, it is that knowledge about people and people as participants in various activities is in continuous development.

Eikeland [2] claims that practice involves patterns of actions with a certain form, direction, purpose, or objective. It is the patterns that indicate 'the ways of doing things' and, in this context, the ways of leading. Several leadership scholars [3–6] have argued that leadership should be understood, researched, and exercised as a practice. Practice-oriented perspectives in leadership indicate that we should relate more to organisational realities as they are 'in practice and in doing, so leadership is a way of doing things in organisations as the exercise of a practice. In fields, such as philosophy, sociology, psychology, anthropology, and technology, there has been a growing interest in recent years in the concept of practice and in studying practice as a social phenomenon (e.g., see [7–13]). Practical knowledge of different forms, as well as the importance of practical knowledge, have been examined since the time of ancient Greece. For both Aristotle and Socrates, practical experience and wisdom were viewed as important when attempting to understand theoretical and professional knowledge [14]. Moreover, the concept of practice has been broadly applied in Marxist philosophy. Marx believed that theory and practice were mutually dependent and had a reciprocal influence on each other. In the humanities in general—and organisational research in particular—practice-oriented studies gained traction during the 1990s. In particular, the field attracted interest in the areas of organisational learning and knowledge management. Researchers emphasised that knowledge could not be separated from action and instead discussed dynamic and social constructs, such as knowledge in practice [15].

However, Barley and Kunda [16] have pointed out that leadership researchers have been less concerned with conducting empirical studies of everyday life within organisations and regarding what leaders actually do. This may have contributed to a possible gap between theory and practice; however, recently, studies have been conducted that focus on leaders' everyday situations and their practices. Rather than presenting idealised notions of what leaders should do, the premise is that leadership is shaped through leaders' actions in their everyday environments. The sum of leadership actions over time constitutes a practice that takes place within a community of practice. This means that leadership is a process and action, and to a certain extent, these elements are disconnected. Accordingly, research into practice is not particularly concerned with identifying individual characteristics and normative models, and thus the focus is shifted from the individual to processes and actions. This positions and this research direction as an alternative to conventional understandings of leadership, which attach importance to a leader's personal characteristics and the importance of the leader's sole actions. Practice-oriented perspectives are also an alternative to neo-charismatic theories. In addition, practice-oriented perspectives add important critical perspectives, and in doing so, they challenge the growing 'managerialism' within leadership studies [17].

In this chapter, I first present the most important theoretical foundations for studying and performing leadership as a practice. Thereafter, the importance of power and its implications for studying practice are discussed. I then discuss the knowing aspect of practicing leadership before considering how leaders should develop their leadership practice. Implications for researching practice are thereafter examined. The chapter concludes with the central arguments for investigating and conducting research on leadership as a practice.

2. The practice turn in leadership

Carlson [18], Mintzberg [19, 20] and Kotter [21] have conducted insightful studies regarding what leaders actually do during their day-to-day activities, and they have established some of the grounds for practice-oriented leadership studies. Also worth mentioning is Luthans, Rosenkrantz and Hennessey's [22] quantitative and qualitative study over a two-week period of 52 leaders in three organisations. These researchers determined empirically which activities successful leaders perform, such as politicking, networking and conflict management, rather than what they were theoretically supposed to do.

More recent studies on leadership in practice have largely concentrated on the behaviour of leaders in everyday settings. Findings include the pressures and expectations leaders face, the complex and often ambiguous work environment, the uncertainty leaders must deal with the hectic pace, the processual and adaptive ways of leadership work, the collectiveness of leadership and the informal and symbolic activities leaders need to engage in to succeed [5]. Research suggests that successful leaders are more efficient than less successful leaders in improvising, learning from experience, recognising opportunities and taking advantage of serendipities. Researchers have also pointed to the challenging realities within organisations that leaders often must deal with to succeed, though these realities are rarely discussed in textbooks and research articles. This includes demanding everyday challenges, such as confusion, emotions, politicking, dubious ethics and selfish behaviour, often observed in organisations.

The practice turn in leadership has also given rise to a specific research direction, commonly referred to as 'leadership-as-practice' (L-A-P). The premise comprises the processes and actions with a form of direction, purpose, or meaning that determine whether leadership is exercised. Leadership is exercised through the conversations and discussions that take place between people and the patterns that develop over time between those involved in collaborative working. Crevani, Lindgren and Packendorff [23] hence argue that leadership researchers need to place the analytical focus on leadership as it is practiced in daily interactions rather than on individual leaders. They claim that leadership should be understood as processes, practices and interactions, and the empirical study of leadership should be based on process ontology. Leadership emerges from social practices rather than from the mind of an individual. One should, therefore, focus on leadership in activities rather than on the traits and heroics of individual actors [24].

Nevertheless, practice-oriented research is still scarce. This has led to the critique that some of the claims made by L-A-P researchers have less substantial supporting evidence and that nothing new is presented that is not already addressed in studies of post-heroic leadership [25]; however, some recent empirical research exists. Findings show that leadership is not only contextually influenced but also context-producing practice in which the leader's micro-actions are important for context and overall success [26]. Researchers have also shown how different types of talk relate to different phases of leadership practice [27]. Other findings highlight power differences and demonstrate that participants are not given equal scope to exercise power within the emerging and hybrid agency orienting the flow of leadership [28].

Practice-oriented perspectives are broader in scope than presented in L-A-P. Moreover, a common theoretical framework has not been established. Nonetheless, the various practice-oriented research directions and studies do have some features in common. First, researchers attach more importance to how framework conditions, guidelines and contexts influence the exercise of leadership. Second, researchers are more concerned with how leadership is shaped through actions in everyday organisational operations. They are also interested in leadership actions, *per se*, and in how people exercise leadership in certain situations. In general, they pay less attention to appointed leadership roles and the qualities that a leader should have and instead focus more on processes and patterns of action. Third, there is a greater focus on realities within organisations, meaning the demanding everyday situations within which organisational groups and leaders operate, and the day-to-day actions that are performed. Fourth, practice-oriented researchers are in most cases not seeking universal truths or normative methods but instead believe that leaders should develop their own practices. In other words, it is a view that leadership emerges through experience and practice, moving from the abstract to the realisation of rehearsed, specific and perfected actions.

A practice-orientation involves a shift from a functional to a process-oriented understanding of leadership. Actions and team-working by and between leaders and co-workers are integrated into structures and contexts. Structures in organisations' social systems become constructed and reconstructed by leaders and co-workers during the team-working process [29]. Accordingly, context, structure and practice become both the medium and the result of their actions and exist because the actors continue to reinforce them. The challenge becomes one of distinguishing between what leaders do when working with others and what it is that they and others do that generates leadership. Often, this includes leadership actions on a micro-level—actions that have little visibility and that do not necessarily have a large immediate impact but that over time can be aggregated to create direction, meaning, cohesion and trust to deliver results within organisations.

For leaders themselves, a focus on practice means that they need to pay attention to their everyday interactions and the context they operate within, and from this, they must learn to identify and develop their own practice in relation to how to handle the challenges of their job. Hence, leaders should develop reflexive knowledge about their own and others' contributions to leadership processes to exercise influence [28]. Leadership happens in everyday work, often in mundane, subtle acts. It is seldom the extraordinary acts that make the difference over time but rather the everyday handling of matters. No one way of leading—no one way of doing leadership work—may be deemed better than others. Rather, there are different ways depending on the individual leader, relationships, structural boundaries and context.

3. Leaders practising leadership

The practice consists of a diverse range of activities that are a function of an understanding of how things should be done and a framework within which one exercises one's practice [30]. In this way, practice comes to constitute interpersonal actions that are organised around and negotiated into existence as part of a shared understanding of 'how things should be done around here' [31]. As discussed, a leadership practice is not so much developed by a leader acting alone but rather by the organisational community and the context in which the leader is a part as well as what the community and context consider acceptable and effective approaches, knowledge and behaviour. The organisational community abides by a shared meaning system regarding language, culture and structure as well as what constitutes acceptable behaviour and attitudes.

Consider the following empirical example from my own research [32]. A leader needs to prioritise different activities during everyday work. A conventional view of leadership suggests that the leader can 'set the direction' instrumentally by determining priorities based on the organisation's objectives. For most leaders, this is a challenging task because it is difficult to see the connection between everyday work activities and the organisation's overarching goals. As a result, many leaders struggle to explain in specific terms how they set a 'direction' [33]. 'Direction' is also an abstract concept that is difficult to correlate to what leaders do during their day-to-day work. Leaders often instead ask themselves and their teams, 'What have we done before in similar situations? What do we know? What do we know less about? Is there something we should know more about before we make a decision? Can we decide now, or should we wait?'

In this example, prioritisations made are therefore a function of experience using the best knowledge available at the time the decision is made coupled with the use of judgement. Leadership practice is thus constituted by specific actions, often on a micro-level. In this case, practice concerns accessing the available knowledge before priorities are made, as this creates organisational movement toward goals. The act of ensuring the quality of the knowledge base over time creates a practice of how the leader, often in collaboration with others, solves organisational challenges. Over time, such actions aggregate into 'a direction'. Eikeland [2], p186 refers to *experiential reality*, which explains how experimental and gradually rehearsed actions make it possible for the practitioner to master them: '*testing and gaining experience, regarding various organisational phenomena; and acquiring the appropriate language, individually and collectively, in relation to patterns of reaction, power, action, interaction, interpretation and thought*'.

Leadership is the interaction between people and environments that emerges through social systems [34]. Contextual factors, such as trends in society, branch of industry, structure, culture, working environment, colleagues and employees, all play a role in the development of leadership practice. Factors such as learning, feedback culture and psychological security affect the community of practice, which in turn provides guidelines for the leader's individual practice. Leadership practice is, therefore, dependent on the knowledge and skills the leader possesses and the context in which he or she operates. This involves having explicit and tacit knowledge of leadership as an activity and process as well as understanding the tasks and processes for which the leader is responsible. Moreover, it requires an understanding of the branch of industry and other contextual knowledge, such as having knowledge of the organisation, its structure and culture and the characteristics of its value creation. Leaders must also possess capabilities to deal with 'the messiness' of organisational life and everyday challenges, politicking, network building, ad-hoc problem solving, improvisation, managing oneself and making decisions under uncertainty whilst maintaining a level of ethics.

Some may claim that such activities are not leadership but management. While this distinction may have its uses, it is problematic because it excludes the important everyday dimensions of leadership. This is also a distinction that some leadership researchers often invoke to legitimise their field and promote the unique aspects of leadership. Leadership takes place in the midst of everyday matters; it is embedded in managerial work rather than distinct from it. Leadership is, therefore, a practice, not the outcome of such [3]. Leaders commonly find that they cannot always rely on available knowledge, systems, rules and procedures but need to deal with problems in '*the swampy lowland where situations are confusing "messes" incapable of technical solutions*' [35], p42. Relevant knowledge and skills needed for leadership are thus determined by the interface between the leader and the environment in which he/she operates [4].

Given a practice orientation of leadership, the *doing* dimension receives more attention than the *being* dimension. This contrasts with the conventional leadership literature that has devoted much space to how and who leaders should *be*, meaning the qualities leaders should possess to be successful; however, this is not necessarily justified. The '*I*' of leadership is often given too much emphasis at the expense of the '*we*' of leadership. Nevertheless, it can be argued that the leader's identity is of interest, though not to the extent of what is emphasised in parts of the literature or a society characterised by individualism. The leader's identity in collaborative practices involves who the leader is in relation to others [36]. The construction and reconstruction of identity occur when leaders do their job as well as when they reflect upon or talk to others about the leadership job. A leader's identity is, therefore, developed both unconsciously because of the work done and consciously via reflective processes. A leadership identity can also legitimise the archetypal aspect of the leadership role, which in turn can be influenced by leadership ethics as well as the professional values and ethics of the organisation for which they work.

4. Power in processes and relations

In leadership, power is commonly understood positionally. Yukl [37] asserts that most definitions of leadership reflect assumptions that include an individual's ability to influence other people to guide, structure and facilitate activities and relationships in a group or organisation. Such activities imply the use of asymmetrical power. His understanding of leadership reflects conventional assumptions about leadership and concerns the ability of the individual leader to influence others as well as the characteristics, qualities and situational understanding that the individual should have to succeed in his/her endeavours; however, practice-oriented perspectives on leadership differ from Yukl's understanding, particularly regarding how much of this influence can be attributed to the appointed leader and the extent to which the individual's specific characteristics or actions equip him/her with the ability and power to influence others.

Undoubtedly, leaders and other influential individuals in organisations exert greater influence than others, either due to position, power relationships, personal characteristics, knowledge or skills or due to situation-specific conditions. Alvesson and colleagues [3], p3 claim that leadership means '*influencing ideas, meanings, understandings and identities of others within an asymmetrical (unequal) relational context'*. The question is whether asymmetry in groups occurs because someone has more power and legitimacy than others or whether it is because processes and power dynamics in groups of people result in the source of influence that alternates depending on position, people, processes, contextual conditions and external events.

Appointed leaders have more power by virtue of their position but not necessarily more legitimacy. This may be due to personal and relational conditions and because power is a dynamic entity [38]. Within leadership, power is often understood as the capacity of a superior to impose his/her will over a subordinate. The party in the position of power can achieve what he/she wants despite opposition [39]; however, the use of power also depends on legitimacy being granted by the people over whom power is wielded [40]. That is, over time, a leader's use of power will be weakened if those who are exposed to the use of power do not perceive it as legitimate. Striking a balance between exerting authority and earning trust is difficult but necessary to lead with legitimacy [41].

Several leadership scholars have shown that leadership is a relational and co-produced process [42–44]. The underlying premise is that power may also operate relationally as well as be embedded in processes [45, 46]. The power lies in interpersonal relations and in the leadership practice that is collectively created in processes by a group that interacts. In other words, power may be a characteristic of interpersonal relationships [47]. Moreover, power differences in relationships need to be legitimised over time. This means that power is dynamic. It is thus a valid assumption that the influence over people in organisations can originate from different sources and may be due to several factors. Appointed leaders as well as others in a working group influence others and the work they do together, and the interaction results in a dynamic process [48, 49]. Many of the activities carried out by leaders are often described as leadership activities because it is the leaders who carry them out [50]; however, such activities are also done by others in working groups or teams, regardless of whether they are appointed leaders. In other words, when people work together in organisations, many may be involved in leadership activities. The execution of such processes in modern organisations is dependent on the position as well as on the knowledge and skills of individuals and the situational conditions and demands.

5. Developing a leadership practice

Leadership development encompasses the interactions between the leader and the social environment. Thus, leadership development is based on the collective capacity of the people in the organisation [51] and needs to be integrated into everyday practices to be effective. Day and colleagues [52] argue that the ongoing practice through day-to-day leadership activities is where the crux of development truly resides. Rather than focusing on implementing better leadership development programmes or classroom lectures, it is more productive to focus on what happens in the everyday lives of leaders as they practice and develop. This entails that leadership is learned on the job and enhanced by a variety of experiences and challenges. Leadership development programmes and classroom experiences may certainly assist in developing a leadership practice. Such learning interventions, when designed to include organisational realities and everyday challenges, can help leaders make meaning of their experience by encouraging them to reflect on it personally and to share it with their colleagues, but the learning must be carried back to the workplace to have an impact on the organisation.

Practice-oriented perspectives on leadership require leaders to have an inquiring relationship with their own day-to-day practices and that of the organisation and its practice community to which they belong. It is not unusual for leaders to create limitations affecting their own behaviour and effectiveness and thus others' behaviour and effectiveness because they resort to familiar patterns for thinking and acting [53]. It is important to challenge their own thought patterns and assumptions. Furthermore, the practice involves the creation, development and adaptation of relevant knowledge and skills to suit the context within which the leader is operating. Therefore, leaders willing to learn and develop tend to become their own 'research objects' and need to acquire a spectrum of knowledge and skills that will allow them to deal with the challenges and opportunities they encounter. This involves the patterns of leadership actions as an activity as well as the actions inner cognitive and emotional aspects [2].

Consider this example. A leader struggles to create good relationships with his/her employees. Conventional understandings of leadership dictate that he/she should be 'relationship-oriented', a characteristic the leader should possess that presumably will enable him/her to effectively lead. Being 'relationship-oriented' is a relevant ambition for many leaders, but what should the leader do specifically? One possible action is to closely examine the relational processes between himself/herself and others. He/she may then find that his/her relationship orientation is affected by a strong need to be 'liked'. If the leader further examines such patterns, he/she may discover that creating professional relationships may involve vulnerability. The leader may realise that he/she must show trust but also endure rejections, receive criticism and be told that he/she is wrong or is not well-liked. Vulnerability is a challenging demand for leaders, and it is not something the leader necessarily associates with a leader's job. It challenges his/her assumptions about leadership. The leader may eventually discover that he/she needs to overcome fears to establish better relationships. These fears may be related to not meeting the expectations of others and oneself, not being liked, making mistakes or losing control. In other words, the leader's leadership is, therefore, not necessarily about being 'relationship-oriented', an abstract skill that says little about the patterns that unfold between people in the workplace, but rather is about facing up to his/her own fear of not being liked. Thus, over time, dealing with this fear may positively influence relationships.

Mastery and the willingness to invest considerable effort in leadership training over time may be important in this context [52, 54, 55]. In this example, mastering leadership is concerned with the leader's ability to deal with workplace relationships, but mastery is applicable to dealing with a wide range of everyday leadership tasks; however, little research has focused on the mastering of leadership, although the literature does provide some answers. Leadership mastery is related to gaining skills and experience in tackling many organisational tasks [56, 57]. That is, it is not enough to complete a university education or to attend various leadership development programmes. Leadership needs to be practiced regularly and over time to achieve mastery. This brings us back to reflexivity as well as to the ability of leaders to be able to accept feedback, possess self-insight and be willing to work on changing their own behaviour. This is a demanding exercise that often results in many leaders not meeting the challenge or not being willing to invest the time and energy in what it takes to master leadership.

The mastery of leadership is also related to leaders' ability to learn, especially the ability to learn from experience and the ability to adapt to changes [58–60]. Studies have pointed out that having a mastery-oriented approach to learning can be effective. Mastery-oriented individuals ask themselves what they want to learn, and they are not afraid to make mistakes [61]. The interplay between cognition, dialogue and the 'inner conversation' influences leaders' experiences, feelings and behaviour. Repetitions turn into thought patterns and attitudes, which in turn affect knowledge and skills. Mastery orientation is also linked to self-efficacy, meaning the belief in one's ability to accomplish various tasks [62, 63].

6. Researching leadership as a practice

The purpose of leadership ought to be continually questioned rather than taken for granted. To advance such questioning, and to advance the practice and study of leadership, the field of leadership research needs to better connect with organisational realities. This is the aim of practice-oriented leadership. Conducting research into leadership practice involves shifting one's focus away from the individual and toward collaborative activities, to what is happening, how things are done, who is doing what and the context in which all this occurs. Crevani and Endrissat [64] argue that the subject of the analysis should be leadership processes and why actions occur. In their opinion, researchers should focus on everyday activities and on what is being done. Accordingly, they recommend that researchers should investigate questions such as: What exactly is leadership work? How is leadership exercised? Where and how is leadership work carried out? What recurrent patterns of actions can be observed? What roles do individuals play? Methodologically, this means investigating leadership as a 'living experience' rather than as a reported experience reproduced by using questionnaires and interviews.

This approach can be operationalised by introducing three elements that are frequently referred to in practice-oriented literature: 'the what, who and how of practice' [65]. This involves studying three different areas: (i) *What*: By examining the actions through which leadership is exercised. These are actions that describe what leaders and employees do, such as staffing, administrative work, operations, strategy planning, implementation of changes, execution of tasks, problem-solving and the social and symbolic activities that take place in organisations; (ii) *Who*: By identifying and describing which people contribute to and are involved in exercising leadership both individually and collectively, including appointed leaders. The purpose is to examine individuals' contributions to what the group does and the degree of influence they have on groups/other people; and (iii) *How*: By examining the activities and actions that constitute leadership, meaning what people in organisations do and how they act. This is done by identifying the recurring patterns that shape interactions in groups, what groups do, what individuals do and the results they achieve. In addition, researchers should study how contextual framework conditions affect these variables as well as how these variables, in turn, affect the context. This involves analysing how certain factors, such as organisational structure, organisational culture, work environment, values, norms, artefacts, budgets and macro conditions, both facilitate and impose restrictions on the work of groups and individuals.

This can be illustrated by using an empirical example of how decisions are made in a group with a leader [32]. The leader may make decisions in meetings with others, using tools, such as digital boards, where it is important that all those participating offer their views before decisions are made. This should follow a fixed routine depending on the type of decision-making. This reflects decision-making in relation to the pattern of activities that govern how a group as well as its leader make decisions. In other words, we have shifted the attention away from the analytic unit 'a leader' to study 'the interactions that are taking place' as well as how the leader influences the process.

The next level of analysis is to understand who is doing what—the purpose is to study the degree of influence that individuals have on the group. Leadership is created in interaction; it is a process but a process where someone leads, while others allow themselves to be led, in the sense that some individuals have more influence on the interaction that takes place. We can then examine what the leader does that supports the processes in the group. For instance, we may observe that he/she initially adopts a somewhat withdrawn role so that everyone is able to have their say before he/she intervenes. We can attempt to identify the type of knowledge or abilities he/she uses when making decisions. We can check whether the leader follows specific routines when making decisions. For instance, when making certain types of decisions, he/she may listen to the views of one or two of the group members, while for other types of decisions, he/she may allow collective ideas to flow freely. In such situations, we may also observe the body language used by the leader. For example, he/she may adopt a stance centrally in the room and use a confident tone of voice when presenting a decision. He/she, therefore, influences others through position-power, whereas knowing this use of power also ensures legitimacy.

The collected data that emerge when the approach and methods described are used will most likely be richer and provide more interesting information than descriptions of the leader and his/her leadership in isolation (for example, see [66]). Alvesson and colleagues [3] express the view that there is a need for more in-depth studies using observations and follow-up discussions over a period of days, even weeks, that involve various actors who can help verify each other's behaviour as well as analyses that focus on understanding the context in which leadership is exercised. Using such a research design, it would be possible to gain a better understanding of how leadership is exercised and avoid falling into the trap of using idealised models that are disconnected from reality. The goal should be to avoid the social fragmentation of everyday experiences by transcending the artificial distinction between theory and practice related to leadership [67]. Eikeland [2] believes that practice-oriented research, in general, has the methodological potential for changing, articulating and defining theory development.

Practice-oriented research thus involves increased use of certain methods, such as auto-ethnography, shadowing, interviews, time studies, observations, and action research as well as multimethod approaches, such as triangulation, to collect, process, analyse and interpret data in addition to using conventional qualitative and quantitative methods. Practice-oriented studies are often more time-consuming and require more analytical work than conventional studies, which may explain why researchers are often reluctant to study practice. It is a demanding approach and entails research that involves a considerable amount of work. Moreover, it is often the case that it is not valued or prioritised by leading leadership journals. Consequently, choosing to conduct practice-oriented research as a research career path will often not result in rapid academic advancement for researchers compared with more time-efficient conventional qualitative and quantitative research. As a result, practice-oriented research is often given less priority by researchers, which may also explain why there are still few practice-oriented studies on leadership.

7. Conclusion

Applying practice-oriented perspectives contributes important insights to the field of leadership studies in relation to theory, empirical findings and methodological

DOI: http://dx.doi.org/10.5772/intechopen.107467

approaches, as well as valuable advice for leaders themselves. These perspectives are applied to build a bridge between theory and practice—a bridge between ideals and reality. Practice-oriented perspectives on leadership comprise a broad spectrum of literature and research but have some shared features. Researchers often attribute greater significance to context and to how it guides and constrains the exercising of leadership. They argue that leadership is also the result of collaboration and collective processes and that the exercise of leadership and the framework conditions for it are created collaboratively. Leadership can be taken on by different people in turn, but someone will be leading, whether it is the appointed leader or someone else. Influence may come from many sources and is dependent on the collaboration that is taking place, power dynamics, group processes and the actions of other actors. Individuals thus can influence the collaboration that determines whether leadership takes place or not, although power differences apply.

Practice-oriented researchers are thus more interested in the process of leadership in relation to everyday organisational operations and day-to-day actions. There is less emphasis on the leadership role and on what leaders as individuals can achieve. Accordingly, there is less focus on describing desirable attributes for a leader but more focus on how the person(s) who want to lead need to develop their own leadership practices, including supportive knowledge and skills. Practice-oriented research involves shifting some attention away from the individual and toward the collaborative activities that are taking place, studying what is happening, how things are done, who is doing what and the context in which it all takes place. The study object comprises everyday operational, tactical and strategic activities as well as what is actually being done. Accordingly, there is a need for in-depth, longitudinal, observational studies.

For leaders, a practice orientation means being aware of their own practices in addition to being aware of the organisational practices of which they are a part. Developing one's own practices means that one will be able to tackle leadership responsibilities as well as develop the ability to influence others. Practice is a function of the knowledge and skills that leaders have developed. Leaders need to find their own leadership approach by experiencing how their activity patterns and the action patterns of others unfold and develop. There is no single best way to lead—no single best leadership practice—that is universally more effective than others. Rather, there are many ways to lead depending on the individual leader, his or her relationships with other people and the context within which he or she exercises leadership.

Author details

Tom Karp
Kristiania University College, Oslo, Norway

*Address all correspondence to: tom.karp@kristiania.no

References

[1] Riggio RE. Introduction: What's wrong with leadership? Improving leadership theory, research, and practice. In: Riggio RE, editor. What's Wrong with Leadership? Improving Leadership Research and Practice. New York: Routledge; 2015. pp. 1-6

[2] Eikeland O. På Sporet av den Syvende Forfatning. Aristoteles og den Norske Samarbeidsmodellen – Makt, Dialog og Organisasjonslæring. Drammen: New Deal Publishing; 2022

[3] Alvesson M, Blom M, Sveningsson S. Reflexive Leadership. Organising in an Imperfect World. London: SAGE; 2017

[4] Mintzberg H. Managing. Harlow: Pearson; 2009

[5] Tengblad S, editor. The Work of Managers. Towards a Practice Theory of Management. Oxford: Oxford University Press; 2012

[6] Raelin JA. Introduction to leadership-as-practice. In: Raelin JA, editor. Leadership-as-Practice. Theory and Application. New York: Routledge; 2016. pp. 1-17

[7] Bourdieu P. Outline of a Theory of Practice. Nice R, Cambridge: Cambridge University Press; 1977

[8] Dreyfus H. Being-in-the-World: a Commentary on Heidegger's Being and Time, division I. Cambridge: MIT Press; 1991

[9] Foucault M. In: Sheridan Smith AM, translator., editors. The Archaeology of Knowledge. New York: Harper and Row; 1976

[10] Giddens A. Central Problems in Social Theory. Berkeley: University of California Press; 1979

[11] Lyotard JF. In: Bennington G, Massumi B, translators., editors. The Postmodern Condition: A Report on Knowledge. Minneapolis: University of Minnesota Press; 1984

[12] Taylor C. Philosophy and the Human Sciences. Collected Papers. Vol. 2. Cambridge: Cambridge University Press; 1985

[13] Wittgenstein L. Philosophical Investigations. Anscombe GEM, Translator. Oxford: Blackwell; 1953

[14] Eikeland O. Demokrati og Medvirkning Under et nytt Kunnskapsforvaltningsregime – tre foredrag. Oslo: Arbeidsforskningsinstituttet; 1997

[15] Lave J, Wenger E. Situert Læring og Andre Tekster. København: Reitzels Forlag; 2003

[16] Barley SR, Kunda G. Bringing work back in. Organization Science. 2001;**12**(1):76-95

[17] Enteman WF. Managerialism: The Emergence of a New Ideology. Madison: University of Wisconsin Press; 1993

[18] Carlson S. Executive Behaviour. A Study of the Workload and the Working Methods of Managing Directors. Stockholm: Strömbergs; 1951

[19] Mintzberg H. The Nature of Managerial Work. New York: Harper and Row; 1973

[20] Mintzberg H. The manager's job: Folklore and fact. Harvard Business Review. 1975;**53**(4):49-61

[21] Kotter JP. What leaders really do. Harvard Business Review. 1982;**60**(3):156-167

[22] Luthans F, Rosenkrantz SA, Hennessey HW. J What do successful leaders really do? An observation study of managerial activities. The Journal of Applied Behavioral Science. 1985;**21**(3):255-270

[23] Crevani L, Lindgren M, Packendorff J. Leadership, not leaders: On the study of leadership as practices and interactions. Scandinavian Journal of Management. 2010;**26**(1):77-86

[24] Raelin JA. From leadership-as-practice to leaderful practice. Leadership. 2011;**7**(2):195-211

[25] Collinson M. What's new about leadership-as-practice? Leadership. 2018;**14**(3):363-370

[26] Endrissat N, von Arx W. Leadership practices and context: Two sides of the same coin. Leadership. 2013;**9**(2):278-304

[27] Simpson B, Buchan L, Sillince J. The performativity of leadership talk. Leadership. 2018;**14**(6):644-661

[28] Case P, Śliwa M. Leadership learning, power and practice in Laos: A leadership-as-practice perspective. Learning Management. 2020;**51**(5):537-558

[29] Giddens A. Sociology. 4th ed. Cambridge: Polity Press; 2001

[30] Schatzki TR. Practice theory. In: Schatzki TR, Cetian KK, Von Savigny E. The Practice Turn in Contemporary Theory. Oxford: Routledge; 2001. p. 1-14

[31] Gherardi S. Introduction: The critical power of the 'practice lens'. Learning Management. 2009;**40**(2):115-128

[32] Karp T, Filstad C, Glomseth R. 27 Days of managerial work in the police service. Police Pract and Research. 2018;**20**(5):427-443

[33] Alvesson M, Sveningsson S. The great disappearing act: Difficulties in doing 'leadership'. The Leadership Quarterly. 2003;**14**(3):359-381

[34] Day DV. Leadership development: A review in context. The Leadership Quarterly. 2000;**11**(4):581-613

[35] Schön DA. The Reflective Practitioner: How Professionals Think in Action. New York: Basic Books; 1983

[36] Cunliffe A. A Very Short, Fairly Interesting and Reasonably Cheap Book about Management. 3rd ed. London: SAGE; 2021

[37] Yukl G. Leadership in Organizations. 8th ed. New Jersey: Pearson; 2013

[38] Hindess B. Discourses of Power. From Hobbes to Foucault. Oxford: Blackwell Publishers; 1996

[39] Weber M. Wirtschaft und Gesellschaft; Grundriss der Sozialokomomik, Abteilung III. Tubingen: Verlag von J. C. B. Mohr; 1925

[40] Engelstad F. Hva er Makt. Oslo: Universitetsforlaget; 2005

[41] Sørhaug T. Om Ledelse. Makt og tillit i Moderne Organisering. Oslo: Universitetsforlaget; 1996

[42] Uhl-Bien M. Relational leadership theory: Exploring the social processes of leadership and organizing. The Leadership Quarterly. 2006;**17**(6):654-676

[43] Osborn RN, Hunt JG, Jauch LR. Towards a contextual theory of leadership. The Leadership Quarterly. 2002;**13**(6):797-837

[44] Karp T. Co-production of leadership activities: a micro-level perspective on human interaction in public sector organisations. In: Overgaard Thomassen A, Jensen JB, editors. Processual Perspectives on the Co-Production Turn in Public Sector Organizations. Hershey, PA: IGI Global; 2021. pp. 80-99

[45] Foucault M. The subject and power. In: Dreyfus HL, Rabinow P, editors. Michael Foucault: Beyond Structuralism and Hermeneutics. New York: Harvester Wheatsheaf; 1983. pp. 208-226

[46] Elias N. The Civilizing Process. Oxford: Blackwell; 2000

[47] Dahl R. The concept of power. Behavioral Science. 1957;**2**(3):201-205

[48] Hernes T. A Process Theory of Organization. Oxford: Oxford University Press; 2014

[49] Uhl-Bien M, Marion R, McKelvey B. Complexity leadership theory: Shifting leadership from the industrial age to the knowledge era. The Leadership Quarterly. 2007;**18**(4):298-318

[50] Alvesson M, Sveningsson S. Managers doing leadership: The extra-ordinarization of the mundane. Human Relations; Studies Towards the Integration of the Social Sciences. 2003;**56**(12):1435-1459

[51] Marion R, Uhl-Bien M. Leadership in complex organizations. The Leadership Quarterly. 2001;**12**(4):389-418

[52] Day DV, Fleenor JW, Atwater LE, Sturm RE, McKee RA. Advances in leader and leadership development: A review of 25 years of research and theory. The Leadership Quarterly. 2014;**25**(1):63-82

[53] Turesky EF, Gallagher D. Know thyself: Coaching for leadership using Kolb's experiental learning theory. Coaching Psychology. 2011;**7**(1):5-14

[54] Karp T. Lede Godt Nok. Hva ledere gjør i praksis. Oslo: Cappelen Damm Akademisk; 2019

[55] Manger T, Wormnes B. Motivasjon og Mestring. 2nd ed. Bergen: Fagbokforlaget; 2015

[56] Howe MJA. A teacher's Guide to the Psychology of Learning. 2nd ed. Oxford: Blackwell Publishers; 1999

[57] Raaheim K. Problem Solving and Intelligence. Oslo: Universitetsforlaget; 1974

[58] Argyris C. Teaching smart people how to learn. Harvard Business Review. 1991;**69**(3):99-109

[59] Dechant K. Knowing how to learn: The neglected management ability. The Journal of Management Development. 1990;**9**(4):40-49

[60] Marshall-Mies JC, Fleishman EA, Martin JA, Zaccaro SJ, Baughman WA, McGee ML. Development and evaluation of cognitive and metacognitive measures for predicting leadership potential. The Leadership Quarterly. 2000;**11**(1):135-153

[61] Covington MV, Beery R. Self-worth and School Learning. New York: Holt, Rinehart & Winston; 1976

[62] Stajkovic AD, Luthans F. Self-efficacy and work-related performance: A meta-analysis. Psychological Bulletin. 1998;**124**(2):240-261

[63] Bandura A. Perceived self-efficacy in cognitive development and functioning. Educational Psychologist. 1993;**28**(2):117-148

[64] Crevani L, Endrissat N. Mapping the leadership-as-practice terrain.

Comparative elements. In: Raelin JA, editor. Leadership-as-Practice. Theory and Application. New York: Routledge; 2016. pp. 21-49

[65] Jarzabkowski P, Kaplan S, Seidl D, Whittington R. If you aren't talking about practices, don't call it a practice-based view: Rejoinder to Bromiley and Rau in strategic organization. Strategic Organization. 2016;**14**(3):270-274

[66] Kempster S, Gregory S. 'Should I stay or should I go?' Exploring leadership-as-practice in the middle management role. Leadership. 2015;**13**(4):496-515

[67] Rowbotham S, Segal L, Wainwright S. Beyond the Fragments: Feminism and the Making of Socialism. London: Merlin Press; 1979

Chapter 3

Leadership Styles during Disruption: A Multi-Case Study

Alberto Abadia

Abstract

This chapter reviews relevant literature in order to identify the leadership framework and profile that may better characterize entrepreneurs and business leaders that eventually founded or developed disruptively successful firms—popularly known as "unicorns." Next, the chapter describes a conducted multi-case study that demonstrates a strong correlation between the positive checkmarks in the selected leadership framework—visionary leadership—and the profile of the leaders of nine different international corporations that became industry leaders in less than 20 years (Apple, Google, Microsoft, Facebook, General Electrics, Toyota, Alibaba, Tencent, and Inditex).

Keywords: leadership, visionary leadership, visionary, disruptive success, disruptive innovation, discontinuous innovation, revolutionary innovation, entrepreneurship, multi-case study on leadership, unicorn

1. Introduction

During the last two decades, there is an increasing number of leadership theories and frameworks. However, less work has been done in terms of determining which frameworks would suit better some particular organizational outputs. The study described in this chapter explores how some leadership models may be linked to some exceptional occurrences, such as "disruptive success." This label can be applied to startups or more mature—but not yet elite—companies that, at some point, grew fast and became world leaders in a period of less than 20 years.

After giving a quick review of state-of-the-art of the leadership research and theories [1], this chapter shortlists, briefly explains, and finally analyzes the candidate frameworks and chooses the apparently most suitable one. Next, the chapter describes a conducted multi-case study that tested the actual possible correlation between the chosen leadership framework and the profile of the leaders of their "disruptively successful" corporations. The option of the multi-case approach for the testing is the most fitting in the explained context, given the limited number of possible samples and the unquantifiable nature of the analysis. The other most plausible alternative option, direct interviews or direct surveys, would not have been doable, given the challenge of obtaining response from a large number of highly profiled business leaders.

2. Theoretical framework: leadership styles

The article "Leadership theory and research in the new millennium: Current theoretical trends and changing perspectives" [1] provides a review of the state-of-the-art research in terms of leadership research of the last two decades, including most of the theories and frameworks, except that of visionary leadership, which has anyway been included in the analysis [2]. Taking into consideration the profile that could be expected in the context of startups and an innovation-led context [1–3], best framework candidates for further evaluation would be (1) transformational leadership, (2) charismatic leadership, (3) entrepreneurial leadership, and (4) visionary leadership.

2.1 Transformational leadership

The concept of transformational leadership was introduced by James MacGregor Burns in his book Leadership [4] and then further developed in Transforming Leadership: A New Pursuit of Happiness [5]. Another researcher, Bernard M. Bass, expanded on Burns' work by describing the psychological mechanisms behind transforming leadership. He applied the term "transformational" instead of "transforming." Bass argued that transformational leadership has four constitutive parts [6, 7] which are (1) idealized influence, (2) inspirational motivation, (3) intellectual stimulation, and (4) individualized consideration. On the opposite, transactional leaders, which frequently are less successful in terms of outcomes [5], usually adopt four possible approaches which are (1) contingency reward—rewards in exchange of support, (2) management by exception (active)—monitoring and just acting when a corrective deed is necessary, (3) management by exception (passive)—no monitoring and just acting when a corrective deed is necessary, and (4) laissez faire—leadership avoidance [6, 7].

2.2 Charismatic leadership

Long ago, Max Weber described charismatic authority in his book Economy and Society [8], where he identified it as one of three types of legitimate domination. According to Weber, charisma is defined as a set of qualities in a person that allows him or her "to be set apart from ordinary people and treated as endowed with supernatural, superhuman, or at least specifically exceptional powers or qualities ... regarded as of divine origin or as exemplary, and on the basis of them the individual concerned is treated as a leader" [8]. A charismatic leader is a person, who has the ability to influence people and who, consequently, has some controlling power over them [9]. A widely accepted framework developed and tested by Conger and Kanungo [10–13] defines four characteristics in charismatic leaders: (1) possessing and articulating a vision, (2) willing to take risk to achieve the vision, (3) exhibiting sensibility to the needs of followers, and (4) demonstrating noble behavior.

2.3 Entrepreneurial leadership

The definition of entrepreneurial leadership can be traced back to different theories about entrepreneurship [14], entrepreneurial orientation [15, 16], and entrepreneurial management [16]. "Entrepreneurial Leadership is that leadership that creates visionary scenarios that are used to assemble and mobilize a 'supporting cast' of participants who become committed by the vision to the discovery and exploitation of strategic value creation" [17]. The article "Entrepreneurial leadership: developing and measuring a cross-cultural construct" [17] compares all the theories about leadership and entrepreneurship. In the case of entrepreneurial leadership, Gupta, MacMillan, and Surie came up with a list of 19 leadership attributes that appeared to be the most relevant [17]. They grouped the remaining attributes into two "enactments" and five roles that would help the analysis in case that this one is the chosen leadership framework [17].

2.4 Visionary leadership

"Visionary leaders are those who inspire extraordinary levels of achievement in followers through an inspiring vision and through other behaviors" [2]. The article "Characteristics of Visionary Leadership" highlights the relevance of certain management traits in the context of greenfield projects and then associates the following attributes to those of a visionary leader [18]: (1) creators of a positive and inspirational vision, (2) supporters of organized learning and growth inside the organization, (3) innovators, and (4) pioneers.

3. Method

3.1 Framework selection

The four models that were considered potentially suitable for a context of disruptive success—transformational, charismatic, entrepreneurial, and visionary—underwent a further scrutiny in order to determine which one would better suit the context of disruptive success, as it is briefly described in the next paragraph.

The original term "transformational" already implies the existence of some entity that experiences transformation, and it is not so suitable in the context of completely new startups [7, 19]. Charismatic leaders emerge in times of instability, change, or crises, but many critics argue that charismatic leaders tend to forget the group's benefit and try to gain most of the attention for themselves. This reality implies that collective or organizational outputs may not always be prioritized or maximized, since that is not the main objective for this type of leaders [9]. Entrepreneurial leadership framework appears to be a suitable option for the study in terms of effectively measuring the entrepreneurial aspect in leadership, but it does not really screen or measure elements that may impact discontinuous innovation [17], which would be mandatory for the chosen context. Therefore, the framework that appeared to suit the best in terms of analyzing environments that combine entrepreneurship and innovation is that of visionary leadership [20–22]. Eventually, there is no assumption on what the results would have been or would be if some other of these frameworks would have been tested in the study. In the case of the selected framework, the results are the ones that tell if this choice was right.

3.2 Case selection

There are few companies—similar to Apple, Microsoft, or Google—that are really disruptively successful over the span of, for instance, a decade, so it is not possible to collect enough samples as to conduct a statistical study. Besides, the analyzed variables are not quantitative in nature. Multiple theorical and practical studies indicate that the longitudinal multi-case approach is the best one in terms of properly investigating the results of qualitative inputs [23–28]. In order to choose the specific companies or cases, disruptively successful firms, the following three criteria were applied: (1) the pool of chosen companies should be located in, at least, three different geographical realms i.e. North America, Western Europe and Eastern Asia, (2) the chosen corporations should be at the highest possible position in the rank of global top 100 companies as per market value [29], and (2) those firms should have become industry leaders in (a) a relatively short period of time—less than 20 years, and (b) after leveraging some competitive advantage based on discontinuous innovation.

An overwhelming percentage of the disruptively successful companies in the top 100 as per market capitalization are American and, mostly, they are located in Silicon Valley. Nine was the maximum number of samples in the list that allowed to keep a reasonable geographical balance across several geographic realms without mixing firms that were not really comparable in terms of size or level of achievements. Nine is also a number in the range of similar studies conducted in the past. For instance, the number was three in the case of the study "Internationalization of small- and medium-sized enterprises: a multi case study" [30], four, in the case of the study "Competitive product-service systems: lessons from a multi-case study" [31], and 10 in the case of the study "Knowledge management critical failure factors: a multi-case study" [32].

The list of selected American corporations included the top five that could be considered disruptively successful firms as per the rapid growth: Apple, Google, Microsoft, General Electric, and Facebook [29]. The other American companies ranked in-between in the original list were not disruptively successful ones e.g. Exxon Mobil, Berkshire Hathaway, Wells Fargo, and Johnson and Johnson [29].

The only large-enough Western European disruptively successful company that also met the criteria was the Spanish firm Inditex—number 67 as per market capitalization [29]. On the other hand, the Eastern Asian disruptively successful companies that ranked high enough in the global top 100 were Toyota Motors, Alibaba and Tencent—15, 22, and 32 [29].

Therefore, the list of multinationals and leaders included in the study is as follows:

1. Apple Inc.; Steve Jobs. USA

2. Google (Alphabet, Inc.); Larry Page. USA

3. Microsoft Corporation; Bill Gates. USA

4. General Electric; Thomas Edison. USA

5. Facebook, Inc.; Mark Zuckerberg. USA

6. Toyota Motor Corporation; Taiichi Ohno. Japan

7. Alibaba Group Holding Limited; Jack Ma. China

8. Tencent Holdings Limited; Ma Huateng. China

9. Industria de Diseño Textil, S.A. (Inditex, owner of Zara and other clothing retailing chains); Amancio Ortega. Spain

4. Multi-case study: findings

4.1 Rankings of leadership

Table 1 summarizes the findings on rankings associated with the four above-mentioned features.

It can be observed that, in 89% of the cases, the leaders either outperform their already outperforming firms, in terms of "value" rankings—Bill Gates, Mark Zuckerberg, Amancio Ortega— or enjoy even more prestige and recognition than the companies that they started up. Only in the case of Larry Page, the achievements and profile of the leader appears to be, arguably, less remarkable than that of his own company.

4.2 Steve Jobs, Apple Inc.

Apple Inc., a multinational technology company, was founded by Steven Paul Jobs—known as Steve Jobs—in 1977, in Los Altos, California, USA [38]. In 2016, Apple ranked number 1 in the world in terms of market capitalization. Steve Jobs ranked top in the list of the 20 most influential Americans of all times [34].

Jobs was raised by adoptive parents in Cupertino, California—in Silicon Valley. His passions kept changing over the time. He dropped out of Reed College, in Portland, took a job at Atari Corporation as a videogame designer in early 1974, and saved enough money for a pilgrimage to India [39]. In 1976, back in Silicon Valley, Steve Jobs and his former friend, Stephen Wozniak, worked on a computer design of their own, the Apple I [39]. Jobs and Wozniak later designed a far better product, the Apple II [39].

Over the last four decades, Apple has been involved and played a leading role in a number of disruptive and revolutionary innovations. The list includes personal computers, music distribution, tablet computing, mobile phones and digital publishing. Elements of disruptive innovation can be found in at least four of the items in Apple's list: personal computers, music distribution, tablet computing, and digital publishing. iPhones would belong to the category of revolutionary innovations [40–43].

Walter Isaacson, Steve Jobs official biographer, described the founder of Apple as a "creative entrepreneur whose creativity, passion for perfection and ferocious drive revolutionized six industries: personal computers, animated movies, music, phones, tablet computing, and digital publishing" [44]. Jobs, pioneered devices such as iMacs, iPods, iPhones, iTunes, and iPads and initiated projects such as Pixar and Apple computers [18].

Some Jobs' words, recorded in the mentioned documentary Triumph of the Nerds [45], can give a sense of his ability for creating positive and inspirational visions [18]:

> *To me, the spark of that (birth of personal computer industry in Silicon Valley in the early seventies) was that it was something beyond the sort of you see every day. It is the same that causes people to wantna be poets instead of bankers, and I think this is a wonderful thing. And I think that same spirit can be put into products. And these products can be manufactured and given to people and they can sense that spirit [45].*

Regarding the second attribute of visionary leadership [18], which is supporting organized learning and growth within the organization, Jobs spoke eloquently about its importance, from his own point of view:

"The people who are doing the work are the moving force behind the Macintosh. My job is to create a space for them, to clear out the rest of the organization and keep it at bay" [46].

Company name	Rank of most valuable firms [29]	Name of founder/ leader	Rank of richest [33]	Other feature on measuring leadership relevance/impact
Apple Inc.	1	Steve Jobs	Dead	Ranked in the list of the 20 most influential Americans of all times [34]. Several articles and surveys rank Jobs in the top 2 of the greatest innovators of all times [35, 36].
Google (now Alphabet, Inc.)	2	Larry Page	12	
Microsoft Corporation	5	Bill Gates	1	
General Electric	13	Thomas Edison	Dead	Ranked in the list of the 20 most influential Americans of all times [34]. Several articles and surveys rank jobs in the top 1 of the greatest innovators of all times [35, 36].
Facebook, Inc.	17	Mark Zuckerberg	6	Ranked in the top of the greatest innovators of all times according to the Lemelson-Mit Invention Index [36].
Toyota Motor Corporation	15	Tailichi Ohno	Dead	Lean manufacturing, Just-In-Time (JIT), and derivative approaches created by Ohno are still currently used by a large percentage of manufacturing firms [37].
Alibaba Group Holding Limited	22	Jack Ma	33	
Tencent Holdings Limited	32	Ma Huateng	46	
Industria de Diseño Textil, S.A. (Inditex)	67	Amancio Ortega	2	

Table 1.
Feature comparison between studied firms and founders.

DOI: http://dx.doi.org/10.5772/intechopen.108029

> *"Innovation has nothing to do with how many R&D dollars you have. When Apple came up with the Mac, IBM was spending at least 100 times more on R&D. It's not about money. It's about the people you have, how you're led, and how much you get it" [47].*

4.3 Larry Page, Google/Alphabet

Google was started in 1998 in Menlo Park—California, USA. Founders were two students of Stanford University, Sergey Brin, and Larry Page [48]. Google's beginnings were less humble than those of earlier Silicon Valley startups at the time, because the two founders were able to initially raise US$1 million US dollars [49].

Larry Page met Sergey Brin when Larry entered the doctorate program at Stanford. Both students were interested in finding a way for extracting useful information from the mass of data in the Internet. With that purpose, they devised a new type of search engine tool to track the backing links of each site. They called the new search engine Google—a name derived from a misspelling of the word googol [48].

Therefore, Google's initial success was not based on disruptive innovation, but rather on revolutionary innovation—the development of relevancy ranking in the search engine sector [49, 50].

In essence, Google's business model has been labeled as continuous disruptive innovation [51] or continuous innovation [50]. These labels define a concept different than Christensen's. Google's innovation model is based on a hub—Googleplex—that attracts talent; this is the same model than Edison's [50, 52, 53]. Eventually, during the last two decades, this model helped Google to be involved in a relevant number of discontinuous innovations, including Android, YouTube, Google Books, and Google Maps, and some continuous ones, such as Chrome or Gmail [54, 55].

There is some dispute among scholars regarding the quality of Page's leadership strength, especially during his early tenure [56]. Still, there are little doubts that Page congregates the four attributes that define a visionary leader, as several authors already validated in their studies [18, 57, 58]. Several quotes from Larry Page that highlight his visionary skills are as follows:

On being an inspirator: "What is the one-sentence summary of how you change the world? Always work hard on something uncomfortably exciting!" [59].

On his role as a supporter of organized learning and growth inside the organization: "My job as a leader is to make sure everybody in the company has great opportunities, and that they feel they're having a meaningful impact and are contributing to the good of society. As a world, we're doing a better job of that. My goal is for Google to lead, not follow that" [59]. On being an innovator: "Invention is not enough. [Nikola] Tesla invented the electric power we use, but he struggled to get it out to people. You have to combine both things: invention and innovation focus, plus the company that can commercialize things and get them to people" [59]. On being a pioneer: "Lots of companies don't succeed over time. What do they fundamentally do wrong? They usually miss the future. I try to focus on that: What is the future really going to be? And how do we create it? And how do we power our organization to really focus on that and really drive it at a high rate?" [59].

Page's personality traits, like his introverted tendencies, may not fit the profile of a charismatic leader [55, 56, 58, 60], but he definitively does in that of a visionary leader. Eventually, it is interesting to notice that many other leaders analyzed in this study also are, apparently, introvert, e.g. Bill Gates, Mark Zuckerberg.

4.4 Thomas Edison, General electric

General Electric (GE), a multinational technology corporation, was founded by Thomas Alva Edison in 1889, in Schenectady, New York, USA. Since then, GE has been in the lists of top ranked companies in the USA [61].

In 1859, Edison quit school and began working as a train boy on the railroad between Detroit and Port Huron. Edison took advantage of the opportunity to learn telegraphy and, in 1863, he became an apprentice telegrapher. By 1869, he thought that he had made enough progress with a duplex telegraph—a device capable of transmitting two messages simultaneously on one single wire—and abandoned telegraphy for full-time entrepreneurship. At that time, Edison moved to New York City, where he initially partnered with Frank L. Pope, an electrical expert, and produced the Edison Universal Stock Printer [62]. During the next decade, Edison grew fast as successful mogul [62]. By 1889, he had full ownership or participation in many electricity-related companies that got then merged. The resulting corporation was General Electric Company (GE) [61, 63].

From the very beginning, General Electric adopted an innovation development strategy similar to Google's. The actual scheme was not so much based on sparks of disruptive innovation and genius, but on a systematic approach toward producing inventions [64]. This method required concentration of researchers and projects in one spot. The first chosen location was Menlo Park, in New Jersey. Menlo Park hub was then succeeded by a larger laboratory in West Orange, New Jersey [53]. Both hubs developed a long list of innovations [53]. Some of the most relevant ones were the phonograph, the incandescent electric light and power, the motion picture camera, and the alkaline storage battery [53].

Thomas Edison ranks in the top of almost every list of all-time greatest innovators, pioneers, and entrepreneurs. He registered more than 1000 patents in the US alone [53] and founded more than 300 companies [34–36, 53]. Edison's role on the development of these technologies and later commercialization of them clearly qualifies him as visionary, innovator, and pioneer [18]. Edison also was one of the first entrepreneurs to apply the principles of organized teamwork to the process of invention [65].

4.5 Bill Gates, Microsoft

In 1975 William Henry Gates III—known as Bill Gates—, a student then at Harvard University, and his friend, Paul Allen, partnered and founded a developing software company, called Microsoft [66]. First, they adopted BASIC, a programming language used at the time on larger computers, as the core of their work. By 1980, Gates managed to convince a large computer manufacturing multinational, IBM, to depend on Microsoft for every software related to personal computers (PCs). Then, other manufacturers of IBM-compatible PCs also turned to Microsoft in search of its products. By 1990, Gates was the PC industry's king [67].

Microsoft's initial success was based on one disruptive innovation—personal computers and related software [66]. Later, Microsoft also played a key role in another emerging industry: gaming—Xbox [68–70].

Gates is as introverted, similar to Larry Page [45, 55] and, definitively, he is not as charismatic as Steve Jobs [39, 45, 71, 72], but, still, he has been equally visionary. Bill Gates clearly fits in the description of an innovator, a pioneer, and a supporter of organized learning and growth [45, 67, 71–73].

4.6 Mark Zuckerberg, Facebook

On February 4, 2004, Mark Zuckerberg, a Harvard student, launched the face-book.com, a directory in which fellow students entered their information and photos into a template. Within 2 weeks, half of the students had signed up [74]. Then, his two roommates, Chris Hughes and Dustin Moskovitz, helped him add a few features and they made Facebook available to other universities [74]. It differed from other social media sites at the time in the fact that it required real names and e-mail addresses [74]. In 2004, the three partners moved to Palo Alto, California, where venture capitalist Peter Thiel invested in the firm. In May 2005, Facebook received additional money from a venture capital firm (US$12.7 million) [74]. Facebook's initial success was therefore based on one single but relevant disruptive innovation: social media [71, 74].

Among other achievements, Mark Zuckerberg reached the top five in the list of wealthiest people on earth [33]. Again, Zuckerberg is as charismatic as Jobs or Edison [39, 45, 71, 72]. However, he definitively qualifies as a visionary leader. Besides other studies, interviews, and papers that prove this point [55, 71, 72, 75], Zuckerberg produced a number of quotes that support this statement. On being an inspirator: "We look for people who are passionate about something. In a way, it almost doesn't matter what you're passionate about" [75]. On being a supporter of organized learning and growth inside the organization: "I think as a company, if you can get those two things right–having a clear direction on what you are trying to do and bringing in great people who can execute on the stuff–then you can do pretty well" [75]. On being an innovator: "People think innovation is just having a good idea but a lot of it is just moving quickly and trying a lot of things" [75]. On being a pioneer: "In a world that's changing really quickly, the only strategy that is guaranteed to fail is not taking risks" [75].

4.7 Amancio Ortega, Industria de Diseño Textil (Inditex)

The Inditex group is a multinational textile fashion retailer firm founded in 1985 in A Coruña, Spain. Inditex currently owns famous brands such as Zara, Pull & Bear, Massimo Dutti, Bershka, Stradivarius, Oysho, Zara Home, and Uterqüe. Inditex ranked 67 in the global top 100 as per market capitalization [29].

As a youth in A Coruña, Galicia, in northwestern Spain, Amacio Ortega gained an entry into the garment business by working as a delivery boy for a men's shirt store and assistant in a tailor's shop. He later managed a clothing store that catered to wealthy clients. Finally, Ortega saw an opportunity of appealing to a much broader audience by selling garment at extremely competitive prices. His proposal was based on reducing production costs by using less expensive materials and more efficient manufacturing systems. Ortega first applied this approach in a bathrobe business, Confecciones Goa, company that he founded in 1963. Then, in 1975, Ortega started the first Zara's ready-to-wear clothing store. Zara soon became not only an internationally famous chain but also the flagship of the holding company Inditex, which he founded 10 years later [76].

The success of Inditex—and H&M, its main competitor—is ultimately based on a revolutionary innovation called "fast fashion" [77]. Inditex devised a new model of supply chain, the Agile Supply Chain (ASC), that allows its fashion retailer chains to update products just in time [77, 78]. In this process, store managers constantly communicate customer feedbacks to collection designers, who immediately update models and production [77, 78]. Inditex's supply chain operations focus on three aspects: maximizing resources used, minimizing inventory, and minimizing lead times [78]. Inditex produces a significant amount of its production in-house and makes sure that its own factories reserve 85% of their capacity for in-season adjustments [77]. Inditex's business model, which is based on flexibility and speed, requires a vertically integrated value chain that differs greatly from that of other competitors, like Benetton and Mango.

Amancio Ortega, who was the one that directly conceived and engineered the above-mentioned business model, clearly is an innovator and a pioneer [18]. He also supports organized learning and growth inside of his firm. An article in The Economist describes how Ortega works:

> *He has never had his own office, desk or desktop computer, preferring to direct his firm while standing with colleagues in a design room of Zara Woman, the flagship line. One former long-term CEO of Inditex, and Mr. Ortega's business partner for 31 years, José María Castellano, says that his ex-boss's working method is to discuss things intensely with small groups, delegate paperwork, listen hard to others and prefer oral over written communication [79].*

"Ortega eats lunch with his employees in the company cafeteria. He can regularly be found sharing table on the factory floor with some of the designers, fabric experts and buyers" [80]. "Dear colleague, dear friend": these are the words that, both, Ortega and Steve Jobs, used in letters addressed to employees [81].

Ortega also is, as most of the previously analyzed leaders, an introvert. "Reclusive," "secretive," and "reserved" are words frequently used to describe him. Amancio Ortega has guarded his privacy so jealously that his company only released a photograph of him when the firm was first listed [82].

4.8 Taiichi Ohno, Toyota Motor Corporation

Toward the end of the second world war, Taiichi Ohno worked as a production engineer for Toyota, a Japanese car manufacture founded in Japan by Kiichiro Toyoda in 1937 [83]. In those days, Toyota was much less productive than its Detroit-based competitors, the Big Three—General Motors, Ford, and Chrysler [83]. In 1956, Ohno visited the USA to learn their supply and inventory methods. In that trip, he visited one of the supermarkets of the Piggly Wiggly chain [84, 85]. Ohno observed then how customers picked up a number of items from shelves and, in turn, the supermarket quickly and precisely replenished them [84]. This model gave Ohno ideas on how to reduce inventory and simplify assembly lines [84, 86, 87]. Based on the streamlined approach to replenishment, Ohno devised the Toyota Production System, which is more broadly known as lean manufacturing or Just-In-Time (JIT) inventory system. That gave Toyota an edge in terms of productivity and quality [86, 87]. The new system made Toyota the car industry leader. Since that time, the principle of lean manufacturing has been adopted by many firms and industries [84, 86, 87].

Based on this history, there is no doubt that Taiichi Ohno was a visionary, an innovator, and a pioneer [18]. The other quality of a visionary leader, supporting internal growth, was clearly evinced by the way that he spoke about Toyota and its organizational style over the length of his career. For instance, he described Toyota in the following way: "The Toyota style is not to create results by working hard. It is a system that says there is no limit to people's creativity. People don't go to Toyota to work, they go there to think" [88].

In terms of actively supporting internal growth:

> *When you go out into the workplace, you should be looking for things that you can do for your people there. You've got no business in the workplace if you are just there to be there. You've got to be looking for changes you can make for the benefit of the people who are working there [89].*

Unlike the previous cases, Toyota was not a startup at the time of its disruptive success and Ohno was not its founder. Ultimately, though, the combination of Onho's leadership and revolutionary innovation transformed Toyota from being an average car maker in Japan to becoming the number one global leader.

4.9 Jack Ma, Alibaba group holding limited

In 1999, Alibaba Group, an online trading company, was established by Jack Ma, a former English teacher, in Hangzhou City, China [90]. Everything started in 1995, during a trip to the USA, when Jack Ma learned for the first time about website portals and Internet. He immediately realized that the design of portals could be a great business opportunity in the yet-unformed Chinese market, especially in the business segment. After his return to China, Ma founded China Pages, a website page developer for Chinese businesses. However, 2 years later, he closed his first company because of strong competitors such as Chinesepage [91]. For a while, Ma went back to his former job as a public servant, but then, in 1999, Ma persuaded his team at the ministry to go to Hangzhou and found the Alibaba Group [91]. Alibaba's growth was fast. Six years later, in 2005, Alibaba attracted the attention of Yahoo!, which bought a 40 percent stake. In 2007, Alibaba.com raised US$1.7 billion dollars in its initial public offering (IPO) in Hong Kong [91].

Alibaba's business model bets a revolutionary innovation: Ma's belief that the small-business-to-small-business online market offered much greater opportunity than the consumer-to-consumer one, the reason being that, unlike consumers, small businesses are willing to pay a membership fee [91].

Ma's visionary leadership is as uniquely prolific as that of Edison and Jobs. In 2003, Jack Ma created a new company, the consumer-to-consumer online marketplace Taobao (meaning Chinese in "searching for treasure"). Taobao did not charge a fee but made money from online services and advertising. By 2007, Taobao had a 67 percent market share in China and eBay sold its Chinese operations to the media consortium TOM Group.

Some quotes from Ma that also proves his talent as an inspirator and team builder are as follows: "A good boss is better than a good company"; "If we are a good team and know what we want to do, one of us can defeat ten of them"; "We never lack money. We lack people with dreams, who can die for those dreams"; "For most people, they see and believe. We believe, and then we see. For leadership, we have to see things that other people don't see" [92].

4.10 Ma Huanteng, Tencent holdings limited

Tencent Holdings Ltd., also known as Tencent, is a Chinese multinational technology conglomerate holding company founded by Ma Huateng in 1998. Tencent is among the largest video game, social media, venture capital, and investment corporations in the world [93].

Ma Huateng studied computer science at Shenzhen University, where he earned a bachelor of science degree (1993). He then worked as a researcher for China Motion Telecom Development Ltd. before founding Tencent in 1998. In 1999, Ma's company launched QQ service (then called OICQ), which quickly became China's most popular instant-messaging platform. In June 2004, Tencent raised nearly US$200 million in the capital market [94]. By 2015, QQ had 850 million monthly users [94]. WeChat, a mobile instant-messaging application that was introduced in 201, soon gathered 650 million users [94]. Tencent also create Qzone, which boasted 670 million monthly users by 2015 [94].

Tencent started based on a revolutionary innovation, Internet-based QQ service. Later, the company provided users with a range of innovative "online lifestyle services." These services included online media outlets, e-commerce outlets, gaming options, social media sites, online advertising, and an online payment option [94].

Huateng is clearly a pioneer and innovator. In terms of being inspirational and a great team builder. Once, he said:

> *"At Tencent, we may be businessmen, but we are still chasing our IT, our science. We are still striving to create something really cool, trying to create things we couldn't even imagine without our new technologies. I am still clinging to this enthusiasm' [95]. 'For us, it is important to choose a character, super emphasis on this one. This is related to our culture. The founders like to be simple and don't like to be politicized. Including the selection of cadres, the character is very important. The second is to look at professional ability and coordination, intelligence and so on. This is a few principles for us to select talent" [95].*

An interesting quote in terms of leadership style—as a paradigm of invention versus innovation in practice—is this one:

> *"In America, when you bring an idea to market, you usually have several months before competition pops up, allowing you to capture significant market share. In China, you can have hundreds of competitors within the first hours of going live. Ideas are not important in China – execution is" [95].*

5. Conclusions

Unlike other studies [1–3, 30–32], the presented multi-case study focuses on a very specific business context: that of the creation of exceptionally successful firms such as Apple, Google, Facebook, or Tencent. The described multi-case study found the four attributes that define visionary leaders (creators of a positive and inspirational vision; supporters of organized learning and growth inside the organization; innovators; pioneers) in the nine studied cases. This is the first search effort that proves the link between the visionary leadership framework and firms that experienced disruptive success—unicorns.

In regard of the reasons why this type of profile is required in the studied context, one may be the fact that, in the case of disruptive innovation, nobody, even clients, may be able to forecast or imagine items such as the final functions and aspect of the products, the expected demand, and other features. Visionaries may be the only ones that can actually provide some accurate guesses, and, at the same time, put together, motivate, and guide a team in the right direction. In the future, it would be interesting to conduct more targeted research that could, both, give more details on the profile and the role of these leaders in the stated context and further describe the associated leadership attributes. Also, it would be of interest to investigate how the visionary leaders and disruptive-innovation-based environments interact with each other and why this type of leadership helps produce such outstanding results. Finally, it would also be interesting to test how other leadership frameworks fit in the same context and how the same leadership framework fits in the different ones.

Author details

Alberto Abadia
University of Vigo, Ourense, Spain

*Address all correspondence to: alberto.aba@gmail.com

References

[1] Dinh JE, Lord RG, Gardner WL, Meuser JD, Liden RC, Hu J. Leadership theory and research in the new millennium: Current theoretical trends and changing perspectives. Leadership Quarterly. 2014;**25**(1):36-62. DOI: 10.1016/j.leaqua.2013.11.005

[2] Goethals G, Sorenson G, Burns J. Encyclopedia of Leadership. Thousand Oaks: SAGE Publications, Inc.; 2004

[3] Au-Yong-Oliveira M, Costa JP, Gonçalves R, Branco F. The Rise of the Unicorn: Shedding Light on the Creation of Technological Enterprises with Exponential Valuations BT Trends and Advances in Information Systems and Technologies. 2018. pp. 967-977

[4] Burns JM. Leadership. New York: Harper & Row; 1978

[5] Burns JM. Transforming Leadership: Pursuit of Happiness. New York, Grove Atl. Inc; 2003

[6] Bass BM. Leadership and Performance Beyond Expectations. New York: Free Press; 1985

[7] Bass BM, Bass R. The Bass Handbook of Leadership: Theory, Research, and Managerial Applications. New York: Free Press; 2009

[8] Weber M. Economy and Society. Berkeley: Univ of California Press; 1922

[9] Schüppel F. Differences and Similarities between Charismatic and Transformational Leadership. Munich: GRIN Publishing; 2013

[10] Conger JA, Kanungo RN. Charismatic Leadership: The Elusive Factor in Organizational Effectiveness. San Francisco: Jossey-Bass; 1988

[11] Conger JA, Kanungo RN. Perceived behavioural attributes of charismatic leadership. Canadian Journal of Behavioural Science/Revue canadienne des sciences du comportement. 1992;**24**(1):86

[12] Conger JA, Kanungo RN, Menon ST, Mathur P. Measuring charisma: Dimensionality and validity of the Conger-Kanungo scale of charismatic leadership. Canadian Journal of Administrative Sciences/ Revue Canadienne des Sciences de l Administration. 1997;**14**(3):290-301

[13] Conger JA, Kanungo RN. Charismatic leadership in organizations: Perceived behavioral attributes and their measurement. Journal of Organizational Behavior. 1994;**15**(5):439-452

[14] Schumpeter JA. The Theory of Economic Development: An Inquiry into Profits, Capita I, Credit, Interest, and the Business Cycle. New York: Routledge; 5 Jul 2017

[15] Covin JG, Slevin DP. The influence of organization structure on the utility of an entrepreneurial top management style. Journal of Management Studies. 1988;**25**(3):217-234

[16] Stevenson HH. A Perspective on Entrepreneurship. Vol. 13. Boston: Harvard Business School; 1983

[17] Gupta V, MacMillan IC, Surie G. Entrepreneurial leadership: Developing and measuring a cross-cultural construct. Journal of Business Venturing. 2004;**19**(2):241-260

[18] Patrick M. Characteristics of visionary leadership. Chron.com, 2015. Available from: http://smallbusiness. chron.com/characteristics-visionary-

leadership-31332.html. [accessed May 30, 2015]

[19] Wang G, Oh I-S, Courtright SH, Colbert AE. Transformational leadership and performance across criteria and levels: A meta-analytic review of 25 years of research. Group & Organization Management. 2011;**36**(2):223-270. DOI: 10.1177/1059601111401017

[20] Christensen CM. The Innovator's Dilemma: When New Technologies Cause Great Firms to Fail. Boston: Harvard Business Press; 1997

[21] Govindarajan V, Kopalle PK. Disruptiveness of innovations: measurement and an assessment of reliability and validity. Strategic Management Journal. 2006;**27**(2):189-199

[22] Abadia A. The Road to Disruptive Success. In: 6th IEEE International Conference on Logistics, Informatics and Service Science. 2016. p. 7. DOI: 10.1109/LISS.2016.7854563

[23] Rosenbloom RS, Christensen CM. Technological Discontinuities, Organizational Capabilities, and Strategic Commitments. New York: Oxford University Press; 1998

[24] Rothaermel FT. Incumbent's advantage through exploiting complementary assets via interfirm cooperation. Strategic Management Journal. 2001;**22**:687-699

[25] Methe D, Swaminathan A, Mitchell W, Toyama R. The underemphasized role of diversifying entrants and industry incumbents as the sources of major innovations, Strateg. Discov. Compet. New Arenas. 1997. pp. 99-116

[26] Macher JT, Richman BD. Organisational responses to discontinuous innovation: A case study approach. International Journal of Innovation Management. 2004;**8**(01):87-114

[27] Ridder H-G. The theory contribution of case study research designs. Business Research. 2017;**10**(2):281-305. DOI: 10.1007/s40685-017-0045-z

[28] Gustafsson J. Single case studies vs. multiple case studies: A comparative study. 2017. Accessed: Feb. 17, 2020. Available from: http://www.diva-portal.org/smash/get/diva2:1064378/FULLTEXT01.pdf

[29] Keeley L, Walters H, Pikkel R, Quinn B, MacMillan I. Global Top 100 Companies by Market Capitalisation. London: PricewaterhouseCoopers LLP; 2015

[30] Amal M, Rocha Freitag Filho A. Internationalization of small- and medium-sized enterprises: A multi case study. European Business Review. 2010;**22**(6):608-623. DOI: 10.1108/09555341011082916

[31] Durugbo C. Competitive product-serve systems: Lessons from a multicase study. International Journal of Production Research. 2013;**51**(19):5671-5682

[32] Akhavan P, Pezeshkan A. Knowledge management critical failure factors: A multi-case study. VINE. 2014;**44**(1):22-41. DOI: 10.1108/VINE-08-2012-0034

[33] Forbes. The World's Billionaires List – Forbes. Forbes Media LLC, 2016. Available from: http://www.forbes.com/billionaires/list/ [Accessed: 13 May, 2016]

[34] Time. The 20 Most Influential Americans of All Time. Time. 2012. Available from: http://newsfeed.

time.com/2012/07/25/the-20-most-influential-americans-of-all-time/. [Accessed: May 18, 2016]

[35] Allis R. The Twelve Greatest Innovators of All Times. Borgbjergsvej: Startup Guide; 2014. Available from: http://startupguide.com/world/greatest-innovators/. [Accessed: May 18, 2016]

[36] Lemelson-MIT Program. Young Americans Recognize the Impact of Innovation on U.S. Economy. Lemelson-MIT Program. Boston: MIT Press; 2012. Available from: http://lemelson.mit.edu/news/young-americans-recognize-impact-innovation-us-economy. [Accessed: May 18, 2016]

[37] Adeyeri MK, Ayodeji SP, Akinnuli BO, Farayibi PK, Ojo OO, Adeleke K. Development of SMEs coping model for operations advancement in manufacturing technology. In: Advanced Applications in Manufacturing Enginering. Woodhead Publishing; Jan 1 2019. pp. 169-190

[38] Levy S. Apple Inc. London: Encyclopædia Britannica; 2021. Available from: https://www.britannica.com/topic/Apple-Inc. [Accessed: May 17, 2021]

[39] Levy S. Steve Jobs. London: Encyclopædia Britannica; 2021. Available from: http://www.britannica.com/biography/Steve-Jobs. [Accessed: Nov. 21, 2015]

[40] The Editors of Encyclopædia Britannica. Apple. London: Encyclopædia Britannica; 2016. Available from: https://www.britannica.com/plant/apple-fruit-and-tree. [Accessed: Aug. 01, 2017]

[41] Story S. Apple Inc. Success Story - CEO, Founder, History. SuccessfulStory, 2015. Available from: http://successstory.com/companies/apple-inc. [Accessed: May 17, 2015]

[42] Hoekman Jr. R. The Secret To Apple's Long-Term Success? It Always Prepares You For The Future — Co. Design — Business + Design. Fast Company, 2011. Available from: http://www.fastcodesign.com/1665089/the-secret-to-apples-long-term-success-it-always-prepares-you-for-the-future. [Accessed: May 17, 2015]

[43] Elgan M. Why Apple is the Most Successful Company in History—Computerworld. Needham, MA: Computerworld; 2015. Available from: http://www.computerworld.com/article/2883747/why-apple-is-the-most-successful-company-in-history.html [Accessed: May 17, 2015]

[44] Isaacson W. Steve Jobs. New York: Simon and Schuster; 2015

[45] Sen P. Triumph of the Nerds. The United States of America. Portland, Oregon: John Gau Productions and Oregon Public Broadcasting; 1996

[46] Tellis GJ. Unrelenting Innovation: How to Create a Culture for Market Dominance. Hoboken, NJ: Wiley; 2013

[47] Kumar V, Sundarraj RP. Global Innovation and Economic Value. New Delhi: Springer India; 2018

[48] Hosch WLH. Google. London: Encyclopædia Britannica; 2021. Available from: https://www.britannica.com/topic/Google-Inc. [Accessed: May 17, 2021]

[49] Hosch WL. Google Inc. London: Encyclopædia Britannica; 2015. Available from: http://www.britannica.com/topic/Google-Inc. [Accessed: May 18, 2016]

[50] Steiber A. The Google Model: Managing Continuous Innovation in a Rapidly Changing World. New York: Springer; 2014

[51] Catapano C. What is Continuous Disruptive Innovation?. Bridgesphere, 2010. Available from: http://bridgesphere.com/what-is-continuous-disruptive-innovation/. [Accessed: May 18, 2016]

[52] Sun L. Google and Innovation – A History. businessdictionary.com, 2016. Available from: http://www.businessdictionary.com/article/710/google-and-innovation-a-history/. [Accessed: May 18, 2016]

[53] Rutgers. Edison's Patents. The Thomas A. Edison Papers Project. 2012. Available from: http://edison.rutgers.edu/index.htm. [Accessed: May 18, 2016]

[54] Adams S. Leadership Tip: Hire the Quiet Neurotic, not the Impressive Extrovert. Forbes.com. Hong Kong: Whale Media Investments; 2013. Available from: http://www.forbes.com/sites/susanadams/2013/04/11/leadership-tip-hire-the-quiet-neurotic-not-the-impressive-extrovert/#7093139e24ea. [Accessed: May 18, 2016]

[55] Fujioka R. How Bill Gates, Larry Page, and Mark Zuckerberg All Thrive as Introverts. Inc.com. New York: Mansueto Ventures LLC; 2016. Available from: http://www.inc.com/russ-fujioka/how-bill-gates-larry-page-and-mark-zuckerberg-all-thrive-as-introverts.html. [Accessed: May 18, 2016]

[56] Carlson N. The Untold Story Of Larry Page's Incredible Comeback. New York: Business Insider; 2014. Available from: http://www.businessinsider.com/larry-page-the-untold-story-2014-4. [Accessed: May 18, 2016]

[57] Akinyemi S. Leadership style. 2014

[58] Elmer V. What would Larry Page do? Leadership lessons from Google's doyen. Fortune Magazine. New York: Time Inc.; 2011. Available from: http://fortune.com/2011/04/18/what-would-larry-page-do-leadership-lessons-from-googles-doyen/. [Accessed: May 18, 2016]

[59] Hartmans A. Best Quotes From Larry Page, Google Cofounder and Alphabet CEO. New York: Business Insider; 2017

[60] Larry Page Leadership Style. A detailed analysis of its positive and negative impact. 2018. Accessed: May 16, 2021. Available from: https://www.totalassignmenthelp.com/free-sample/larry-page-leadership-style

[61] Encyclopædia Britannica. General Electric Co. (GE). London: Encyclopædia Britannica; 2021. Available from: http://www.britannica.com/topic/General-Electric-Co. [Accessed: May 19, 2016]

[62] Conot RE. Thomas Edison. London: Encyclopaedia Britannica; 2018. Available from. https://www.britannica.com/biography/Thomas-Edison. [Accessed: May 18, 2021]

[63] Essays. The History Of General Electric Company Management Essay. UK Essays; 2018. Available from: https://www.ukessays.com/essays/management/the-history-of-general-electric-company-management-essay.php. [Accessed: Jul. 02, 2019]

[64] Hardy Q. Google's Innovation - And Everyone's?. Forbes.com. Hong Kong: Whale Media Investments; 2011. Available from: http://www.forbes.com/sites/quentinhardy/2011/07/16/

googles-innovation-and-everyones/#60a52aa8331a. [Accessed: May 18, 2016]

[65] Walsh B. The Electrifying Edison. New York: Time Inc.; 2009. Available from: https://time.com/time/specials/packages/article/0,28804,1910417_1910419_1910460,00.html. [Accessed: Apr. 20, 2018]

[66] Zachary GP. Microsoft Corporation. London: Encyclopædia Britannica; 2021. Available from: https://www.britannica.com/topic/Microsoft-Corporation. [Accessed: May 17, 2021]

[67] Augustyn A et al. Bill Gates. London: Encyclopædia Britannica; 2016. Available from: https://global.britannica.com/biography/Bill-Gates. [Accessed: May 18, 2016]

[68] Malerba F, Nelson R, Orsenigo L, Winter S. History-friendly'models of industry evolution: The computer industry. Industrial and Corporate Change. 1999;**8**(1):3-40

[69] Ceruzzi PE, Paul E, Aspray W. A History of Modern Computing. Boston: MIT Press; 2003

[70] Campbell-Kelly M. Not only Microsoft: The maturing of the personal computer software industry, 1982-1995. The Business History Review. 2001;**1**:103-145

[71] Computer History Museum. Mark Zuckerberg & Facebook - Inside Story of the World's Fastest-growing Company 2014. Computer History Museum, Computer History Museum, 2014

[72] Rose C. Charlie Rose - Interview With Senior Facebook Leadership Mark Zuckerberg, CEO, Sheryl Sandberg, COO. CBS. San Bruno: Google LLC; 2014. Available from: https://www.youtube.com/watch?v=Il507j6qojg. [Accessed: May 21, 2016]

[73] Augustyn A et al. Mark Zuckerberg. London: Encyclopædia Britannica; 2016. Available from: http://www.britannica.com/biography/Mark-Zuckerberg

[74] Hall M. Facebook. London: Encyclopædia Britannica; 2021. Available from: https://www.britannica.com/topic/Facebook. [Accessed: May 17, 2021]

[75] Economy P. Mark Zuckerberg: 19 inspiring power quotes for success. Inc.com, Feb. 24. 2020. Available from: https://www.inc.com/peter-economy/mark-zuckerberg-19-inspiring-power-quotes-for-success.html. [Accessed: May 17, 2021]

[76] Orwig SF. Amancio Ortega. London: Encyclopaedia Britannica; 2021. Available from: https://www.britannica.com/biography/Amancio-Ortega. [Accessed: May 18, 2021]

[77] Lu C. Zara's secret to retail success - its supply chain, tradegecko. 2014. Available from: https://www.tradegecko.com/blog/zara-supply-chain-its-secret-to-retail-success. [Accessed: May 20, 2016]

[78] Zhelyazkov G. Agile Supply Chain: Zara's Case Study Analysis. Vol. 1. Glasgow: Strathclyde University of Glasgow; 2011. p. 11

[79] The Economist. The Management Style of Amancio Ortega - Behind the Mask of Zara. London: The Economist Group; 2016. Available from: https://www.economist.com/business/2016/12/17/the-management-style-of-amancio-ortega. [Accessed: Jul. 02, 2019]

[80] Marlow B. The Humble Life of Zara Owner Amancio Ortega is to be Admired. London: Telegraph Media Group;

2015. Available from: http://www.telegraph.co.uk/finance/newsbysector/retailandconsumer/11656753/The-humble-life-of-Zara-owner-Amancio-Ortega-is-to-be-admired.html. [Accessed: May 20, 2016]

[81] Novoa Ojea O. Madera de líder. Madrid: El Mundo; 2011

[82] Reuters, The Reclusive Billionaire: Secret Life of Zara Boss Amancio Ortega and His 'Fast Fashion' Empire. Reuters. Sydney: The Sydney Morning Herald; 2013. Available from: http://www.executivestyle.com.au/the-reclusive-billionaire-secret-life-of-zara-boss-amancio-ortega-and-his-fast-fashion-empire-2fhne. [Accessed: May 20, 2016]

[83] Kaizen Institute. Taiichi Ohno's Contribution. Ellisbridge: Kaizen Institute India; 2013. Available from: https://kaizeninstituteindia.wordpress.com/2013/10/17/taiichi-ohnos-contribution/. [Accessed: May 21, 2016]

[84] Toyota. Taiichi Ohno. Aichi: Toyota Motor Corporation; 2004. Available from: http://www.toyota-global.com/company/toyota_traditions/quality/mar_apr_2004.html. [Accessed: May 21, 2016]

[85] Bruce M. Piggly Wiggly: An Inspiration for the Toyota Way. Montreal: X Ray Delta; 2011. Available from: https://xray-delta.com/2011/10/12/piggly-wiggly-an-inspiration-for-the-toyota-way/. [Accessed: May 21, 2016]

[86] Schuman M. Toyota Production System (1988), by Taiichi Ohno, Time. 2011. Available from: http://content.time.com/time/specials/packages/article/0,28804,2086680_2086683_2087688,00.html. [Accessed: May 21, 2016]

[87] Ohno T. Toyota Production System: Beyond Large-Scale Production. London: Productivity Press; 1988

[88] Maurya A. Running Lean. Sebastopol, CA: O'Reilly; 2012

[89] Shimokawa K, Fujimoto T. The Birth of Lean. Cambridge, MA: Lean Enterprise Institute; 2009

[90] Alibaba Group. History and Milestones. Hangzhou: Alibaba Group; 2021. Available from: https://www.alibabagroup.com/en/about/history. [Accessed: May 17, 2021]

[91] Gregersen E. Jack Ma. London: Encyclopædia Britannica; 2021. Available from: https://global.britannica.com/biography/Jack-Ma. [Accessed: May 22, 2016]

[92] Aditya S. 17 Brilliant Jack Ma quotes on leadership and success – AirTract. Airtract. 2019. Available from: https://www.airtract.com/article/18-Brilliant-Jack-Ma-Quotes-On-Leadership-And-Success. [Accessed: Jul. 02, 2019]

[93] Peili R. A brief history of tencent holdings and its rise to the blockchain era. Crptos.com. Jul. 24, 2020. Available from: https://cryptos.com/a-brief-history-of-tencent-holdings-and-its-rise-to-the-blockchain-era/. [Accessed: May 17, 2021]

[94] Hollar S. Ma Huateng. London: Encyclopædia Britannica; 2016. Available from: https://global.britannica.com/biography/Ma-Huateng. [Accessed: Sep. 20, 2015]

[95] Alizila. West Point Invites Jack Ma to Talk Leadership. Alizila. Hangzhou: Alibaba Group; 2019. Available from: https://www.alizila.com/west-point-invites-jack-ma-to-talk-leadership/. [Accessed: Jul. 02, 2019]

Chapter 4

Emotional Intelligence: Constraints and Possibilities in Leadership Practices

Doris M. Dickerson

Abstract

Once the COVID-19 pandemic was over, the issue of educational disparities in outcomes for marginalized students in all fields revealed a systemic process of educational disparities. This has amplified economic inequality among ethnic groups. Accommodating the diversity of student needs while also helping to create leaders has now become a critical priority. Addressing this necessitates implementing inclusive leadership practices which need novel leadership abilities. Principals can expand their inclusive leadership talents by including emotional intelligence (EI) expertise in their repertoire. I believe that taking on new leadership challenges, such as ethics, diversity, equity, inclusion (DEI), creativity, and innovation, will support developing inclusive leadership habits, which will aid in providing education and academic triumphs to all underprivileged students while also bringing in lasting human capital growth. Therefore, this chapter takes note of the connection between transformational leadership and the principal's capabilities when it comes to leading.

Keywords: emotional intelligence, leadership, diversity, equity, inclusion, creativity, innovation, change

1. Introduction

Among educational policymakers, researchers, and practitioners, there is a consensus that effective principals contribute to the success of student academic achievement and other school outcomes, such as attendance, discipline, and high school graduation. However, research indicates systemic and persistent educational disparities in educational outcomes at all levels for minoritized students [1]. Black students from low SES homes, when compared to their Caucasian middle-income counterparts, despite the numerous federal mandates and school improvement initiatives to increase academic success for these students. For example, the results Post-COVID-19 pandemic revealed that student loss of learning during the shutdown, expatiated the systemic educational inequalities of minoritized students in public schools [2]. In addition, the long-term learning loss—gap will result in 3% lower income over their lifetimes [3]. Such factors contribute to economic disparities between Black and students of color.

The results of post-COVID-19 pandemic also revealed that principals are faced with increased challenges of teacher shortage, teacher burnout, teacher turnover, emotional safety, and well-being, primarily due to political interference in some states that caused inconsistencies in following CEC guidelines for safe school reopening [2]. This suggests that principals should employ the same leadership skills during the disruption and gradual reopening, of schools; empathy, compassion, collaboration, and support. Such leadership skill reflects emotional intelligence (EI) competencies. Simply stated, EI is defined as the ability to understand and manage individual emotions, as well as recognize and influence the emotions of others around you [4–6].

Moreover, the results of a comprehensive report identified four major themes that pose new challenges for leadership and principals, in particular: ethnicity, diversity, equity, inclusion (DEI), creativity, innovation, and change [7]. The identified themes mirror principals' existing leadership challenges and post-COVID-19 pandemic leadership challenges.

This chapter discusses the principal's use of EI skills as a vehicle to improve their inclusive leadership skill sets. In the process, I question whether EI competencies facilitate leadership effectiveness. Therefore, I collect related literature and find the connections among these variables. Next, the conceptual framework for studying the effects in the context of the four new leadership variables was drawn to confirm the connections among these variables. Finally, the four challenges for principals to improve leadership effectiveness in the post-COVID era were concluded. I believe the reader can identify the relationships between EI competencies and leadership effectiveness, which can be improved through EI competencies and inclusive leadership skills.

2. Literature review

2.1 Transformational leadership skills in a new era

Einstein [8] famously said, "Insanity is doing the same thing and expecting different results." Covey [9] commented similarly along the same vein: "If we carry on in our usual way, we will continue to get what we have." The aftermath of the COVID-19 pandemic revealed a persistent educational disparity for marginalized students, which supports the notion that race and socioeconomic status can determine a student's success. People who work with economic policy, researchers, and practitioners all agree that these persisting educational inequalities necessitate new leadership skills embracing inclusivity to increase all students' academic achievement.

In general, scholars and practitioners consider transformational characteristics and behaviors important when assigning leadership roles. This was first discussed by Burn [10] who noted that it "entails a process where leaders and followers raise each other to high levels of motivation and morality" (p. 20). Bass [11] later expanded the principals' role, which was inspire, motivate, establish a commitment to a vision and work collaboratively with stakeholders. However, Grissom and Loeb [12] reported that recent studies have found only minimal effects of transformational leadership behaviors relative to instructional leadership.

By contrast, a quote by Kouzes and Posner [13], "Exemplary leaders know that if they want to gain commitment and achieve the highest standards, they must be models of the behaviors they expect of others" supports the notion of transformational leadership in the context of organizational management. This concept of organizational management is also supported [13, 14]. Kouzes and Posner [13], share leadership lessons from 25 years of experience and research on what makes successful leaders. Also, they embody five key transformational skills for effective leadership behavior and practice: model the way (role model), inspire a shared vision (illustrate your vision), challenge the process (experiment and take risks), enable others (teamwork, trust, and listen), and encourage the heart (reward and celebrate). The leadership challenge inventory is an assessment that identifies distinctive features related to transformational leadership theory, seen as a playbook. This inventory also defines leadership behavior and characteristics that can help build successful leadership abilities with an emphasis on purposeful and effective change management.

In this same vein, Fullan [15] identified several issues that contribute to change leadership, According to Fullan, organizational growth is contingent upon change leadership from a moral point of view. Consider the adage "if it ain't broke, don't fix it"—it neglects the altering demographics and assorted educational requirements, while maintaining educational differences amongst marginalized students. Change can help promote innovation and avoid stagnation. Besides having a moral basis, building relationships, and establishing shared liability requires school leaders to clearly depict the core competencies of alteration, understand change, build correspondence, form knowledge, produce consistency and get agreement from associates to make goals. Also necessary are leadership capabilities such as creating coherence and working together.

Nevertheless, transformational leadership skills are widely accepted among scholars and practitioners and are touted to increase leadership effectiveness in addressing challenges that lead to organizational change. For example, research backs the perception that efficient leadership qualities include forming long-term and attainable goals and objectives, stirring commitment by executing strategies to enhance a positive climate, and communicating a definite vision for the school district. Contrarily, scholars claim that long-term aims result in burnout among staff members. Long-term ambitions are normally tough to realize and may be postponed due to unforeseen issues. Shorter objectives are realistic and can be achieved more easily, allowing personnel to observe swift results in their labor, as outlined by Lucas and Venckute [16]; Jex and Britt [17].

Two schools of thought exist on leadership abilities. While some researchers and professionals believe that transformational leadership skills are obtained naturally, many leadership preparation courses tend to focus on the theories of leadership instead of providing leaders with opportunities to practice such skills [18, 19].

By comparison, the plea for leadership aptitudes that portray inclusivity is endorsed by the study that has steadily revealed the broad accomplishment hole between high-social class and low-social class students and the disparities in opportunity (e.g., top-notch direction, admittance to propelled school readiness courses) that power these accomplishment holes. The achievement hole for students from low socioeconomic homes encompasses the expanding US pay equality financial gaps. Likewise, it attracts thoughtfulness regarding an expansion in understanding the connection between understudy scholarly achievement and labor force preparedness for monetary worldwide rivalry [3].

In the DEI era, there is a growing need for principals to demonstrate leadership skills and practices that provide structures that afford underrepresented students the opportunity to compete in a diverse and inclusive global economy [3]. A growing body of research calls for new leadership skills that focus on inclusive leadership behavior and practices that increase positive school outcomes for all students [20].

Early research on culturally responsive teaching was to support minoritized students. However, it was later argued that culturally responsive practices should be extended to all aspects of education, including school leaders. Previous and current research indicates that principals can and do contribute to student academic success, understand school resources, and are in the best position to promote and support school improvement initiatives. In this same vein, they are accountable for progress or lack thereof, Khalifa et al. [21]. Besides, principals are primarily responsible for instructional support to empower teachers to make intentional changes in their teaching practices that lead to improvement in student academic outcomes [22].

Harvey and Allard [23] observed that it can be challenging to foster diversity in the workplace through organizational change and management practices. Leaders can assist by utilizing methods such as active listening, forming connections, and recognizing and comprehension impediments. For instance, social scientists discovered that enforced education, warnings, and regulations had little effect. Procedures that promote variety at work embrace voluntary teaching, setting up self-regulating teams, a mixture task force, and diversity supervisors.

2.2 Emotional intelligence

> *Anyone can become angry-that is easy. But to be angry with the right person, to the right degree, at the right time, for the right purpose, and in the right way-this is not easy.*
>
> —*Aristotle, The Nicomachean Ethics*

A consensus is that EI has been an important and controversial topic during the last few decades. Its significance and its correlation with many domains of life have made it the subject of expert study. EI is the appendage for feeling, thinking, learning, problem-solving, and decision-making [24]. Although there is an increasing demand for EI, the accuracy of its varied measurements as well as its relevance in terms of worth and merit are often questioned. Various types of EI tests may hold potential, but their standards, evidence from neuroscience literature regarding EI, and the link between leader EI and followers all require further research [25, 26]. EI competencies expand the skill set leaders possess to create equitable outcomes for all students through more inclusive practices [3–6, 27].

Mayer and Salovey [4, 28] introduced the concept in 1990 to define EI "as the ability to monitor one's own and other's emotions, to discriminate among them, and to use the information to guide one's thinking and actions. Successfully developing EI affords one the ability to use emotions to direct thoughts and behavior and to understand their own feelings and others' feelings accurately. Goleman [5, 29] extended the concept to include general social competence and suggests that EI is key for the success of one's life.

Notwithstanding, Mayer and Salovey [28], suggested that EI is a cognitive ability, which is separate but also associated with general intelligence. Mayer and Salovey [30] revealed that EI consists of four skill dimensions: (1) perceiving emotion (i.e., the ability to detect emotions in faces, pictures, music, etc.); (2) facilitating thought with emotion (i.e., the ability to harness emotional information in one's thinking); (3) understanding emotions (i.e., the ability to understand emotional information); and (4) managing emotions (i.e., the ability to manage emotions for personal and interpersonal development). These skills have a key role in facilitating thinking, understanding emotions, and managing emotions, and evolve contingent upon maturity.

Moreover, Drigas and Papoutsi [24] studied a variety of learning theories from multiple researchers creating a nine-layer pyramid that encompasses EI Ability and EI Trait. This pyramid acts as a graphic presentation to depict what must be accomplished for someone to attain the apex of EI—emotional unity. This highest level is associated with awareness, gratification, and vastness. Models seven and eight, depicting self-actualization and transcendence, appear to draw from Maslow's pyramid of needs. The pyramid appears to combine emotional, cognitive, and metacognitive capabilities with personal progression toward growth and wants [24].

Similarly, research indicated that a growing body of evidence on research on EI has been divided into two distinct areas in terms of conceptualizing emotional competencies and their measurements: the trait EI [30] and the ability EI model [31]. Research evidence has consistently supported this distinction by revealing low correlations between the two [29–36].

In a novel standpoint, Humphrey et al. [37], proposed to combine studies on leadership and EI for the benefit of both. By examining various mainly theoretical approaches, it was concluded that leadership behavior is an emotional process triggered in everyday work settings. The five-tier multi-level model of emotions and leadership developed by these authors included: (1) within the person's internal changes; (2) differences in responses to events; (3) interpersonal attention such as contagion, dyadic leadership, and emotional labor; (4) groups/teams where contagion takes place; and (5) organizational culture/regulation rules. In detail, each tier offered advantages to the fields of both leadership study and EI research. Moreover, merging the two topics proposes that researchers should extend their aim to take into further consideration aspects of quality research as well as expand empirical research area [37].

Bradberry and Greaves [6] categorize EI competencies into two areas personal and social; identified four EI competencies that align with their 2.0 EI Assessment A brief description of the EI competencies is included below.

1. Self-awareness: A personal competence is defined as a leader's ability to accurately perceive individual emotions in various situations and to understand tendencies across them. Such skill requires being aware of reactions to specific occurrences, events, circumstances, and people. Making sense of individual emotions including the ability to tolerate the discomforts of focusing on possible negative feelings. Moreover, these authors posit that leader with self-awareness clearly understand their strengths and weakness, and motivations, and can identify people and situations that trigger their emotions. In this same vein, extant research has found that self-awareness skill is fundamental and that learning about oneself is not contingent upon a crisis, but rather, the daily conditions that situations that occur in worsening.

2. Self-management: The second personal skill and competence, describes as leaders' ability to use awareness of emotions, remain flexible, and direct behaviors positively. Managing emotions includes reacting to situations and people positively. For example, being able to tolerate uncertainty while exploring emotions and options. Self-management is evidenced by being able to understand and build comfort with individual feelings. Benefit of self-management skills is being able to defer momentary needs to pursue larger more important and sustainable goals. Additional competencies and avenues to assess effective relationship management skills include providing resources support and encouragement in

developing others, applying ethical decisions in conflict management, and successfully serving as a catalyst for change in the organization [13, 15].

3. Social awareness: Parallel to self-awareness, social awareness, is a fundamental skill that refers to a leaders' ability to accurately access emotions in other people and understand the underlying nature of the emotions, as well as empathizing with others, although the point of view may be different. Also, social awareness includes the ability to remain focused and absorb critical and relevant information. Essential to social awareness is listening and observing, while fully engaged in the process, yet remaining detached from personal feelings and beliefs that might influence a leaders' thinking. The ability to adjust to different situations, build relationships, as well as the ability to spot and address the elephant in the room is also essential social awareness skills. Lastly, evidence of social awareness supports team-building skills and involves staff in problem-solving process [13, 15, 23].

4. Relationship management: The second component of social awareness is Relationship Management skills, which is the awareness of individual emotions, and those of others, and to manage interactions successfully. Managing interactions successfully ensures clear and intentional communication and effective conflict-resolution skills. Relationship management skills afford leaders the opportunity to see the benefits of connecting with diverse groups, which include those who think differently. This skill requires the ability to initiate direct, constructive communication which avoids stress that leads to disengagement and conflict in the workplace [38] Also, relationship management skills require asking questions to gain a clear focus on the nature of the issue, which leads to being initiative-taking, rather than reactive. In this vein, self-management reflects a growth mindset, as evidenced by exercising flexibility, embracing challenges, viewing failure as an opportunity to gain experience, and believing mistakes are an essential part of learning [13, 38].

2.3 Emotional intelligence and leadership challenges

2.3.1 Leadership for change

Consequently, the world is transforming to an altered way of life during an epidemic, which is true for schooling. It has been asserted by investigators that confronting the aftermath of COVID-19 and its influence will be one of the significant tests for educational leaders in this age. By leaving a door open and exchanging ideas with one another, school leaders are utilizing data and modern tools to rapidly adjust and traverse the difficulties brought on by the pandemic. This "new normal" won't just be a brief event but instead will have continuous and powerful results in education and school direction. Additionally, educational leaders can use insights to b Accordingly, the world is adjusting to "new" life during a pandemic, and the same is true for the education sector. Researchers argue that responding to the COVID-19 pandemic and its aftermath will be one of the biggest challenges for school leaders in this era. By being open and sharing insights with each other, school leaders are using data and the latest tools to quickly adapt and navigate COVID-19 challenges. More than just a trend, this "new normal" will have lasting and powerful effects on the future of education and school leadership. Also, school leaders can use data to make a change that is impactful and sustainable [1, 2, 7].

Conversely, a review of the literature reported that effective leadership is key to successful organizational change [2, 11, 13, 15, 19, 22]. For example, effective leadership and change management behaviors and practices facilitated positive organizational change and innovations for organizational growth and sustainability. Effective leaders must be able to understand and apply change management theory such as applying the three stages: (1) adapting to change, as evidenced by determining stakeholders readiness and willingness to commit to change, (2) controlling change, which include determining the degree of implementation such as piloting a program, to gather data to identify issues and areas of concerns prior to fully implementing innovation, and (3) effecting change, means that school leaders begins with the understanding that change is a personal choice [15]. Researchers concluded that effective leadership behavior and practices, which facilitate change in the work setting includes building trust with stakeholder and employing strategies to implement an organizational culture that reflects trust and honesty, which results in a sense of belonging. Such strategies reinforce a commitment to organizational change [7, 15, 17, 39].

2.3.2 Ethically leadership

Ethical challenges of Leadership: Casting light or shadow. C.E. Johnson

Moreover, a lack of knowledge, skills, or experience might cause leaders to unintentionally "cast shadows". For example, a lack of understanding digital equity, which goes beyond access, as equity includes literacy and identifying the digital gap. In this same vein, application of ethical perspectives or frameworks to be applied to ethical dilemmas requires under understanding emotions, which are critical to decision-making and actions. Consequently, a lack of self-awareness can misguide in making appropriate ethical choices [40]. Continuous research concerning ethical leadership is taking place within multiple contexts of educational leadership, such as detailed defining of ethical leadership, which aptly portray an ethical leader as one who respects truthfulness and models their actions in line with their values and beliefs [39, 41]. Nonetheless, past studies on the effectiveness of leadership mostly emphasized traits and behaviors. Furthermore, strictly concentrating on leadership behaviors may mask unethical destructive behaviors which necessitate followership.

For instance, a scandal related to testing in a nearby metro school district caught my attention. The superintendent (who has since passed away) was responsible for orchestrating it back then. Most teachers were among the followers who manipulated test scores for pupils experiencing academic difficulty across the area. Although the superintendent had to refund capital earned from high-test scores for the district to the state government, great damage had ensued: lack of trust by learners, parents as well as citizens alike and subsequent blaming of instructors that disturbed learning progression. This situation reminded me of an old saying: "We believe what we see more than what we hear". Similarly, early research on transformational leadership was crucial for understanding how connection between leaders and their followers results in increased motivation and morale [11, 13, 15]. Furthermore, conceptualized transformational leadership via group purpose which aids in recognizing constituents' individual objectives can stimulate rethinking of entrenched thought process leading to organizational adjustment [11, 13]. Researchers reported that creating relationships enables transformational leaders to pick up high-order values, which are guided by ethics resulting in moral behavior. Highlighted that only when leaders satisfy ideal requirements and display moral values do they become transformational leaders. This study investigated how ethical management secures psychological safety thus promoting corporate social responsibility at a micro level connecting with employees' awareness, perspectives, or strategies [10, 11, 15, 19, 39]. Research has also purported that the personal integrity of leaders contributes to ethical behavior and practices, which requires developing character and is developed by experiencing personal trauma, such as career setbacks and personal losses which allows leaders to examine his/her inner self. Revisions maintains my intended meaning [11, 13, 19].

2.3.3 Leadership for diversity, equity, and inclusion

School leaders are charged with producing tangible outcomes such as higher test scores and graduation rates (n.d.) School culture, the environment, and the organizational change adversely impact school leaders' cognitive behaviors. A study focused on how secondary principals conducted decision-making related to federal and state mandates. The results revealed that over half of the principal's decision-making process on mandates was guided by their values and beliefs, which requires thinking and reasoning, a cognition process. This study supports the notion of how self-awareness helps understand triggers that evoke emotions and the importance of identifying strategies to address such emotions [15, 30, 32, 34].

The advantage of hiring people who look different from the existing majority, and think differently, is that leaders are provided an opportunity to develop and exercise collaborative intelligence, which is a "road less traveled". For example, many leaders are traditionally taught to focus on the gulfs between us rather than valuing the intellectual diversity that key players bring to the setting [27]. This approach supports leaders in developing competence in self-management skills, such as demonstrating active listening and patience.

Likewise, cultural competency is essential for diversity to thrive in the workplace, which begins with self, by acknowledging stereotypes and biases, and understanding cultural values and norms of the groups he/she serves [23, 25, 42]. Importantly, leaders should also acknowledge that cultural competency is an ongoing learning process. Social awareness skill also supports the importance of leaders' acknowledging their own bias and limitations [6].

Authors Flore and Bagwel [43] extended the discourse on social justice and leadership to promote inclusion. Accordingly, inclusion has previously been limited to students with disabilities, by which instruction was provided in the least restrictive environment. However, the persistent inequalities among underrepresented students, linguistically diverse students, and LBGTQ students, are increasingly challenging the traditional notion of inclusion. The ongoing academic gaps and educational disparities are the center of attention in most school districts, which suggest inclusive leadership practices to be employed as social justice leadership and to expand the capacity of beginning school leaders to become champions for social justice in their schools [18, 43].

A case study of two principals, in a large urban school district elected to implement social justice model in their assigned schools. Data collection included interviews, observations in each school, and the development of themes that described the barriers and resistance to social justice in their schools [38], reported that understanding a clear definition of social justice leadership begins with a recognition of the unequal circumstances of underrepresented groups and how policies and procedures, economic, political, and societal beliefs regarding race, class, gender, and other variables to successful perpetuate inequalities in schools and classrooms [43, 44].

2.3.4 Leadership for creativity and innovation

Research reported that education systems are quickly recognizing the significance of creativity. Even though scholarship around leadership in schools is vast, there isn't much on leading for creativity. A study highlighted how engaging people with varying backgrounds leads to greater intellectual innovation for leaders. Moreover, a recent examination determined if servant leadership actions and practices could influence creativity, as well as if participation and knowledge sharing improved it. Data was accumulated from 247 employees and 57 managers employed at Chinese commercial enterprises. It showed that servant leader behaviors such as establishing an atmosphere where personnel feels appreciated and respected can help provoke creative thought by facilitating knowledge sharing [45].

A unique perspective on creativity and the field of educational leadership examined creativity discourses in the educational leadership journal, .and found a limited number of peer-reviewed journals, with a limited direct focus on the topic of creativity in the major professional educational leadership journals. This chapter concluded by suggesting an invitation for the field of educational leadership rather than providing conclusions or setting aims to be achieved.

Previously, studies on leadership and creativity have focused on organizational problem-solving to improve product performance and to maintain a competitive edge in an increasing complex global economy. However, research indicated that problem-solving is a complex cognitive process that requires time and attention of leaders. Tenets of creative problem solving include defining and constructing a problem, producing relevant information, generating, and evaluating a diverse set of solutions. The duration of time for pursuing creativity in the workplace requires commitment and support from leadership. Also, these authors noted that identifying and understanding various models of creativity demonstrate leadership commitment and support [43, 46].

Hao and Yazdanifard [47] reported that communication patterns are another important variable that fosters creativity in the workplace. For example, the inclusion of diverse teams of members from a wide background and experiences in problem-solving is based on previous experiences. Subsequently, diverse teams increase the possibilities of including multiple and diverse problem construction. Likewise, planning was identified as an integral part of performing complex tasks in organizations during the creative for performance process. For example, an examination of alternative models of planning as well as how planning might uncover errors should be included in this process. In this same line of thinking, the evaluation of ideas might minimize errors, especially as the problem-solving process is more cylinder [45]. As previously indicated, this process requires leadership support and guidance. Also, leadership should articulate what criteria are being evaluated and identify barriers to use as a guide to help cognitive processes such as time for planning and implementation. Recommendations included providing feedback that includes strengths, weaknesses, and future challenges [45, 46].

2.3.5 Leadership for change

Accordingly, the world is adjusting to a "new" life during a pandemic, and the same is true for education sector. Researchers argue that responding to the COVID-19 pandemic and its aftermath will be one of the biggest challenges for school leaders in this era. By being open and sharing insights with each other, school leaders are using data and the latest tools to quickly adapt and navigate COVID-19 challenges. More than just a trend, this "new normal" will have lasting and powerful effects on the future of education and school leadership. Also, school leaders can use data to make change that is impactful and sustainable [1, 2, 7].

Conversely, a review of the literature reported that effective leadership is key to successful organizational change [2, 11, 13, 15, 19, 22]. For example, effective leadership and change management behaviors and practices facilitated positive organizational change and innovations for organizational growth and sustainability. Effective leaders must be able to understand and apply change management theory such as applying the three stages: (1) adapting to change, as evidenced by determining stakeholders readiness and willingness to commit to change, (2) controlling change, which include determining the degree of implementation such as piloting a program, to gather data to identify issues and areas of concerns prior to fully implementing an innovation, and (3) Effecting change, means that school leaders begin with the understanding that change is a personal choice [15]. Researchers concluded that effective leadership behavior and practices, which facilitate change in the work setting includes building trust with stakeholder and employing strategies to implement an organizational culture that reflects trust and honesty, which results in a sense of belonging. Such strategies reinforce a commitment to organizational change [7, 15, 17, 39].

As previously stated, the adage "If it ant broke don't fix it," is still prevalent among some stakeholders in today's work settings. This notion reflects a lack of establishing clear goals by linking goals to school improvement plans or analyzing data from multiple sources to develop school-wide goals. Educational leaders provide stakeholders the opportunity to understand the 'why' and what is truly "broken" [13, 23].

"Moving the vision from the wall to the hall" is reflected in this line of thinking Kouzes and Posner [13]; Fullan [15] reported that modeling beliefs and values demonstrate involvement, which results in commitment from stakeholders. Also, studies have found that a lack of involving stakeholders in decisions that affect them increases the risk of stalled change efforts (as previously noted, change involves a personal decision). Involving stakeholders in the decision-making process strengthens relationships and provides estimations on timetables and duration of goals, expectations, and commitment. These strategies increase leaders' effectiveness in successfully managing change in the workplace [13, 21].

3. Summary

The data from the literature review, previous educational leaders in K-12 public school settings, and teaching experience in higher education in recent years are collected. In summary, there are two central concepts to the conceptual framework for studying EI competencies and the four variables for leadership challenges. The model represents the relationships among EI competencies, principals' behaviors for each EI competency, and variables of leadership challenges in post-COVID-19 pandemic.

The second establishes an operational path for establishing the relationship between EI competencies and the variables of the leadership challenges. It also illustrates how the EI competencies affect principals' leadership behavior and practices and subsequent leadership skills. Variables that mediate (explain) how effects influence leadership behavior and practices and principals' leadership skills. A basic model, shown in **Figure 1**, is proposed and is used in all empirical casual studies.

The model represents the relationships among EI competencies, principals' behaviors for each EI competency and variables of leadership challenges. As shown

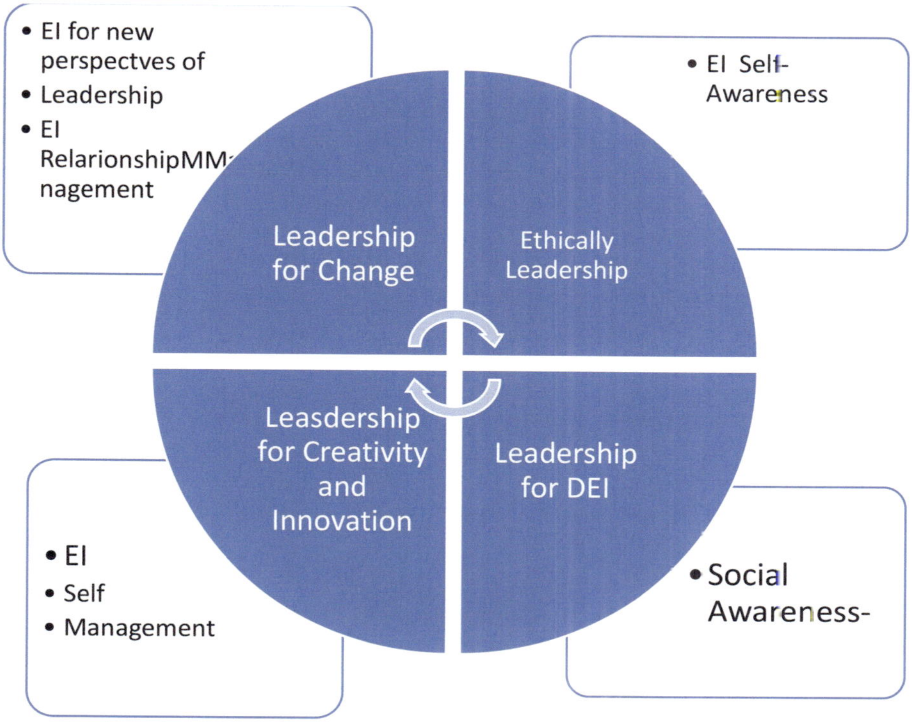

Figure 1.
Data collection is the basis of principals' leadership skills. Principals' influence student academic success and other school outcomes such as attendance, discipline, and high school graduation rates. Data collection should also include teacher observations for culturally responsive teaching practices and teacher, student, and parent surveys. These data can be considered true and measurable. Principals can expand the lens by seeing how teacher practices support DEI. Also, data can be used for principals to work collaboratively to identify and develop professional development activities, develop instructional goals, and to initiate a professional learning community. These steps suggest that principals should increase EI competencies to increase inclusive leadership skills that support teaching and learning, which leads to increased learning opportunities and positive school outcomes for all students.

in **Figure 1**, a theory of action for principals' increasing ethical leadership behavior and practices, EI competencies, inclusive leadership skills, culturally responsive leadership practices, developing and initiating creative innovations to reflect change leadership practices and developing a community of practice

In **Figure 1**, principals can apply EI competencies to develop inclusive skillsets to identify the leadership challenge that speaks to the specific needs of the individual school to move the needle toward increasing student academic success for all students; increase leadership effectiveness in implementing innovations to increase educational opportunities for marginalized students.

4. Conclusion

Research step 1 proves that EI competencies can support principals' personal core values in making ethical decisions. For example, implementing policies that support social justice for underserved students and increasing access to high-quality instruction [18, 19].

Research step 2 illustrates that EI competencies can support principals' personal core values in increasing self-awareness in self-management skills to guide in staying the course for creativity and innovation. For example, risk-taking and using challenges as opportunities. Also, remaining focused on the benefits of creativity, which includes retaining quality employees, and fostering imagination leads reflects intellectual capital, which leads to problem solving in the work setting [16].

Research step 3 shows that EI competencies can support principals' social-awareness in leading for DEI skills. For example, culturally responsive schools begin with intentional leadership practices and inclusive leadership skills that support teaching and learning practices that foster motivation, build relationships, and support rigorous and relevant instruction [3, 20, 21].

Research step 4 delineates that EI competencies can support principals lead change, which requires self-management, trust, collaboration, and relationship building [2, 7, 12, 18]. For example, applying the ADKAR model created by Jeffery Hiatt [48], limits resistance, by implementing incremental change, incorporates employee feedback, and keeps the goal in front. A (awareness of the need to change); D (desire to change); K (knowledge of how to change); A (ability to change); R (Reinforcement to keep the change in place).

Author details

Doris M. Dickerson
Concordia University Portland, OR, USA

*Address all correspondence to: ddickerson31@gmail.com

References

[1] Harris A, Jones M. COVID 19 - school leadership in disruptive times. School Leadership and Management. 2020;**40**:243-247. DOI: 10.1080/13632434.2020.1811479

[2] Zhao Y. COVID-19 as a catalyst for educational change. Prospects. 2020;**49**:29-33. DOI: 10.1007/s11125-.au020-09477-

[3] Barak MEM. Managing Diversity: Toward a Globally Inclusive Workplace. Los Angeles, CA: Sage Publication; 2016

[4] Salovey P, Mayer JD. Emotional Intelligence. Imagination, Cognition and Personality. 1990;**9**(3):185-211. DOI: 10.2190/DUGG-P24E-52Wk-CDG

[5] Goleman D. Emotional Intelligence. New York, NY: Bantam Books Publishers; 2005

[6] Bradberry T, Greaves J. Emotional Intelligence 2.0. San Diego, CA: Talent Smart Publications; 2009

[7] Sekiguchi T, De Cuyper N. Addressing new leadership challenges in a rapidly changing world. Applied Psychology. 2022;**40**(4):243-247. DOI: 10.111/apps.1240

[8] Einstein A. The Ultimate Quotable Einstein. Princeton University Press; 2010. p. 479

[9] Covey S. https://youtu.be/CZtWG0yWYTU Steven Covey Gracious Quotes

[10] Burn JM. Leadership. New York, NY: Harper & Row Publishers; 1978

[11] Bass B M. Leadership and Performance Beyond Expectations. New York, NY: Free Press; 1985

[12] Grissom JA, Loeb S. Triangulating principal effectiveness: how perspectives of parents, teachers, and assistant principals identify the central importance of managerial skills. American Education Research Journal. 2011;**48**(5):1091-1123. http //aer.sagepub.com/content/early/2011/03/26/0002831211402663

[13] Kouzes JM, Posner BZ. The Leadership Challenge: How to Get Extraordinary Things Done in Organizations. San Francisco: Jossey-Bass Publications; 2017

[14] Cummings TG, Worley CG. Organization Development and Change. Mason: Ohio South-Western College Publications; 2001

[15] Fullan M. Change Leader: Learning to Do What Matters Most. San Francisco, CA: Jossey-Bass; 2011

[16] Lucas B, Venckutė M. Creativity–a transversal skill for lifelong learning. An overview of existing concepts and practices. In: Kampylis P, Cachia R, editors. Literature review report. EUR 30405 EN, Publications Office of the European Union, Luxembourg, 2020. ISBN 978-92-76-23323-7. DOI: 10.2760/557196, JRC121862

[17] Jex SM, Britt TW. Organizational Psychology: A Scientific-Practitioner Approach. 3rd ed. Hoboken, NJ: John Wiley & Sons Publications; 2015

[18] Kuhnert KW. In: Bass BM, Avolio BJ, editors. Transforming Leadership. Hoboken, NJ: John Wiley & Sons Publications; 1994. pp. 10-25

[19] Souba W. Perspective: a new model of leadership performance in health care.

Academic Medicine. 2011;**86**:1241-1252. DOI: 101097/AcM.ob013e31822c0385

[20] Adhikari T, Groeoneveid S, Kuipers B. The role of inclusive leadership in support inclusive climate in diverse public sector teams. Review of Personnel Administration. 2020. DOI: 10.117/0734371X19899722

[21] Khalifa MA, Gooden MA, Davis JE. Culturally responsive school leadership: a synthesis of the literature. Review of Educational Research. 2016;**86**(4):1272-1311. DOI: 10.3102/0034654316630383

[22] McCall MW. Highfliers: Developing the Next Generation of Leaders. Boston, MA: Harvard Business School Press; 1998

[23] Harvey C, Allard MJ. Understanding and Managing Diversity: Readings, Cases, and Exercises. Denver, CO: Prentice Publications; 2015

[24] Drigas AS, Papoutsi C. A new layered model on emotional intelligence. Behav Sci (Basel). 2018;**8**(5):45. DOI: 10.3390/bs8050045. PMID: 29724021; PMCID: PMC5981239

[25] Antonakis J, Ashkenazy NM, Dashborough MT. Does leadership need emotional intelligence? The Leadership Quarterly. 2009. DOI: 10.1016/jeaqua.2009.01.006

[26] Cole WF, Humphrey MS. Emotional intelligence: Sine qua non of leadership or folderol? American Psychological Association. 2011;**25**(1):45-59. DOI: 10.5465/AMP.2011.59193449

[27] Hanson E, Court B. Bridging the leadership gap. Performance Improvement. 1998;**37**(1):8-14

[28] Mayer JD, Salovey P, Caruso DR. Emotional intelligence: new ability or eclectic traits? American Psychologist. 2008;**63**:503-517. DOI: 10.1037/0003-066X.63.6.503

[29] Spector PE. Introduction: emotional intelligence. Journal of Organizational Behavior. 2005;**V26**(14):409-410. DOI: 10.1002/job.316

[30] Mayer JD, Salovey P. Emotional intelligence, and the construction and regulation of feelings. Applied and Preventive Psychology. 1995;**4**:197-208. DOI: 10.1016/S0962-1849(05)80058-7

[31] Brackett MA, Rivers SE, Salovey P. Emotional intelligence: implications for personal, social, academic, and workplace success. Social and Personality Psychology Compass. 2011;**5**:88-103. DOI: 10.1111/j.1751-9004.2010.00334.x

[32] Mikolajczak M, Luminet O, Menil C. Predicting resistance to stress: incremental validity of trait emotional intelligence over alexithymia and optimism. Psicothema. 2006;**18**:79-88

[33] O'Connor RM Jr, Little IS. Revisiting the predictive validity of emotional intelligence: self-report versus ability-based measures. Personality and Individual Differences. 2003;**35**:1893-1902. DOI: 10.1016/S0191-8869(03)00038-2

[34] Pérez JC, Petrides KV, Furnham A. Measuring trait emotional intelligence. In: Schullze R, Roberts RD, editors. Emotional Intelligence: an International Handbook. Ashland, OH, USA: Hogrefe & Huber Publishers; 2005. pp. 181-201

[35] Warwick J, Nettelbeck T. Emotional intelligence is ...? Personality and Individual Differences. 2004;**37**:1091-1100. DOI: 10.1016/j.paid.2003.12.003

[36] Gardner HE. Intelligence Reframed: Multiple Intelligences for the 21st

Century. London, UK: Hachette UK; 2000

[37] Humphrey RH, Burch GF, Adams LL. The benefits of merging leadership research and emotions research. Frontiers in Psychology. 2016;7, Article 1022. DOI: 10.3389/fpsyg.2016.01022

[38] Manovich D, MacArthur A. Collaborative Intelligence: Thinking with People Who Think Differently. New York, NY: Spiegel & Grau Publications; 2015

[39] Voegttin C, Schere AG, Stahl. Hawn, O. Grand societal challenges and response. Journal of Management and Studies. 2022;**59**(1):1-28. DOI: DOI/10.111/joms.12785

[40] Johnson CE. Meeting the Ethical Challenges of Leadership: Casting Light or Shadow. 6th ed. Thousand Oaks: CA, Sage Publications; 2018

[41] Monahan K. A review of the literature concerning ethical leadership in organizations. Emerging Leadership Journeys. 2012;**5**(1):56-66

[42] Grissom AR. The alert collector: workplace diversity and inclusion. Reference & User Services Quarterly. 2018;**57**(4):243-247. DOI: 10.5860/rusq.57.4

[43] Flore C, Bagwell J. Social justice leadership as inclusion: programming inclusive practices to ensure equality for all students. California Association of Professors of Education Administration; 2021 ERIC No: EJ13185-16

[44] Matthews D, Mawhinney HB. Social justice leadership and inclusion: exploring challenges in urban district struggling to address inequalities. Educational Administration Quarterly. 2014. DOI: 10.1177/0013161X13514440

[45] Chen M, Zada M, Khan J, Saba NU. How does servant leadership influence creativity? Enhancing employee creativity via creative process engagement and knowledge sharing. Front. Psychol. 2022;**2022**. DOI: 10.3389/fpsyg.2022.947092

[46] Munford MD. Performance in planning: process, requirements, and errors. Sage Journal. 2001;**5**(3). DOI: 10.1037/1089-2680.5.3.213

[47] Hao MJ, Yazdanifard R How effective leadership can facilitate change in organizations through improvement and innovation. Global Journals USA. 2015;**15**(9):9 Online ISSN: 2249—4588

[48] Hiatt J. ADKAR: A model for change in business and our community. River Grove Books. Levelland, CO; 2006

Section 3

Leadership Styles

Chapter 5

Shepherd Leadership: A Review and Future Research Directions

Majda I. Ayoub/Al-Salim

Abstract

This chapter is important because Shepherd leadership is not much taught in popular business or leadership textbooks. There is inadequate understanding and practice of compassionate care-Shepherd leadership quality-in sectors such as education and healthcare. Education is an important sector as it impacts students' learning. Teachers with Shepherd leadership qualities motivate students to outperform, and be creative and work persistently to improve themselves, their communities and society. Healthcare is an important sector because providing healthcare has significant impact on personal and public health, development and economic growth to attain major employment. Additionally, research reveals that caring and compassionate leadership is lacking in organizations because it forms resilience, nurtures a team spirit, enhances engagement, and may reduce employee turnover. This chapter sheds light on the importance of compassionate and caring leaders in religious and educational organizations, healthcare, the army, and business organizations. This chapter will discuss mainly Shepherd leadership and aims to define it and will explore where it is mostly utilized and in what type of organizations has this leadership been applied and successful. This chapter also compares Shepherd leadership with Servant leadership, a closely related leadership, and other popular leadership styles in today's organizations. Lastly, this chapter will touch on the challenges of Shepherd leadership.

Keywords: Shepherd leadership, Servant leadership, Secular leadership, Spiritual leadership, Shepherd leadership challenges, Compassionate leadership

1. Introduction

A great leader is the one who sparks the followers' passion and brings out the best in them. In many cases when trying to explain why such leaders are very effective, many tend to give credit to their perfect strategy, vision or to their innovative ideas. In reality however, such leaders are effective because they share their compassion with their followers as they work through the emotions, irrespective of what they are set out to accomplish. Those leaders' success relies on 'how' it is being done therefore, if those leaders fail to share their compassion, care and drive their emotions in the right direction; nothing will work as anticipated [1]. Additionally, there is so much confusion about spirituality in public education and how educators may generate the right environment to adopt spirituality as a form of diversity, as an aspect of leadership at secular institutions. When educational institutions encourage and support the students' spiritual walk without biases, this may extend students connectedness to self, others and the community at large. Also, when spiritual leadership is practiced, it may harvest the skills that are demanded by employers once those educational institutions nurture students' spiritual development [2].

Several recent clinical studies concluded that there is inadequate understanding and inadequate practice of compassionate care in the healthcare industry as an example-the physical and the mental health; a more profound understanding of crucial behaviors and attitudes that bring better health to patients through compassionate care is in great need [3, 4].

Shepherd leaders, serve their followers with compassion, they know how to build themselves up through their spirituality as well as build and encourage their followers; to have compassion is when you serve others as a leader and not wait to be served [5]. There are real world examples that prove that when a type of Spiritual leadership is in place in business organizations, positive outcomes are harvested. The Ynna Conglomerate group, a Moroccan holding company led by a Spiritual leader Miloud Chaabi. Basically all his decisions at work were taken based on his ethical convictions; he was a shepherd before he established his organization. Chaabi was listed on Forbes Magazine among the top 40 billionaires in the continent of Africa [6]. Mrs. Shiprah Gichaga, is another example among many women in Africa, who was the executive director of the Kenya chapter of African Women Educationalists; lobbied for educational equality of access for girls, especially in marginal communities [7]. The hope Mrs. Shiprah had, kept her motivation going, even when the figures presented only minimal progress; it is the hope as a major element of spiritual leadership, as it provides persistence and resilience to continue until the goal is accomplished [7].

In this chapter the author advances a position regarding the current state of leadership and how it can be improved in multiple sectors; this is done through a theoretical lens of Shepherd leadership. The author will argue that through careful application of Shepherd leadership, organizations regardless of the sector can better motivate their employees and reap great success. The author aims to unlock some insights in Shepherd leadership by shedding light on the humane aspects of the real purpose of the organization and its people, besides maximizing profits, that is almost absent in today's business world [8]. Being caring and compassionate not only is the right thing to do, but it is also good for the firm's bottom line.

The author advances her position by starting with a theoretical framework that defines the Shepherd leadership model. Following, the author continues then with literature review to include Shepherd leadership in religious organizations where it is widely utilized, a brief comparison of Shepherd leadership with very similar leadership such as Servant leadership, followed by a comparison of Shepherd leadership with popular leadership approaches. Then the author goes on to discuss the success of Shepherd leadership in churches, education, healthcare, business sector, and the army followed by the discussion of drawbacks or challenges of Shepherd leadership.

2. Theoretical framework

Shepherding is one of the most ancient professions of humankind, the image of a shepherd as leader goes back since thousands of years and is a widespread image.

The Shepherd leader' symbol is a perfect way through which to understand leadership in general [9]. According to Merriam-Webster dictionary, the history of the word was taken from the Middle English word Sheepherde which comprises of the two words, sheep and herd [10].

The sufficient credentials that define a good leader is a 'good Shepherd' who has the best interest at heart for the flock [11]. A shepherd leader is a Spiritual leader who displays an honest character and demonstrates good moral behavior as he/she holds high respect for human dignity. Spiritual leadership appears to be an all-inclusive view in comparison with Servant and Shepherd leadership approaches. Spirituality in leadership emphasizes progress based on worldwide values like morality, integrity, love, compassion, thankfulness that have an influence on the leader's behavior, ability and attitude. Such spiritual values are desired for generating accountable and ethical actions, as they control what to think, who the person is and what he/she does [12].

A Shepherd leader portrays humility while leads by example with patience, he/she encourages values and ethics, cares about the flock, with sound judgment and always seeks justice for all. The sincere character of Shepherd leaders stems from their fundamental beliefs [13]. The Shepherd leader is expected to sincerely care and demonstrate concern for others. The shepherd leader repeatedly evaluates the essentials of the herd and have empathy and go beyond the call of duty to support his/her followers [14]. As the Shepherd leader spends a plethora of time with his/her flock; he/she becomes very knowledgeable of their needs. Therefore, the shepherd leader develops great communication skills in order to guide, counsel and motivate his/her flock as well as provide accountability. Additionally, the shepherd leader provides the needed security to encourage stability, safety, innovation, and motivation to advance the organization [13].

The origin of the Shepherd leadership could trace back to the early biblical record, according to the Judeo-Christian faith, when God validated a preferential option for shepherds. This started in the Old Testament Bible and persists throughout the New Testament. Genesis 4:2 which is in the first book of the Old Testament, explains that Abel was a shepherd and Cain was a farmer and it revealed that Abel's sacrifice was one of his firstborn lambs that was preferred by God while Cain's sacrifice of his crops was not preferred by God; which clearly revealed a favored option for the shepherd's sacrifice [15]. A potential explanation would be as Cain was a 'tiller of the ground', he engaged in a more industrially innovative work than his brother Abel, since agriculture became the basis of the very first cultures or civilizations in recorded history. Shepherding, on the other hand, was the job of nomads and thereby set apart from the trappings of civilization [16]. As a result, through the Old Testament record, God often used the role of the shepherd to form His chosen leaders. Likewise, the leader as a shepherd is stressed as well, when Jesus Christ reveals himself as "the Good Shepherd" and compares the role with both hired laborer and the robber [16].

At the surface, the business world today may look at Shepherd Leadership style as an over-simplified style of leadership however, King David, one of Israel's pronounced leaders, stated in Psalm 23, a book in the Old Testament Bible, that before he was seated as king of Israel, he was a shepherd. In today's society, we may think of shepherding as a serene and peaceful activity, King David on the other hand may have disagreed with this simplification [17]. For King David, shepherding was much more than a peaceful activity; it was a hazardous and difficult business. The humility of Shepherd leaders is a difficult thing to be and it is established in their inclination to work silently behind the scenes, devote time on minor things, and make, seemingly unimportant decisions unrewarded and unobserved [18]. Furthermore, ruthless shepherding may destruct a family's financial well-being if for example the quality of the flock's meat, wool, skin, or milk is being degraded [17]. Therefore, from this viewpoint, David's writings about shepherding may look more applicable to today's business leaders [17]. However, the reader of David's writings can sense the satisfaction and respect of the shepherd follower [17].

Shepherd leadership vision, with hope and unselfish love, offer the foundation for strong intrinsic motivation through identifying of goals and task involvement since it fits in the higher order needs category of individuals, such as feeling autonomous, self-efficacy, proficiency, and relatedness. Through empowerment, Shepherd leaders may free employees from fear, force, and over control. This allows employees to utilize their talents when needed while Shepherd leaders also benefit by focusing on strategic matters in this ever-changing environment [19].

The follower-leader in Shepherd leadership creates value similarity all across the empowered team which is very nurturing. Higher S**piritual leadership**s such as Shepherd leadership proposes a promise as a catalyst, for a new model of **leadership theory** where theories and practice combine and outspread charismatic and transformational leadership theories along with values-based theories [20].

3. Literature review

The main objective of this chapter is to define Shepherd leadership and have a better understanding of such leadership, and which organizations are known to be utilizing and applying Shepherd leadership. Also this chapter compares Shepherd leadership with other similar leadership styles such as Servant leadership as well as other popular leadership styles. In addition, this chapter will aim to examine the applicability of Shepherd leadership in both, religious and secular sectors while touching on the challenges and potential drawbacks of such leadership.

3.1 Shepherd leadership in religious organizations

This term-Shepherd leadership is widely recognized and practiced in most churches, a Christian house of worship, all over the world. The Shepherd Leadership is when a church calls for a leader who is able to walk side by side with his flock in regular communication and care, all while teaching them self-adequacy [21]. The more self-sufficient a church becomes, the pastor functions as a true shepherd. It is worthy of noting that faith fixated Shepherd leaders give credit to God when a sermon touches the heart of the hearer. As it is believed that the Shepherd leader is used by God to feed, encourage and support the flock and when great accomplishments take place, the Shepherd leader never takes credit, but gives it all to God [22].

3.2 A brief comparison between shepherd leadership with servant leadership

There is a substantial link between Shepherd Leadership and Servant Leadership; it may exist as a model of Servant leadership in a parallel fashion where spiritual leadership is advanced as a model of Servant leadership. Robert Greenleaf originally presented this concept in his paper in 1970 [23]. The Servant leader is the opposite of the oppressive and authoritarian leader, who is mainly occupied with controlling his followers and gathering wealth; one who has confidence in the idea that leaders should be first. While, Servant leaders may not be concerned with individual glorification and self-interest, their focus is on others; they care about and empower individuals and act as facilitators, and long for all of their followers to be successful [24]. In order to lead, a servant leader has a duty to serve, mentor and teach followers; this is considered the main motto that is indicative of Servant leadership. Servant leadership is the methodical process of developing the needs of followers ahead of those leaders which may potentially be found inside many organizations. Shepherd leadership however, provides individual followers with empowerment and encouragement to do well [25]. The value sought from effective leadership is grounded in the sharing of accountability, respect, care, and being practical with the people, not against them. Thus, in Shepherd leadership, delegation is essential and must be handled wisely with a goal in mind which may fundamentally equip, empower and inspire followers in their efforts [26]. There is an evident overlap of Servant, Spiritual and Shepherd leaderships. To point out a leader, the Bible uses the Shepherd metaphor; according to the Old Testament Bible, Prophet Moses was chosen as a leader due to his tenderness and caring character as he was a shepherd; he fed his sheep and made sure they never went astray [15]. Meanwhile the Servant leader is the one who delights his followers with tenderness and compassion; in many cases, leaders are shunned for being insensible or indifferent with their followers which strip them from influencing them into ethical standing [27].

Servant leadership explains the reason behind the motivation of the shepherd in fulfilling his/her responsibilities. Servant leaders are committed to put their followers' needs before their own which allows for relationship formation with their followers as it provides leverage to be influential; with such influence, a culture is recognized [17]. Shepherd and Servant leaderships can be both considered Spiritual leadership which may be recognized as faith-based leaderships; such leadership styles compel the leader to follow his/her vision to make a difference in the organization as part of the leader's calling which provides meaning and purpose to the leader's life [19].

Table 1 gives a brief comparison of servant leadership attributes and shepherd leadership attributes.

3.3 Comparing Shepherd leadership with other popular leadership styles!

There are noticeable differences between Shepherd leadership and other popular leaderships. The first difference is that most popular leadership approaches can be manipulating as they aim to influence, guide or control followers' behaviors in order to accomplish the firm's objectives. Secular leadership models put emphasis on the leader overpowering his/her followers through demanding work while Shepherd leadership utilizes power via kind and gentle service [28].

Furthermore, Shepherd leadership is about building relationships and demonstrating sincere love as the highest inspiration and transformational force. It pursues to work on maturing the leader-follower unity of purpose and change the followers' hearts while they joyfully complete their tasks. Other popular leadership approaches rely on their followers to complete tasks; Shepherd leadership on the other hand, gets the tasks done through building relationships and transforming individuals [29]. The second difference is that popular leadership approaches are usually transactional and demand followers' commitment through the use of rewards, intimidations or coercions [29].

Servant leadership attributes VS. Shepherd leadership attributes	
1. Listening	1. Best interest at heart for the flock
2. Empathy	2. Accountability Sharing
3. Healing	3. Honesty
4. Awareness	4. Good moral behavior
5. Persuasion	5. Has sincere character
6. Conceptualization	6. Humility
7. Foresight	7. Leads by example
8. Stewardship	8. Patience
9. Commitment to people growth	9. Sound judgment
10. Building community	10. Seeks justice for all
	11. Sincerely cares
	12. Listens, cooperates to create harmony, security, stability and safety

Table 1.
Servant leadership attributes versus Shepherd leadership attributes [17].

Popular leaderships are usually based on the concept of **reciprocity**; which brings mutual benefits; therefore subordinates perform their parts to benefit the leadership while they can benefit from a good evaluation or a bonus at the end of the term. The view of rewards/punishment or fear of vengeance frequently motivates, since it provokes positive or negative feelings within followers. The relational view of leadership understands that the individual role is powerful, and at the same time is always performed in the context of the whole belief system, practices, and action logic that form how mutual direction, order, and commitment are generated [30]. Shepherd leadership however, is **relational** and neither relies on possibilities of rewards nor threats of consequences, and followers do their tasks and go the extra mile to please their leader; as they expect the leader's steadfast care and love for them [31]. Finally, Shepherd leadership is a whole-person kind of leadership approach, and has little to do with completing tasks in a particular way; it is a leadership that benefits from a transformed character that makes his/her followers' interests, the leader' priority [19]. Shepherd leadership relies on the belief that what people do does not define them, but rather what people are; which is echoed in people's behavior. Accordingly, Shepherd leadership is all about first becoming and then doing, and not the other way around; sincere leadership is a lifestyle, not a system or method [31]. **Table 2** below

Shepherd Leadership Popular Leaderships	
1. Kind and gentle	1. Manipulating to accomplish objectives
• Builds relationships	• Puts emphasis on leader overpowering followers
• Demonstrates sincere love as the force	• Relies on followers to complete tasks
2. Pursues Leader-follower unity of purpose	2. Transactional and demand followers' commitment
• A leader benefits from a transformed character	• Reliant on reciprocity
3. What people are defines them	3. What people do, defines them

Table 2.
Brief comparison between Shepherd leadership and other popular leaderships.

DOI: http://dx.doi.org/10.5772/intechopen.108324

summarizes the main differences between popular leaderships in the twenty first century and Shepherd leadership.

4. Method

This chapter assumes a critical review method to advance an understanding of Shepherd leadership. This work was demonstrated based on the most noteworthy literature in the field. The focus of this chapter is to generate a clear understanding of Shepherd leadership in the secular and non-secular arenas. Also this chapter, through the use of a critical lens, will touch on how Shepherd leaders can influence their followers by referring to the current literature and practice.

5. Discussion

5.1 Shepherd leadership in churches

The Shepherd-like leadership of Joel Osteen at Lakewood Church in Houston, Texas can be a good example of very successful Shepherd leadership in religious organizations [25]. Lakewood Church is the largest congregation church in the United States and Joel Osteen's message had been described as positive and optimistic. Regardless of Joel Osteen's leadership successes, he continues to display humility and down to earth character, his message always aims to create harmony as he does not harp on conflicting views, while many of his followers perceive sincerity in character; which is consistent with Shepherd leadership qualities [25].

According to study findings, there is a strong direct relationship between the shepherd leadership characteristics, when present, and tithing. Tithing is essential for churches to survive and thrive. The study collected Shepherd leadership scores of multiple churches, which experienced growth in major areas as a proof of ministry effectiveness and success; the top five churches that had their attendance go up as well as their finances improve, had very high scores in relationship and duty grouping [32]. Thus, the Shepherd leader's relationship with his/her flock is the main element that produces ministry effectiveness. Also, the findings show that a strong relationship between effective leaders and the capability to create and sustain relationships with their followers [32].

5.2 Shepherd leadership in education

Shepherd Leadership has been successfully utilized in the education sector as well. Shepherd leaders provide a learning environment in higher education that is favorable in creating optimum performance from the faculty members, administrative employees, and students alike [33]. Also within the educational institution, teachers may 'lead from behind' although they may not hold any leadership title [34]. Shepherd leadership for example deemed successful in enhancing online class participation for Asian students; it helped them overcome cultural barriers and were able to get the students involve in online critical thinking. A shepherd leader knows his/her flock adequately to practice effective and compassionate care in order for their followers to progress [35]. In the classroom where teachers practice Shepherd leadership, a teacher only intercedes or redirects the students if they are moving outside the allowed perimeters; this is considered compassionate and caring attributes of a good Shepherd leader. Moreover, according to current research, teachers possess the greatest impact on student learning. Metaphorically, just as the good Shepherd pays great deal of attention in the form of caring for the flock, good teachers pay a great deal of attention to their students [36]. For example, religious higher education generally offers theological college students with the expertise required to practice their calling, such expertise should form a share of a multifaceted competency that embraces Shepherd leadership qualities mentioned earlier in this chapter as well as discipleship fundamentals, teamwork, and empowerment [33]. Secular higher education also, may prosper and become a success in a learning community where faculty members are treated justly and with reverence so to share their wisdom and knowledge with their students. In the meantime, these students may share their learning experiences and character building with their families, loved ones, and their communities at large [33].

Shepherd leadership is also practiced in secular education; when we closely examine informal teacher leadership style, as teachers practice humility in character and focus on building caring relationships with students and their communities. Teachers in this informal leadership setting do not have a hierarchical role with their students where they do not have a formal title as being the students' superiors [37].

5.3 Shepherd leadership in healthcare

Shepherd leadership has been successful also in healthcare organizations. Many studies in healthcare institutions concluded that compassionate care impacted the health of patients. When receiving compassionate care from nurses, doctors and those who interact with patients, it assisted in their recovery process. Moreover, according to institutional reports from psychiatric therapists in social work, they specified that because of the use of compassionate care, patients felt heard and understood; patients were improving noticeably [38, 39].

5.4 Shepherd leadership in the business sector

Empirical studies in the field of Shepherd leadership as part of Spiritual leadership, has proven this leadership to be productive and demonstrated positive relationships between spirituality on multiple organizational variables. One study who surveyed 225 non-executive workers in one firm, they have concluded, among other things, that their results propose a direct causal relationship between spirituality in the workplace and a constructive and efficient leadership [40]. Another study also concluded causal relationship between successful leadership and spirituality [41]. another relevant research where 1234 participants were surveyed to detect how faith-based values in secular organizations, impact business ethics and judgments; their findings indicate a greater level of moral judgment on behalf of participants with strong spiritual beliefs [42]. Additionally, other researchers studied the relationship between job satisfaction and spirituality and found a solid and positive correlation between organizational commitment and spirituality [43]. Also, research concluded a positive relationship between workplace spirituality and job involvement [44].

In practice, Shepherd leadership concepts have been successful in a group of companies in the country of Turkey. A group of small and medium firms in Turkey recognized as' The Anatolian Tigers' has been investigating and trying new methods of integrating care and compassion within their organizations. The group mainly focused on Shepherd leadership concepts such as spirituality, ethics and sustainability, in order to create compassionate and caring organizations which led to their financial success [45].

Spiritual leadership was also examined through China and Taiwan societies and three main Chinese industries which included manufacturing, financial institutions, and retail sectors. Factors of spiritual leadership like vision, hope and faith, and unselfish love-also called **altruistic** love- were found to be facilitated by the employee' spiritual attribute towards several things like work, calling, work-team, and towards his/her inner self such as self-esteem. The latter was found the most impactful on the firm's performance [46].

Another practical example is JW Marriott Surabaya, is one of Marriott International subsidiaries; is a successful application of Shepherd/servant leadership concepts. Their leadership is voluntarily submissive, transformative inspiration as they practice moral responsibility, genuine character, unparalleled spirituality, relational promises, and supervision capabilities. Also, the Marriott leadership displays understanding, mindfulness, listening, community building, staff growth commitment, and persuasion; are among the major depictions of the Marriott leadership [47].

There are a plethora of successful organizations that apply Shepherd/Servant leadership concepts, in addition to the Marriott International, such as FedEx, AFLAC, Southwest Airlines, Starbucks, Nestle, Men's Warehouse, UPS, and GE to name a few. Consequently, Shepherd leadership harvests results in many industries in our unceasingly changing environment. Although all leaders serve their firms however, merely exceptional leaders serve the best interests of others; and that is the central reason behind these companies success [48].

5.5 Shepherd leadership in the army

There is evidence that Spiritual leadership seems effective in the army. An in-depth study took place in the United States army division with specific leaders with good reputation being positive and optimists who enticed voluntary individuals from other programs to wish to join this particular division. The study investigated the leadership practices and concluded that organizational commitment within the leaders division may have positively impacted followers through exhibiting spiritual leadership attributes [49]. Another study took place in an Apache operational army unit in Texas; it also concluded that Spiritual leaderships, such as Shepherd leadership, proposes a promise as a catalyst for a new paradigm for leadership model and practice offered that it incorporates and extends charismatic, transformational leadership and values-based models [20].

5.6 Drawbacks/challenges of shepherd leadership

To shepherd human flock may not be as easy as shepherding animals; due to the high standards and it is cumbersome to find someone who satisfies the requirements. Only the select few appear to shine at this human shepherding task. A spiritual shepherd leader for example, can be a devout, talented, multi-skilled person of integrity, yet he/she ought to uphold a meek conduct of a shepherd. There are great responsibilities when leading human flock; although there is tremendous blessing from such responsibilities; there is potential to tremendous judgment [50]. Also, trying to explain spirituality in a scientific sense is very challenging [51]. Some scholars argue that the concept of a spiritual leader in the business world is flawed. Leaders are anticipated to perform in a moral and ethical manner, yet it should not be confused with successful or failing business leaders and relate it to the firm's action. Therefore, wrong corporate decision may be addressed as a matter of poor judgment or miscalculation as opposed to a spiritual or ethical deficit. Thus, spirituality at work, according to some research, is not a productive leadership and it's a deceptive framework that serves as an instrument to control followers [51, 52]. Also, it is a challenge for many Spiritual leaders such as Shepherd leaders to be bold in order to face serious situations which could threaten the well-being of followers. The leader must always be prepared to make exceptions on certain issues, for example boldness to face a complicated situation [53]. It is not easy for Shepherd leaders to lead in fast-changing or intimidating environments. Many times followers forget that the Shepherd-leader is also a human being who is not perfect. This leadership role may mandate facing false accusers and assisting victims of unfair attacks; in many cases this can be challenging [53]. Nevertheless, for future research, its recommended that more empirical research of the psychometric properties of Shepherd leadership to measure behavior, is needed to further develop and validate this approach.

6. Conclusions

6.1 Practical implications

Shepherd leadership, as a type of Spiritual leadership, is utilized in the business world which means that leaders ought to find basis of a higher purpose especially within perplexing situations. A spiritual leader instead of zooming in on the challenge at hand, he/she looks to inspire her followers through a higher purpose or calling in order to overcome the challenge. Thus, dependence on a higher purpose allows leaders to overcome individual and the surrounding environment, by instigating activities that would serve the community. Once the individual's attitude is molded to a higher purpose-related societal cause than simply adhering to guidelines and procedures; it would help individuals not have pity on themselves and aim to help others [54].

Moreover, Shepherd leadership contributes to the advancement of positive behaviors and conduct in followers as they demonstrate Organizational Citizenship Behavior [55].

The author's position is that Shepherd leadership, as a Spiritual leadership, may work successfully in any sector, whether religious or secular, once employees and leaders have a shared belief system with the whole organization. These shared beliefs create harmony, understanding and intrinsic motivation which lead to compassion to do the job well because they truly believe in their organization and its higher purpose.

7. Conclusions/limitations

This study concluded that Shepherd leadership as a form of Spiritual leadership have been successfully utilized in different types of sectors including religious organizations, education, physical and mental healthcare, the army, and business organizations. Also, Shepherd leadership is not without flaws or challenges, some scholars believe that this type of leadership is flawed due to the fact that the Shepherd leader may use spirituality to control her followers. Also, the Shepherd leader is always held to very high standards where there is always potential for tremendous judgment once he/she makes a miscalculated decision in such fast-changing environments [56].

This chapter is not without limitations; the author had to select articles and exclude others, and was not able to include great details which may have resulted in a not completely all inclusive study.

Acknowledgements

I would like to thank the almighty God for everything and for everyone that He had placed in my life. I like to thank my loving husband for believing in me and encouraging me. Also, I would like to thank this book publisher, staff and editors, IntechOpen, for their very supportive staff and for being patient with me and giving me this opportunity to contribute to this leadership book.

Conflict of interest

The author declares no conflict of interest.

Author details

Majda I. Ayoub/Al-Salim
American University of Madaba, Amman, Jordan

*Address all correspondence to: m.ayoub@aum.edu.jo;
majda-phr@hotmail.com

References

[1] Goleman D, Boyatzis RE, McKee A. Primal Leadership: Unleashing the Power of Emotional Intelligence. Boston, Massachusetts: Harvard Business Press; 2013

[2] Nolan-Arañez SI, Ludvik MB. Positing a framework for cultivating spirituality through public university leadership development. Journal of Research in Innovative Teaching & Learning. 2018;**11**(1):94-109

[3] Cochrane BS, Ritchie D, Lockhard D, Picciano G, King JA, Nelson B. A culture of compassion: How timeless principles of kindness and empathy become powerful tools for confronting today's most pressing healthcare challenges. In: Healthcare Management Forum 2019. Los Angeles, CA: SAGE Publications

[4] Sinclair S, Norris JM, McConnell SJ, Chochinov HM, Hack TF, Hagen NA, et al. Compassion: A scoping review of the healthcare literature. BMC Palliative Care. 2016;**15**(1):1-6

[5] Engstrom T, Cedar P. Compassionate Leadership. Ada, Michigan: Baker Books; 2011

[6] Hassi A, Storti G. Authentic leadership: The case of Miloud chaabi, a shepherd who became a business legend. Emerald Emerging Markets Case Studies. 2014;**4**(6):1-12

[7] Ngunjiri FW. Lessons in spiritual leadership from Kenyan women. Journal of Educational Administration. 2010;**48**(6):755-768

[8] Ellis T. The Era of Compassionate Capitalism. Greenlands, UK: Henley Management College; 2004

[9] Swalm JE. The Development of Shepherd Leadership Theory and the Validation of the Shepherd Leadership Inventory (SLI). VA, USA: Regent University; 2010

[10] Merriam Webster. 1st ed. Merriam Webster. 2014 [cited 26 August 2022]. Available from: http://www.merriam-webster.com/dictionary/authentic

[11] Keller WP. A Shepherd Looks at psalm 23. Grand Rapids, MI

[12] Samul J. Spiritual leadership: Meaning in the sustainable workplace. Sustainability. 2019;**12**(1):267

[13] Brodie EF. The Leader as a Shepherd: A Case Study of Ecclesiastic, Business, and Education Leaders. AZ, USA: Grand Canyon University

[14] Gabriel Y. The caring leader–what followers expect of their leaders and why? Leadership. 2015;**11**(3): 316-334. Genesis chapter 4 verse 2

[15] Testament O. The holy bible. New International Version Book of the Old Testament

[16] McCormick B, Davenport D. The leader as shepherd. Executive Excellence. 2004;**21**(2):6

[17] Adams AW. Shepherd Leadership of Church of God Pastors and How This Relates to Ministerial Effectiveness. AZ, USA: University of Phoenix

[18] Iorjaah I. Jesus' servant-shepherd leadership framework as springboard to the Nigerian national project. Ilorin Journal of Religious Studies. 2014;**4**(2):27-40

[19] Fry LW. Toward a theory of spiritual leadership. The Leadership Quarterly. 2003;**14**(6):693-727

[20] Fry LW, Vitucci S, Cedillo M. Spiritual leadership and army transformation: Theory, measurement, and establishing a baseline. The Leadership Quarterly. 2005;**16**(5): 835-862

[21] Hernandez E. Review of oversee God's people: Shepherding the flock through administration and delegation, by Brian croft and Bruce Butler. Journal of Applied Christian Leadership. 2018;**12**(1):102-103

[22] Stowell JM. Shepherding the Church: Effective Spiritual Leadership in a Changing Culture. Chicago, IL: Moody Publishers; 1997

[23] Greenleaf RK. The Servant as Leader Indianapolis: South Orange, New Jersey: The Robert K. Greenleaf Center; 1970. pp. 1-37

[24] Greenleaf RK. Servant leadership: A Journey into the Nature of Legitimate Power and Greatness. Mahwah, NJ: Paulist Press; 2002

[25] Peyton GL, Ross DB. Servant and shepherd leadership in higher education: Empowerment and mentorship. In: Key Factors and Use Cases of Servant Leadership Driving Organizational Performance. Hershey, Pennsylvania: IGI Global; 2022. pp. 272-292

[26] Savage NR. Empowering the Priests in the Pew: The Shepherd Leader Delegates to Multiply Ministry. WI, USA: Wisconsin Lutheran Seminary

[27] Lynch J, Friedman HH. Servant leader, spiritual leader: The case for convergence. Journal of Leadership, Accountability and Ethics. 2013;**10**(2):87-95

[28] Resane KT. Leadership for the Church: The Shepherd Model. HTS Teologiese Studies. 2014;**70**(1):1-6

[29] Khanin D. Contrasting burns and bass: Does the transactional-transformational paradigm live up to Burns' philosophy of transforming leadership? Journal of Leadership Studies. 2007;**1**(3):7-25

[30] Palus CJ, Harrison S, Prasad JJ. Developing relational leadership in Africa. In: Creative Social Change. Bingley, UK: Emerald Group Publishing Limited; 2016

[31] Chiseyengi JM. The Nexus between Shepherd Leadership and Modern Leadership Models: A Systematic Literature Review. Journal of Economics, Finance and Management Studies; 2022:1692-1694

[32] Jeffress MS. A study of the demographics, exposure levels, and perceptions of the viewing audience of Pastor Joel Osteen, America's most popular preacher. Journal of Media Critiques. 2017;**3**(12):291-309

[33] Russell RF, Stone AG. A review of servant leadership attributes: Developing a practical model. Leadership & Organization Development Journal. 2002;**1**:145-157

[34] Anderson N. Leadership is not about position: Leading from behind. In: TESOL Symposium on Leadership. Utah, USA: Brigham Young University; 2005

[35] Chiu YC. Facilitating Asian students' critical thinking in online discussions. British Journal of Educational Technology. 2009;**40**(1):42-57

[36] Key S. The good shepherd: Lessons for teacher education. International Christian Community of Teacher Educators Journal. 2015;**10**(2):5

[37] Anselmus DZ. Informal teacher leadership: Lessons from shepherd leadership. International Journal of Leadership in Education. 2021;**13**:1-30

[38] Van der Cingel M. Compassion in care: A qualitative study of older people with a chronic disease and nurses. Nursing Ethics. 2011;**18**(5):672-685

[39] Lloyd M, Carson A. Making compassion count: Equal recognition and authentic involvement in mental health care. International Journal of Consumer Studies. 2011;**35**(6):616-621

[40] Sanders JE, Hopkins WE, Geroy GD. A causal assessment of the spirituality-leadership-commitment relationship. Journal of Management, Spirituality & Religion. 2005;**2**(1):39-66

[41] Allen KE, Cherrey C. Systemic Leadership: Enriching the Meaning of our Work. Lanham, Maryland: University Press of America; 2000

[42] Longenecker JG, McKinney JA, Moore CW. Religious intensity, evangelical Christianity, and business ethics: An empirical study. Journal of Business Ethics. 2004;**55**(4):371-384

[43] Danish RQ, Usman A. Impact of reward and recognition on job satisfaction and motivation: An empirical study from Pakistan. International Journal of Business and Management. 2010;**5**(2):159

[44] Word J. Engaging work as a calling: Examining the link between spirituality and job involvement. Journal of Management, Spirituality & Religion. 2012;**9**(2):147-166

[45] Karakas F, Sarigollu E. The role of leadership in creating virtuous and compassionate organizations: Narratives of benevolent leadership in an Anatolian tiger. Journal of Business Ethics. 2013;**113**(4):663-678

[46] Chen CY, Yang CY, Li CI. Spiritual leadership, follower mediators, and organizational outcomes: Evidence from three industries across two major Chinese societies 1. Journal of Applied Social Psychology. 2012;**42**(4):890-938

[47] McCormick B, Davenport D. Shepherd Leadership: Wisdom for Leaders from Psalm 23. Minneapolis, Minnesota: Fortress Press; 2020

[48] Setiawan R, Eliyana A, Suryani T, Osito LO. World-class Hospitality Management In Tourism Strategy: The Implementation of Servant Leadership. Jawa Timur, Indonesia: Petra Christian University

[49] Novikov V. Spiritual leadership within an army acquisition program management context. Journal of Leadership, Accountability, and Ethics. 2017;**14**(2):81-94

[50] Allen GP, Moore WM, Moser LR, Neill KK, Sambamoorthi U, Bell HS. The role of servant leadership and transformational leadership in academic pharmacy. American Journal of Pharmaceutical Education. 2016;**25**:80

[51] Nicolae M, Ion I, Nicolae E. The research agenda of spiritual leadership. Where do we stand? Revista De Management Comparative International. 2013;**14**(4):551

[52] Ruth D. Leader as priest: Plucking the fruit of a flawed metaphor. Leadership. 2014;**10**(2):174-190

[53] MacArthur JF. Pastoral Ministry: How to Shepherd Biblically. Nashville, TN: Thomas Nelson

[54] Klaus L, Fernando M. Enacting spiritual leadership in business through ego-transcendence. Leadership & Organization Development Journal. 2016;**37**(1):71-92

[55] Sendjaya S, Sarros JC, Santora JC. Defining and measuring servant leadership behaviour in organizations. Journal of Management Studies. 2008;**45**(2):402-424

[56] Zondervan KE, Khan SE, Chaudhry AG. Impact of servant leadership on workplace spirituality: Moderating role of involvement culture. Pakistan Journal of Science. 2015;**67**(1):109-113

Chapter 6

Dyadic Relationship Quality (DRQ) – Describing the Development of Leader-Follower Relationship Quality: A Qualitative, Longitudinal Study

Julie Wilson

Abstract

For the last 20 years, Leader-Member Exchange theory (LMX) has been associated with the quality of relationships between leaders and followers, accounting for quality through the four dimensions of contribution, affect, loyalty and respect. This paper contributes to our understanding of relationship quality by presenting an extension to LMX theory. With a more comprehensive view of the development of leader-follower relationship quality than existing LMX theory, we propose the explanatory construct of Dyadic Relationship Quality (DRQ) development. The DRQ model demonstrates how trusting behaviours have hitherto been overlooked as the key to positive initial interactions. We show how performance and relationship quality are active dimensions of relationship development rather than outcomes of the relational process. The paper elaborates the experiential nature of leader-follower relationship quality by utilising a relatively rare methodology in LMX studies, a longitudinal qualitative study of leaders and followers in high-tech start-up organisations.

Keywords: relationship quality, followers, leaders, LMX, trust

1. Introduction

What exactly is exchanged in relationships of different qualities? ([1], p. 415).

The number of studies into quality of leader-follower relationships grows year on year, for which researchers often rely on the perceived explanatory power of Leader-Member Exchange (LMX) theories [2–4]. Despite the dominance of LMX to explain these relationships [1], the construct has come under critique (see [5] for an overview). The majority of studies are quantitative, based on surveys [6] and single time-point studies that focus on the four main dimensions of LMX (explained later) and describe antecedents, outcomes and mediating/moderating variables of leader-follower relationships [7]. Too few qualitative studies have been undertaken that elaborate the experiential nature of relationship quality and how it may be constructed through a 'two-way interactional process' ([8], p. 15). In addition: 1. The majority of LMX studies relating relationship quality and performance are based on the perceptions of leaders or followers with few matched dyads being explored [9]; 2. There is relatively little research on factors disrupting relationship quality [10]; and 3. The role of time on relationship quality is under-researched [2]. Importantly, whilst trust is acknowledged as essential to the leader-follower relationship [11], most existing studies position trusting behaviours, performance and relationship quality as *outcomes* of relationship development and focus on the factors influencing a leader's trust of his/her followers [12]. As Wang and Clegg [13] state, dyadic LMX relationships are complex, and more research needs to be done on how both leader and follower behaviours and perceptions influence trust. 4. Therefore, from a practitioner perspective, understanding how leader-follower relations function and what can disrupt them is potentially valuable [14]. Without being cognisant of the effect of reciprocal leader and follower perceptions and behaviours, relationship development can be adversely affected [15]. This study provides examples of how the leader-follower relationship can completely crumble when either party, but particularly leaders fail to understand the impact of their behaviours on those who follow them. Here, I offer practical perspectives on protecting and enhancing dyadic relationship quality and how this improves organisational outputs such as commitment, engagement, discretionary effort, etc.

Please note that whilst leaders and managers are different constructs where managers effect their authority and leaders exercise influence [16], we use the terms interchangeably here as the context for the study was the start-up environment where teams were small and those in leadership positions also enacted management activities [17].

This paper addresses a number of critiques of LMX theory, particularly the need as highlighted by Sheer [5] to address LMX as a construct that is applicable to real-world situations. Following Benson et al [18], we are interested in exploring the meanings that leaders and – in our case – also followers ascribe to their relationship: meanings that 'cannot be isolated from the context in which they are embedded' (p. 951). We explain how leader-follower relationship quality develops over time and is based on trusting assessments and behaviours of both leaders and followers. In doing so, we propose three additions to current LMX theory and the new construct of Dyadic Relationship Quality (DRQ). The three additions are that: 1. Trust and trusting behaviours occur at the beginning of relationships rather than just as outcomes of relationship stability; 2. *Both* leader and follower make assessments of trust and each other's performance early in the relationship, which are integral to relational quality; 3. The perceptions of relationship quality influence the development of leader-follower relationships in both positive and negative ways, from early within a relationships and are linked to perceptions of performance and trust. Additional dimensions of communication, commitment, transactional/contractual terms, emotions, initial impressions were also found in the data and, although not novel, are reported in brief.

By including additional dimensions of trust, performance, perceived relationship quality, etc. we offer a more comprehensive view of the development of relationship quality than existing LMX theories and introduce the explanatory construct of Dyadic Relationship Quality (DRQ) development. DRQ explains more fully the dimensions required to describe the development of relationship quality over time. We conceptualise DRQ development as:

> *The temporal leader-follower relationship development process where relationship quality is influenced by the perceptions of both leaders and followers of initial and on-going interactions; trustworthiness, trusting behaviours and performance; communication; socio-emotional and transactional aspects of the relationship; and perceptions of the quality of the relationship.*

The findings are based on a longitudinal qualitative research study consisting of in-depth sequential interviews of 12 leader-follower dyads over a 6–9-month period. The study's overarching research question of

> *What factors influence the quality of leader-follower relationships within workplace contexts?*

provided the basis for identifying and explaining the various factors that influence how relationship quality develops over time. An important addition to LMX research is that we suggest relationship quality encompasses the perceptions and actions of *both* leaders and followers in relation to: trustworthiness, trusting behaviours, performance, perceptions of relationship quality and commitment to each other. The study provides concurrently a broader and a more in-depth qualitative understanding and a more detailed and nuanced view of how relationship quality develops.

The paper is organised as follows: First, we discuss why there is a need to extend Leader-Member Exchange Theory (LMX), we then explain the methodology and study findings, offering an explanatory construct for relationship quality development. Finally, we discuss the implications for theory and practice.

2. The need to expand theorising on leader-follower relationship quality

While leadership and trust literatures discuss how relationships between leaders and followers develop, little qualitative work has been done on elaborating the nature of relationship quality and the factors that contribute to, or detract from, its development. The theory most commonly used to describe the quality of relationships between leaders and followers is Leader-Member Exchange theory, where:

> *'The so-called quality of these leader-member exchange (LMX) relationships is assumed to reflect the extent to which leader and subordinate mutually exchange resources and support.'* ([19], p. 534).

LMX theorists suggest that leadership is effective when relationships are characterised by high levels of trust, affect (liking), loyalty, respect and contribution [20, 21]. High-quality relationships are likely to be long-term in focus, with quality growing over time unless negative events derail the relationship development process [22]. Poor quality exists when relationships are seen instrumentally as a way of improving productivity and are characterised by transactional interactions [23, 24]. This results in low trust and low levels of affect, loyalty and respect.

2.1 Definitional, theoretical and methodological issues with LMX

LMX offers a useful way of describing the quality of leader-follower relationships; however, there are still definitional, theoretical and methodological issues [5], pointing to the need for further in-depth experientially based qualitative research.

2.1.1 Definitional issues

LMX is defined and employed in many ways, with each definition addressing different aspects of the dyadic relationship [25]. This can be seen in the confusing array of descriptions of how leaders and followers relate including: leader-follower exchanges (i.e. anything that passes between leader and follower), exchange quality (the quality of anything that passes between leader and follower), relationship exchange quality (the quality of the exchanges within the relationship) or relationship quality (the quality of the relationship itself) [5]. This lack of clarity about the nature of the relationship being explored results in theoretical confusion, for example, whether the focus is on leaders, followers or both, on exchanges, perceptions of exchanges or on perceptions of relationship quality. As Hiller et al. [26] argue, leader-member relationships are multidimensional, and it is important to find a way of exploring and mapping their temporal and multifaceted nature. From these definitional problems, theoretical issues then arise.

2.1.2 Theoretical issues

Today, LMX is seen as a key construct in the leadership realm ([25], p. 3), and many measures and variables link it with a range of other variables (see, for instance: [27–29]). By 1995, LMX was seen as synonymous with relationship quality despite the absence of theoretical or empirical links between them. Sheer describes how this link was probably derived from the need to 'to capture a cocktail of attributes that include leader characteristics, relationship quality, and exchange-related attributes' creating a 'tautological fallacy' which 'nullified a central thesis of the theory' (2015: 217). The four main LMX dimensions of contribution, affect, respect and loyalty are mainly used as core dimensions of quality, and while they are a useful start, they fail to capture other aspects of high-quality relationships such as high trust, interaction, support and rewards ([22], p. 257), honesty, openness, advice and socio-emotional influences such as friendship [30–32].

A further theoretical shortfall emerges in relation to the role of trust. Trust appears in the LMX literature in early works such as Dienesch and Liden [33] who identified trust as important to exchange relationships. However, the role and influence of trustworthiness, trusting behaviours and communication in relationship quality have remained unclear [34], and theory is largely unsupported by empirical studies [30, 35, 36].

Finally, existing studies theorise trust, performance and relationship quality as *outcomes* of relationship development and of leader interventions. While taking an outcome view of relationship development has value [7], it can lead to a focus on an instrumental input-output view. Research is needed around the processes that affect the emergence of these outcomes ([7], p. 55). We argue that experientially, dimensions of relationship quality such as performance and perceptions of quality are not outputs, but interdependent constituents of an iterative and emergent process relationship development. Theoretical concerns impact on how research is conducted and the methods employed in empirical work.

2.1.3 Methodological issues

While leader-member exchange is conceptualised as a dyadic social relationship with important consequences for performance and well-being [37], studies of the quality of LMX relationships are mainly quantitative based on measurement scales and surveys of the individual perceptions of either leaders or followers at a point in time [6]. As a result, the focus lies on generalised structures or mechanisms divorced from the particularities of specific relationships. Two issues arise: First, agency (the ability to act and influence) and trust are mainly located with the leader [9], even though follower perceptions are measured, therefore the ability of the follower to influence relationship quality remains under-considered [7]. Second, longitudinal studies of the development of relationship quality over time are rare [2], which means that relationship quality is often defined through the outcomes – *not the process* – of exchanges. As Nahrgang and Seo [10] note, the empirical evidence for LMX development continues to be a 'critical area of investigation and [...] fruitful ground for future research'. We argue that leader-member relationships are experientially complex and that LMX currently does not account for the complex, nuanced nature of leader and follower relationships. This study extends the concept of relationship quality by explaining how leader-follower relationships develop over time and how interpersonal trust (trustworthiness and trusting behaviours), communication, emotion, performance and perceptions of relationship quality by both leaders and followers influence this development. Acknowledging the issues outlined above, Wilson designed a qualitative longitudinal study to go beyond LMX by exploring the perceptual and temporal nature of the development of leader-follower relationships and the various dimensions.

3. Methodology

The research was based on a qualitative longitudinal study of 12 leader-follower dyads consisting of 21 individuals across eight hi-tech start-up firms in England. The context was chosen because leader-follower relationship quality is important in new technology firms which 'are known to be volatile dynamic organizations whose innovations are subject to short life cycles and product imitability' ([38], p. 27). The high-tech environment also offers an alternative to the majority of leadership research, which is carried out in corporate firms [39]. This context therefore offers a fresh perspective on how relationship quality functioned between leaders and followers.

The world of hi-tech start-ups is a fairly closed community, generally accessed through recommendation and personal introductions [40] because of the competitive/sensitive nature of their business, therefore a snowball sampling technique was used to gain access to a group of individuals who are unlikely to respond using cold contact methods.

Sixty semi-structured interviews took place, with each leader-follower dyad (members of each dyad being interviewed separately) carried on a 3-monthly cycle. The questions were informed by the theory but left open so that additional issues could emerge. The interviews took place in a variety of locations, depending on convenience and the need for privacy for respondents. These venues included local coffee shops, work-space offices and where necessary over Skype or telephone. All conversations were recorded digitally, anonymised to maintain confidentiality, and the transcript was shared with each respondent to ensure they were happy with the information they had provided. Liden et al. ([3], p. 415) note that to answer the question of how LMX develops, it is important to identify and examine new dyads early in the life of the relationship and that such studies are rare. The initial leader-follower dyad interviews in this study were carried out soon after recruitment. In total, 60 interviews were recorded resulting in over 35,000 words to be analysed.

Data were interpreted inductively through thematic analysis, which allowed the identification of issues that participants saw as important [41]. This involved a fine-grained reading of each interview transcript, identifying 304 primary themes within each interview that related to the research question [42]. These themes were then compared across the data set, related to theory and grouped into 14 (secondary) themes. Of these, three themes were additional to current theory; others (also reported here) corroborated existing literature and as a result, have received less attention in this paper. The themes were reviewed iteratively against each interview to identify specific salient statements and examples and to check the veracity of each theme. The themes are defined and elaborated in the following section through excerpts from the interviews.

This qualitative methodology facilitated an in-depth exploratory discussion of the perceptions and experiences of leaders and followers around the nature of their relationship. The longitudinal qualitative methodology provides a contrast with current LMX research, which is mainly quantitative and tends to focus on one timepoint [6].

4. The development of relationship quality between leaders and followers

Three major themes of trust, performance and ongoing assessment of relationship quality emerged from the data analysis. These themes constitute important differences from the majority of LMX research, highlighting the temporal and interactional nature of relationship quality. Specifically: (1) Assessments of trustworthiness and trusting behaviours were present from the initial interaction of the leader and follower onwards, rather than being an outcome of relationship development; (2) *Both* leaders and followers assessed each other's performance continuously, thus moving performance to a key element in the development of relationship quality rather than an outcome; (3) The perception of relationship quality is temporal and iterative based on ongoing assessments by *both* leaders and followers that may support or disrupt their relationship. In addition, and in accordance with current literature, the quality of relationships between leaders and followers encompasses socio-emotional and transactional aspects as well as involving respect, loyalty and commitment. We explain these findings below and illustrate them with salient excerpts from the interviews. The leader is represented with a pseudonym followed by (L) and the follower with a pseudonym followed by (F).

4.1 Theme 1: trustworthiness and trusting behaviours

In LMX theory, trust is extended from leaders towards followers, resulting in high LMX and outcomes such as the empowerment of subordinates [13]. Here, trust is theorised as a psychological state where one individual is willing to make themselves vulnerable to another [43]. Assessments of trustworthiness are made on the basis of the other party's: (1) ability to fulfil a role; (2) benevolence, i.e. kindness, support and consideration; (3) integrity, i.e. fair, ethical, honest, etc. [36] and (4) predictability/reliability [44]. Trusting behaviours are conceptualised as risk-taking actions by which leaders or followers make themselves vulnerable to the actions of the other [45]. Such leader behaviours include the disclosure of information, delegation or autonomy, support for progression and promotion and the introduction of followers to social and professional networks. Trusting behaviours of followers include offering discretionary effort, disclosing information and benevolent actions towards the leader [45]. While these trusting behaviours were identified by study participants, they additional actions included being open about fears and problems and being willing and trusted to deal with difficult tasks and issues. Both leaders and followers made their decision to act based on their assessment of the trustworthiness of the other party – as can be seen in the excerpts below, which illustrate how assessments of trustworthiness and the enactment of trusting behaviours were perceived.

Trustworthiness was evident in Ken's (F) and Lloyd's (L) first interviews. Lloyd felt from their initial meeting that Ken was honest and that there was no 'bullshit':

> **Lloyd (L):** *'You've got to be likable, but generally I think that if you're honest, you're generally going to be likable... I think it's mostly about being honest, articulate and being clever as well...'*

For Ken, Lloyd's initial openness about the company, disclosure of its financial position and the vision for its future were evidence of his honesty and integrity:

> **Ken (F):** *'Lloyd was very transparent about [the company's] plans. I was able to ask him questions about the business, where its planning to go... he was very open in terms of the plans and where they want to be [and where Ken could progress to] in six months, twelve months, two years, five years down the line...'*

Ken and Lloyd's comments illustrate the reciprocal and subjective (individually perceived and context-related) nature of trust – that Lloyd saw Ken as honest and likable and in return Ken trusted Lloyd's transparency and willingness to follow through. In addition, while the literature suggests that trusting behaviours only tend to appear once a relationship has developed, the interviews above (and below) present a different picture, suggesting that trusting behaviours occur during initial interactions between leaders and followers. This is important because it places trusting behaviour as essential to the early relationship-building process – to whether the leader and/or follower might trust the other and invest in the relationship – rather than as an outcome of relationship development. This represents a significant departure from existing theories (e.g. [44]) that posit trusting behaviours occurring as the relationship matures in response to a bank of events and experiences between both parties.

In another dyad, Lance (L) decided during the interview processes that he trusted his new recruit, Adrian (F), and as a result gave him access to the company's most prized asset – the code base – the software that allows customer access to the company's product online. This was significant because developments in code are commercially sensitive and have a financial value in a market where competitors are racing to produce better applications and web experiences. This was a potentially vulnerable – and very visible – action on Lance's part, reciprocated by Adrian returning this trusting behaviour by signing an employment contract that gave Lance control of any material that he produced outside of work hours. In the first interview, a week after he'd accepted a position at Lance's firm, Adrian (F) recalled that by signing the employment contract anything he produced in or outside of work would be owned by the firm. Adrian viewed signing the contract as evidence of his trust that Lance would not take advantage of this legal relationship.

When asked if he trusted that Lance would not take advantage, Adrian's response was: 'Yes', thus indicating that they trusted each other as a result of open communication in terms of clarifying rights of intellectual property. Both Lance and Adrian's actions also indicate a degree of risk-taking on both parts that the other can be trusted to reciprocate and engage in trusting behaviours – an issue we will discuss later.

Another example of trusting behaviour and risk-taking based on initial perceptions of both leader and follower occurred at the start of Lisa and Izzy's relationship. Izzy (F) had returned from the USA and wanted an internship. She contacted Lisa (L), whose company she had recently researched, feeling it offered an exciting opportunity that she would like to be involved with. At their initial meeting, Lisa was aware of Izzy's lack of formal experience but took the risk of giving her a job, trusting that she could do it.

> **Lisa (L):** *'She had some experience of social media stuff but she hadn't worked in the technology sector or anything like that before.'*

From Izzy's perspective, she was prepared to offer her services for free on the basis of her first impressions of Lisa's talent and energy, trusting that she would eventually be financially rewarded:

> **Izzy (F):** *'I'd seen pictures in articles... [they] made me think, OK you're not only doing this by yourself, but you're so young... so I knew she had the energy and drive to make it happen... so, yeah, quite inspiring'*

Her decision was based not only on an assessment of Lisa's achievements so far, but also on her feelings of admiration for how much had been accomplished and the women-focused social ethos of the company, which Izzy found appealing.

Lance and Adrian, Lloyd and Ken, and Lisa and Izzy's relationships illustrate the complexity of trust. The interviews highlighted a significant departure from much of the trust literature, which suggests that trusting behaviours will only occur after a period of time during which one party assesses the trustworthiness of the other and then decides that they trust enough to engage in risk-taking behaviours [46]. We contest this view of trusting behaviours. Instead, we find that they occur during the initial interaction and early phases of relational development between leader and follower. The interelated nature of trust and risk-taking is particularly important in the context of high-tech start-ups where the rapid pace of developments makes speed and effective interaction with others important, and investing in people is a major decision. The trusting behaviours described above (sharing confidential information, being open about intellectual property, making public statements of confidence, offering to work for free) demonstrate that leaders and followers make positive assessments and act on these during the first meeting. Such actions have two explanations in the literature, although we also suggest a third alternative here.

The first recognition of early trusting behaviours is found in work on predispositions to trust (see [47]), followed up by more recent work on the influence of prior knowledge before leaders and followers meet. McKnight et al. suggested that individuals were more predisposed to trust if they had both a general 'faith in humanity' and a 'trusting stance' (where benefits derive from treating others as though they are trustworthy until proved unreliable). This work was expanded upon by Delgado-Márquez et al. [48], who used laboratory methods to argue that a trustor's prior knowledge about a trustee influences trusting behaviours because initial knowledge reduces uncertainty and allows a trustor to more accurately determine how a trustee might behave in future situations. Certainly, in this study, both leaders and followers made crucial assessments in their initial meeting about the trustworthiness of the other and whether they could behave in a trusting manner.

However, whilst our data support these findings that prior knowledge in the form of information about the company and some respondents in the data volunteered a position on their predispositions to trust, the extent of trusting behaviours exhibited in this data set requires a more robust explanation than predispositions and efforts to gather prior information can reasonably account for.

A second explanation for these findings is that they are a function of the start-up context. Scarbrough et al. [49] looked at the relations between entrepreneurs and angel investors. They found that the display of risk-taking, trusting behaviours during the initial interaction and early relationship stages was linked to greater success in terms of gaining funding for new ventures. The suggestion is that such behaviours relfect the high-risk environment in which investors and entrepreneurs meet. However, it is unclear whether early trusting behaviours are a purely phenomenon of the start-up environment rather than a feature of relationships more broadly and again, this explaination is not convincing.

Our third explanation is that the initial display of trusting behaviours has been under-explored. Whilst in this study, participants acted on early trust-based assessments of what the relationship might offer in the long-term, it could well be that all relationships begin with behavioural signals around trust. When these are displayed by something as simple as sharing personal information or taking the time to listen to the other party, the relationships gets off to a good start; when absent, leaders and followers are likely to be more cautious and trust will take longer to develop. The trust literature is largely based on the results of quantiative surveys, which are confirmatory rather than exploratory by nature. The deductive models on which quantitative studies are based have largely ignored trusting behaviours at the beginning of relations, so trusting actions have largely gone un-noticed. We suspect that early trusting behaviours are prevalent in all relationships. Their absence in the literature is a 'blind spot' resulting from a preponderence of confirmatory research approaches, but more empirical material is required to substantiate our asssertion.

Our findings coroborate the less explored body of work on the longitudinal process of trust development [50]. Whereas much trust research focuses on how followers demonstrate how they trust leaders or engender trust from their superiors, our data suggest that trust can be mutually developed depending on how leaders and followers interpret each others' words and actions.

Although the study contained mostly positive assessments of trustworthiness leading to trusting behaviours early in the relationship, the opposite did occur and relationship quality was disrupted [10]. Sadly, Lloyd (L) and another employee, Maddie (F), quickly learned not to trust each other. For Lloyd, this related to his feelings and assessment relating to Maddie's signs of extreme discomfort when she felt under stress:

> **Lloyd (L):** *'Crying at work ... at various times, you'd see her go to the toilets and crying... and that's when I thought it was all my fault. Oh my god, what have I done? I can't believe I've ruined someone's life, this is just awful... She really wanted to do a good job ... she wanted to do too much and got upset when things weren't going well on the project. In a small company you've got to do lots of things... and you've got to do them well but you don't have time to focus on one thing and I think she wasn't suited to that.'*

From Lloyd's perspective, Maddie's lack of ability to multitask and cope with stress was the undoing of their relationship and caused him to reflect on his own judgement. While from Maddie's perspective, she felt she was asked to take unacceptable shortcuts:

> **Maddie (F):** *'There'll be parts [of a project] that won't work but you can still get it through ... which I'm not comfortable with ... so my standards are a little bit lower ... It really doesn't sit well with me and because I feel that my role has ... not been properly defined or changed, I don't have that much respect and doubt the integrity of the company at the moment.'*

The quality of their relationship quality suffered because Maddie felt that Lloyd had let her down – she had trusted him to provide a role that she could fulfil and he had failed to behave in a way that protected her interests or supported her to act with integrity towards clients. Lloyd felt that Maddie was unable to cope with the work and that her personal standards were more important than the company's needs. Both withdrew trusting behaviours, Lloyd stopped delegating any tasks that were above routine, and Maddie resigned shortly after the interview, thus showing the dark side of trust and how it may decrease over time and disrupt relationship quality.

To summarise, Dietz and Den Hartog [44] argue that trust is based on an assessment that the other person will eventually engage in trustworthy behaviour following a positive decision to act. The relationships described here recount trusting actions and draw attention to the willingness of both parties to take a risk. All four dyads illustrate that ability, benevolence and integrity are key aspects of trustworthiness [51–53] in both positive (trusting) and negative (non-trusting) ways. While there are questions in the literature around whether ability, benevolence and integrity have a unique or collective impact [54], our findings are that they are mutually implicated and that trust is an issue for both leaders and followers.

The study also draws attention to *when* trusting behaviour occurs and *by whom*. Trusting behaviours have generally been viewed as outcomes of the relationship development process [46]. The data indicate that on first meeting, *both* leaders and followers assessed trustworthiness – the integrity, ability and benevolence – which then influenced decisions and led to trusting behaviours occurring at that point.

4.2 Theme 2: performance, disruption and relationship quality

While no specific questions were asked about performance, the topic emerged inductively. Comments from participants indicated that they constantly assessed each other's performance and that this was embedded in the development of relationship quality from day 1. Leader and follower dyads identified a number of positive aspects of performance, which included liking and loving the job, being proud of achievements, being organised, having skills and talent, growing in ability, having experience and working hard. Negative perceptions of performance included assessments by *both* leaders and followers of poor results and undesirable behaviours such as introversion, dismissiveness and disinterest.

Consequently, the data show that positive perceptions of performance reassure both leaders and followers and impact confidence in the quality of the relationship. Jeremy's (F) relationship with Lois (L) is a good example of mutual appreciation and affect based on performance. Jeremy viewed Lois almost as a superwoman in terms of what she managed to do and how she contributed to the business, attributing company results to Lois and the team's input. The assessments they made of each other's performance started early in the relationship, as both recounted being impressed with the other's ability to perform.

This initial and continual assessment of ability to perform by both leaders and followers was evident in other leader-follower relationships. Nine out of the 12 dyads echoed Jeremy and Lois's experiences, where an assessment of performance and ability occurred in the initial interaction and was re-evaluated throughout the relationship. For example, Laurence's (L) early positive assessment of Fred's (F) ability to perform was upgraded as they got to know each other better over time, and by the last interview, he had complete faith in Fred based on a set of judgements made over the preceding months:

> **Laurence (L):** *'I've seen that Fred [is] actually really good at his job ... he's one of the nicest guys I ever met, like he's got great morals and he's not a pushover. He's [...] not too nice, [...] he's not gonna get walked over or anything like that ... I think better of Fred every day.'*

Laurence valued not only Fred's ability to perform but also his integrity as a moral human being and someone who would stand up for himself. This was reciprocal, Fred was aware of being appreciated and also respected Laurence's abilities as a leader in creating success:

> **Fred (F):** *'I feel like I have a lot of pride in my work and I want us to be really good ... I guess that's probably quite useful to have in an employee [...] I think the fact that I'm just determined to get anything done, [he's created] the company ethos and that's what people want to do at this company [...] his leadership has contributed to [our] success as well.'*

This suggests that performance assessments are reciprocal and involve more than work outcomes, they encompass perceptions of personal factors such as integrity ('great morals') and an ability to bring people together to create a culture of success. Consequently, these perceptions played an important part in the development of relationship quality as confidence in each other increased.

However, for Edward and Leon, the opposite also occurred and relationship quality disrupted. Soon after Edward (F) began his position, Leon (L) learned that he was struggling with the numeracy aspect of his work. Their relationship quickly took a downturn as Leon's faith in Edward's ability to perform diminished and trusting behaviour in the form of autonomy was withdrawn:

> **Leon (L):** *I look at him as a cost centre of about £115k a year including his on-costs. So he's either got to be generating fantastic results ... there's not really a lot of room for the senior management team to be carrying somebody ... . He didn't like the fact that*

> *his bonus is based on performance [...] he said: 'I don't like this' [...] He's in a really difficult position because he can't afford to be performing poorly, so I was amazed when he offered to resign, but I think it was also an empty gesture.*

Edward was aware of being under pressure with metrics being used to measure his performance. This increased his sense of being undervalued:

> **Edward (F):** *Because of the criticisms I've received ... I don't know, he keeps saying he values me but I don't see evidence of it ... You know the comments about how he's not gonna get rid of me makes you think that he's obviously talked about it and has wanted to and that doesn't fill you with confidence.*

This change in the leader's and follower's perception of each other's ability to perform led to a deterioration in both relationship quality and trust, which resulted in Edward seeking alternative employment and leaving Leon's firm.

Likewise, Lisa (L) and Izzy's (F) relationship – which started off on a positive footing (see page 11) – was disrupted and relationship quality decreased. In the final interview, Lisa was struggling with Izzy's inability to perform, despite providing mentoring and training. Her comments highlight how being able to trust an employee to perform is crucial:

> **Lisa (L):** *'For me, this is kind of the last thing, if she can't do this I'm gonna let her go... the business is entering a different phase, it's like people have to take shit, own it and get it done and push things forward. [...] There's only so many times that I can ask her to try and do things and then she doesn't do them [...] We're a start-up and there's six people [...] I can't do her part of the business as well as my part of the business.'*

Izzy was made redundant a few weeks after this interview as Lisa restructured the team.

In the three examples of the disruption and deterioration of relationship quality over time (Edward, Izzy and Maddie), it appeared that negative assessments of performance by leaders and/or followers led to a decline in trust, and their view of the relationship was downgraded. There came a point where after a reassessment of performance and relationship quality, one member of the dyad decided to terminate the relationship. Edward (F) and Maddie (F) resigned, Lisa (L) made Izzy redundant. This finding accords with recent literature where trust is a predictor of performance (e.g. [55]) but supplements the considerably fewer studies exploring how performance may be a predictor of trust (e.g. [56]).

4.3 Theme 3: the development of relationship quality over time

The study highlights two important issues that supplement current LMX theory: the iterative and temporal nature of relationship quality. Whereas most measures of LMX are based on single point surveys aimed at predicting outcomes, the surveys do not offer detailed explanations of the development and fluctuations in leader and follower relationships over time. Nor do they offer insights on the interactional and iterative nature of the relationship. The value of a longitudinal qualitative study lies in highlighting how leaders and followers make assessments of each other on an ongoing basis and those assessments may support or disrupt relationships, i.e. result in high- or low-quality relationships. In our study, relationship quality remained fluid and emergent for far longer than the 6 months suggested by Nahrgang et al. [22] and was seen to improve or deteriorate in response to specific events, behaviours and/or actions that took place between leader and follower.

The examples in the previous section show how perceptions of relationship quality are fluid, temporal and interdependent with other dimensions in relationship development.. All but one of the participants volunteered comments on the quality of their relationship with their leader or follower at each of the three interviews over the 6–9 month period. Most perceptions of relationship quality were positive and appeared to strengthen over time, but as seen in above, three of relationships were disrupted through negative assessments (Leon and Edward; Maddie and Lloyd; Lisa and Izzy). Based on the data, we argue that ongoing assessments of the relationship's value, by both leaders and followers, are an integral part of the development of relationship quality. Such assessments include subjective perceptions of trustworthiness, performance and trusting behaviours, all of which interact to shape opinions about the relationship's current quality.

As Lloyd (L) commented about Ken (F), in the final interview, his estimation of the quality of their relationship was based on a number of factors:

> **Lloyd (L):** *'I've known him from being a junior member of staff to somebody that I need to rely on ... he's enthusiastic [...] with Ken we work as a team to get things sorted and it's great. [...] I'd trust his opinion. He is someone who is cheerful, hard-working, reliable, capable, somebody who naturally gets on with others. He believes in what he's doing and he's enjoying it ... It's a good relationship for me, I think this is priceless.'*

For Lloyd, relationship quality is based on a number of factors he has experienced in working with Ken over a period of time, and on that basis he was keen to promote him. In particular, his comments illustrate affect (liking), performance (he's hard working), respect (he's capable) and socio-emotional qualities (cheerful, getting on with others). Trust also appears to be important in their relationship in terms of Ken's reliability. As a result, Ken was promoted, indicating benevolence and trusting behaviours on Lloyd's part.

In contrast, Edward's (F) and Leon's (L) experiences became increasingly negative over time. Leon commented that the Board had no faith in Edward, leaving Edward insecure and unhappy:

> **Edward (F):** *'... that was the point when I thought this is it I can't just keep doing this... I received quite a lot of criticism, the relationship between Leon and myself had become quite strained I just thought, do you know what? I've had enough. ... I just said to Leon why don't I resign and he said 'let's park that ... and look at it Mid-May'*

Because their perception of the benevolence, performance, commitment and trustworthiness of the other decreased, so did their relationship quality and their relationship development took a downturn, indicating the interdependent nature of perceptions of trustworthiness, trust in action and relationship quality. For Edward and Leon, neither party seemed to feel that the relationship could be restored and their increasingly negative views of each other were expressed though their social and emotional interactions.

The data therefore show that relationship quality is temporal, emerging and changing over time in both positive and negative ways and reciprocal in terms of involving both leader and follower assessments.

4.4 Additional themes in the data: socio-emotionality, transactional elements, communication, loyalty and respect

A number of themes appeared in the data that support current LMX literature. As a result, they are noted here rather than described in detail. These themes were: (1) the role of affect and socio-emotional elements; (2) feelings of respect and loyalty; and (3) the role of transactional aspects of the relationship (4) The value of communication. These are each described briefly below, starting with affect and socio-emotional dimensions.

First, LMX studies of relationship quality often include 'affect' or liking as a dimension, and Social LMX theory expands this to include socio-emotional elements of fun, laughter, commitment, benevolence and mutual trust [57, 58]. Our data indicate that socio-emotional aspects of relationships are important and that they interact with the other dimensions described so far. The findings are in line with recent literature around workplace relationships where affect and leadership are closely linked [59]. In addition, friendship is associated with positive emotions at work and personal growth links to life satisfaction [60] higher creativity, performance and reduced staff turnover [57, 61]. They also appear to confirm Dysvik et al. [62] findings that the better the quality of socio-emotional relations, the greater the likelihood of co-operation and information exchange between leaders and followers.

Secondly, respect and loyalty, two dimensions of multi-dimensional LMX [20], appeared strongly in the data. Both leaders and followers made comments regarding respect, including: 'having respect for each other', 'admiring' the other party and feeling respected where role-boundaries were clear and maintained. Loyalty took the forms of 'not wanting to let the other party down', responding favourably to or delegating tasks, and 'doing well' for the other person. Perceptions of both dimensions had a temporal aspect, growing more positive over time unless there was a negative event that disrupted the relationship development process.

The third additional theme relates to transactional (or economic) relationship dynamics, which are more contractual, self-interested relationship dimensions with relatively short-term tangible economic-based pay-offs (e.g. [63]). Positive assessments occurred where promises had been fulfilled, and contractual terms upheld. Negative perspectives included feelings of having been let down, demotivated or over-managed (on the part of employees), of promises or contracts being broken. The extent to which this influenced relationship quality, performance and trust depended on the calibre and style of leadership and procedures for management. Where these transactions involved share options and share values, there was a slight improvement over time if both parties felt that the firm's performance was increasing share value in the long term.

Finally, the extent to which individuals perceived their relationship to be good was reinforced by their view of the quality of the communication between their leader/follower. Our findings agreed with Abu Bakar and Sheer [64] and Sheer [5] where positive perceptions were linked to commitment, support, trust, transactional dimensions and individual performance.

In summary, we suggest that relationship quality is interrelated with: trustworthiness, risk-taking, trusting behaviours; subjective perceptions of relationship quality;

and an individuals' ability to perform their roles. In addition, a range of dimensions covering both transactional and socio-emotional aspects of working life feed into this relationship development process. Additionally, as Kuvaas et al. [65] note, socio-emotional relationships are 'characterized by a long-term orientation, where the exchanges between leaders and followers are on-going and based on feelings of diffuse obligation, and less in need of an immediate "pay off"." These sentiments were reflected in our data: where relationships were positive both leader and follower wanted it to continue. When asked if Jeremy would like to continue working with Lois, even if the company were bought out, his answer was an unequivocal:

Jeremy (F): 'Yes...'

Assessments of these dimensions are made continually throughout the relationship's lifetime rather than being outcomes that occur after a period of time. The concept of trust and relationship quality as interdependent is not new in the literature, but there are no qualitative empirical studies that explain how trust, performance, leader-follower perceptions and relationship quality are interrelated and develop over time. We now discuss how each is connected and present a model for Dyadic Relationship Quality (DRQ) that encapsulates the dimensions of relationship development.

5. Discussion

Participants in the study were clear that a good-quality relationship existed where leaders and followers liked each other (affect), where they considered the other trustworthy and where the other's ability to perform was enacted, acknowledged and valued. The contribution to LMX theory based on the data indicates that both leaders and followers identified a number of influences on the quality of their relationship and that relationship quality started to develop from their initial interaction (see **Figure 1** below). If both parties anticipate trust and perceive trusting behaviours, then along with a sense of liking, admiring and/or assessing the other party as open, positive first impressions are formed. These first impressions can influence the relationship for some time to come [29, 66, 67] unless a disruption occurs, i.e. no trusting behaviours appear, performance expectations of either leader or follower are not met, or either party's liking and/or respect for the other deteriorates. Then the quality of the relationship is affected in a negative way. This underlines the need for more longitudinal studies of relationship quality.

In much LMX-based research, performance is seen as an outcome of relationship development. Findings from this study indicate that performance (whether potential

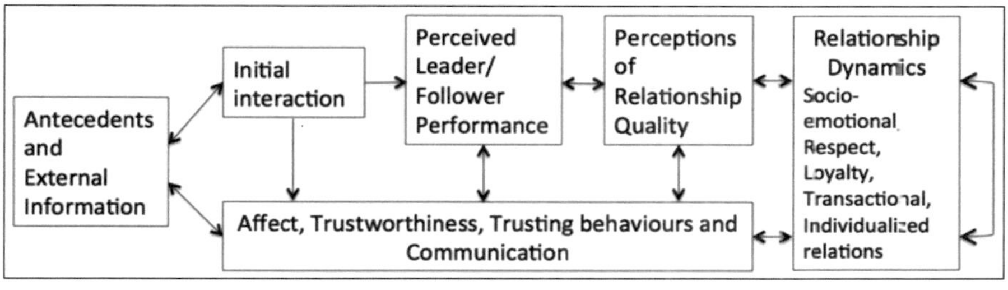

Figure 1.
Dyadic relationship quality process over time.

or realised) is assessed from the beginning of the relationship and that this changes how relationship quality is viewed. Where performance is strong, relationship quality, trust and relationship dynamics remain positive, where performance fails (as for Edward and Izzy), then parties lose faith in the relationship and the other dimensions also start to fall in quality terms.

Based on the empirical data, we propose the following definition for Dyadic Relationship Quality (DRQ) development:

> *The temporal leader-follower relationship development process where relationship quality is influenced by the perceptions of both leaders and followers of initial and on-going interactions; trustworthiness, trusting behaviours and performance; communication; socio-emotional and transactional aspects of the relationship; and perceptions of the quality of the relationship.*

Figure 1 (see below) maps the interrelationship of the various influences on leader-follower relationship quality over time – emphasising its temporal nature. This process generally starts before leader and follower meet, where through personal, social or media networks both parties are likely to have prior knowledge of the other, their achievements and previous employment history. With this knowledge, and each person's antecedents, the initial interaction takes place.

During the first encounter, each party decides whether they think they can or do like the other person (affect), whether they think they are trustworthy and easy to communicate with and crucially takes a risk in displaying some form of trusting behaviour. In the study, this took the form of offering/accepting an unpaid job (Lisa and Izzy) and access to the code base/signing an intellectual property agreement (Lance and Adrian). These four dimensions (affect, trustworthiness, communication and trusting behaviours) impact the relationship for the remainder of its lifespan and interact with all other dimensions of relationship quality.

Findings also suggest that both leaders and followers assessed the actual or potential performance of their leader/follower and the relationship quality over time, ascribing value, based on their experience of the relationship. This assessment considered perceptions of: trust, communication, liking and emotions. In some dyads, the relationship developed in a mutually constructive way, for others, in a negative direction. Participant comments also illustrate that relationship quality is more complex and multifaceted than conceived of by LMX theory. In addition to trust, both leader and follower perceptions of the socio-emotional aspects of their relationship and their assessment of each other's performance interact to influence relationship quality. These dimensions (as described above) are generally treated as outcomes of relationship development but were, in this data set, active influences on the emergence of relationship quality over time – in both supportive (e.g. Jeremy and Lois) and disruptive (e.g. Edward and Leon) ways.

Another major difference between this study and much existing work on LMX and interpersonal trust is that rather than looking for determinants and dependent and independent variables of interpersonal trust or increased performance, we argue that trust, relationship quality, performance and ongoing leader and follower assessments of each other and their relationship quality are interdependent, iterative and embedded in the context in which they work. The picture of how relationship quality develops and is maintained, therefore, is far more complex and nuanced than current descriptions of the types of leader behaviours that will induce follower trust (e.g. [12]), or how trust improves outcomes [68–70].

6. Conclusion: further considerations

The significance of the study lies in the conceptualisation of relationship quality not as an outcome, but as integral to ongoing assessments made by both leaders and followers based on many factors. The findings show that these multiple factors continue to influence perceptions of relationship quality over time and that both leaders and followers review their perceptions and assessments throughout the development process. Significantly, perceptions of relationship quality are not an outcome of dyadic relations but part of the relationship quality development process itself, interdependent and potentially changing through the lifetime of the relationship.

A wholistic approach will be required to fully understand how workplace experiences, relationships and productivity function, within relationship contexts and treating the combination of these elements as interdependent and emergent.

The study also suggests that contrary to many LMX studies, relationship quality cannot be determined by surveying leaders and followers separately on the basis of four dimensions. Rather, the entwined, personal and lived nature of leader-follower relationships and the agency of both leaders and followers in assessing, influencing and acting upon subjective perceptions of relationship quality suggest that qualitative longitudinal research on how both leaders and followers perceive their relationship would be beneficial in furthering the development of theory [71]. This should also offer organisations with practical opportunities to improve relationship quality and performance at work.

The practical implications of this study lie in the immediate applicability to the workplace. If leaders are aware of and demonstrate trusting behaviours as new hires are inducted, and also know what to look for, they can both support positive relationship beginnings and recognise when reciprocal behaviours occur. Likewise, understanding the value of social, emotional, respect and good communication will help to 'oil the wheels' of relationships as they progress [72]. Conversely, if leaders and followers note the absence of these key dimensions of relationships, they are then equipped to describe how a relationship is lacking, take remedial action to improve and/or end the relations in the workplace. Key to empowering leaders and followers to recognise and act on positive or negative behaviour patterns will be leadership training and development [73].

Finally, this study examined vertical relationships between leaders and followers in a high-tech start-up context in the United Kingdom. Future work could extend qualitative and quantitative studies across different contexts with more diverse settings, paying attention to the lenses of gender, race, ethnicity and sexual identity. In addition, it may be interesting to address whether similar results might result in relation to horizontal, co-worker relationship quality.

Acknowledgements

Firstly, thank you to the entrepreneurs and their staff who took part in the research: for their time, honesty and openness. Secondly, to Ann Cunliffe for her indomitable determination and cheerful guidance. Finally, to my ever-supportive family and friends for their enduring patience.

Conflict of interest

The author declares no conflict of interest.

Acronyms and abbreviations

LMX	leader-member exchange
DRQ	dyadic relationship quality

Author details

Julie Wilson
Eastshaw Consultancy, The Derwent Flour Mill, United Kingdom

*Address all correspondence to: eastshaw@gmail.com

References

[1] Erdogan B, Bauer TN. Leader-member exchange (lmx) theory: the relational approach to leadership. In: Day DV, editor. The Oxford Handbook of Leadership and Organizations. New York: Oxford University Press Inc.; 2015. pp. 407-433

[2] Day D, Miscenko D. Leader-member exchange (LMX): Construction evolution, contributions, and future prospects for advancing leadership theory. In: Erdogan B, editor. The Oxford Handbook of Leader-Member Exchange. Oxford, UK: Oxford University Press; 2015. pp. 9-28

[3] Liden RC, Wu J, Cao AX, Wayne SJ. Leader-member exchange measurement. In: Bauer TN, Erdogan B, editors. The Oxford Handbook of Leader-Member Exchange. New York, USA: Oxford University Press; 2015. pp. 29-54

[4] Carsten MK, Bligh MC, Kohles JC, et al. A follower-centric approach to the 2016 US presidential election: Candidate rhetoric and follower attributions of charisma and effectiveness. Leadership 2019;**15**(2):179-204

[5] Sheer VC. Exchange lost in leader-member exchange theory and research: A critique and a reconceptualization. Leadership. 2015;**11**(2):213-229

[6] Stentz JE, Plano Clark VL, Matkin GS. Applying mixed methods to leadership research: A review of current practices. The Leadership Quarterly. 2012;**23**(6):1173-1183

[7] Dinh JE, Lord RG, Gardner WL, Meuser JD, Liden RC, Hu J. Leadership theory and research in the new millennium: Current theoretical trends and changing perspectives. Leadership Quarterly. 2014;**25**(1):36-62

[8] Kabalo P. David Ben-Gurion's leadership as a "two-way interaction process". Leadership. 2017;**13**(3):320-342. DOI: 10.1177/1742715015589645

[9] Tourish D. Leadership, more or less? A processual, communication perspective on the role of agency in leadership theory. Leadership. 2014;**10**(1):79-98

[10] Nahrgang J, Seo JJ. How and why high leader-member exchange (LMX) relationships develop: Examining the antecedents of LMX. In: Bauer TN, Erdogan B, editors. The Oxford Handbook of Leader-Member Exchange. New York, USA: Oxford University Press; 2016. pp. 37-118

[11] Bligh MC, Kohles JC. Do I trust you to lead the way? Exploring trust and mistrucst in leader-follwer relations. In: Leonard JPHS, Lewis R, Freedman AM, editors. The Wiley-Blackwell Handbook of the Psychology of Leadership, Change and Organizational Development. Oxford, UK: John Wiley & Sons, Ltd.; 2013. pp. 89-112

[12] Hernandez M, Long CP, Sitkin SB. Cultivating follower trust: Are all leader behaviors equally influential? Organization Studies. 2014;**35**(12):1867-1892

[13] Wang KY, Clegg S. Managing to lead in private enterprise in China: Work values, demography and the development of trust. Leadership. 2007;**3**(2):149-172

[14] McCauley CD, Palus CJ. Developing the theory and practice of leadership development: A relational view. The Leadership Quarterly. 2021;**32**(5):101456

[15] Ayoko OB, Tan PP, Li Y. Leader–follower interpersonal behaviors,

emotional regulation and LMX quality. Journal of Management & Organization. 2022:1-18. DOI: 10.1017/jmo.2022.26

[16] Planchy RJ, Smunt TL. Rethinking managership, leadership, followership, and partnership. Business Horizons. 2022;**65**(4):401-411

[17] Oberer B, Alptekin E. Leadership 4.0: Digital leaders in the age of industry 4.0. International Journal of Organizational Leadership. 2018

[18] Benson AJ, Hardy J, Eys M. Contextualizing leaders' interpretation s of proactive followership. Journal of Organizational Behavior. 2016;**37**:949-966

[19] Le Blanc PM, González-Romá V. A team level investigation of the relationship between leader–member exchange (lmx) differentiation, and commitment and performance. The Leadership Quarterly. 2012;**23**(3):534-544

[20] Schyns B, Day D. Critique and review of leader – member exchange theory: Issues of agreement, consensus, and excellence. European Journal of Work and Organizational Psychology. 2010;**19**(1):1-29

[21] Graen GB, Scandura TA. Toward a psychology of dyadic organizing. Research in Organizational Behavior. 1987

[22] Nahrgang JD, Morgeson FP, Ilies R. The development of leader–member exchanges: Exploring how personality and performance influence leader and member relationships over time. Organizational Behavior and Human Decision Processes. 2009;**108**(2):256-266

[23] Dansereau F, Cashman J, Graen G. Instrumentality theory and equity theory as complementary approaches in predicting the relationship of leadership and turnover among managers. Organizational Behavior and Human Performance. 1973;**10**(2):184-200

[24] Martin R, Guillaume Y, Thomas G, Lee A, Epitropaki O. Leader-member exchange (LMX) and performance: A meta-analytic review. Personnel Psychology. 2015:1-55. DOI: 10.1111/pepa.12100

[25] Bauer TN, Erdogan B. Introduction to this handbook. In: Bauer TN, Erdogan B, editors. The Oxford Handbook of Leader-Member Exchange. New York, NY: Oxford University Press; 2016. pp. 3-8

[26] Hiller NJ, DeChurch LA, Murase T, Doty D. Searching for outcomes of leadership: A 25-year review. Journal of Management. 2011;**37**:1137-1177

[27] Bernerth JB, Walker HJ, Harris SG. Rethinking the benefits and pitfalls of leader-member exchange: a reciprocity versus self-protection perspective. Human Relations. 2016;**69**(3):661-684

[28] Boon C, Biron M. Temporal issues in person-organization fit, person-job fit and turnover: The role of leader-member exchange. Human Relations. 2016;**69**(12):2177-2200. DOI: 10.1177/0018726716636945

[29] Hu J, Wayne SJ, Bauer TN, Erdogan B, Liden RC. Self and senior executive perceptions of fit and performance: A time-lagged examination of newly-hired executives. Human Relations. 2016. DOI: 10.1177/0018726715609108

[30] Bernerth JB, Armenakis A, Field HS, Giles WF, Walker HJ. Leader – member social exchange (LMSX): Development and validation of a scale.

Journal of Organizational Behavior. 2007;**28**:979-1003

[31] Buch R, Kuvaas B, Dysvik A. If and when social and economic leader-member exchange relationships predict follower work effort. The moderating role of work motivation. Leadership and Organization Development Journal. 2014;**35**(8):725-739

[32] Buch R, Kuvaas B, Dysvik A, Schyns B. If and when social and economic leader-member exchange relationships predict follower work effort: The moderating role of work motivation. Leadership & Organization Development Journal; 2014

[33] Dienesch RM, Liden RC. Leader-member exchange model of leadership: a critique and further development. Academy of Management Review. 1986;**11**(3):618-634

[34] Ikonen M. Trust development and dynamics at dyadic level: A narrative approach to studying processes of interpersonal trust in leader-follower relationships. [Thesis Dissertation, Pulications of the University of Eastern Finland, No. 53]. 2013

[35] Dulebohn JH, Bommer WH, Liden RC, Brouer RL, Ferris GR. A meta-analysis of antecedents and consequences of leader-member exchange: Integrating the past with an eye toward the future. Journal of Management. 2011;**38**(6):1715-1759

[36] Nienaber AM, Hofeditz M, Romeike PD. Vulnerability and trust in leader-follower relationships. Personnel Review. 2015;**44**(4):567-591

[37] Schermuly CC, Meyer B. Good relationships at work: The effects of leader-member exchange and team-member Exchange on psychological empowerment, emotional exhaustion, and depression. Journal of Organizational Behavior 2016;**37**(5):673-691

[38] Gannon MJ, Pillai R. Understanding Global Cultures: Metaphorical Journeys through 34 Nations, Clusters of Nations, Continents, and Diversity. Sage Publications; 2015

[39] Ayman R, Korabik K. Leadership: Why gender and culture matter. The American Psychologist. 2010;**65**:157-170

[40] Browne K. Snowball sampling: using social networks to research non-heterosexual women. International Journal of Social Research Methodology. 2005;**8**(1):47-60

[41] Crist JD, Tanner C. Interpretation/analysis methods in hermeneutic interpretive phenomenology. Nursing Research. 2003;**50**(3):202-205

[42] Braun V, Clark V. Using thematic analysis in psychology. Qualitative Research in Psychology. 2006;**3**(2):77-101

[43] Rousseau D, Sitkin SB, Burt RS, Camerer C. Not so different after all: A cross-discipline view of trust. Academy of Management Review. 1998;**23**:393-404

[44] Dietz G, Hartog DN Den. Measuring trust inside organisations. Personnel Review. 2006;**35**(5):557-588

[45] Wasti SA, Tan HH, Erdil SE. Antecedents of trust across foci: A comparative study of Turkey and China. Management and Organization Review. 2011;7(2):279-302

[46] Dietz G. Going back to the source: why do people trust eachother? Journal of Trust Research. 2011;**1**(2):215-222

[47] McKnight DH, Cummings LL, Chervany NL. Initial trust formation

in new organizational relationships. Academy of Management Review. 1998;**23**(3):473

[48] Delgado-Márquez BL et al. Does knowledge explain trust behaviors and outcomes? The different influences of initial knowledge and experiential knowledge on personal trust interactions. The International Journal of Human Resource Management. 2014;**July**:1-16

[49] Scarbrough H et al. Exploring the role of trust in the deal-making process for early-stage technology ventures. Entrepreneurship: Theory and Practice. 2013;**37**(5):1203-1228

[50] Van der Werff L, Buckley F. Getting to know you: A longitudinal examination of trust cues and trust development during socialization. Journal of Management. 2017;**43**(3):742-770

[51] Colquitt JA, Scott BA, JA LP. Trust, trustworthiness, and trust propensity: A meta-analytic test of their unique relationships with risk taking and job performance. The Journal of Applied Psychology. 2007;**92**(4):909-927

[52] Frazier LM, Tupper C, Fainshmidt S. Where are you going? A comparative analysis of job and career change intentions among USA IT workers. Journal of Organizational Behavior. 2016. DOI: 10.1002/job.2091

[53] Mayer RC, Gavin MB. Trust in management and performance: Who minds the shop while the employees watch the boss? Academy of Management Journal. 2005;**48**(5):874-888

[54] Poon JML. Effects of benevolence, integrity, and ability on trust-in-supervisor. Employee Relations. 2013;**35**(4):396-407

[55] Gupta N, Ho V, Pollack JM, Lai L. A multilevel perspective of interpersonal trust: Individual, dyadic, and cross-level predictors of performance. Journal of Organizational Behavior. 2016;**37**(8):1271-1292. DOI: 10.1002/job.2104 A

[56] Peterson RS, Behfar KJ. The dynamic relationship between performance feedback, trust, and conflict in groups: A longitudinal study. Organizational Behavior and Human Decision Processes. 2003;**92**(1-2, 112):102

[57] Buch R, Kuvaas B. Capitalizing on Creativity at Work: Fostering the Implementation of Creative Ideas in Organizations M. Skerlavaj et al. (eds) Cheltenham UK: Edward Elgar. Publishing Ltd; 2016

[58] Buch R, Dysvik A, Kuvaas B, Nerstad CG. It takes three to tango: Exploring the interplay among training intensity, job autonomy, and supervisor support in predicting knowledge sharing. Human Resource Management. 2015;54(4):623-635

[59] Rowold J, Borgmann L. Interpersonal affect and the assessment of interrelationship between leadership constructs. Leadership. 2014;**10**(3):301-325

[60] Colbert AE, Bono JE, Puranova RK. Flourishing via workplace relationships: Moving beyond instrumental support. Academy of Management Journal. 2015. DOI: amj-2014

[61] Little LM, Gooty J, Williams M. The role of leader emotion management in leader-member exchange and follower outcomes. Leadership Quarterly. 2016;**27**(1):85-97

[62] Dysvik A, Buch R, Kuvaas B. Knowledge donating and knowledge collecting. Leadership & Organization Development Journal. 2015;**36**(1):35-53

[63] Kuvaas B, Buch R, Dysvik A, et al. Economic and social leader–member exchange relationships and follower performance. The Leadership Quarterly. 2012;**23**(5):756-765

[64] Abu Bakar H, Sheer VC. The mediating role of perceived cooperative communication in the relationship between interpersonal exchange relationships and perceived group cohesion. Management Communication Quarterly. 2013;**27**:443-465

[65] Kuvaas B, Buch R, Dysvik A, Haerem T. Economic and social leader–member exchange relationships and follower performance. The Leadership Quarterly. 2012;**23**(5):756-765

[66] Liden RC, Wayne SJ, Stilwell D. A longitudinal study on the early development of leader-member exchanges. Journal of Applied Psychology. 1993;**78**(4):662-674

[67] Kangas HM. The development of the LMX relationships after a newly appointed leader enters an organization. Human Resource Development International. 2013;**16**(5):575-589

[68] Werbel J, Henriques P. Different views of trust and relational leadership: Supervisor and subordinate perspectives. Journal of Managerial Psychology. 2009;**24**(8):780-796

[69] Yang J, Mossholder KW. Examining the effects of trust in leaders: A bases-and-foci approach. The Leadership Quarterly. 2010;**21**(1):50-63

[70] Zhu W, Newman A, Miao Q, Hooke A. Revisiting the mediating role of trust in transformational leadership effects: Do different types of trust make a difference? The Leadership Quarterly. 2013;**24**(1):94-105

[71] Cunliffe A, Eriksen M. Relational leadership. Human Relations 2011;**64**(11):1425-1449

[72] Adams BG, Meyers MC, Sekaja L. Positive leadership: Relationships with employee inclusion, discrimination, and well-being. Applied Psychology: An International Review. 2020;**69**(4):1145-1173

[73] Cunliffe A, Wilson JA. Can Leadership be Taught. In: The Routledge companion to leadership. s.l.: Routledge; 2016. pp. 527-566

Chapter 7

An Introduction to High-Reliability Leadership Style in Healthcare

Maryam Memar Zadeh

Abstract

Hospitals, urgent care units, outpatient clinics, and long-term care facilities constantly keep tightening their safety measures by adopting new interventions. As a result of these efforts, nowadays, fewer patients injure or die from accidental injections, medication errors, falls, or serious healthcare-acquired infections. Yet, many service providers still frequently find themselves at the center of criticism by the media and advocacy groups for their inefficacy in making drastic systematic changes that last. More recent advancements in the field have called for the emulation of the principles of High-Reliability Organizations (HROs) for creating safer services through more radical changes. Building upon this research and juxtaposing it with the leadership literature, our study takes this call one step further by introducing and conceptualizing a leadership style which we call high-reliability leadership style. The chapter also provides a starting point for the advancement of research and practice in healthcare by providing an in-depth exploration of the characteristics of high-reliability leaders. Healthcare organizations can use the findings presented in this chapter for selecting and developing individuals into leadership roles capable of ensuring the sustainable reliability of their care delivery systems.

Keywords: leadership, healthcare delivery systems, patient safety, reliability, high-reliability leadership style, high-reliability leaders

1. Introduction

Since the United States Institute of Medicine published "To Err is Human" to highlight the extent of patient safety deficiencies within the healthcare industry [1], research in the patient safety field has proliferated exponentially. The result of this vast research expansion was the dissemination of a variety of safety interventions, in the form of technological advancements and standardized best practices, to improve the reliability of health service delivery processes [2]. Despite an increase in the adoption of these quality and safety improvement interventions, service provider failures remain a major public concern across all health provision sectors. In fact, the efficacy of these interventions in preventing care delivery failures seems to have reached a plateau due to the gradual escalation in the complexity of healthcare services, which has emerged in more recent decades as a result of a combination of unprecedented factors, such as increased patient acuity and increased human life expectancy [3, 4]. Healthcare service providers' failures are now considered among the leading causes of injury and death in the United States [5]. Only hand hygiene failures of service providers contribute to the 1.7 million annual cases of healthcare-acquired infections, which are estimated to cost Americans $45 billion [6, 7].

While these types of failures in the healthcare industry are not entirely avoidable [8], in more recent years, an alternative and more promising safety approach have been adopted by some healthcare settings. This safety approach originates from a sub-category of complex socio-technical systems, widely known as high-reliability organizations (HROs), that operate under hazardous conditions with the potential for catastrophic failures. Yet, despite operating in such demanding and failure-prone environments, HROs have developed a capability to sustain nearly failure-free operations over very long periods of time. Some classic examples of HROs that are documented by management scholars are: air traffic control systems [9], nuclear power plants [10], nuclear aircraft carriers [11], navy SEALs [12], and space shuttle programs [13, 14].

As healthcare organizations are extremely prone to service provider failures, in the healthcare industry, the emulation of HROs' safety approach has shown astonishing positive outcomes in some settings such as intensive care units, emergency departments, and operating rooms [15, 16]. Despite these recent developments, the characteristics of HRO leaders remain understudied, both among social scientists and healthcare scholars. In particular in the healthcare context, given the complexity and variety of health provision settings, there is still no agreement on how HROs are operated by leaders whose characteristics are different from the traditional leadership roles.

The clarification of this leadership style is a necessity for improving care safety and quality outcomes. First, the noticeable lag of many healthcare settings—such as long-term care organizations—in adopting the HRO principles, to some extent, is ascribable to the ambiguities surrounding the leadership role. The past research advocates that the successful adoption of the HRO approach in healthcare requires a top-down approach, all the way from the leadership to the frontline, to ensure embedding a high-reliability mindset and practices in the day-to-day function of organizations [3]. Second, many healthcare organizations still treat the HRO approach as a framework for incremental improvements and, as a result, they miss the opportunity for creating the foundational changes necessary for operating with high reliability. Therefore, as soon as a key person leaves the organization or a new safety approach is introduced, the organization tends to revert to its old practices and HRO processes disappear [17].

The purpose of this chapter is to shed light on the fundamental role of high-reliability leaders in infusing healthcare organizations with high levels of patient safety. Our research revealed four major characteristics of high-reliability leaders in the healthcare industry: mindfulness, participative tendencies, integrity, and ambidexterity. In the following sections, we first discuss why the high-reliability leadership style is required for creating lasting changes in the operational reliability of healthcare organizations. Then we elaborate on each dimension of high-reliability leaders' characteristics.

2. Leadership in healthcare

A substantial body of literature has charted the evolution of healthcare leadership styles that, over years, unfolded in response to arising opportunities and challenges, including: the increased complexities of patients' care, ongoing shifts in the care delivery systems, emergence of new technological advancements, recognition of the formerly overlooked organizational goals (particularly patient safety outcomes), and unprecedented challenges of providing care for the aging population [18–24]. This literature discusses the adoption of a variety of leadership theories in healthcare including trait theories, contingency theories, as well as the transactional, transformational, and servant leadership styles.

While emulation of some of these leadership styles occasionally has led to dysfunctional accountability and poor outcomes in the healthcare industry [25, 26], the transformational leadership style has received extensive attention from scholars for its potential for tackling the complex and evolving environment of most healthcare settings. This leadership style has been associated with enhancing the work-oriented values of the caregivers, their self-efficacy, commitment, job satisfaction, building successful teams, and, generally, improving organizational citizenship [27, 28]. Moreover, transformational leadership processes are known to contribute the most to operational objectives such as patient safety and process quality [29, 30].

Traditionally, predominant reliability frameworks for improving safety and quality outcomes in the healthcare industry were created utilizing evidence-based best practices, which are converted into highly standardized operating procedures [31]. These reliability frameworks originate from continuous improvement methodologies, such as Plan-Do-Study-Act (PDSA) cycle. Yet the effectiveness of these traditional reliability frameworks is contingent upon the application of an appropriate leadership approach in conjunction with the implementation of the reliability framework to reap its expected benefits. More often than not, due to the lack of engagement of the staff or due to their resistance to changes, these types of safety and quality improvement frameworks tend to fail [20].

This explains why the application of the transformational leadership process can play a critical role in the success of these traditional improvement frameworks. Under the leadership of transformational leaders, the staff is more likely to act in alignment with organizational goals. Transformational leader strives for creating enduring transformation in their followers by expanding their vision and understanding of the organizational goals, and, thereby, they can alter the trajectory of their organizations in the long run [32, 33]. In this context, a leader will be considered transformational if he/she exhibits four characteristics of role modeling, inspirational motivation, intellectual stimulation, and individualized consideration of followers' needs and concerns [32, 34–36]. As a result of these characteristics of transformational leaders, the followers would have the motivation to act in alignment with organizational goals. As such, in a healthcare setting, the followers of transformational leaders might significantly contribute to improving safety outcomes of the care delivery system by adhering to the requirements of the adopted reliability frameworks.

Despite the fact that the transformational leadership style is extremely impactful in mitigating some major barriers to reliability enhancement in healthcare organizations, this reliability improvement leadership approach is not entirely sufficient in creating fundamental changes necessary for operating failure-free. The problem arises from the fact that the traditional reliability frameworks are, in nature, inadequate for tackling the operational risk of health provision settings. As mentioned earlier, the traditional reliability frameworks are designed based on the principles of continuous improvements philosophy. As a result, no matter how closely followed by the clinical staff, the implementation of these reliability frameworks would essentially create only incremental changes within the health delivery system [31].

The fast-paced evolution of both the care complexities (as evidenced by the recent COVID-19 pandemic) and the care delivery system integration and interactivity—coupled with the dramatic socio-technical changes in the industry—make healthcare systems extremely volatile and unpredictable [3]. Therefore, the implementation of incremental changes, by utilizing the traditional reliability frameworks in conjunction with the adoption of transformational leadership processes to reinforce them, may seriously lag the pace of the healthcare industry's evolution. In response to the ever-shifting healthcare service delivery environment, this research suggests the adoption of the high-reliability leadership approach, which could enhance patient safety outcomes by creating fundamental and philosophical changes in organizations.

3. Methods

To assess the underlying process and characteristics of the high-reliability leadership style in healthcare, we critically reviewed leadership literature in healthcare and juxtaposed them with the HRO literature. For this purpose, we conducted two rounds of search in the PubMed/Medline database to identify the relevant research published between 2002 and 2022 (see PRISMA flow diagram in **Figure 1**, for the number of studies screened, assessed for eligibility, and included in the review). In the first round, the primary search keyword was "patient safety AND leader". The result of this process was identifying a total of 176 articles. After the initial screening of their abstracts, 108 articles were selected for the detailed assessment. We considered

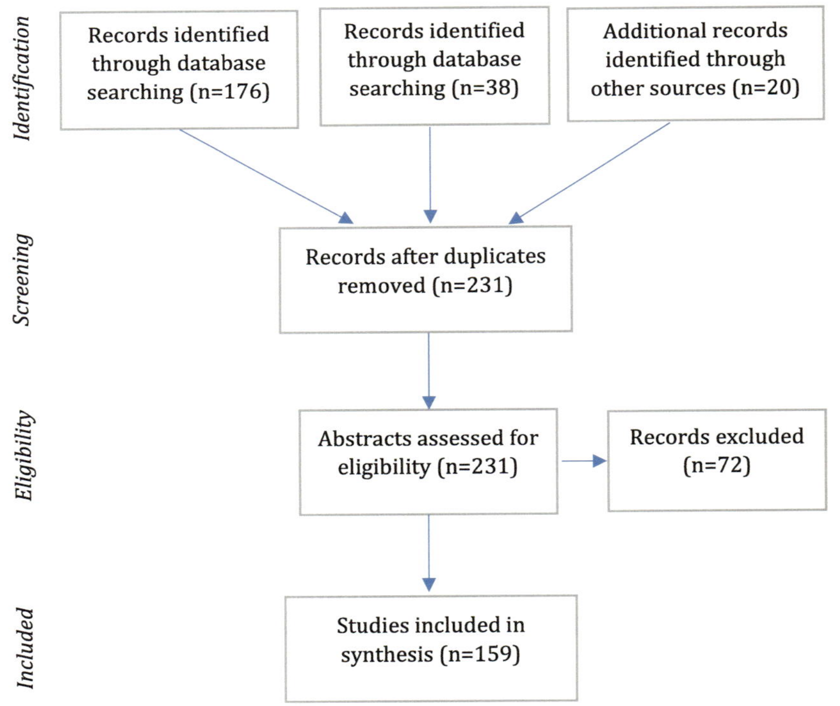

Figure 1.
PRISMA flow diagram. Adopted from [37].

four exclusion criteria when reviewing abstracts: papers that discussed policy-level interventions and contained no (or very little) information about the leadership at an organizational level, papers that were too technical (i.e., specialized in certain subject matter such as laboratory tests or application of FMEA risk management technique) to the extent that the findings were not easily generalizable to other health sectors, papers that had not elaborated adequately on the top level leadership role in organizations, and papers with overall lower quality of the publication.

During the second round, the search keyword "high-reliability organizations AND leader" was used to identify a total of 38 articles of which 34 were deemed suitable for informing our research. Among these 34 articles, three were common between round one and round two. As such, in total, the literature search process yielded 139 healthcare articles which were reviewed to make conclusions on the nature of leadership requirements in healthcare. In addition to this set of articles in healthcare, we also reviewed the seminal literature on HROs (additional 20 publications) to understand the specific principles that allow these organizations to operate with high levels of reliability. Then we used these principles to contextualize and specify characteristics of healthcare leaders that would be conducive to the implementation of the HRO principles. Additionally, this review process allowed us to identify the leadership process which must be devised to translate the HRO theory into practice in healthcare.

4. High-reliability leadership style in healthcare

4.1 HRO principle and healthcare adoption

HROs are systems that despite operating in high-risk, unpredictable, multifaceted, and turbulent environments, exhibit virtually failure-free operations over long periods of time [38]. The enhanced reliability in these systems is the result of an optimum combination of leveraging technical barriers to failures and deploying interventions that underpin a safe operations philosophy and culture. While the application of technical barriers is often idiosyncratic to each industrial context (and therefore is not easily transferable to other industries uniformly), the philosophical interventions appear in form of processes and principles that impact the human/social factors in these organizations, and as a result, are more readily documentable and, therefore, transferrable. Previous HRO research has identified five major HRO principles that are known to be the foundation of HROs' reliable performance [9–14, 38–41]:

Principle 1: HROs maintain a preoccupation with failures. These organizations are always skeptical about their operating reliability and, therefore, are never content with their own performance. Instead, they are constantly occupied with seeking, identifying, and addressing areas of weakness. Due to this characteristic, HROs are known to be distinctive from traditional organizations because they have created a culture of *perfection-seeking* instead of *being perfect* [3, 38, 39].

Principle 2: HROs have developed a collective sensitivity to operations. HROs leverage heightened awareness of the technical aspects of frontline operations to spot and address minor issues before they escalate into more serious failures. Based on this principle, not only the frontline staff but also all organizational actors (including top/senior managers), should maintain an awareness of the ongoing state of any critical frontline processes [39, 40].

Principle 3: HROs demonstrate a reluctance to simplify interpretations. Based on this principle, operating with high reliability requires a non-stop questioning of accepted rules and assumptions. In other words, as HROs often operate in highly complex and uncertain conditions, simplification is not recommended. Rather, organizational actors are encouraged not to take anything for granted, in particular, when assessing trivial issues and near misses [9–14, 38].

Principle 4: HROs are committed to resilience. According to this principle, HROs must develop the capacity for containing any arising crises and bounce back from them quickly. Additionally, they must investigate failures and re-incorporate the learned lessons into the operating procedure to prevent similar failures in the future. This level of commitment to resilience also requires the development of a culture of failure tolerance toward trivial deviations [9, 12, 38, 40].

Principle 5: HROs defer to expertise. This principle requires organizations to value and prioritize experts' insights. Regardless of their rank, authority, or seniority, experts, with the most pertinent knowledge of time-sensitive processes, should have the necessary autonomy to make quick decisions, without the need for authorization of their senior managers. This prevents insignificant issues from turning into major failures [38–41].

Operating based on these principles has enabled HROs to attain well-coordinated decision-making ability across their organization, which is necessary for avoiding errors with disastrous consequences [42]. These HRO safety principles were first adopted by the healthcare industry over 20 years ago [43]. With the publication of "To Err is Human," which highlighted some major causes of compromised patient safety such as system fragmentation and the lack of a solid safety culture, the urgent need for adoption of a structured safety approach such as HRO principles became evident. Although certain characteristics of healthcare organizations (e.g., high contact with the service consumers or extensive mobility of the caregivers) make the adoption of HROs' principle slightly challenging in the healthcare context [44], many promising improvements have been reported by healthcare providers that dared to venture to the realm of HRO philosophy. For example, following a comprehensive adoption of the HRO philosophy, some hospitals have experienced a significant reduction in adverse events, ranging from 55 to 100% [44]. The reported improvements are not limited to enhanced safety outcomes. For instance, Hilliard and colleagues [45] report on significant cost savings and financial growth as a result of improved reliability.

4.2 High-reliability leadership in healthcare

While the successful adoption of HRO principles has led to encouraging results, still the assimilation of the HRO philosophy remains scarce, unstructured, and often incomprehensive among healthcare provision settings [3]. Unfortunately, as it is often assumed that emulating HROs is extremely costly and that the financial gains do not offset the adoption cost, there is major resistance to the adoption of HRO principles, in particular among the small- and medium-sized care providers. Some other healthcare organizations are reluctant because they assume that they should be prioritizing other improvement frameworks such as the implementation of electronic health record (EHR) systems [44]. Yet, these types of assumptions are not necessarily accurate. For instance, Memar Zadeh and Haggerty [3] have reported significant complementary effects between the implementations of EHR and HRO frameworks in the context of long-term care facilities.

One crucial factor that seems to be contributing to this lag, fragmentation, inconsistency, and hesitancy in emulating the HRO principles among healthcare providers is the lack of a high-reliability leadership, which is supposed to be the driving force for the establishment of a robust safety culture. The presence of the right leaders in this context is essential for enhancing the reliability through the creation of the necessary structure (e.g., investing in a wide array of communication technologies to facilitate the sensitivity to operations) and infrastructure (e.g., developing policies surrounding deference to expertise or resilience) for successful adoption of the HRO philosophy. Past research shows that in healthcare organizations, one of the five most commonly reported requirements for successful adoption of HRO principles is the adoption of a corresponding leadership style that infuses the organization with a collective priority of safety [44].

The role of leaders in creating the foundation for operating with high reliability has long been acknowledged in many HRO publications. The leadership commitment to HRO principles is known to be a major facilitator of successful adoption [4, 31, 46–49]. Despite the emphasis of the literature on the critical role of leadership in HROs, studies that investigate the nature of a leadership style corresponding to the leadership of HROs are scant. One notable exception is Martínez-Córcoles' [50] conceptual study in which the author identifies two leadership mechanisms, i.e., leading by expansion and leading by reaction, by which leaders manage the reliability of their systems. While this study is very valuable in paving the research road in studying the concept of high-reliability leadership, it does not elaborate on the personal characteristics of the leaders in HROs. Moreover, to date, no healthcare research has specifically attempted to identify the high-reliability leaders' characteristics necessary for improving patient safety outcomes.

In order to further explore the nature of high-reliability leadership style and the characteristics of high-reliability leaders in the healthcare context, it is crucial to first distinguish between the two concepts of leaders and leadership. Following the recommendations of leadership scholars [33, 51, 52], we recognize the necessity of making a conceptual distinction between the two notions of leaders and leadership. Investigating the concept of leaders requires understanding the "intrapersonal characteristics" associated with individuals who fit this categorization [33]. Whereas leadership is referred to as the "process" through which leaders persuade followers to operate in congruence with their organization's vision and goals [51, 52]. Following this logic, we conceptualize high-reliability leadership as the process through which the vision, values, and actions of organizational actors are aligned with the intention of the organization in terms of operating with utmost reliability to pre-empt the risk of any potential harm to patients.

As such, high-reliability leadership is a top-down process of influencing followers by their leaders. It encompasses all practices and activities that are designed by healthcare organizations' leaders to influence individuals' decisions and ensure that their actions are in accordance with the principles of high-reliability organizations. Undoubtedly, to achieve this, first and foremost, there is a need for the leadership commitment to the transformation of the organization into a reliability-seeking one. Without leadership commitment at all levels (including boards of trustees and senior clinical and administrative managers), no organizational initiative, including the HRO reliability improvement framework, cannot succeed [4]. The high-reliability leadership process should also gradually infuse the healthcare organization with reliability through the following micro-processes: 1. embedding reliability-oriented measurable goals into the vision and mission of the organizations, 2. allocating the necessary budget for achieving these goals, 3. Creating the necessary structure and infrastructure for achieving the goals, 4. identifying and coordinating lines of responsibility, 5. monitoring the outcomes, and 6. reassessing the effectiveness of the current structure and infrastructure in attaining the goals.

It is noteworthy that, as a result of the preoccupation with the failures principle of HROs, one salient trait of these organizations is that they are unstoppable in "seeking" reliability [39, 53] and, regardless of how reliable their operations are, they never assume that they have already attained high reliability. In other words, there is no room for complacency or satisfaction with the state of reliability in HROs. As a result of this principle, to make operating with high reliability a sustainable goal, the high-reliability leadership process in healthcare must necessarily reflect this reliability-seeking trait. Thus, it is essential for such healthcare organizations to continually regenerate their reliability-oriented goals and reiterate the above-mentioned process of infusing the organization with higher levels of reliability.

If designed appropriately, this high-reliability leadership process could lead to instilling a safety culture, collective mindfulness, and continuous learning, which will help the organizational actors to be constantly preoccupied with failures, sensitive to frontline operations, reluctant to simplify, resilient when facing failures, and reliant on expertise—or, simply, operate based on the principles of HROs. As such, establishing the high-reliability leadership process, over time, would result in the transformation of a traditional healthcare organization into a high-reliability one that constantly reinvents itself and generates long-lasting improvements in process reliability and patient safety outcomes.

4.3 High-reliability leaders' characteristics in healthcare

While high-reliability leadership encompasses the process by which the leadership team influences the followers to collectively understand and agree on what needs to be done to prevent adverse events, high-reliability leaders are individuals who play critical roles in accomplishing this. These individuals transform a traditional healthcare organization into a high reliability-seeking one, which is untiring in its endeavors to prevent failures and improve patient safety outcomes. Drawing on the HRO and healthcare literature, we have identified four characteristics of high-reliability leaders that enable them to continually drive their organizations toward higher states of reliability: mindfulness, participative tendencies, integrity, and ambidexterity. These characteristics are discussed here.

4.3.1 Mindfulness

One of the most prominent characteristics that any high-reliability leader should demonstrate is mindfulness. The HRO literature conceptualizes mindfulness as attentiveness or awareness [53, 54]. In the context of healthcare organizations, mindfulness represents the state of being aware of the ongoing evolution of the messy and fluxing care delivery system. As mentioned earlier, nowadays, healthcare operational systems are characterized by the utmost volatility and unpredictability. To tackle this evolving nature of healthcare operations, high-reliability leaders are required to be able to maintain mindfulness by being fully present (i.e., grounded in the now moment wherever they are), standing by the frontline staff as much as possible (either in-person or virtually through a variety of communication technologies), and prioritizing high-risk frontline processes and giving undivided attention to the details of these processes. To possess this characteristic, essentially, leaders require to have a fair amount of technical knowledge of the frontline processes, so they know where to place their attention to prevent adverse events.

Leaders' mindfulness characteristic facilitates harnessing the first two HRO principles, discussed in Section 4.1. First, the preoccupation with failures principle requires the mindfulness of high-reliability leaders so that they can provide the necessary support for the frontline staff in spotting trivial shortcomings and addressing them before they turn into system-wide failures. Second, the sensitivity with operations principle requires all organizational actors collectively create a "big picture" of the ongoing status of the critical frontline processes. Leaders' mindfulness characteristic facilitates the development of this big picture by allowing them to get actively involved in resolving the work-systems challenges that frontline staff constantly deal with.

This intentional engagement of high-reliability leaders with the frontline also helps in the construction of the safety culture by promoting reliability-enhancing work practices among the frontline staff. Other benefits of the mindfulness characteristic of high-reliability leaders include: providing real-time feedback to the staff, detecting previously unknown areas where staff training could improve patient safety, and selecting, developing, and promoting the right employees for future leadership succession plans [4, 45, 55]. Finally, it is noteworthy that while leaders' mindfulness requires their involvement in the frontline processes to be on the same page with their staff and help them in constructing the big picture, it does not mean that leaders should micromanage their subordinates. In fact, based on the fifth principle of HROs (deference to expertise), high-reliability leaders can trust that their subordinates are well trained and know their jobs [15].

4.3.2 Participative tendencies

With the ever-increasing complexities of care delivery systems, participative tendencies of high-reliability leaders are essential for creating a channel of information from the frontline to the top of the organization. This characteristic of high-reliability leaders represents their propensity for allowing and promoting the engagement of subordinates in making sense of operational issues (e.g., near misses) to help managers in their operational decisions. Leaders with participative tendencies are comfortable with shifting some of the responsibility and authority to the frontline staff.

In the majority of healthcare organizations, the frontline is composed of clinical staff (often physicians and registered nurses) and non-clinical staff (often personal support workers). The clinical staff usually have extensive specialized education, which qualifies them for some degrees of autonomous decision-making. The non-clinical staff, on the other hand, while they might lack extensive education, often work closely with patients (e.g., to help them with bathing) and this allows them to learn about the potential operational issues firsthand. As a result, they have access to valuable information that leaders could use in spotting potential areas of weakness which make the service delivery system susceptible to adverse events.

Moreover, to establish the third principle of HROs, high-reliability leaders should demonstrate such participative tendencies. The third principle, i.e., the reluctance to simplify, requires the organizational actors to recognize and acknowledge the complex nature of their operations and never take anything for granted. As opposed to traditional organizations in which simplification is highly valued to increase focus on key performance areas, HROs forestall oversimplification. Instead, HROs encourage organizational actors to collectively build a nuanced, detailed, picture of the complex, unpredictable, and unknowable environment that they deal with [40].

Nowadays, many healthcare organizations leverage huddle meetings to achieve this [3]. Yet, without the participative tendencies of leaders, a huddle meeting, by itself, cannot guarantee that staff would share what they know. What gives the voice to subordinates to share their ideas and thoughts is the propensity of high-reliability leaders to encourage the active participation of their followers. Leaders' participative tendencies allow them to welcome a diverse range of, not only, farfetched ideas and thoughts but also constructive criticism and skepticism from their followers.

4.3.3 Integrity

Another characteristic of high-reliability leaders is integrity. Generally, management scholars conceptualize the integrity characteristic either as a normative or positive construct [56–58]. The normative view evaluates an entity's integrity subjectively and as the quality of advocating for ethical and moral principles and acting upon these principles [59, 60]. Whereas the positive view considers integrity as a morally neutral concept and assesses it objectively and in terms of the degree of congruence between an entity's principles and its actions [57, 61, 62].

In our study, we adopt the positive view and conceptualize the integrity characteristics of high-reliability leaders in terms of their ability to adhere to their advocated principles and standards. Thus, in our definition, whether or not these principles and standards are infused with morality and ethics is irrelevant to the integrity characteristic of high-reliability leaders. Instead, what matters here is that the leaders' advocated standards and principles originated from the principle of HROs. Therefore, the integrity characteristic of a high-reliability leader is determined by the degree to which a leader adheres to the designed high-reliability protocols and standards of their organization. Put simply, a high-reliability leader who demonstrates integrity characteristic "walks his/her talk" in terms of adherence to the adopted reliability standards of the organization.

The importance of leaders' integrity characteristic arises from the fact that by exhibiting this characteristic, a high-reliability leader sets the standard for followers to adhere to the safety and reliability protocols of their organization. Therefore, this characteristic is crucial for cultivating a safety culture in healthcare organizations. For building this culture, high-reliability leaders need to gently persuade their followers to place patient safety as a priority in everything that they do and when they do this themselves, they act as role models for their followers.

It is also important to note that high-reliability leaders who exhibit high levels of integrity, voluntarily, make themselves vulnerable. According to the fourth HRO principle, i.e., commitment to resilience, all near misses must be reported so that the organization can learn their lessons and re-incorporate these lessons into renewed operating policies and protocols to prevent similar failures in the future. When high-reliability leaders encounter a fault within their own actions, they would never attempt to hide their failures. Instead, they would use their own failures to show their followers that their organization is a safe place for the staff to discuss their shortcomings and help others to learn from them.

4.3.4 Ambidexterity

The final characteristic of high-reliability leaders is their ability to be ambidextrous. At an organizational level, the literature defines ambidexterity as the ability of an organization to stay ahead of the innovation game in a cost-effective fashion in a high-velocity market, through the exploitation of existing resources/capabilities and, simultaneously, exploration of novel resources/capabilities [63–65]. In more recent years some leadership scholars have extrapolated the ambidexterity characteristic to individual leaders' level and argue that when in an organization two diverging operating modes are required simultaneously, the leaders should necessarily exhibit ambidexterity to lead their followers through intricacies of both operating modes [66].

In the HROs context, due to extreme complexity, tight-coupling, and uncertainty of HROs' environment, these organizations must effectively deal with two contrasting operating modes simultaneously: (1) adhering to the standardized operating procedures and routines under the normal condition and (2) improvising to find unique solutions and creative ideas when facing unpredictable situations. HROs leverage standardization to reduce deviations (and thereby unnecessary wastes) and increase productivity. At the same time, to maintain preparedness for unforeseen issues, they never stop questioning the status quo to find and address weaknesses in their system. So, when the unexpected happens, they intentionally deviate from routines to create the space necessary for tackling the issue from a whole new perspective.

Neither of these operating modes is more important than the other, and it is the responsibility of high-reliability leaders to strike a balance between these two operating modes by leading their subordinates to strictly follow the routines and, simultaneously, by encouraging them to improvise when necessary. Achieving this balance, therefore, requires high degrees of ambidexterity on the leaders' part. On the one hand, leaders must have the ability to guarantee their followers' procedural integrity. In a healthcare setting, this means that leaders must control deviations from planned routines (e.g., patients' care plans) by ensuring that the care delivery staff precisely follows procedures just as planned. On the other hand, leaders must proactively manage unanticipated disruptions in plans by giving situational flexibility to their staff to navigate uncertainty through the improvision of idiosyncratic solutions. This ability of leaders to allow and encourage improvision is aligned with the fifth principle of HROs, i.e., deference to expertise, in which the expert staff, regardless of their rank or seniority, are encouraged to act almost autonomously and spontaneously when the organization's reliable performance is threatened by an unfamiliar/unforeseen situation.

5. Discussions

Given human limitations, healthcare experts generally agree that care provider failures are inevitable and can never be completely eradicated [8]. Even the title of the published reports by the Institute of Medicine, i.e., "To Err is Human", confirms the harsh reality of compromised patient safety due to the inevitability of human errors. Taking these limitations into account, healthcare research and practice have primarily relied on the implementation of a diverse array of best practices and interventions for reducing the frequency and severity of failures. Yet, as discussed in this chapter, our research reveals that the traditional reliability frameworks in healthcare often do not address more fundamental safety issues, such as cultural transformation, which are necessary for creating lasting changes

[4, 31]. Moreover, the introduction of these reliability frameworks often lags behind the ongoing drastic environmental changes within the healthcare industry. As a result, transformational leadership, which used to be the predominant healthcare leadership style for handling these safety frameworks, is no longer perfectly compatible with the current complexity and pace of the evolution of healthcare delivery systems [25–30].

By introducing and conceptualizing high-reliability leadership, our study makes important contributions to the research. First, as discussed in this chapter, cultivating a safety culture, which is conducive to sustainable reliability in healthcare operations, requires a more radical and proven approach to reliability. Thirty years of research on HROs has documented the outstanding performance of these organizations in terms of operating failure-free in the long run and an extremely volatile environment. Thus, adopting the HROs' principles and practices can be potentially a key to creating lasting reliability in healthcare too. However, research shows that healthcare organizations have struggled in the process of translating HRO theory into practice [67]. Our research takes a major step in facilitating this process by shedding light on the role of high-reliability leadership in infusing the organization with a reliability-seeking mindset and practices that not only do not deteriorate easily but also become stronger with the passage of time.

Second, while the past HRO research recognizes the critical role of leaders in cultivating reliability, no prior healthcare research specifies the characteristics of high-reliability leaders that are necessary for turning a traditional healthcare organization into a reliability-seeking one. Our research identified these overlooked characteristics of high-reliability leaders given the specific attributes of service delivery systems in healthcare organizations. This makes our study particularly interesting for healthcare scholars, practitioners, and policymakers in that we tailored the proposed dimensions of high-reliability leaders' characteristics specifically to healthcare settings. As a result, these findings can be applied as the basis for creating leadership education and training programs to prepare future high-reliability leaders.

A potential shortcoming of this study, however, is the lack of empirical evidence to ground the findings. Future research should assess the impact of our proposed high-reliability leadership process in action research. Characteristics of high-reliability leaders should also be examined through survey instruments to develop measures of high-reliability leaders in healthcare organizations. Another potential area for research is the application of multiple case studies for comparing these characteristics in various healthcare sectors to uncover more specific details on high-reliability leaders given the specific attributes of each category of the healthcare sector.

6. Conclusion

Extensive research has been done in the area of HROs. Yet, the characteristics of high-reliability leaders have not received the necessary attention among the field's scholars. In particular, as more and more healthcare organizations are seeking to emulate the principles of HROs, the identification of high-reliability leaders' characteristics has become of paramount importance to help this industry in its quest for improving patient safety outcomes. This chapter aimed at specifying the leadership characteristics that are vital for leading healthcare organizations toward operating with higher degrees of reliability. Juxtaposing the past research in leadership, healthcare, and HROs areas, we introduced the high-reliability leadership style and discussed why the adoption of this specific leadership style lies at the heart of preventing frequent healthcare service failures and improving patient safety outcomes. We also specified the characteristics of high-reliability leaders in the healthcare context. Mindfulness characteristic of high-reliability leaders is a necessary attribute for ensuring that a healthcare organization can maintain both a preoccupation with failure and a sensitivity to the care delivery processes. Leaders' participative tendencies are essential for preventing the simplification of assumptions that could allow near-misses or trivial system weaknesses to escalate into irreversible, system-wide, failures. The integrity characteristic of high-reliability leaders is what makes leaders role models for their followers and, thereby, helps organizations to learn from failures and attain resilience. Last, but not least, the ambidexterity characteristic of leaders is crucial for empowering them to handle the unique dual mode of healthcare operations, which requires the staff simultaneously comply and improvise. Healthcare practitioners can use our findings to enhance patient safety outcomes in their organizations by adopting the high-reliability leadership process discussed in this chapter and by fostering these four characteristics in the future generation of their leaders.

Acknowledgements

This manuscript draws on research supported by the University of Winnipeg's Major Research Grant (#31611) and the Covid-19 Discretionary Grant (#31484).

Conflict of interest

The author declares no conflict of interest.

Notes/thanks/other declarations

The author would like to thank Dr. Joseph Crawford for his valuable insights and suggestions on the contents of this chapter.

Author details

Maryam Memar Zadeh
The University of Winnipeg, Winnipeg, Canada

*Address all correspondence to: m.memarzadeh@uwinnipeg.ca

References

[1] Kohn LT, Corrigan JM, Donaldson M. To Err Is Human: Building a Safer Health System. Washington, DC: Institute of Medicine; 1999

[2] Ghaferi AA, Myers CG, Sutcliffe KM, Pronovost PJ. The next wave of hospital innovation to make patients safer. Harvard Business Review. 2016;**94**:1-8

[3] Memar Zadeh M, Haggerty N. Improving long-term care services: Insights from high-reliability organizations. Leadership in Health Services. 2021;**35**(2):174-189

[4] Chassin MR, Loeb JM. The ongoing quality improvement journey: Next stop, high reliability. Health Affairs. 2011;**30**(4):559-568

[5] Makary MA, Daniel M. Medical error—The third leading cause of death in the US. BMJ. 2016;**353**:i2139

[6] Klevens RM, Morrison MA, Nadle J, Petit S, Gershman K, Ray S, et al. Invasive methicillin-resistant Staphylococcus aureus infections in the United States. Journal of the American Medical Association. 2007;**298**(15):1763-1771

[7] Mørkeberg J, Sharpe K, Belhage B, Damsgaard R, Schmidt W, Prommer N, et al. Detecting autologous blood transfusions: A comparison of three passport approaches and four blood markers. Scandinavian Journal of Medicine & Science in Sports. 2011;**21**(2):235-243

[8] Gallagher TH, Waterman AD, Ebers AG, Fraser VJ, Levinson W. Patients' and physicians' attitudes regarding the disclosure of medical errors. Journal of the American Medical Association. 2003;**289**(8):1001-1007

[9] Weick KE. The vulnerable system: An analysis of the Tenerife air disaster. Journal of Management. 1990;**16**(3):571-593

[10] Schulman PR. The negotiated order of organizational reliability. Administration & Society. 1993;**25**(3):353-372

[11] Weick KE, Roberts KH. Collective mind in organizations: Heedful interrelating on flight decks. Administrative Science Quarterly. 1993;**38**:357-381

[12] Fraher AL, Branicki LJ, Grint K. Mindfulness in action: Discovering how US navy Seals build capacity for mindfulness in high-reliability organizations (HROs). Academy of Management Discoveries. 2017;**3**(3):239-261

[13] Vaughan D. The Challenger Launch Decision: Risky Technology, Culture, and Deviance at NASA. University of Chicago press; 1996

[14] LaPorte TR. Institutional issues for continued space exploration: High-reliability systems across many operational generations, requisites for public credibility. In: Dick SJ, Launius RD, editors. Critical Issue in the History of Space flight; 2006. pp. 403-427

[15] Roberts KH, Madsen P, Desai V, Van Stralen D. A case of the birth and death of a high reliability healthcare organization. BMJ Quality & Safety. 2005;**14**(3):216-220

[16] Vogus TJ, Sutcliffe KM. The safety organizing scale: Development and validation of a behavioral measure of

safety culture in hospital nursing units. Medical Care. 2007;**45**:46-54

[17] Desai V, Madsen PM, Roberts KH. High-reliability organizations in health care. In: Handbook of Human Factors and Ergonomics in Health Care and Patient Safety. Boca Raton: CRC Press, Taylor & Francis; 2012

[18] Jivraj S, Goodman A, Pongiglione B, Ploubidis GB. Living longer but not necessarily healthier: The joint progress of health and mortality in the working-age population of England. Population Studies. 2020;**74**(3):399-414

[19] Casida J, Parker J. Staff nurse perceptions of nurse manager leadership styles and outcomes. Journal of Nursing Management. 2011;**19**(4):478-486

[20] Kumar RD. Leadership in healthcare. Anesthesia & Intensive Care Medicine. 2013;**14**(1):39-41

[21] Stefl ME. Common competencies for all healthcare managers: The healthcare leadership alliance model. Journal of Healthcare Management. 2008;**53**(6):360-373

[22] Calhoun JG, Dollett L, Sinioris ME, Wainio JA, Butler PW, Griffith JR, et al. Development of an interprofessional competency model for healthcare leadership. Journal of Healthcare Management. 2008;**53**(6):375-390

[23] Denis JL, van Gestel N. Medical doctors in healthcare leadership: Theoretical and practical challenges. BMC Health Services Research. 2016;**16**(2):45-56

[24] Hargett CW, Doty JP, Hauck JN, Webb AM, Cook SH, Tsipis NE, et al. Developing a model for effective leadership in healthcare: A concept mapping approach. Journal of Healthcare Leadership. 2017;**9**:69

[25] McAuliffe E, Ward M, DeBrun A, Cunningham U. ISQUA17-2839 collective leadership and safety cultures: Developing an alternative model of leadership for healthcare teams. International Journal for Quality in Health Care. 2017;**29**(suppl_1):52-53

[26] Al-Sawai A. Leadership of healthcare professionals: Where do we stand? Oman Medical Journal. 2013;**28**(4):285

[27] Perez J. Leadership in healthcare: Transitioning from clinical professional to healthcare leader. Journal of Healthcare Management. 2021;**66**(4):280-302

[28] Millward LJ, Bryan K. Clinical leadership in health care: A position statement. Leadership in Health Services. 2005;**18**(2):xiii–xxv

[29] Boamah SA, Laschinger HK, Wong C, Clarke S. Effect of transformational leadership on job satisfaction and patient safety outcomes. Nursing Outlook. 2018;**66**(2):180-189

[30] McFadden KL, Henagan SC, Gowen CR III. The patient safety chain: Transformational leadership's effect on patient safety culture, initiatives, and outcomes. Journal of Operations Management. 2009;**27**(5):390-404

[31] Polonsky MS. High-reliability organizations: The next frontier in healthcare quality and safety. Journal of Healthcare Management. 2019;**64**(4):213-221

[32] Bass BM, Avolio BJ, editors. Improving Organizational Effectiveness through Transformational Leadership. Thousand Oaks, CA: Sage; 1994

[33] Siangchokyoo N, Klinger RL, Campion ED. Follower transformation as the linchpin of transformational

leadership theory: A systematic review and future research agenda. The Leadership Quarterly. 2020;**31**(1):101341

[34] Bass BM, Riggio RE. Transformational Leadership. Erlbaum, Mahwah, NJ: Psychology press; 2006

[35] Van Knippenberg D, Sitkin SB. A critical assessment of charismatic—Transformational leadership research: Back to the drawing board? Academy of Management Annals. 2013;**7**(1):1-60

[36] Ng TW. Transformational leadership and performance outcomes: Analyses of multiple mediation pathways. The Leadership Quarterly. 2017;**28**(3):385-417

[37] Moher D, Liberati A, Tetzlaff J, Altman DG, PRISMA Group. Preferred reporting items for systematic reviews and meta-analyses: The PRISMA statement. Annals of Internal Medicine. 2009;**151**(4):264-269

[38] Roberts KH. Some characteristics of one type of high reliability organization. Organization Science. 1990;**1**(2):160-176

[39] Vogus TJ, Welbourne TM. Structuring for high reliability: HR practices and mindful processes in reliability-seeking organizations. Journal of Organizational Behavior: The International Journal of Industrial, Occupational and Organizational Psychology and Behavior. 2003;**24**(7):877-903

[40] Sutcliffe KM. High reliability organizations (HROs). Best Practice & Research Clinical Anaesthesiology. 2011;**25**(2):133-144

[41] Weick KE, Sutcliffe KM. Managing the Unexpected: Resilient Performance in an Age of Uncertainty. San Francisco, CA: Jossey-Bass, John Wiley & Sons; 2011

[42] Bogue B. How principles of high reliability organizations relate to corrections. Federal Probation. 2009;**73**(3):22-27

[43] Roberts KH. HRO has prominent history. The Newsletter of The Anesthesia Patient Safety Foundation. 2003;**18**:13-14

[44] Veazie S, Peterson K, Bourne D. Evidence brief: Implementation of high reliability organization principles. Evidence Synthesis Program. Washington, DC, USA: Health Services Research and Development Service, Office of Research and Development, Department of Veterans Affairs; 2019. VA ESP Project #09-199. Available from: https://www.hsrd.research.va.gov/publications/esp/reports.cfm

[45] Hilliard MA, Sczudlo R, Scafidi L, Cady R, Villard A, Shah R. Our journey to zero: Reducing serious safety events by over 70% through high-reliability techniques and workforce engagement. Journal of Healthcare Risk Management. 2012;**32**(2):4-18

[46] Alavosius MP, Houmanfar RA, Anbro SJ, Burleigh K, Hebein C. Leadership and crew resource management in high-reliability organizations: A competency framework for measuring behaviors. Journal of Organizational Behavior Management. 2017;**37**(2);142-170

[47] Bierly P, Gallagher S, Spender JC. Innovation decision making in high-risk organizations: A comparison of the US and soviet attack submarine programs. Industrial and Corporate Change. 2014;**23**(3):759-795

[48] Nembhard IM, Edmondson AC. Making it safe: The effects of leader inclusiveness and professional status on psychological safety and improvement efforts in health care

teams. Journal of Organizational Behavior: The International Journal of Industrial, Occupational and Organizational Psychology and Behavior. 2006;**27**(7):941-966

[49] Ruchlin HS, Dubbs NL, Callahan MA, Fosina MJ. The role of leadership in instilling a culture of safety: Lessons from the literature. Journal of Healthcare Management. 2004;**49**(1):47

[50] Martínez-Córcoles M. High reliability leadership: A conceptual framework. Journal of Contingencies and Crisis Management. 2018;**26**(2):237-246

[51] Crawford JA, Dawkins S, Martin A, Lewis G. Putting the leader back into authentic leadership: Reconceptualising and rethinking leaders. Australian Journal of Management. 2020;**45**(1):114-133

[52] Pilbeam C, Doherty N, Davidson R, Denyer D. Safety leadership practices for organizational safety compliance: Developing a research agenda from a review of the literature. Safety Science. 2016;**86**:110-121

[53] Weick KE, Sutcliffe KM. Mindfulness and the quality of organizational attention. Organization Science. 2006;**17**(4):514-524

[54] Weick KE, Putnam T. Organizing for mindfulness: Eastern wisdom and Western knowledge. Journal of Management Inquiry. 2006;**15**(3): 275-287

[55] Kanerva A, Kivinen T, Lammintakanen J. Collaborating with nurse leaders to develop patient safety practices. Leadership in Health Services. 2017;**30**(3):249-262

[56] Becker TE. Integrity in organizations: Beyond honesty and conscientiousness. Academy of Management Review. 1998;**23**(1):154-161

[57] Erhard WH, Jensen MC, Zaffron S. Integrity: A positive model that incorporates the normative phenomena of morality, ethics, and legality (abbreviated version). Routledge: Integrity in Business and Management; 2017. pp. 11-39

[58] Monga M. Integrity and its antecedent: A unified conceptual framework of integrity. The Journal of Developing Areas. 2016;**50**(5):415-421

[59] Parry KW, Proctor-Thomson SB. Perceived integrity of transformational leaders in organizational settings. Journal of Business Ethics. 2002;**35**(2):75-96

[60] Heineman BW Jr. High Performance with High Integrity. Boston, MA: Harvard; 2008

[61] Jensen MC. Integrity: Without it nothing works. Rotman Magazine: The Magazine of the Rotman School of Management, Fall. 2009:16-20

[62] Simons T. Behavioral integrity: The perceived alignment between managers' words and deeds as a research focus. Organization Science. 2002;**13**(1):18-35

[63] Benner MJ, Tushman ML. Exploitation, exploration, and process management: The productivity dilemma revisited. Academy of Management Review. 2003;**28**(2):238-256

[64] Luger J, Raisch S, Schimmer M. Dynamic balancing of exploration and exploitation: The contingent benefits of ambidexterity. Organization Science. 2018;**29**(3):449-470

[65] O'Reilly CA III, Tushman ML. Organizational ambidexterity: Past, present, and future. Academy

of Management Perspectives. 2013;**27**(4):324-338

[66] Kassotaki O, Paroutis S, Morrell K. Ambidexterity penetration across multiple organizational levels in an aerospace and defense organization. Long Range Planning. 2019;**52**(3):366-385

[67] Goldenhar LM, Brady PW, Sutcliffe KM, Muething SE. Huddling for high reliability and situation awareness. BMJ Quality & Safety. 2013;**22**(11):899-906

Chapter 8

Chameleon Leadership and Traits to Serve on a Global Scale

James Williams

Abstract

Global business equates for billions and billions in revenue. Yet, global business brings a diverse complexity with the nature of its operations. In order for businesses to operate on a global scale, leaders must have the ability and wherewithal to understand environments of this magnitude. Chameleon leaders embody traits that give them the knowledge and style to serve on a global scale. Chameleon leaders are adaptive and blend into diverse work environments while creating a conducive environment that promotes equity and inclusion, to promote successful and impactful leadership. Chameleons do not change their core, but they do have the mechanisms to alter their dimensions to blend in and to survive in unfamiliar environments. Chameleon leaders maneuver in a similar fashion by blending into new or different environments while maintaining the core values and traits that accompany their leadership style. Most organizations operate domestically and globally, so it is crucial to fabricate leaders who can lead and thrive in global surroundings. Chameleon leaders can emerge when businesses ensure that leaders lead with seven key core competencies.

Keywords: chameleon leadership, leadership, global leadership, traits, soft skills

1. Introduction

What is leadership and its relevance to organizations?: *Leadership* has been a trending topic for decades. Leadership is discussed in elementary school middle school, high school, university, and industry. There is no sector or no area of life where leaders are not needed [1]. Leaders are essential to the evolution of life and the progression of organizational development. Yet, leadership is required from a broad perspective and an inclusive viewpoint [2]. When an individual leads their followers or others, it is crucial to welcome disparate outlooks rather than their invested tunnel vision. A global stance is all-encompassing and involve an interconnected slant. Some might argue that this angle encourages empathy, inciting leaders to raise their level of awareness and to walk in other people shoes or to embrace their perspectives.

This form of leadership creates a dichotomy that enables leaders to vacillate between following and leading in a given environment. In other words, it provides leaders with the ability to engage in decentralized management rather than centralized management approach. Decentralized management transfer decision-making power from upper-level management to middle and lower-level management [3]. This empowers employees to make decisions in a more efficient and effective fashion while centralized management limits power to upper-level management. When leaders lead from a global perspective, leaders tend to welcome diverse opinions and attitudes for the overall good of a collective goal or team. This global paradigm shift demand leaders who are willing to embrace and to adopt other culture norms to produce buy-in from different people.

2. Chameleon leadership impact in today's organizations

What is a chameleon? This is the question that should drive anyone who chooses to read this chapter. This rudimentary question sets a foundation for one's understanding of *chameleon leadership* and for some advantageous principles derived from a chameleon. A chameleon is a reptile that has the ability to change its skin, and these changes can enable this creature to adapt and to blend into different environments. Some would argue that many people act as Chameleons, by the way they change their clothes, attitudes, and/or behaviors to placate cultures and subcultures to survive, psychologically and/or materialistic matters [4]. Chameleon leadership started as a conceptual idea, and this concept focused on leaders' abilities to adjust their attitudes and behaviors to lead unique environments. This conceptual idea was published in 2011, but since then, there have been several authors/researchers who defined chameleon leaders in a disparate fashion.

One author depicts chameleon leaders as deceptive individuals who employs chicanery and deceptive practices to appear effective and efficient as leaders. For example, this particular author surmises that these leaders create chaos and crisis, and then, use their leadership skills to solve those self-created issues. I have an issue with this author's synopsis because I do not perceive those cute little reptiles as deceptive and capable of promoting chaos. On the contrary to deceptive manners, chameleons are quiet and provides a hint of stillness and calmness to an environment [5, 6]. From my experience, calm leaders tend to observe, listen, and think prior to making complicated decisions. Who would not want a leader who possess those attributes? Chameleon leaders will be viewed as adaptable and welcoming to unpredictable situations; they will embody a fearlessness approach towards change. These individuals view change as a necessary corollary to organizational progression and personal development.

Today's businesses have faced constant change, from a pandemic, politics, and economy, to name a few. These issues have impacted local and global economies, requiring today's leaders to be strategically reactive and proactive, to ensure that their organizations survive and thrive in the modern era of doing business. Chameleon leadership offers individuals an opportunity to mirror different cultures, behaviors, attitudes, and communication patterns while leading from an authentic presence. The idea is for one to develop a fearlessness approach towards change and to envision change as a necessity to future success. Ultimately, this notion incites the individual to adapt and to adopt the change appropriate for their interactions. This paradigm shift is similar to situational leadership, but chameleon leadership focuses on altering one's traits and leadership tactics rather than their leadership style. More specifically, *situational leadership* encourages leaders to choose the right style for the right people.

For example, a general in the air force might tend to utilize an *autocratic leadership* to tell younger airmen with minimal experience how to comport themselves in war situations. However, this same general might change his/her leadership style to a *democratic leadership* style when he is working with other generals to formulate an invasive strategy in a war zone area. Chameleon leaders do not shift their leadership styles, instead, they tend to embody traits that creates commonality in their known or unknown environments. Chameleon leaders are vastly different from Machiavellian leaders and transformational leaders. Machiavellian [7] leaders apply personal power to lie, manipulate, and coercion to persuade others to serve their set objective, meaning the "ends justify the means". Transformational leaders focus on bringing the best out of individuals and building them to be leaders. Transformational leaders encourage and inspire their followers to align their attitudes and actions to create meaningful change [8].

Chameleon leaders welcome change and blend in to chaos and crisis situations while they continue to use their strengths to guide their followers. Yet, chameleon leaders are not trying to manipulate others, and they are not focusing on changing followers' behaviors. Chameleon leadership is about the leader and the leaders' attitudes and actions.

2.1 Method of chameleon leadership

Chameleon leadership is conceptual idea that became a phenomenon. In 2011, Williams et al. [9] coin chameleon leadership as a fearlessness approach to change management situations. There were 20 various managers from North Carolina who shared their lived youth sport and management experiences. The researchers used a phenomenological study to explore managers' experiences and interpretations showed patterns of managers having a proclivity to welcome challenges in complex organizations and in diverse working groups [10]. Participants were selected through a purposeful sampling due to the nature of the study. Managers were sought who played youth sports and who held a management position in North Carolina, for 3–5 years.

A snowball technique was employed from a personal contact being interviewed; the personal contact provided names of other potential participants who displayed required attributes for this qualitative study. Denzin and Lincoln [11] created this systematic process to ensure purposive sampling remain effective and efficient for acquiring participants. Researches utilized semi-structured face-to-face interviews during two separate interview sessions to reach saturation. Participants were assigned a code to protect their identities, and interviews were tape-recorded while the researcher took personal notes of verbal and nonverbal behavioral cues. Interviews were analyzed, interpreted, and coded for themes and patterns using Nvivo.

2.2 Global traits that are tied to successful leadership

Effective leadership traits are not just paramount to leading small organizations, but they are traits employed to successfully lead companies on a global scale [12]. These traits are the underpinnings of all impactful leadership styles. Depending upon the research study, there can be as many as 15 different traits. Yet, for this chapter, there are 10 that should be integrated in every leadership style. Leadership traits are principles that guide leaders' attitudes and behaviors towards decision-making and relationship-building. These principles can help to ensure leaders remain authentic, effective, and efficient when managing processes and inspiring colleagues in their respective organizations and/or environments. Global leaders have the same productive traits, but they think from an intentional DEI (diversity, equity, and inclusion) outlook.

Colleges and universities design curriculum that provide students with core competencies needed to succeed and to make a positive impact in hospitality and tourism businesses [13, 14]. NACE (National Association of Colleges and Employers) uses data to determine the core competencies for a productive and career readiness workforce. Those seven core competencies are global traits recommended for future leaders. The following are the core competencies: self-managing, communication, critical thinking, equity & inclusion, professionalism, teamwork, and technology [15]. However, these traits cannot come alive and thrive until individuals learn how to self-manage themselves and to comport themselves in an authentic fashion.

2.3 Self-managing

Self-managing is a crucial trait of chameleon leadership. This trait ensures a leader governs their own actions, attitudes, and behaviors. Meaning, self-managing is anchored in accountability. The notion associated with this trait surmises that an individual must first manage self before they can manage or guide others. Chameleon leaders blend into environments while maintaining their authenticity and handling stress, to create a balance, personally and professionally. Many students tend to enter colleges and many entry-level employees tend to enter work environments assuming that they are not leaders. Most people assume leaders are created when someone in higher authority anoints them with some official title [16, 17]. This misconception surmises that leaders are tethered to someone with *authoritative power* rather than *influential power*. What is the difference between the two powers and how do they relate to self-managing in chameleon leadership? *Authoritative power* is bestowed to an individual to execute decisions while *influential power* is one's ability to persuade others to align to their collective goal or idea.

Chameleon leaders are adept at managing challenges and utilizing empathy when they deal with employees who might struggle during high-pressure situations. Exceptional leaders do not rely on authoritative power to adapt to difficult tasks, situations, and interactions; yet, influential power provides individuals with the wherewithal to inspire followers to buy-in and to align to their set objectives. Self-managing should be perceived as "self-mastery," which means leaders maintain self-control and sustain discipline in their actions. However, chameleon leaders do not enable this self-managing trait to restrict their pliable nature to pivot in diverse environments. Effective leaders know that leadership begins and ends as a personal journey, so it is pivotal for leaders to engage in self-managing to become the best version of themselves. Once leaders understand one's self, they must transmute that maturity into effectual communication, to inspire their followers.

2.4 Communication

Communication furnishes leaders with a medium to deliver information vital to their organization [18]. This information can be essential to demonstrating a leader's competency level, assisting in proffering one of the four traits that researchers suggested followers saw in their leaders. Those four traits were *honesty, forward-looking, inspiring, and competent*. These traits are essential to exchange information, ideas, facts, and outlooks with individuals inside and outside of their milieus. Communication seems simple when we breakdown the process. Communication requires a sender and a receiver; the sender encodes their message by choosing verbal and nonverbal cues. The receiver decodes the message and interpret it for understanding and for feedback. Leaders must be able to communicate with active listening skills, persuasive rhetoric, and influencing nonverbal and verbal tactics [19, 20].

DOI: http://dx.doi.org/10.5772/intechopen.108325

Chameleon leaders have the ability to organize their thoughts and to couch conversations that match unique settings. Chameleon leaders frame discourse to welcome diversity of thought and learning styles, employing varied communication styles and cultural differences. One of the most important aspects of chameleon leaders is to ask questions to gather specific information, to ensure information aligns with set objectives to present contextual outcomes that might benefit the greater good of the team. Chameleon leaders use their honesty, vision, persuasion, and intellect to lead during crisis and chaotic situations. Chameleon leaders need critical thinking to deliver their messages with clarity and to inform followers how to perform assigned tasks.

2.5 Critical thinking

Critical thinking has been a constant trait for leading globally. Critical thinking has also been a buzz word for resumes and for universities, to appeal to and to attract the best and brightest scholars. Critical thinking is more than an attractive word; critical thinking is a skill associated with action and proactive behaviors. Leaders are expected to diagnosis problems and/or situations and to respond according to the situational context and information be presented. This effort requires a basic understanding of self and an ability to communicate in all types of settings. Chameleon leaders blend in and take a fearlessness approach due to their ability to judge and to read situations based on limited data and to react appropriately. In global environments, there are many variables that might influence the overall situational context. Chameleon leaders operate with logical and rational reasoning by gathering and analyzing all information being presented prior to making a sound decision.

Chameleon leaders remain poised while combing through information, to ensure followers maintain a level of calmness. This is extremely important in global leadership because nonverbal cues that indicate stress or panic can present more challenges in global environments. The language barrier and compounding stress cues can create a level of distrust and ultimately an uninspired work environment. Critical thinking could enhance one's ability to welcome and to embrace followers or employees from diverse backgrounds. Critical thinking challenges leaders to be open-minded and to view challenges as opportunities while understanding the holistic makeup of people and situations [21]. Chameleon leaders utilize critical thinking on a daily basis to assess familiar and unfamiliar situations without losing motivation and without diminishing their confidence. This trait enhances their ability to circumvent some situations and to broach some situations head-on.

2.6 Equity and inclusion

What is equity and inclusion? Prior to answering this question, diversity needs to be discussed. Diversity is the state of including or involving people from different backgrounds, ethnicities, races, genders, or etc. Simply put, it is seeing the beauty of different people and welcoming them to the same space. Does this approach ensure equity and inclusion? The answer is "no," and it is now appropriate to discuss equity and inclusion and what it takes to ensure equity and inclusion happens in organizations or shared spaces. Everything begins with the individual, the leader, so a chameleon leader must utilize their awareness, attitude, knowledge, and skill ensure equity for all members. Chameleon leaders should actively engage in anti-racist practices by designing systems and policies that eliminate racism and promote different local and global cultures [22, 23]. Equity focuses on providing resources to match an individuals' needs and is based on others' resources or opportunities rather than providing individuals with the same resources (equality).

Inclusion involves giving equal access to opportunities and resources for people who tend to be excluded and/or marginalized in specific spaces. As chameleon leaders, equity and inclusion must serve as the undergird of their decision-making [24]. This collective outlook serves as effectual tactics for productive global leadership. When everyone feels valued and vested in an organization, they develop an unconditional love and a desire to see the organization progress [25–27]. This universal investment and attitude is the key to ensure leaders can serve and thrive in global environments. Chameleon leaders have the ability to weave in this equity and inclusion perspective to establish and sustain success in all settings.

2.7 Professionalism

Chameleon leaders should model behavior that is indicative of an inclusive work environment. An environment that practices civility, collegiality, and equity. All work environments have policies and procedures that builds should build a culture that promotes integrity and individual accountability. This culture should encourage and act with individual and collective integrity and accountability, to maintain extreme accountability and positive personal brand. Professionalism requires leaders to know effective work habits and actions in the interest of the workplace. Chameleon leaders stay present and arrive prepared to raise their level of awareness, to demonstrate accountability. Employees mirror productive behavior when leaders reinforce those behaviors with positive rewards. Chameleon leaders learn to prioritize tasks according to the level of organizational goals and/or importance.

Chameleon leaders do not merely complete goals, they exceed goals and expectations. These leaders embody discipline and stay consistent while paying attention to detail and showing high level of commitment towards doing a great job. Chameleon leaders strive for excellence and inspire followers to strive for a high-level of excellence. Professionalism extends beyond one's appearance and ability to speak appropriately in their work environment. Chameleon leaders exhibit influential power and motivate followers to align their attitudes and actions to the work culture. Productive work habits play a significant role to conducive equity and inclusion. Professionalism incites a collective team approach, and chameleon leaders are the consummate team players. Global leadership relies on collaborative and successful teamwork [28, 29].

2.8 Teamwork

Global leadership requires all hands-on deck. It is a team effort that ensures organizations expand their reach, domestically and globally. Teamwork focuses on collaborative relationships that strive to achieve common goals while including disparate outlooks in an equitable environment. Chameleon leaders focus on serving and supporting team members by placing them in positions that highlight and placate their strengths. This can only happen when chameleon leaders are willing to listen intently and to give grace throughout the process. Followers or employees feel more relaxed, and they are more willing to elaborate on challenges or issues that might impede the organization's mission. Chameleon leaders should ask questions without interrupting and defending their position. When conflict arise, and it will arise; chameleon leaders mitigate conflict by respecting diverse personalities and by meeting unclearness with transparency. Chameleon leaders demonstrate to team members how to hold themselves accountable in the confines of their team and how to focus on team responsibilities and deliverables.

Chameleon leaders set members up for success by aligning their talents and strengths with comparable tasks, to complement the efforts of other team members. Chameleon leaders compromise to placate the needs of employees or situations, to exhibit a pliable frame of reference regarding workplace challenges. This behavior empowers and encourages followers to maneuver in the same fashion. Chameleon leaders make sure to involve key stakeholders prior to making a decision, to create buy-in and to show a willingness to collaborate with others to achieve a common goal. Chameleon leaders are responsible for generating optimism and positivity in their work environment, to build strong and positive working relationships [30, 31]. Chameleon leaders can exhibit this attitude in face-to-face interactions, group settings, and email messages. Technology plays a vital role in setting the tone for leadership in today's culture and work environments.

2.9 Technology

Technology is a tool utilized for enhancing our business practices and for accomplishing our collective goals. Technology should enhance collaboration, equity, and efficacy in work environments. Yet, technology can serve as a distraction and a hinderance when it is not properly introduced or people are not trained to handle new technologies. Chameleon leaders are responsible for integrating new technologies into work environments by being well-versed on its capabilities and by providing training sessions, to demonstrate its abilities and to address in concerns from team members. Chameleon leaders ensure team members learn how to navigate change and learn how to incorporate new technologies into their day-to-day business practices. It is important for leaders to remain open to learning new technologies because it might inspire team members to follow suit. Chameleon leaders must maintain patience as followers learn to adapt to unfamiliar new technologies. Chameleon leaders have to show that this new technology serves the greater good of the team and works towards established objectives and strategic goals.

Chameleon leaders need to distinguish between technology trends and organizational needs. This can serve as a guide for transparent communication and team collaboration. Chameleon leaders blend into environments and make them function according to industry needs and standards. However, they carry out these functions while inspiring team members to adapt and to adopt new changes that provides their organization with a vantage point over competition. Chameleon leaders view technology as a tool that proffers support to the mission and vision of the team.

3. Conclusion

Leadership is an essential skill set needed to ensure organizations build for a global scale. There requires an exceptional leader to lead teams to think more broadly and to function on a global scale. Chameleon leaders take the time to learn their strengths and weaknesses and to employ this information to guide team members towards collective goals. Various industries have created a task force in 2017 to decide what traits were needed to be career ready for undergraduate students. Chameleon leaders embody all traits mentioned by NACE. Chameleon leaders develop self-awareness to self-manage, communicate with transparency, think critically, lead with equity and inclusion, manage with professionalism, collaborative teamwork, and integrative technology. Chameleon leaders utilize these traits to welcome and to embrace diverse perspectives and cultures. Chameleon leaders should have the ability to adapt to conflict and crisis situations while using traits that prepare them to lead on a global scale.

In the future, there will be situations that require leaders to blend into unfamiliar environments and situations while be able to positively impact their work place. The way to ensure leaders remain productive; leaders must be willing to blend in and to employ productive traits for a global market.

Acknowledgements

I am grateful for the University of Tennessee for providing me with leadership responsibilities and opportunities to enhance my leadership outlook. Also, I appreciate the computer and space to create this intellectual property.

Notes/thanks/other declarations

Thank you to my lovely wife (Latoya Williams) for providing me with the time and space to work and to create this book chapter. She has been the greatest support to my career.

Author details

James Williams
University of Tennessee, Knoxville, TN, USA

*Address all correspondence to: jwill316@utk.edu

References

[1] Baran B, Shanock LR, Miller L. Advancing organizational support theory into the twenty-first century world of work. Journal of Business and Psychology. 2012;**27**:123-147

[2] Aperion Global. What is Global Leadership?. 2021. Available from: https://www.aperianglobal.com/what-is-global-leadership/

[3] Posner B, Kouze J. The Leadership Challenge. 6th ed. Hoboken, NJ: Jossey-Bass; 2017

[4] Agle BR, Nagarajan NJ, Sonnenfeld JA, Srinivasan D. Does CEO charisma matter? An empirical analysis of the relationships among organizational performance, environmental uncertainty, and top management team perceptions of CEO charisma. Academy of Management Journal. 2006;**49**:161-174

[5] Eisenberger R, Stinglhamber F. Perceived Organizational Support: Fostering Enthusiastic and Productive Employees. Washington, DC: American Psychological Association; 2011

[6] Mhizha A. Application of the chameleon survival strategy model in the study of strategic Management in Small and Medium-Scale Enterprises. International Journal of Innovative Research and Development. 2014;**3**(6):216-225

[7] Belschak FD, Muhammad RS, Den Hartog DN. Birds of a feather can butt heads: When Machiavellian employees work with Machiavellian leaders. Journal of Business Ethics. 2018;**151**(3):613-626

[8] Siangchokyoo N, Klinger RL, Campion ED. Follower transformation as the linchip of transformational leadership theory: A systematic review and future research agenda. The Leadership Quarterly. 2020;**31**(1):101341

[9] Williams J, Roberts C, Bosselman R. Youth sports and the emergence of chameleon leadership. Journal of Leadership Studies. 2011;**5**(3):6-12

[10] Williams J, Bosselman R, Hurst JL, Zheng T. Passive leadership is unlikely among hospitality managers with high-level youth sports participation. Journal of Hospitality & Tourism Education. 2013;**25**:22-28

[11] Denzin N, Lincoln Y. Handbook of Qualitative Research. Thousand Oaks, CA: Sage; 1994

[12] Hinkin TR, Tracey JB. An analysis of human resources practices among fortune's best companies to work for. Cornell Hospitality Quarterly. 2010;**51**:158-170

[13] Brownell J. Leading on land and sea: Competences and context. International Journal of Hospitality Management. 2008;**27**(2):137-150

[14] Brownell J. Women in hospitality management: General managers' perceptions of factors related to career development. International Journal of Hospitality Management. 1994;**13**(2):101-117

[15] NACE. National Association of Colleges and Employers. 2022. Available from: https://www.naceweb.org/career-readiness/competencies/career-readiness-defined/

[16] Allen NJ, Meyer JP. The measurement and antecedents of affective, continuance

and normative commitment to the organization. Journal of Occupational Psychology. 1990;**63**:1-18

[17] Thakur A, Kumar N. The effect of perceived organizational support, role related aspects and work involvement on work-life balance: Self-efficacy as a moderator. International Journal of Scientific and Research Publications. 2015;**5**(1):1-8

[18] Neves P, Eisenberger R. Management communication and employee performance: The contribution of perceived organizational support. Human Performance. 2012;**25**(5):452-464

[19] Jacobs W. Speaking the Lower Frequencies: Students and Media Literacy. Albany, NY: State University of New York Press; 2005

[20] Plester B. Take it like a man: Performing hegemonic masculinity through organizational humour. Ephemera. 2015;**15**(3):537-559

[21] Williams J. Finding a voice: An autoethnography of my odyssey in the hospitality academy. Journal of Negro Education. 2021;**90**(2):173-182

[22] Morrell R, Jewkes R, Lindegger G. Hegemonic masculinity/Ies in South Africa: Culture, power and gender politics. Men and Masculinities. 2012;**15**:11-30

[23] Williams PJ. The Alchemy of Race and Rights. Cambridge, MA: Harvard University Press; 1991

[24] Savery LK. Men and women in the workplace: Evidence of occupational differences. Leadership & Organization Development Journal. 1990;**11**:13-16

[25] Eisenberger R, Huntington R, Hutchison S, Sowa D. Perceived organizational support. Journal of Applied Psychology. 1986;**71**:500-507

[26] Flammer A. Self-efficacy. International Encyclopedia of the Social & Behavioral Sciences. 2015;**2**:504-508

[27] Moreo A, Woods R, Sammons G, Bergman C. Connection or competence: Emotional labor and service quality's impact on satisfaction and loyalty. International Journal of Contemporary Hospitality Management. 2019;**31**(1):330-348

[28] Antonakis J, Avolio BJ, Sivasubramaniam N. Context and leadership: An examination of the nine-factor full-range leadership theory using the multifactor leadership questionnaire. The Leadership Quarterly. 2006;**14**:261-295

[29] Bandura A. Self-efficacy: Toward a unifying theory of behavior change. Psychological Review. 1977;**84**:191-215

[30] Avolio BJ, Zhu W, Koh W, Bhatia P. Transformational leadership and organizational commitment: The mediating role of psychological empowerment and the moderating role of structural distance. Journal of Organizational Behavior. 2004;**25**:951-968

[31] Blake-Beard SD. Taking a hard look at formal mentoring programs. Journal of Management Development. 2001;**20**(4):331-345

Section 4

Developing Leadership Practices

Chapter 9

Leadership Coaching to Drive Transformation in the Experience Economy

Marcela Fang

Abstract

Coaching has been recognized as a valuable developmental approach in the field of leadership development, able to support aspiring leaders to attain their personal and professional goals, as well as support their teams in a rapidly changing, increasingly uncertain, and complex business environment. Coaching programs have the potential to support the creation of culture norms that can better support optimal working attitudes and behaviors, contributing to improved performance through evolved leadership capacity. However, the use of leadership coaching in the experience economy, and specifically the tourism and hospitality industries, is mostly unreported. In a case study of coaching tourism and hospitality managers and educators in Vietnam, the intentional change theory was used to support the development of coaching behaviors. The program learning evidence from a six-week long coaching program showed that those participants who aspire to become effective leaders can engage in coaching behaviors through leadership identity, engagement in intentional leadership development, and through more mindful and collaborative actions. This chapter presents a starting point for other "leader as coach" programs, advancing the field of evidence-based tourism and hospitality leadership development. Theoretical and practical implications are also discussed.

Keywords: coaching, leadership development, experience economy, intentional change theory, managerial coaching

1. Introduction

Coaching has attracted vast interest from leadership development scholars and practitioners over the past three decades, contributing to the leadership development field's scientific research base across different industry sectors [1]. Day [2] defined coaching as a goal-oriented experiential process aimed at the development of leadership skills to improve performance and organizational outcomes. Organizations in the experience economy, predominantly tourism and hospitality organizations that provide experiences rather than goods and services [3] and rely heavily on human and face-to-face interactions between customers and staff, are finding it increasingly challenging to attract, engage, and retain talented staff [4, 5]. In addition, tourism and hospitality organizations have been the most severely hit by the disruptive nature of the COVID-19 pandemic [6]. Two and half years into the pandemic, many tourism and hospitality organizations now experience deep-rooted challenges associated with prolonged labor shortages and high turnover rates. The seasonal nature of tourism and hospitality jobs and low pay further add to these challenges [7]. Researchers highlighted that the lingering pandemic triggers business decisions that also lead to different organizational structures and how jobs are performed as consumer demand changes [6]. Since the reopening of global borders in 2021, employees are finding in the current tourism and hospitality workplace to do more with less, under more stringent policies, and also under elevated levels of stress and anxiety [6].

While most tourism and hospitality leadership literature advocates positive leadership styles and behaviors, such as transformational leadership, servant leadership, and empowering leadership [8], the changed and uncertain environment and under-resourced organizations, however, may make it increasingly challenging to apply these leadership styles and associated behaviors, specifically when managers work under a higher level of stress and anxiety for an extended period. The pressure to produce results may be paralyzing for many managers and front-line workers alike, debilitating any well-established high-performance work practices [9]. In such a context, stress may contribute to burnout, intention to leave, and high turnover [10]. It has been argued that changes that fundamentally affect members of society in a radical way may have profound effects on how individuals construct their identity and find meaning in life [11], potentially leading some individuals to question their future in the tourism and hospitality industries [12]. This has potentially devastating effects on the organizations from the human resource management standpoint as this may significantly compromise the organizational leadership capacity. Coaching managers for development in such a social context may therefore offer new solutions to deal with the challenges of modern times [11]. It is perhaps even more vital in the "new normal" to help managers undertake personal development that will assist in the reset to help reduce the overwhelm experienced by many in the workplace and to continue driving more sustainable human resources practices in their organizations.

This study refers to managerial coaching through which organizational managers could elevate their leadership skills and abilities. The aims of this study are to (i) explore how a coaching program designed for junior to mid-level managers can drive change in coached managers, and (ii) identify how and when the change occurred during the program. The question that directed this study is: How can coaching training support the development of managers, consequently supporting their efficacy to lead in the new normal? The study's purpose is influenced by the fact that the cultural norms in today's tourism and hospitality businesses and organizations have changed as the result of the COVID-19 pandemic and that there is a need for different and more effective leader development interventions, such as managerial coaching, to reduce the pain and friction associated with staff and labor shortages and turnover intention.

2. Coaching for managerial development

An early definition of coaching pointed to "unlocking a person's potential to maximize their own performance. It is helping them to learn rather than teaching them" ([13], p. 8). In this assertion, coaching was linked to individual's internal state, highlighting the importance of drawing one's focus to self-awareness and taking personal responsibility for change [13]. Other researchers stressed that coaching is a distinct form of human development and different from other interventions driving change (e.g., counseling and mentoring) [14]. The coaching process is underlined by a dialog between the coach and the individual being coached, which is mostly one-on-one dialog, where the coach asks open questions, aiming to stimulate the coached individual's self-awareness and personal responsibility. Similarly, Stelter [11] suggested that coaching is "a form of dialogue [that] offers the coachee a space for self-reflection; for revising and refining positions and self-concepts" (p. 52). Overall, most definitions shed light on coaching as a process in which the coach and the coached individual engage in interpersonal interaction that leads to an exchange of knowledge and the development of insights, leading to growth. It is during this process that the coached individuals are supported by the coach to see themselves in a new light. Researchers stress that the coaching interpersonal interaction should be focused on the coached individual's goal [15], and the coaching dialogs need to support the achievement of the goal to foster positive behavioral change [16].

Coaching is seen as an attractive approach within the leadership development field as the demand for high-quality managers in the more uncertain business environment grows [17]. Increasingly, managers are expected to use a coaching style in their daily managerial practice [18, 19] and to support a collective development of an organizational coaching culture important for improved organizational outcomes [20]. McCarthy and Milner [21] argued that coaching in the organizational context can lead to employee engagement, improved performance, responsibility, and trust in the organizational context. Overall, coaching, as a form of development, has been perceived as an important and effective managerial activity as it can support the growth and performance of those being coached [22]. As highlighted in the literature, coaching has been studied in relation to organizational outcomes such as job satisfaction [23], service quality and turnover intention [24], and individual and organizational performance [25].

Weller and Weller [26] noted that coaching as an approach to leadership development is particularly valuable as the coaching intervention can be customized to the needs of different managers and the contexts within which the managers exist. In terms of managerial coaching, Hawkins and Smith [27] suggested four types of coaching directions to support others' growth and development—coaching for skills, coaching for performance, coaching for development, and coaching for transformation. However, despite the growing popularity of coaching in the organizational context, theoretically, the empirical evidence outlining how and why coaching leads to change in behaviors is limiting the advancement of the field [28, 29]. For example, the lack of underpinning theoretical coaching models and theories in coaching programs and interventions, such as managerial coaching, can lead to unjustified evidence and misconceptions of what is being developed, when and how. Previously, calls have been made to empirically investigate the elements that can predict effective coaching outcomes [26, 30]; the coaching antecedents (e.g., coaching and the coached individuals' characteristics); the coaching process (e.g., the coaching approach and the coaching relationship); and different levels of outcomes (e.g., individual, team, organizational) [31].

3. Intentional change theory

Intentional change theory is an integrated theory of change, unifying elements from leadership development, emotional and social intelligence, cognitive emotion, social complexity, and psycho-neurobiology [32–35]. Intentional change theory was specifically developed for the leadership development field, as other theories of change could not effectively explain why a change occurred during a given leadership development intervention and how it could sustain the new behaviors over time, a phenomenon labeled as the "black box" [36].

According to intentional change theory [37], individuals who embark on an intentional journey of desired change need to achieve sustained change in their behavior, thoughts, feelings, and perceptions, which requires an evolved progression through five vivid phases of discovery: (i) the ideal self, (ii) the real self, (iii) development of learning agenda and plan for intended change, (iv) experimentation and practice of new behaviors, thoughts, and feelings to move closer to the ideal self, and (v) the discovery derived from conversations with others during the learning process, leading to a noticeable change. Overall, the intentional change theory suggests that the enactment can enable behavioral change and progress through the delineated five phases of discovery, which are integral to finding oneself, who one is, and what is the ideal self that the individual wants to develop and rise to their purpose. Boyatzis [37] asserts this to be an iterative process of discovery as individual cycle through the different discovery phases in a nonlinear manner until the gap between the ideal self and real self is reduced.

During this developmental process, the coach's role is to meaningfully guide and support the coached individuals through the process of self-discovery, to awaken their drive, extrinsically and intrinsically, through coaching, questioning, and listening, consequently increasing the prospects of them being able to achieve sustainable behavioral change. For example, if managers' agenda is to use the coaching practice as a form of practice in their organization, these managers would need to engage in this coaching practice on a consistent and continuous basis. Boyatzis [38] stressed that an individual's internal motivation is, however, the key to one's intentional change, as others cannot force the change upon them. This suggests that only individuals who are committed to developing the needed qualities, such as traits, mindsets, and behaviors of effective managerial coaches, would be able to attain the desired change for longer. It is possible that less committed individuals may acquire such qualities, however, only for the short-term [36]. In other words, if the desire for sustained change is not present during the coaching development intervention, it may require friction for an individual to suddenly notice the need for intentional change [39].

Over the past 30 years, intentional change theory has been empirically tested and increasingly integrated into various professional and educational programs globally, including leadership development programs and coaching interventions [40]. While the extant intentional change theory research started to document some insights into how the model's five phases of discoveries can support the emergence of new behaviors—from the real self to the ideal self—more is to be done to fully explore the "black box" phenomenon. In addition, intentional change theory is yet to be applied in the experience-based context of tourism and hospitality interventions intended to foster managerial coaching. Specifically, in relation to managerial coaching, how can the theory support the effective development of junior and middle-level managers at this level of management?

4. The coaching approach

While suitable change theory such as the intentional change theory can inform the coaching intervention design, it is also necessary to apply a suitable coaching approach to help propel the development of the coached individuals, so they are able to help others through their managerial coaching in their organizations. Boyatzis [33] suggested that intentional change theory can be used as the underpinning developmental theory driving leadership development interventions as well as a suitable model to guide the coaching intervention and process. In terms of the coaching process, the coach plays an important support role for the individual being coached to progress through the five intentional change theory phases. The coach's role is also to help reignite the coached individuals' will, through continuous discussions, to sustain their intended and desired managerial coaching change. Hence, the coaching approach also calls for a trusting and collaborative coaching relationship that could support the coached individual's sense of identity, as well as reinforce the coached individual's accountability for change, to reduce the potential for relapse [40]. In this sense, the coaching relationship and approach can be viewed as the key elements to the transformative process [41] as the coached individual engages in a reinterpretation of perceptions, experiences, and meaning-making [11]. It is the coach's facilitation capacity that helps trigger the change process through conversations, which consequently elicits the coached individual's shift in mindset or perspective. It is the coaching relationship, the rapport, collaboration, commitment, and the trust established between the coach and the coached individual—the psychological safety—that supports the coaching process and the development of the desired behavior [42].

Hence, coaching might be used as one of the approaches to foster leader development. The coach-coaching relationship and process can facilitate the intended behavioral change and goal attainment, such as optimal functioning, well-being, and improved personal and professional performance [41].

In terms of the coaching approach, several researchers suggested that an effective coaching approach consists of a designated yet flexible set of questions to enable the coached individuals to think for themselves, encouraging them to move toward their identified goals [43–45]. Hence, it is through the coach's questions, active listening, and continuous encouragement that the coached individual can engage in self-reflection, experimentation, and formation of plans to learn about the self, others, and the environment within which they exist. Thus, coaches expediate the learning process instead of giving advice [44].

Differently, Boyatzis et al. [46] suggested coaching for compassion, which requires a caring relationship between the coach and the coached individual. This type of relationship calls for both parties to be on the same emotional wavelength (e.g., feelings) and holds a commitment to each other [40]. Relationships with a greater level of trust, respect, and loyalty seem to add to the coaching benefits. Therefore, if coaches do not have a caring relationship with the coached individual, the coaching interactions may lead to added stress for the coach and the participant. To help sustain managers' energy and focus, organizations may consider coaching for compassion as an approach to organization's culture – culture where emotional intelligence is fostered through compassionate coaching. Compassion should be therefore incorporated in the leadership development interventions [40, 47].

Boyatzis [33] further discovered that compassionate coaching leads to more effective coaching outcomes than does coaching for compliance. Compassion in coaching was conceptualized as an understanding of the feelings of others, caring for the coached individual, and having the willingness to act in response to the coached individual's feelings [33]. Boyatzis and colleagues highlighted that coaching done with caring conviction about the individual's development in mind acts as the antidote for stress as compassion in coaching can stimulate the psychophysiological response driving this state [33, 47]. Thus, it is important that coaches do not see the participants as a burden or responsibility and emphasize organizational reasons for coaching as this would escalate the coached individuals' stress levels and close the individuals to engage in learning and high performance [33].

During the coaching process, coaches use a wide range of tools and developmental techniques to help the coached individuals achieve their goals and improve their performance. For example, in the field of coaching psychology, researchers emphasize the use of psychological theories, approaches, and application of behavioral science to promote evidence-based practice in human-focused coaching development, aimed at the non-clinical population [48].

However, evidence-based managerial coaching insights are a few and still in their infancy [19, 49], which limits the understanding of how the mainstream coaching models and approaches contribute to coaching and performance outcomes, and specifically in the dynamic organizational context within the experience-based tourism and hospitality industries. Studying leadership coaching initiatives in the context of experience economy offers current and future tourism and hospitality organizations the opportunity to gain new insights into the relationship between managerial coaching and organizational outcomes. Whether and how such leadership development interventions can support the development of more sustainable human resource practices in the experience economy through managerial coaching and, subsequently, an organizational coaching culture. Hagen [29] suggested that to better understand managerial coaching, qualitative studies are needed, as so far, few quantitative studies have only shaded light on the relationship between managerial coaching and various outcomes. Little is also known about coaching in the eastern context, as most studies have been conducted in the US [18]. This chapter presents initial findings from a coaching program developed for tourism and hospitality managers and educators in managerial roles in Vietnam to foster their managerial coaching practice at a time the global economy started to open after the international border restrictions linked to the COVID-19 pandemic were lifted in 2022.

5. The Australia-Vietnam coaching program

The Australian-Vietnam coaching program design was underpinned by intentional change theory. The program consisted of four learning modules and, along with the coaching approach, aligned with the intentional change theory model. The modules included content on "the ideal self," "the real self," "learning agenda," and "coaching" (with a leadership development coach and peer-coaching).

The once-a-week six-hour residential workshops of an overall six-week delivery were facilitated by an Australian faculty member and supported by one Vietnamese faculty member. The development was further supported with coaching sessions: a one-on-one coaching session with an Australian facilitator and a peer coaching session. The training was conducted in a trusting and supportive environment, underpinned by psychological safety and coach-peer-relationships that promoted participants' openness to learning and discoveries. Throughout the coaching program, participants were required to experiment and practice, and consequently reflect on their learning experiences, noting down any tipping points leading to new discoveries in behaviors, thoughts, or perceptions.

DOI: http://dx.doi.org/10.5772/intechopen.108104

6. Method

The aim of this study was to conduct a preliminary assessment of the coaching program and its impact on behaviors developed by tourism and hospitality managers and educators through the six-week leadership coaching program underpinned by the intentional change theory and what and when contributed to the developed behaviors during the intervention. The coaching program contained the following topics-leadership styles, emotional intelligence, personal vision, values, and balance sheet, and coaching; and included the following methods: workshops (six one-day sessions); action learning reflections (participants reflecting on experimentation and practice in their workplaces—weekly individual and group reflections); and coaching (two sessions of 45 minutes).

The first one-on-one coaching interaction was between a female coach (also the Australian program facilitator, who was an experienced coach with an extensive background in leader and leadership development and organizational management). The second coaching session was a triad coaching interaction between the program participants – participants taking turns to coach, be coached, and act as observers and feedback providers. The one-on-one coaching session was built around the participants' personal vision—"the ideal self." The triad coaching was related to strengths identified during the coaching program and at the discretion of the coach and the coached participants.

6.1 Participants

Participants were tourism and hospitality professionals—junior to middle-level managers and educators—located in Vietnam who completed the Australia-Vietnam leadership development program funded by the Australian government as an initiative to upskill mostly female managers in the tourism and hospitality sectors in the "new normal." An Australian educational institution was selected to design and delivery the program for the Vietnamese context. All participants were interested in leadership and were required to undertake all learning components in English. Twenty participants engaged in the coaching intervention and volunteered to participate in the study. Among these participants, all completed reflective writing and 14 participants completed an end-of-program questionnaire. The final sample comprised 13 females and one male program participant; 8 participants were between 31 and 40 years, 5 between 20 and 30 and 1 between 41 and 50 years of age. Most participants (n = 11) had less than 5 years of management experience. Seven participants were from the tourism and hospitality education sector, and the other seven were employed by large tourism and hospitality organizations.

6.2 Procedure

Participants completed six one-day workshops with four key topics linked to coaching. These topics anchored the guided exploration and identification of the real and ideal self, identification of personal/ professional goals, and agenda for each participant's desired behavioral change. Consequently, all participants were scheduled for two coaching sessions. Each participant had the opportunity to discuss the ideal self with the coach and the agenda they had intentionally set for themselves to achieve in due course (post-program).

The data were collected from the participants' end-of-week individually written reflections and one end-of-program questionnaire. The questionnaire was used to assess the participants' coaching program experience and the extent of their coaching development—the perceived improvements and attainment of new behaviors—through open and closed questions. The study was approved by the institution's Human Research Ethics Committee.

6.3 Data analysis and findings

Weekly individually written reflections from all the coaching program participants ($n = 20$) and an end-of-program survey from 14 participants were analyzed. The reflections were linked to the weekly program content and the open-ended survey questions related to the participants' learning experiences, including what outcomes the participants perceived attaining at their individual level and in the context of their organizations. Themes were noted through thematic analysis, using a deductive approach [50, 51]. A deductive approach was used to create categories which the reflection-based and open-ended survey data were coded into, using themes linked to the intentional change theory [51].

The researcher first read all the documents to gain familiarity with the data. Next, the researcher started the coding process, coding data relevant to the research question, and the phases of the intentional change theory across the dataset. The codes were then reviewed, and similar codes were merged and, in the end, put into categories representing a given theme of the intentional change theory. An interpretation of data followed, capturing the meaning of how the participants gained insights from their classroom and workplace learning experiences, how the discoveries were processed and applied in their work and life, and the outcomes these actions contributed to by the time the program finished. The five themes that inform this study are ideal self-category, real self-category, learning agenda category, experimentation and practice category, supportive relationships category, and outcomes.

6.3.1 Ideal self-category

Throughout their lives, managers seek developmental opportunities to optimize their performance and help others to do the same in the organizational context. As managers pause from their busy working life and take the opportunity to visualize what their ideal self may look like over the next 5 years, it becomes evident that several goals appear on their list—a mix of personal and professional goals. Within this study, all participants noted that goals, in general, are helpful for performance but that it is harder to decide which goals to focus on at any one time. Having clarity on what goals to pursue emerged as the tipping point for the participants. For example, one participant says: "*[...] Before the program, I had lots of goals...I lived in chaos without direction for my career... during the program, I gradually found my direction... I had that 'Oh' moment that I should go this way... I can now organize all the things to focus on that I should follow*" (Participant 20). Indeed, the idea of a clear goal appears enlightening to most participants, as one participant says: "*[...] So many ideas running through my head... I can now narrow the lens and focus on my target*" (Participant 17). It becomes evident that having a clear goal for these participants also means a sudden surge of ideas that could potentially lead to ways of accomplishing their goals. Another participant also expresses that goal setting can lead to more purposeful living: *"[...] It strengthens the ability to experience life, look forward, set a journey for the boat of my life, and be on the right track to the future with life values"* (Participant 12).

The participants' perceptions reveal that the coaching program, and specifically the one-on-one coaching experience, contributes to discoveries that lead to purposeful visions in which the future or the ideal self appears attainable. With coach's support and mindful questioning, the participants can figure out what to do to achieve their short- to long-term goals. However, it is not often the case in the Vietnamese context that managers are presented with a coaching opportunity to speak openly to a coach about their personal goals, struggles, and aspirations to lead in the post-COVID-19 era.

6.3.2 Real self-category

While many participants speak of their self-discoveries that contribute to understanding their current selves, there is an overwhelming perception that transformational and servant leadership behaviors frequently play out in their everyday lives. One participant says: *"[...] Through the result of transformational leadership, I realized that this type of leadership is the one I often apply in my job... servant leadership is also my favorite"* (Participant 11).

The analysis further uncovered the sub-theme of personal values. The participants realized that their values underscore their actions and behaviors. One participant expresses this idea by saying that: *"[...] developing my awareness of my values helped me to be true to my values, reducing conflict and making my work more enjoyable and fulfilling... It helps me to improve my leadership skills and to communicate with the team better. I will continue to develop my self-awareness to lead myself and others"* (Participant 20).

However, many more insights emerged through the work conducted in the area of emotional intelligence, another distinct sub-theme within this category. One participant expresses that leaders need to manage their emotions: *"interactions with colleagues can often be confusing, not to mention a source of stress. When you are a leader, you need to learn how to control your emotions in all cases in your workplace and your life"* (Participant 1). It is evident that most participants support the idea that managers can control their emotions during difficult times, as one participant says: *"I realized that when I'm angry or upset about something, I should not argue about it, I better go off somewhere, calm down and be prepared to agree or disagree and only then deal with it... I have a choice about whether I let these emotions take over or whether I lead a healthy life"* (Participant 2). Another participant also expresses similar sentiment and highlights how emotional intelligence leads to better social interactions: *"our openness to emotions and our ability to read our own and others' emotions can accurately give us important knowledge about how we are feeling whether we are communicating effectively and about the quality of our relationships"* (Participant 20).

The participants' reflective insights reveal that class activities, such as discussions around their leadership styles, values, and strengths, contribute to greater self-awareness, which further stimulates the thoughts and actions in their everyday lives. This illustrates how sustained reflective practice fostered through a training program can continue to elevate one's self-awareness and develop the ability to understand the real self through everyday experiences. However, this ability is reinforced through interpersonal feedback and supportive relationships as one cannot entirely rely on own personal beliefs [33].

6.3.3 Learning agenda category

The analysis indicates that the program activities linked to the exploration of the ideal and real self also set the base for the development of personal learning agenda—a specific plan developed by each participant to action their personally set goals. Indeed, most participants are driven by clearly defined goals, as one participant says that: *"[...] I gradually discovered and learned how to achieve my goal. What steps should I take first.... I know how to develop my learning agenda to align reality with my vision. The development not only helped me to clarify my vision, but also to find my direction"* (Participant 20).

Most participants are driven to embark on meaningful projects, either aligned to the opportunities in their current organization or the idea of starting a business. In either case, it is evident that all participants want to continue to grow as leaders and, in that process, also to grow their teams to achieve better performance and succeed on their projects. These participants appreciate their strengthened self-awareness, propelling their confidence to attain their aspired goals. One participant expresses this idea by saying: *"[...] I fully appreciate the value of self-awareness. With that, I can change and also see the change in my life" (Participant 12).*

6.3.4 Experimentation and practice category

The analysis further reveals that the sustained reflective practice presents meaningful insights into participants' experiences of how they take the opportunity to apply the learned concepts and methods in their daily working environments. Most participants seem preoccupied with challenging customer interactions and interactions involving their colleagues from other departments and their subordinates and managers at higher levels. This also represents the everyday working environment within the tourism and hospitality sectors, highlighting the significance of emotions in working life. It is noted that most participants experiment and practice their emotional self-control before leaning into conversations with others. As one participant states:

> *"[...] I hold back a moment to think carefully to make sure I will not say or do any impulsive thing. After that, I take time to review if I did well or what I should improve. So far, I evaluate myself that in most situations, my ability to control my anger is improved; I gradually become more patient with people and problems and do not let emotions overwhelm reason... I realized that in every situation, keeping calm is a must—"cold head and warm heart" is the key to overcoming a hard time" (Participant 9).*

In addition to trying to control their own emotions for personal benefit, most participants are also mindful of how their emotions impact their teams, as one participant says: *"[...] I realised that emotions could affect the team's spirit in working, so I must carefully use my words and commands"* (Participant 19).

Overall, the participants' reflective insights show how they continuously strived to experiment with different thoughts and behaviors as they started to feel more confident in doing so, including within their workplaces. Throughout the program, many participants try practice emotional intelligence, seeing it as the foundation for more effective individual and team performance. The participants continue to practice dealing with their work colleagues and customers to progress to their ideal level of mastery. By the end of the coaching program, most participants express that they are "better able to perform their job tasks," are "more confident to show up as leaders" when at work, and overall, are "more interested in leadership."

6.3.5 Supportive relationship category

Coach support is perceived by several of the participants as a much-desired aspect of the training experience. The participants point to the coaching relationship, the interactions, questioning, and conversations as important triggers helping them to gain new insights and ideas and to realize their self-identified potential. Through the coaching support, the participants note they can better identify strategies to answer their own questions, and solve problems to their workplace issues and overall other challenges. The participants appreciate the coaching approach as it is unique and different from their prior experiences. Others could not lead them to meaningful insights and answers, only more confusion, making them question the coaching approach. The participants note that coaches need to be professional and able to work with the coached individuals' needs and understand their context rather than closing their motivation to change. One participant notes that:

> *"[...] I think like the way the coaching session was done on the program, we were asked questions, but through these questions, we figured out by ourselves what we needed to do... But with some coaches, the quality is not there. Some local coaches ask questions that are nonsense... it doesn't help with anything at all... like we don't need someone to tell us what we need to do. Like some coaches even say, 'you need to do that, you need to do this', and it makes us feel no, we're not children anymore. So, finding a good coach is really hard... Coaches really need a high level of IQ and emotional intelligence."*

However, some participants also note that the leader development process can include other forms of support to navigate the journey of self-discovery. One participant says that: *"[...] Most of the time, I process the leadership by myself... I also get feedback from my colleague, who I usually work with... Then, I try to find support from people around me. So, I've never been alone"* (Participant 9). One participant also notes how she works with her husband to gain insights. She says: *"[...] I usually share with my husband. He can give me some advice, and he can share with me what he feels about my change, and he can give me advice on what I should do, this or this or this"* (Participant 20).

6.3.6 Outcomes

The six-week-long coaching program focused on developing coaching skills and behaviors, in which 20 managers from the tourism and hospitality and education sectors showed that engagement in reflective practice, emotional intelligence, visioning, self-discovery, goal setting, and learning to coach could raise the participants' leadership identity, self-efficacy, and better workplace effectiveness. The specific change that occurs for them is that they can clearly see the type of leaders they are and how they want to present themselves to others—a form of leadership identity. For example, this idea is expressed by one participant that says: *"I'm always the one who likes to inspire people, inspire, and anchor and support them to help people what they really want to do, what makes them happy in a job or life. I try to give good energy, not negative energy.*

I want to be an inspirational person...never be rude to others to make them lose their positive energy in life... always listen to people before making judgments" (Participant 9).

Most participants have strengthened their resourcefulness through emotional and social competencies, improved strategic choices to deal with conflict, and deepened their essence to help others develop and feel good in the process. One participant says that: "*[...] I realized that my hidden abilities were much stronger than I thought. If I want to make my dreams come true, I have to be passionate and dedicated. If I want to succeed, I must constantly learn, improve, and practice physical and mental health*" (Participant 16). Another participant also expresses a similar sentiment and says: "*[...] I had a different mindset after each session*" (Participant 12). Yet another participant shows how the other orientation—being there to serve others—can lead to more pleasant feelings and satisfaction at work. She says: "*[...] I care more for others, not just myself, but think for them. This makes me more open and able to keep good relationships with others like senior colleagues, junior colleagues, guests... I can better manage my stress and be there for my team... think from their shoes, making them my friends for life, not just colleagues at work*" (Participant 18).

It is evident that most participants support the idea of managerial coaching in the tourism and hospitality context in Vietnam. One participant expresses this as such: "*[...] I began to think about my leadership style and found the proper styles for me. Then, I began to focus on teamwork, interact with my colleagues, accept differences, and motivate my team. Especially, I tend to think bigger and share the vision with my whole team to make sure they know their role and responsibilities of the general goal*" (Participant 20).

While the above outcomes shed light on the early impact of the coaching program (during the program), the analysis also points to when and how the various personal changes occur. The weekly reflections provide important means of understanding participants' experiences through their insights of highlighted events during each week as the participants continue to apply their learning at work, how they start to change their thinking and reinforce new behaviors. Each topic provides an opportunity for the participants to focus and strengthen their desired behaviors in a scaffolded way. Evidently, the participants continue to practice what works for them, leading to improved habits week by week, as noted by one participant: "*[...] I became stronger and calmer... I can now overcome challenges in my work and life*" (Participant 16).

In terms of the end-of-program survey completed by 14 participants, the analysis identified up to three workplace-level outcome examples in this category. There were 39 responses in total, which fell into 7 themes. The top four behavioral outcomes comprised "working collaboratively with others to achieve common goals," "spreading leadership knowledge," "motivating and influencing others," and "coaching others."

7. Discussion

This study contributes to the management literature, hospitality and tourism sectors, and broadly, the experience economy by shedding light on the process of managerial coaching underpinned by intentional change theory. This study aimed to explore how a coaching program designed for junior to mid-level managers can drive change in coached managers and how and when the change occurred during training. These objectives were to fundamentally help address the gap in the managerial coaching literature by examining how coaching training can support the development of managers in the post-pandemic times, to lead effectively in "the new normal."

The findings indicated that the six-week coaching program facilitated the emergence of incremental discoveries through deepened self-awareness, such as the essence of clarity around the ideal and real self, associated with self-efficacy beliefs at the end of the coaching program. This is in line with prior research that showed executive coaching increased self-efficacy [52]. Self-efficacy to lead has been derived through the program's learning content and two coaching sessions. Specifically, the key discovery was triggered by the one-on-one coaching sessions with the leadership development coach as it enabled the program participants to clarify their visions and build an agenda around these self-determined visions. These findings enrich the intentional change theory by demonstrating the implications and effects of one's desired state of visioning and exploring the ideal self [53], and how the coaching approach with a high-quality coaching interaction can help facilitate and reinforce the coached individuals' drive, agency, and determination to transcend and transform the conventional ways of working.

The study also revealed that the participants' evolved emotional intelligence was also the critical element to their resourcefulness, and that the participants have strengthened the ability to control and manage their emotions before engaging in actions and interactions with others, thus choosing the right mindsets and strategies to deal with issues and challenges more effectively. The context of managerial coaching, emotions' role, and their impact on leaders' efficacy and other outcomes in the Vietnamese setting had not yet been explored in the extant research. These preliminary findings therefore suggest that the desire to help others on their path to evolve their leadership skills and behaviors (e.g., coached managers wanting to coach their colleagues and teams) can help transcend the self, leading to more positive mindsets and engagement at work. Hence, when the participants feel in control of their emotions and connect with their visions, the more they are able to work effectively and foster collaborative practices in their organizations. Hence, the results are in agreement with the studies on coaching with compassion [47].

The cycling through the intentional change theory dimensions of discoveries also contributed to the strengthening of the leadership identity through experimentation (emotional, social, cognitive), reflection, and insights gained from the learning and workplace environments. The results are in agreement with Ibarra's findings [54] that leadership development is an opportunity to establish a "new working identity."

7.1 Theoretical implications

Intentional change theory in the context of leadership development has been well-explained by Boyatzis [36] and, to some degree, studied empirically in the organizational context [55] and individual leader level [53]. This study provides qualitative insights into the impacts of intentional change theory at the individual level—junior and mid-level managers in Vietnam, specifically as the guiding approach to coaching in the experience economy that relies on distinctive and high-quality interactions between customers and front-line employees. The study demonstrated that awareness of the self and the presence of purposeful goals and sustained drive to the continued development of the self, and the essence of developing others positively influenced the coached managers' mindset and attitude toward high-performance work practices and others orientation. Hence, this study adds to the literature and theory related to managerial coaching and leader development. In line with the five intentional change theory phases, when the coached individuals' mindset to engage is self-identified and meaningful, it can lead to improved individual and team-related working performance and working behaviors.

7.2 Practical implications

This study shows that coaching underpinned by intentional change theory leads to the gradual strengthening of self-awareness and clarification of one's goals, leading to individual choices and actions that contribute to more collective forms of leader's behavior at the workplace (e.g., teamwork, collaboration, collective problem solving, and decision making) and leader self-efficacy (e.g., self-awareness, emotional and social intelligence, mindfulness). Several implications can be drawn for managers in the experience economy. This study demonstrates that coaching is a distinct form of managerial and leader development that can help strengthen coached managers' emotional capacity and contribute to more effective social interactions and individual, team, and organizational outcomes. The findings suggest that the development of emotional intelligence could contribute to competitive advantage as human interactions supported through employee performance and quality customer service have been linked with success in the experience economy. Therefore, investment in developing managers at the individual level could contribute to outcomes at the organizational level [56].

The findings further suggest that managers who undergo coaching training with the understanding that they can develop further as leaders and can help support the growth of others within their organization leading to realization of their strengths, values, and career aspirations and goals, which internally drive their engagement in the intentional change process. The belief that these aspiring leaders can contribute to something more significant and in the context of their organizations leads to more compassionate engagement with front-line workers, colleagues, and customers and, in turn, seem to contribute to greater job satisfaction and lowered intention to leave, for their subordinates and themselves. Dweck [57] highlighted that coaching is an essential tool that can foster employee development and productivity. Thus, to use coaching in the experience economy to develop human resources and performance, coaching interventions should be offered to aspiring leaders to support their leadership development rather than as a requirement to improve performance. As stressed by Wood and Gordon [58], during disruptive times, managers need to be provided with guidance (not instructions) and be equipped with coaching skills to help drive developmental cultures and help strengthen the weaker human resources.

Boyatzis [33] argued that "when leaders experience compassion through coaching the development of others, they experience psychophysical effects [that] can restore the body's natural healing and growth processes, thus enhancing their sustainability" (p. 1). Considering the stressful nature of tourism and hospitality roles in the current post-pandemic times, managers could engage in compassionate coaching interventions, not coaching for compliance interventions, to not only benefit from the restorative capacity gained through the coaching practice and experience but also to add value to their organizations by developing the human resources, and overall strengthening the leadership capacity for competitive advantage.

7.3 Limitations and future research

This study is linked to one manager coaching program designed for tourism and hospitality managers in Vietnam. Hence, the findings may not be generalized to all coaching interventions. The leadership development context in Vietnam might be unique to the tourism and hospitality sectors within the broader experience economy. The cultural context in Vietnam is characterized by high power distance and collectivism [59]. Coaching managers as part of leadership development is an emerging practice, and the consideration of these elements, along with emotions and emotional intelligence, is yet to be thoroughly investigated.

This study only considered the coaching evidence that emerged during the training program (participants' weekly reflections) and immediately at the end of the coaching at 6 weeks (end-of-program survey). Future research can examine the impact of coaching and leadership development programs on post-coaching training behaviors to understand the process of sustained change. To help understand how coaching and leadership development initiatives lead to participants' attainment of the ideal self and their visions and goals.

8. Conclusion

The experience economy in the "new normal" calls for leaders at all levels as staff shortages, high-staff turnover rates, and lack of skilled workforce deepened by the COVID-19 pandemic drive the need for revised and more sustainable human resource management practices, including new ways of leading and working, to achieve competitive advantage. This qualitative study provides new insights into the coaching of managers' process in the experience economy. The study highlighted how intentional change theory could guide the coaching intervention and the coaching process to help aspiring managers (re)discover their passion through the visioning and setting meaningful goals for development. Through compassionate coaching and questioning, managers can become more self-aware of their strengths and weaknesses and use their strengths and values to activate their plans and strategies in a self-determined way. In doing so, managers can pursue attaining the ideal self in a more sustained manner. The study also examined the coaching topics that reinforced the coached managers' ability to engage in intentional change, evidently leading to improvements in individual performance and the performance of others in the managers' workplace context. The findings of this study demonstrate that coaching that is underpinned by a change theory from the leadership development field and that incorporates emotional intelligence can contribute to individual and team outcomes in a six-week-long coaching program.

Funding

The author received no financial support for the research, authorship, and publication of this article.

Conflict of interest

The author declares no conflict of interest.

Author details

Marcela Fang
William Angliss Institute, Melbourne, Australia

*Address all correspondence to: marcela.fang@angliss.edu.au

References

[1] Segers J, Dries N, Versées D. Coaching. In: Hartung PJ, Savickas ML, Walsh WB, editors. APA Handbook of Career Intervention. 2nd ed. Washington, DC: APA; 2015. pp. 397-411

[2] Day D. Leadership development: A review in context. The Leadership Quarterly. 2001;**11**(4):581-613

[3] Pine BJ II, Gilmore JH. Welcome to the experience economy. Harvard Business Review. 1998;**78**:97-105

[4] King C, Madera JM, Lee L, Murillo E, Baum T, Solnet D. Reimagining attraction and retention of hospitality management talent—A multilevel identity perspective. Journal of Business Research. 2021;**136**:251-262

[5] Madera JM, Dawson M, Guchait P, Belarmino AM. Strategic human resources management research in hospitality and tourism: A review of current literature and suggestions for the future. International Journal of Contemporary Hospitality Management. 2017;**29**(1):48-67

[6] Kwok L. Labor shortages: A critical reflection and a call for industry-academic collaboration. International Journal of Contemporary Hospitality Management. 2022. DOI: 10.1108/IJCHM-01-2022-0103

[7] Kravariti F, Voutsina K, Tasoulis K, Dibia C, Johnston K. Talent management in hospitality and tourism: A systematic literature review and research agenda. International Journal of Contemporary Hospitality Management. 2022;**34**(1):321-360

[8] Arici HE, Arici NC, Kö̈seoglu MA, King BEM. Leadership research in the root of hospitality scholarship: 1960-2020. International Journal of Hospitality Management. 2021;**99**:103063. DOI: 10.1016/j.ijhm.2021.103063

[9] Cheng BH, McCarty JM. Understanding the dark and bright sides of anxiety: A theory of workplace anxiety. Journal of Applied Psychology. 2018;**103**(5):537-560

[10] Azem SM, Nazir NA. Role of stress and burnout among nurses in the private hospitals. International Journal of Academic Research in Business and Social Sciences. 2014;**4**:420-428

[11] Stelter R. Third generation coaching: Reconstructing dialogues through collaborative practice and a focus on values. International Coaching Psychology Review. 2014;**9**(1):51-65

[12] Goh E, Baum T. Job perceptions of generation Z hotel employees towards working in Covid-19 quarantine hotels: The role of meaningful work. International Journal of Contemporary Hospitality Management. 2021;**33**(5):1688-1710

[13] Whitmore J. Coaching for Performance: GROWing People, Performance and Purpose. London: Nocholas Breley; 1992

[14] Passmore J, Mortimer L. The experience of using coaching as a learning technique in learner driver development: An IPA study of adult learning. International Coaching Psychology Review. 2011;**6**(1):33-45

[15] Grant AM, Stober DR. Introduction. In: Stober DR, Grant AM, editors. Evidence Based Coaching Handbook: Putting Best Practices to Work for your Clients. Hoboken, NJ: John Wiley and Sons; 2006. pp. 1-14

[16] Lai Y, McDowall A. A systematic review (SR) of coaching psychology: Focusing on the attributes of effective coaching psychologists. International Coaching Psychology Review. 2014;**9**(2):120-136

[17] Bowles SV, Picano JH. Dimensions of coaching related to productivity and quality of life. Consulting Psychology Journal: Practice and Research. 2006;**58**(4):232-239

[18] Beattie RS, Kim S, Hagen MS, Egan TM, Ellinger AD, Hamlin RG. Managerial coaching: A review of the empirical literature and development of a model to guide future practice. Advances in Developing Human Resources. 2014;**16**(2):184-201

[19] Ellinger AD, Hamlin RG, Beattie RS. Coaching in the HRD context. In: Bachkirova T, Spence G, Drake D, editors. The SAGE Handbook of Coaching. London: SAGE; 2016

[20] Schein E. Organisation Culture and Leadership. 5th ed. San Francisco, CA: Jossey Bass; 2017

[21] McCarthy G, Milner J. Managerial coaching: Challenges, opportunities and training. Journal of Management Development. 2013;**32**(7):768-779

[22] Bartlett CA, Ghoshal S. Building competitive advantage through people. Sloan Management Review. 2002;**43**(2):32-74

[23] Ellinger AD, Ellinger AE, Keller SB. Supervisory coaching behavior, employee satisfaction, and warehouse employee performance: A dyadic perspective in the distribution industry. Human Resource Development Quarterly. 2003;**14**(4):435-458

[24] Slåtten T, Svensson G, Sværi S. Service quality and turnover intentions as perceived by employees: Antecedents and consequences. Personnel Review. 2011;**40**(2):205-221

[25] Hannah C. Improving intermediate skills through workplace coaching: A case study within the UK rail industry. International Journal of Evidence Based Coaching and Mentoring. 2004;**2**(1):17-45

[26] Weller K, Weller D. Coaching and performance: Substantiating the link. LIA. 2004;**24**(2):20-21

[27] Hawkins P, Smith N. Coaching, Mentoring and Organisational Consultancy: Supervision and Development. Maidenhead: Open University Press; 2006

[28] Bennet JL. An agenda for coaching-related research: A challenge for researchers. Consulting Psychology Journal: Practice and Research. 2006;**58**(4):240-249

[29] Hagen M. Managerial coaching. A review of the literature. Performance Improvement Quarterly. 2012;**24**(4):17-39

[30] Feldman DC, Lankau MJ. Executive coaching: A review and agenda for future research. Journal of Management. 2005;**31**(6):829-848

[31] Baek-Kyoo BJ. Executive coaching: A conceptual framework from an integrative review of practice and research. Human Resource Development Review. 2005;**4**(4):462-488

[32] Boyatzis RE. Core competencies in coaching others to overcome dysfunctional heavier. In: Druskat V, Mount G, Sala F, editors. Emotional Intelligence and Work Performance. Location: Publisher; 2002

[33] Boyatzis RE. An overview of intentional change from a complexity

perspective. Journal of Management Development. 2006;**25**(7):607-623

[34] Boyatzis RE, McKee A. Intentional change. Journal of Organizational Excellence. 2006;**25**(3):49-60

[35] Boyatzis RE. Developing emotional intelligence. In: Cherniss C, Boyatzis RE, Elias M, editors. Developments in Emotional Intelligence. San Francisco: Jessey-Bass; 2000

[36] Boyatzis RE. Leadership development from a complexity perspective. Consulting Psychology Journal: Practice and Research. 2008;**60**(4):298-313

[37] Boyatzis RE. Developing emotional intelligence competencies. In: Ciarrochi J, Mayer JD, editors. Applying Emotional Intelligence: A Practitioner's Guide. Psychology Press; 2007. pp. 28-52. DOI: 10.4324/9781315782935

[38] Boyatzis RE. How and why individuals are able to develop emotional intelligence. In: Cherniss C, Goleman D, editors. The Emotionally Intelligent Workplace. San Francisco, CA: Jossey-Bass; 2001. pp. 234-253

[39] Goleman D, Boyatzis RE, KcKee A. The emotional reality of teams. Journal of Organizational Excellence. 2002;**21**(2):55-65

[40] Boyatzis RE, Cavanagh KV. Leading change: Developing emotional, social, and cognitive competencies in managers during an MBA program. In: Keefer KV, Parker JDA, Saklofske DH, editors. Emotional Intelligence in Education. The Springer Series on Human Exceptionality. Cham: Springer; 2018. pp. 403-426. DOI: 10.1007/978-3-319-90633-1_15

[41] Illeris K. Transformative learning in the perspective of a comprehensive learning theory. Journal of Transformative Education. 2004;**2**:79-89

[42] Ely K, Boyce LA, Nelson JK, Zaccaro SJ, Hernez-Broome G, Whyman W. Evaluating leadership coaching: A review and integrated framework. The Leadership Quarterly. 2010;**21**:585-599

[43] Griffiths KE, Campbell MA. Discovering, applying and integrating: The process of learning in coaching. International Journal of Evidence-Based Coaching and Mentoring. 2009;**7**(2):16-30

[44] Bluckert P. Critical factors in executive coaching—The coaching relationship. Industrial and Commercial Training. 2005;**37**(7):336-340

[45] Griffiths KE. Personal coaching. A model for effective learning Journal of Learning Design. 2006;**1**(2) 55-65

[46] Boyatzis RE, Smith ML, Blaize N. Developing leaders through coaching and compassion. Academy of Management Learning and Education. 2006;**5**(1):8-24

[47] Boyatzis RE, Smith ML, Beveridge AJ. Coaching with compassion: Inspiring health, well-being, and development in organizations. The Journal of Applied Behavioral Science. 2013;**49**(2):153-178

[48] Passmore J, Lai Y-L. Coaching psychology: Exploring definitions and research contribution to practice? International Coaching Psychology Review. 2019;**14**:69-83

[49] Lawrence P. Managerial coaching—A literature review. International Journal of Evidence Based Coaching and Mentoring. 2017;**15**(2):43-69

[50] Patton MQ. Qualitative Research & Evaluation Methods. 4th ed. Thousand Oaks, California: SAGE; 2015

[51] Braun V, Clarke V. Using thematic analysis in psychology. Qualitative Research in Psychology. 2006;**3**(2):77-101

[52] Moen F, Skaalvik E. The effect of executive coaching on performance psychology. International Journal of Evidence Based Coaching and Mentoring. 2009;**7**(2):31-49

[53] Boyatzis RE, Akrivou K. The ideal self as the driver of intentional change. Journal of Management Development. 2006;**25**(7):624-642

[54] Ibarra H. Identity transitions: Possible selves, liminality and the dynamics of career change. INSEAD Faculty and Research Working Paper. 2007:1-57. Available from: https://sites.insead.edu/facultyresearch/research/doc.cfm?did=2720

[55] Van Oosten E. Intentional change theory at the organizational level: A case study. Journal of Management Development. 2006;**25**(7):707-717

[56] Van Rooj DL, Alonso A, Viswesvaran C. Group differences in emotional intelligence scores: Theoretical and practical implications. Personality and Individual Differences. 2005;**38**(3):689-700

[57] Dweck CS. Mindset: The Psychology of Success. New York, NY: Random House; 2006

[58] Wood B, Gordon S. Linking MBA learning and leadership coaching. International Coaching Psychology Review. 2009;**4**(1):87-104

[59] Hoang HT, Ho NTT, Nguyen N. The influence of leadership commitment to service quality on hotel employees' brand citizenship behavior: A mediation and moderation analysis. Journal of Hospitality Marketing & Management. 2022;**31**(3):369-395

Chapter 10

What Offshore Sailing Captains Teach Us about Leadership

Lee Ann Avery

Abstract

This qualitative and exploratory study examines how leadership is demonstrated in the context of offshore sailing through the sea stories of sailing captains' experiences where there was potential for massive physical, psychological, or material consequences to the crew and/or the boat. The analysis of their stories shows that offshore sailing captains demonstrate the characteristics of *in extremis* leaders, consistent with prior research, which include inherent and intrinsic motivation, effective sense-making and sense giving during the extreme event, and developing a collaborative team without hierarchy built on trust engendered from demonstrating competence and confidence. The study also revealed a model of how these captains demonstrate dynamic system leadership through continuous learning and acting which prepares the captains to prevent or minimize the effects of the extreme situations they encounter at sea. Through their self-development, technical skills, emotional intelligence, planning and preparation, team management, and constant scanning of the environment they build situation awareness for quick risk assessment and decision-making in moments of *in extremis*. The captain's goal at all times is to keep the crew and the boat safe, both physically and psychologically, through normal conditions and during *in extremis* events, using appropriate decisions and actions, and always remaining calm.

Keywords: leadership, *In extremis* leadership, situation awareness, emotional intelligence, decision-making

1. Introduction

This research examines an exceptional set of leaders I discovered during an offshore sailing trip from Newport, Rhode Island to Bermuda and on to St Martin in 2001. I considered these leaders worthy of research because many of them saw their crews safely through a Force 10 gale with dangerous winds of 50 miles per hour and up to 30-foot waves. They managed the boat, the crew, and the conditions in such a way that the crew felt safe and had a life-affirming experience despite the terror of the conditions. I felt that if these leaders could successfully lead through these conditions with a positive outcome, they would have lessons to teach other leaders who are trying to deal with increasingly complex environments and systems in a world that is increasingly volatile, uncertain, complex and ambiguous. I wanted to know how they developed their leadership to this level, and the actions and behaviors they used to lead their crews. During my research period, covid hit and many businesses were not prepared for this major change in our world. Those that adapted were able to survive, and some to flourish, while others fell by the wayside. If these captains can handle the always changing ocean, failures of the boat systems, extreme weather, and often inexperienced crew, they have a lot we can draw from to always look forward, adapt to conditions, and prepare for the worst possibilities that now seem to be more probable.

2. *In extremis* leadership as an initial theoretical framework

As I began to prepare this research, I was looking for a leadership concept that might fit these leaders as a starting point. I discovered *In extremis* leadership through Thomas Kolditz' book based on his research at WestPoint with Army soldiers and their elite parachuting team [1]. In his thought on future research, he listed offshore sailing captains as potential *in extremis* leaders. This concept of *in extremis* leadership was further expanded on by Sean Hannah et al. in 2009 by developing a conceptual framework for *in extremis* leadership, and in 2010 by advancing a research agenda for studying *in extremis* leadership. *In extremis* leadership is leading as if your life depends on it. *In extremis* events and environments are those where the potential for serious risk of damage to life and property, even death, are possible [2]. These events create unique constraints, contingencies, and causations making these situations inherently contextualized with leadership where leadership actions can either improve or intensify the danger. More than a crisis, *in extremis* threats may reach an intolerable level where goals of life and safety are not just a high priority, but imperative; and, where the trust → performance linkage between leaders and followers is essential. Hannah et al. [3] have suggested that research needs to investigate *in extremis* leadership from a multi-level approach recognizing that leadership is a dynamic system of complex social interactions within the system, and between the system and its environment.

I propose that the leadership character and actions required in this pressurized *in extremis* system can teach us how leaders should act because in many ways our current world has become an *in extremis* environment. Pandemics, ground wars in Europe, climate instability, and economic hardship globally should wake us up to pay attention to how we behave in organizations. Laying people off and failing in business have serious consequences to peoples' lives, and the Great Resignation has shown us that people do not want to participate in unhealthy organizations with poor management and toxic cultures [4].

Some of the main characteristics of *in extremis* leaders based on current research are [1–3] as follows. The ability to sense make in the midst of extreme events may be one of the most critical characteristics because most extreme events are unique, ill-defined, and emergent, and the leader must help the team make meaning out of complex, traumatic, and ever-changing danger. Inherent and intrinsic motivation drive these leaders to take responsibility and find a way in any situation to achieve the best possible outcome. Trust is one of the critical factors in leader-follower relationships and in certain *in extremis* situations trust may not be optional, and without it, a leader's influence may be nil. Trust is built on demonstrated competence and confidence to the point where followers are willing to put their lives in his/her hands. There is no hierarchy. The leader builds comradery and cohesion through an understanding that "we are all in this together". They are clear in their communication and assigning of roles and tasks, and will take command when the situation is urgent based on their expertise and trust rather than ego or authority.

I believed the sailing captains I was studying demonstrated these behaviors, so my research questions were: Do these offshore sailing captains demonstrate *in extremis* leadership? And, what more can they teach us about *in extremis* leadership and other aspects of leadership?

3. Methodology

Because I wanted to understand all that I could about the sailing captains, I used an exploratory approach to my research soliciting their sea stories through a semi-structured interview process in which I asked them to tell me stories of when they had gone through *in extremis* events beginning from the preparation for the trip through to the successful outcome. Because the captains downplayed the extremity of the events that they had experienced, I probed with questions such as "Tell me about the worst storm you went through", "What was your worst experience with a crew member?", "Was there ever a time that you feared for your life?" Additional probing questions were used to guide them through the timeline of the story as well as demographic information to understand their background and how they entered their sailing careers.

Although I solicited for captains from several on-line professional captains' directories and organizations, my sample was mainly a sample of convenience from Offshore Sailing Opportunities, with additional captains added from their suggestions. I especially requested their suggestions for younger captains, as my initial sample was skewed toward the more mature captains. The maturity of the sample was intentional and appropriate as I wanted to study good captains and good leadership. The younger captains were added to give me a sense of whether the same leadership qualities also carried into the younger generations.

The Zoom interviews lasted between one and 2 hours and were recorded and then transcribed. The transcribed interviews were open-coded with descriptions and categories developed as I progressed in keeping with this exploratory research. I used QDA Miner to code and analyze the interviews, and to develop main themes and categories. My initial analysis was comparing my results to the *in extremis* literature. My subsequent analysis was to discover what other literature also pertained and to see if there was an overall story that the data was telling me.

4. The sailing captains

I interviewed 18 sailing captains, three of whom were female. The ages ranged from 35 to 73, with the average age being 58½. Half of the sample is married, four were divorced, and five never married. The geographic dispersion was concentrated on the East Coast of the United States from Florida to Maine with pockets in the sailing communities of Newport, Rhode Island and Annapolis, Maryland. Also included were interviews from Sweden, New Zealand, and South Africa where captains were on their travels or at part-time residences. Most of the sample was American, although three of the captains had been born in Australia or the UK.

I had sailed with about half of these captains before, and several had been part of the trip to St Martin where we encountered the Force 10 gale just north of Bermuda which inspired this research. One of the unique aspects of these captains was that most of them had sailed with crew members that they had just met or who had paid to be on the trip. This created a need to develop instant trust and rapport. It also further pressurized the system as they headed offshore, some for the first time. Another interesting aspect of these captains was that many of them did not believe they had stories to tell that would fit the *in extremis* definition. On probing further, they were able to tell stories which included cyclones and hurricanes (7 incidences), unpredicted serious weather (6), very high winds over 35 mph (13), high waves up to 35 feet with the occasional higher one, or confused seas (11), Gulf Stream and heavy currents with contrary winds (8), and large mammals (3). These conditions can result in taking on water (6), knock downs (5) when the boat tips over sideways and the mast hits the water, and torn sails (2). As opposed to high winds, you can also be becalmed and go nowhere or drift backwards for days. Captain Murray actually drifted back 16 miles in 1 day. In addition, there are other ships and man-made obstacles such as buoys and windmills that can be hit or be near misses (11). Boats are fallible, and these captains encountered problems due to bad boat design and unfamiliar layout (10), major equipment or boat failures (32), engine problems and failures (9), loss of electricity and electronic instruments including communications (4), and fires on board (2). As Captain AJ remarked, it's not a vacation and there is no PAUSE button.

Captain Mary said, "it's like childbirth, you suffer and then it's over and the rest is beautiful." She also believes that everyone has a different tolerance for terror. Three of the captains accounted for this lack of immediate memory of *in extremis* events as more of a normalization process. Over their career, situations that were difficult or extreme when they first started out as a captain, and which they handled adequately, were not as difficult when encountered later in their career, and might even seem tame in retrospect.

Based on the above findings, the sailing captains I interviewed qualified for leading in an *in extremis* environment. The potential for serious environmental, boat, and crew risks identified provided a lens for studying leadership in a dynamic system with these captains where mistakes or miscalculations could result in consequences ranging from an uncomfortable trip to a life-threatening disaster. My findings also compared favorably with pervious findings related to *in extremis* leaders, including the attributes listed above and exhibited in the detailed findings outlined below. Captain Adam explained the attitudes that make some captains unsuccessful *in extremis* leaders:

> *I've worked with some particular ones [captains] who were really, really good [sailors], but God, they're fucking just shitty leaders. You know, they don't know how to work with people: they don't know how to bring a crew together. They just don't have this sense of "Hey, we're all here together. We're all here for each other."*

More than experience or skill, Captain Adam says that someone who "just kind of naturally wears the weight well is easier to follow than somebody skilled and maybe has more experience, ... but just doesn't have that sense of like, yeah, I'll go into battle with you." On the sea, it is all up to these captains. The crew is dependent on them for a safe trip. The captains, like any *in extremis* leader, cannot hide behind layers of bureaucracy or policy manuals. Their competence and authenticity are entirely exposed through *in extremis* events.

The lesson for leadership in general is to promote into potential leadership roles people who have a natural sense of command and a high tolerance for the risky and unknown. Find those who can take their previous experience in difficult situations and learn from them, and normalize them into their way of sensemaking and sense giving in every situation so that the outcome is favorable for the whole team and organization.

5. The sailing captains' dynamic system of leadership

In addition to finding that the sailing captains exhibited previously researched and identified attributes of *in extremis* leadership, I found a picture of how these captains participated in an iterative system of learning and development, supported by their actions and experience, in this complex environment. **Figure 1** provides an overview of the complexity involved in any offshore sailing trip. This is the system that these captains operate in. The model I derived from the sailing captains' stories of dynamic system leadership (**Figure 2**) shows the process by which the sea captains develop themselves and manage this complex undertaking.

In extreme situations, it has been shown that followers want someone who they trust because of their competence and integrity to take charge and be decisive with swift action. Recent research shows that a "both-and" approach to leadership in the complex demands and paradoxical situations of today is perceived as most effective balancing the times for participative versus decisive behavior [5]. During times outside of crisis, these captains like to collect input, share information and consult, and empower and challenge the crew to take responsibility (6). When an extreme event occurs, they transition from teacher and collaborator to leader and commander in a way that inspires confidence and cooperation. As a personally responsible leader (8), they are able to take command and make swift decisions because they are in tune with the boat and all its systems and people (25). They are a fully integrated part of the system and have a natural leadership and command presence. They are comfortable in their authority (15). They know that they are the captain, and the best person for the job (7).

This model represents a dynamic system of learning and leadership action reflecting how these captains live as leaders as seen from a high level and holistic

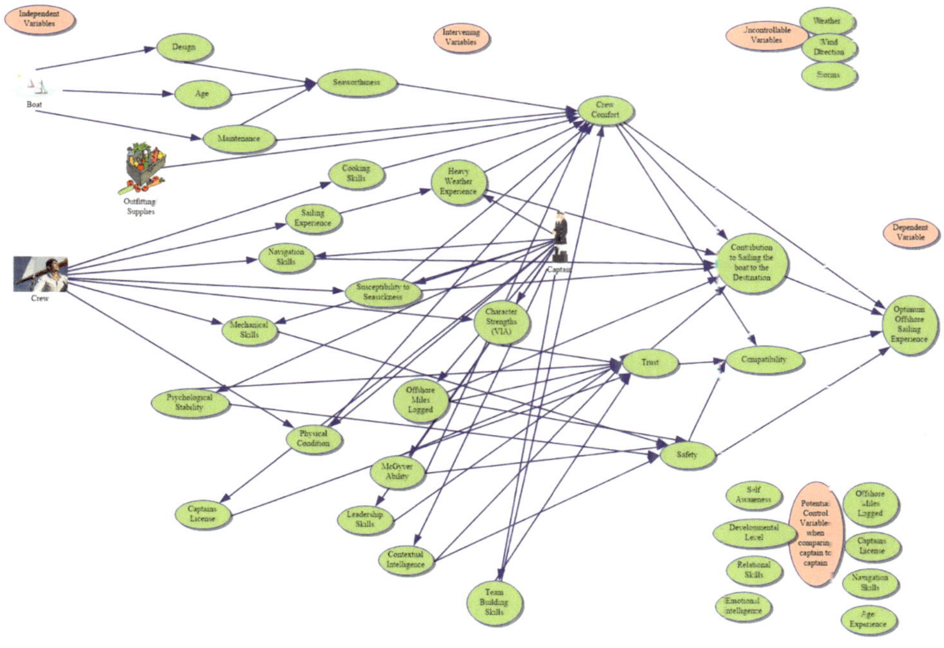

Figure 1.
The complex dynamic system of an offshore sailing trip.

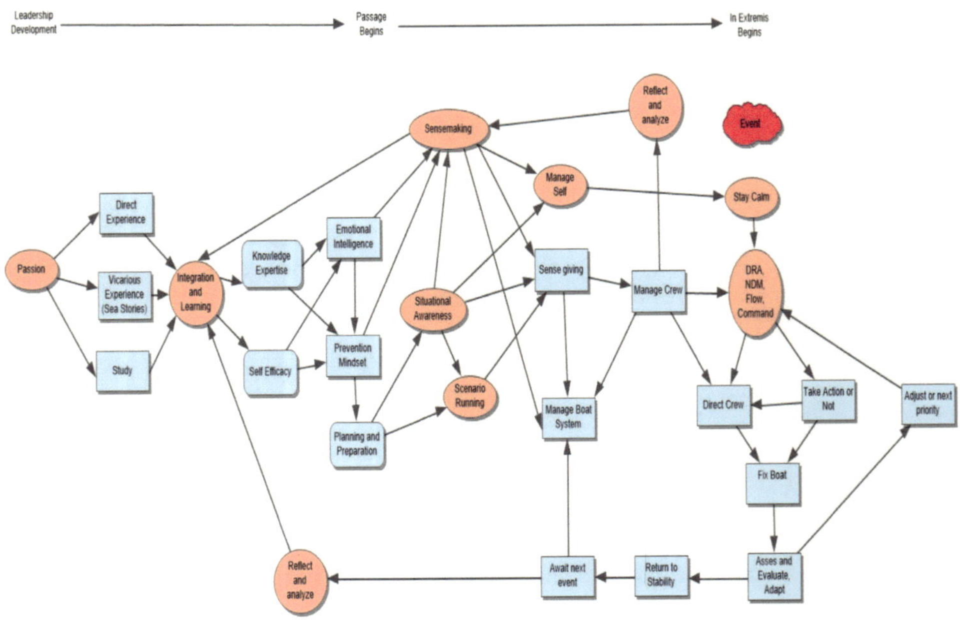

Figure 2.
Dynamic system leadership of sailing captains.

perspective. It is a leader-centric model focusing on how the sea captains develop themselves into reliable captains that their ever-changing crew can trust to keep them safe. It is a model of personal responsibility for their leadership development. My preferred definition of leadership includes the requirement that followers be willing to follow them during tough situations. On the leader's part, this requires them to develop those qualities that will result in followers trusting their competence and care for their safety as their captain.

There are three major components of the model roughly reflecting learning and development, the dynamics of the stable offshore passage, and the extreme event dynamics. The system is complete or closed in that all of the activities also circle back and contribute to learning and development in a continuous feedback loop and learning process. Key skills or talents are highlighted in each component (blue boxes), and internal cognitive processes (pink ovals) show how they are integrated or brought together. Because the real-world dynamics of what happens in offshore passages are so complex, this model only represents a sliver of all of the possibilities reinforcing that leadership is a complex, diverse, emergent, ever-changing relational process. The model, therefore, just represents a two-dimensional attempt to represent a segment of this complexity and provide one layer of understanding.

6. What happens before an offshore trip

The world we live in is a dynamic system. The world of offshore sailing that these captains operate in is a dynamic system. One might say that the captains' system is a limited one because it is just sailing offshore with only a few people at a time for a week or so. That is true, but it is a highly compressed system, and the captains have maximized the way that they lead and deal with their *in extremis* environment. In the world of *in extremis*, failure to anticipate, address, and conquer problems as they arise can lead to death of oneself and others. The ability to cope with and manage crises and extreme events does not happen in the moment, at least not very often without divine intervention. There is a significant buildup to that moment, a lifelong buildup that prepares one to become an *in extremis* leader. That development appears to be wholly self-instigated and matured as these captains recognized an internal call to be a captain, and recognized their natural ease with command. They took the responsibility to learn as much as possible and to keep learning everything that would help them take care of their followers and accomplish the mission of bringing them back safely.

The careers of these sea captains is built on their passion for the sea, being a captain, and helping others experience the joy they have in what they do. Captain AJ expressed the wonder he feels:

> *But it is adventurous, and boy it is beautiful. ...You'd see stuff that nobody sees. You know, the night times, I've seen so many, I can't even tell you all the spectacular things I've seen at night. During the day, waves coming from nowhere, swirls, fishes, whales, stuff. You know, it's just crazy out there when you get out in the middle. Rainbows and quick thunder storms in the morning. It's just, you can't explain that to your friends.*

This passion is vital in driving a leader's growth, and resonates with the Third Factor/Winning Factor [6]. Peter Jensen has studied self-initiative toward learning and developing while working with Olympics coaches and athletes. He sees it as the third factor in the development of individual human beings that transcends culture, upbringing, and genetics. He has called this the winning factor, which is the role individuals choose to play in their development beyond nature and nurture. It is the factor of choice that determines what we become. Jensen uses the term "third factor" to talk about self-direction and the development of self-awareness and self-responsibility which encourages people to get passionate about developing themselves.

Life experiences and their response to them is critical in how a leader is formed and the kind of leaders they become [7]. These experiences need to be analyzed, reflected on, and incorporated into their self-construct as a leader so they can be drawn upon later. The captains spent time questioning and reflecting on their experiences (8). At least two had written books about their experiences which formalized their reflections and shared them with the rest of the world. What they learned was also put into practice at every opportunity (20); on the boats they command, running a sailing school, teaching at several large sailing schools, and coaching a university-level sailing team (11). Hands-on training was very important as a student and teacher (11).

In addition to passion as a motivator, becoming a great leader is largely a matter of conscious choice [8]. Many of the captains reported that they read and studied about sailing, sailing history, and seamanship (11). All of the interviewees requested a copy of the study when it was completed.

6.1 Development of self-efficacy

A leader's belief in their self-efficacy to perform well in a crisis is driven by many factors including prior and vicarious success experiences [9]. Bandura's [10] social learning model proposes that prior successful experiences (enacted experience), vicarious experience (modeling), persuasion, and emotional arousal all add to someone's self-efficacy for a particular task. Other forms of vicarious learning are running scenarios (13), a form of modeling, and hearing other people's sea stories (9), a form of embodied narrative sensemaking [11] which is an ongoing embodied process of interpretation of self and experience in which we cannot separate ourselves, our senses, our body, and emotions. They are the captain.

Crisis leader self-efficacy is also benefited by divergent thinking which is a key component of creative thought and flexibility in problem solving under various conditions, mainly in the generation of multiple alternative solutions [9]. The captains practiced critical thinking (12) as well as challenged others' unquestioned patterns of thinking (9), and challenged their crew to do the same (2). A lot of what they learned about leadership was through observation, evaluation, and emulation (7), another form of modeling. Sailing with other experienced sailors and captains (7) added to their direct and vicarious experience.

6.2 Mental and emotional resources

All of this initial and ongoing learning was integrated into their self-construct and provided them with self-efficacy for being a captain, as well as mastery of the skills of sailing and seamanship. It also provided them with the emotional intelligence with which to manage themselves (11) and their crew (39). It also developed a preventative mindset of leaving nothing to chance (18), which led to their many practices of thorough planning and preparation before each passage.

Dr. Tony Kern writes in his book, Blue Threat: To Err is Inhuman, "The world seems stable, so our situation awareness grows dull, and we lose our respect for things that can bite" [12]. He believes it is easier for us to address The Red Threat, which are external threats such as those found in an *in extremis* environment, than The Blue Threat which he used to collectively refer to the internal obstacles such as poor planning, inadequate communication, and other "human errors." He believes The Blue Threat is responsible for more failed outcomes than external factors, and the transition from complacency to catastrophe can occur in 20 seconds or less. Complacency creeps in through the illusion of control, overreliance on past experience, tolerance of errors that seem to have no consequences, apathy and loss of respect for the environment, compromised personal discipline and casual noncompliance, and normalization of deviance. There are clear examples of this happening in our world today. The awareness of The Blue Threat that these captains have experienced within themselves may be part of what has motivated their learning and development, the resulting preventative mindset (18), and the attitude that they leave nothing to chance (2).

Captain Adam's near-death experience, when his boat hit a wave and fell out from under him, taught him to never assume that you are safe, and always follow the safety protocols of wearing a life jacket and being attached to the boat by a harness and tether, especially when on watch alone. Captain AJ's comments show how seriously he takes The Blue Threat and safety:

> *Look at last year's --- Race. ... They were, in my opinion ... it was probably the most inexperienced group of people out on --- boats. You know, they really opened it up to, not inexperienced sailors, but inexperienced in ocean sailing. And, how many people didn't have life jackets? Every time I saw a video, and they're doing 20 knots at sea in open water, and nobody's wearing a life jacket? That's all new because, you know in the past couple years that never would have happened. And, it was just a mindset where, you know, until something, until Vesuvius blows again, people will forget about it.*

These captains know Mount Vesuvius will erupt again. They know that it is as irresponsible to ignore The Blue Threat, as it is to ignore The Red Threat, and they try to make their crews aware of their personal Blue Threat by challenging them. Captain Andy says, "One of my first questions to the crew is, 'What is going to keep you on the boat offshore?' And, inevitably, everybody answers, 'Oh, my life jacket and my tether.' And that answer's wrong. I say to them, 'What is going to keep you on the boat is you, and your ability to keep yourself on the boat.'" He emphasizes this because he knows that

> *The biggest emergency that I worry about, the two things that we cannot do, and this is how I've been training my skippers as we expand the business; the two sort of highest risk things that we have to prevent at all costs: number one is a man overboard situation. We just cannot allow that to happen. And, number two is an accidental gybe, because an accidental gybe can cause a man overboard or can bring down a mast. You know, those are two very high consequence things. If we avoid doing those two things, then we'll probably have a successful passage.*

6.3 Emotional intelligence

Many, many studies have researched emotional intelligence as a key component of good leadership, and show that emotion can serve rationality rather than interfere with it, as was first theorized. Emotional intelligence, as defined by Salovey et al. [13] is the ability to perceive and express emotions, and to understand and use them to foster personal growth. It is the ability to perceive, appraise, and express emotions accurately; the ability to access and generate feelings to facilitate thinking; the ability to understand emotionally laden information; and use emotion relevant knowledge to manage one's own emotions and the emotions of others. The intelligence in emotional intelligence is to use this ability to promote growth, well-being, and adaptive social relations.

Although not measured with a recognized instrument in this study, attributes of emotional intelligence were displayed by the captains in remaining calm and positive in dangerous situations (27) both to maintain their own emotional control (11), and because they knew that it would impact the emotional state of the crew. This showed a deep understanding of their responsibility to be a cogent decision maker as well as a touchstone for the crews' emotions. They admitted that they had often been afraid, but they had managed that fear (19) so that they did not show it to the crew, and remained calm and in control. The captains actively managed the attitudes of the crew (39) and saw that as one of their biggest responsibilities. They even downplayed the danger and risk to the crew (24) knowing nothing would be gained by fear. Captain Adam's quote reflects emotional intelligence as well as self-efficacy:

> *I] feel like it's a natural fit for me. And, I think that helps a lot of people when they come on the boat. They see the ease and confidence, and competence of the skipper, I think it helps the crew be better crew because then it's just one less thing we can be acrimonious about. I mean, if you're going offshore with somebody that you have some reservations about you're putting energy into your reservations and you're questioning your guy, you're not putting your energy into, let's say prep. So managing the boat, and managing the crew, then managing yourself and being aware of your situation, and spatial awareness and situational awareness, and weather and learning, and all that. Because all of that doesn't matter if the one person in charge of the group you have doubts about.*

All of these experiences and learning have instilled in these captains the knowledge that the most important work they do is before the trip starts, which is discussed next.

6.4 Planning and prevention mindset

The key to any safe passage is planning and prevention. As most of the captains stated, they have two goals for a passage: Get the crew there in one piece and get the boat there in one piece. As Captain Andy puts it, "it's ironic that you want to hear people's sea stories, when my whole motivations are, how do we prevent having those kinds of sea stories in the first place."

Eighteen times having a preventative mindset was mentioned, and 19 times it was mentioned that the captains plan to avoid potential dangers and problems. Planning to avoid risks, in particular, waiting for a good weather window was mentioned 16 times. Practicing good seamanship was also often brought up (16). Seamanship is the code and practice of excellence for all mariners and includes all the aspects of boating. As Oxford defines it, it is the skill, techniques, or practice of handling a ship or boat at sea. It is the bible or operators' manual for all mariners. Many of the captains mentioned good seamanship as being essential to being a good captain (12). Two key components of good seamanship and prevention are preparation before the trip and situation awareness during the trip.

The prevention of extreme events was a pervasive theme in every captain's modus operandi and was particularly important in the planning and preparation before the trip. As Captain Andy puts it, preparation is 99% of the work we do in getting the boats ready, which the crew never sees; "The passage itself is the execution. If you've done all the preparation, the execution's the easy part." Those that run their business from their own boats, or are fulltime paid captains on sailboats, have total control over the preparation of the boats before a passage. However, delivery skippers often see the boats they will deliver for the first time just before the trip. Several of the captains (3) told stories of turning down boats because of missing safety equipment or the unsafe condition of the boat.

The inspection, attention to, and care of essential equipment on the boat were mentioned 16 times by the captains. Bringing spare parts, additional safety equipment, and provisioning fuel and food based on a worst-case scenario, was also brought up 14 times. The captains (3) have their own essential kits that they bring on board with them including sea anchors (used to hold the boat steady against the waves in a storm), GPS, radios, satellite (sat) phones, and so forth. One captain even brings a spare pump with him in case they take on water. Captain Murray had brought a substantial wooden plug with him on the way back from Japan to Australia, and it became essential when the boat sprung a significant leak after a patchwork, glued-on piece of the hull was blown out by a wave. Loading the boat properly for balance, but also in reverse order of need, was also mentioned as well as lashing and stowing everything so that objects will not be flying around or go overboard when the boat starts flailing in bad weather (2).

Several captains (4) talked about having checklists for many different aspects of the trip just to get everything they need to remember out of their heads and onto paper so that nothing is overlooked. The captains have a set of practices and mantras that also help them keep safety at the forefront, and they emphasize to the crew how important it is to pay attention to safety. Many of the captains mentioned constantly running scenarios in their minds of what could happen and how they would deal with it (13), and one also uses "what-if" scenarios to get the crew engaged in the joint responsibility of keeping everybody and the boat safe. They also mentioned contingency plans (7), and several have written emergency protocols (2) that they post near the navigation station next to the watch schedule. Taking care of the small things before they become big things (9), and getting control of and containing problems as soon as possible (17) are also cardinal rules. They have seen how small things, like a missing stopper knot (a knot at the end of a line that prevents the line from going through a hole) can cascade into really bad situations when that line goes overboard, gets caught in the propeller, and disables the boat.

One of the essential practices, especially since many of these captains sail with a relatively inexperienced crew, is Wake the Captain (15). This is stressed over and over because the captain has to be quick to handle any emergent situation. So, they ask to be woken up if anything changes, if the crew sees something unusual, or if they just do not know--wake the captain. This is critical because the captain cannot handle a situation about which they are unaware. Captain Murray mentioned being woken up 17 times on one trip by a woman who was just learning about sailing offshore. When she apologized at the end of the trip for waking him up so much, he told her he had never felt safer and more comfortable sleeping because he knew she would wake him up if there were a problem. Sleeping is essential on any long voyage, and captains know that they may be up for days if there is a significant situation or storm. Many have learned to reserve themselves for those emergencies so they can always be ready and have clear judgment when events happen (5), and by not standing a regular watch so they can be awake and available to all watches.

Communication is a key component of prevention. Several captains have regularly scheduled crew meetings en route to keep everybody informed of the current weather situation, the boat's course and sail plan, and to keep everybody on the same page, "because information shared is power" and people can react correctly and quickly if they are fully informed. Captain Dave cooks dinner each day and has a crew meeting over dinner. Captain Kelsey uses group communication meetings to have people share what they think is going well and what could be improved directly with the person next to them, and even orchestrates these meetings to address and resolve crew interaction problems.

Constant monitoring of the weather is essential for captains and is much easier these days with satellite phones and laptops and more marine weather available online. The captains mentioned being prepared for weather upfront (8), and also mentioned that they are much more conservative now and more quickly go to reduced sail area to keep the boat under control (13) to prevent damage and be a more comfortable ride for the crew. Slowing the boat down (5), or heaving-to (6) to stop the boat by back-winding the sails and setting the rudder in the opposite position causing the boat to drift in place, allows them to wait out serious wind and waves and has become more of a ready option. Captain Murray has been reported to heave-to and cook dinner in 70 knots of wind. Captain Richard has gotten into the routine of prepping and rigging the storm sails before any trip, even if no bad weather is expected, because he does not want to leave anything to chance.

This derived model of dynamic system leadership of sea captains' documents that intentional and purposeful self-development toward mastery, through various and many methods of learning, builds self-construct and self-efficacy. This is the foundation on which these captains practice dynamic leadership of the complex system outlined in **Figure 1**. Their complex self-construct and self-efficacy enable them to manage the system and the crew through more normal times and also rise to the occasion to see everyone safely through *in extremis* events.

As stated before, this derived model is simplistic when compared to the actual complexity of managing any human system in an extreme environment or our VUCA (volatile, uncertain, complex, and ambiguous) world. However, it attempts to show a long-term, longitudinal, and high-level view of some of the components and aspects that contribute to how these leaders develop into successful offshore sailing captains. The model represents a system of continuous learning and acting that reflects the captains' lived experience, as told in their sea stories.

There are several key lessons for leadership in general we can take from this analysis. Anticipate all possible situations and problems and develop plans to deal with them including having the right equipment and backups readily available. Inform and prepare your team for future possibilities including soliciting additional scenarios from them. Prevent or minimize the consequences of potential future events by setting up systems to deal with them and ways of adapting as events unfold. A covid lesson as well. Keep everybody informed and participating in all aspects of the organization so that they can be aware of the goals, know what actions to take in many cases, and be prepared to follow commands when urgency requires it. Build trust, communication, and cohesion when things are stable so they are accessible when things get rough.

6.5 Situation awareness and scenario running

After you have anticipated and prepared for as many potential risks and situations as you can, you then need to monitor the environment for the current situation and to anticipate as things may be changing. Captains are constantly vigilant and always scanning for information and changes in the environment (17) and assessing their whole system (11). They are trying to spot emerging signals (7) and anticipate what is ahead and what could happen (17). They know where everybody is and what they are doing (4). While they were racing one Thursday evening, Captain Hank's wife said to him, "It doesn't matter how many people you have on-board, and how much you drink, you always know where everybody is and what's going to happen, you know, when you tack or gybe." Captain Mary believes that skill is hardwired in her, maybe from being a mother. Captain Niles says, "You can never let your guard down. That's it, that's it. You can never let your guard down. And I actually never do. I'm kind of always, you know, was it my daughter called me a meerkat because I'm always sticking my head up and looking around."

The captains' situation awareness is aided by being in complete tune with the boat and the whole system (26). The captains say they sleep with one eye open (6), and Captain Dave reported even hearing a pin drop:

> *The biggest failure we had on the boat, I think, was the main sail outhaul shackle pin dropped out and fell on the deck, which interestingly enough, when the pin hit the deck it was right over my head while I was in the aft cabin sleeping. And the person on watch didn't hear it, and it woke me up from a sound sleep.*

The continuous learning and awareness include recognizing the physical and mental states of the crew and helping them manage their health and even their fears by giving them a job or focusing them on a task, even if it is meaningless, like pumping water to nowhere (Captain Kelsey). The wisdom of the captains was demonstrated by the ease with which they discussed their mistakes and what they had learned from them (35). When asked when they knew they were "a sailor," two of these longtime skippers said they were still not there.

7. Managing the routine part of the passage

Once a passage begins, the captain is sensemaking continuously first by evaluating his or her crew (10) as resources, continually scanning the environment and the boat system to gain and keep situation awareness (21), and running scenarios through their mind of all possibilities that could happen (13). A key part of that sensemaking is the crew's mental and emotional health. Captain Hank describes the process of managing the crew, and how he uses his emotional intelligence throughout the trip:

> *Well, one of the big things you can control is just your attitude about it and how you treat other people. You see how easily it could spiral out of control, and when there is an issue going on and all of a sudden, the people aren't getting together, you know, to work on an outcome. So, you know, certainly you've got to hold yourself or watch yourself when stupid things happen, that you don't get into the blaming thing, and you just deal with what you've got and get through it. So, that's really all you can control after things start going bad, is just your attitude, and how you keep the crew together as opposed to letting things fall apart. So, that's really all you've got there, all you've got control of. The biggest one is really just don't ask anybody to do something that you wouldn't do. I've found just by jumping in or getting things started, it's how you get things done rather than delegating so much. I've seen the skippers that do just kind of stand there and point and tell, and that might work for some people, but I've found that usually jumping in and then doing it, and then having people work along with you towards the common goal is my better way of doing things, rather than just delegating all the time. And, I think people appreciate that too.*

Captain Nick also finds a way of including even the non-functioning members of the crew to keep them emotionally part of the team:

> *But that's really what it's about. It's taking in what's there--your resources. Certainly, keeping your own cool to manage them, because that's your crew. And, of course we do all of these things with no professional crew, just OPO people, they're just people. Even professional crew is just people. It's more observation. ... It starts there managing and learning about people ... who's gonna be an asset and who's not and when I take newbies... I take newbies that are eager, able-bodied newbies that want to learn. ... So, you build your crew from there ... And, you look at people, especially if you're stuck in port for a day or two, and see if they're resourceful, see if they pitch in, see how well they get along with other people, and you just build your own thing. But everybody has assets, and you have to learn how to use them. And, it makes them fulfilled as well.*

During the passage, the captains focused on managing their crew, taking care of their well-being, compensating for their inexperience, managing those who were emotionally hijacked by the experience, and generally trying to make the trip as pleasant and meaningful as possible. They prepared the crew, kept everyone informed of what was going on, and tried to balance safety with allowing people to try things and learn. What enables them to do all that and keep things as normal as possible is their hyper-vigilance to maintain situation awareness, and their constant scenario running to prepare themselves to act automatically, or with automaticity, when extreme things happen.

For these sea captains, part of who they are is scanning and assessing their environment (17) looking for anything that will forewarn them of a coming problem (19), and performing a continuous risk assessment of the whole system (11). They are in tune with the whole boat system and the crew (26). Captain Patrick describes it:

> *So, just knowing the sounds and the roll and the rhythm, and the smashing of the waves ... I had a pretty good sense of what was happening topside, and especially with the voices. ... But, just the sounds from the crew, and the boat, everything sounded pretty well. ...Even on pleasant sailing days, you have to know where everybody is on the boat, and pretty much what they're doing, especially when they're topside. ... So, you're, you're always looking ahead for danger signals. That is situational awareness--making sure that nobody screws up that's going to hurt somebody else.*

The following are lessons I believe can be applied to all leadership. Always maintain situation awareness even when things seem calm or normal because there will be a storm or problem just over the horizon, and you need to train yourself to look ahead and recognize emerging patterns so you can anticipate how to handle them. During routine times, prepare your followers for what might be ahead. Enlist them in brainstorming possible events or changes to the environment and the business, and how to best adapt to any changes. Build your systems and business practices to be nimble and easily adjust to new business conditions. Always keep your followers in the loop on all that is happening in the business tactically and strategically so they can independently adjust their areas of responsibility to the course and keep the whole organization in alignment. Never fall behind in your housekeeping and maintenance tasks so there are no distractions or interference when you have to act urgently.

8. Evaluating, managing, and leading the crew

Crew reactions and actions can contribute to the difficulties captains have to manage, or they can provide real help and positivity. Captains report different ways that they assess their crews for physical fitness, sailing competency, and psychological stability. The captains that run sailing expeditions as a business send out questionnaires to their paying crew to find out what their fitness routines are, and if they can do basic things like getting up and down from sitting and crawling on all fours. Sailing resumes are often part of the selection of crew members, but many captains discount them for sailing experience on lakes or close to shore or sailing courses taken on weekends. Skype and phone interviews are also used to select the crew (4). Many captains would rather have someone steady and eager than "experienced" sailors because they principally need them to be able to follow direction and stand a watch.

Captain Murray claims that he can tell within 5 minutes if a crew member knows anything about sailing. In an emergency, most captains will handle problem solving, and just need a crew member to drive the boat or pump water. Their assessment/evaluation of the crew tells them whom they can rely on in those situations, and to what extent, both physically and for boat handling. The captains assess the crew through observation (6) particularly on the helm (steering wheel), asking questions (5), and boat handling exercises and drills (4), among other things.

8.1 Crew behavior and incidents

The reason that these captains do the above assessments is that they want to avoid some of the incidents that they reported in their sea stories. The majority of captains say that they have had good crews for the most part (12). They found some exceptional crew members that demonstrated competence and confidence (5), were cheerful, came up with ideas to solve problems (4), felt that they had a life-expanding experience (6), or had just gone to "graduate school" for offshore sailing (2). However, they also reported crew members with debilitating seasickness which made them unable to function (12) even though captains (5) reported stressing taking seasickness medicine before the trip. There were 11 incidents of crew members ignoring the captain's safety briefings and warnings and doing unsafe things. Other problem crew members were the racers, know-it-alls, idea men, instructors, and alpha dogs (11) whose egos interfered with their listening and learning from the captains. Fortunately, they were more annoying than dangerous in most cases.

More dangerous were the crew members who became belligerent, passive/aggressive, experienced extreme stress and freaked out or shut down (21), or thought they were going to die (4). Drugs and alcohol problems were minimally reported (3). The captains also feel it is their responsibility to monitor the crew for dehydration, proper eating, and sleeplessness and fatigue (9) so that they do not become ill during the trip. They see that as part of their role as caretaker or mother for the crew (13). In the middle, there were crew members who just became immune, adapted, or just accepted whatever happened, and even laughed after the tension was released (4).

There were also crew members whose behavior and mistakes could have had very serious consequences for the safety of the whole crew and the boat, including sleeping or inattentiveness at the helm when driving the boat resulting in near-miss collisions (4), and accidental gybes (when the main sail's heavy metal boom swings across the boat in an uncontrolled manner) which can severely damage the boat and injure the crew (7). The captains reported 11 cases where they had to restrain or contain a crew member including confining them to their cabin and in one case, having to physically restrain someone. Captain Richard reported, "And, as we lost sight of Monhegan, one of my crew guys went nuts. He attacked the helmsman. He wanted to go back. So, I tied him up because he was violent and put him in his bunk, and we went back to Monhegan, and I put him off the boat and said, 'How you get home, pal, is your problem. You're a threat to the boat.'"

Even though the captains have had to take quick and decisive action to protect themselves, the crew, and the boat, they are relatively sanguine about it. In some cases, the person has apologized. Still, the captains seem to understand that not everyone can handle "the wilderness," as Captain Mary calls it, recognizing that "most people have no desire to be out in the middle of the ocean with strangers on a boat." Captain Murray is still friends with someone who fell off his boat three times and had to be retrieved, even though he called him a "dickhead" and banned him from his boat. Several captains (3) mentioned blacklisting crew members that they would not want on their boats again for various reasons. Captain Reggie had to deal with a revolt: "So, when you have a revolt on board, the thing is then to confine those sectors, those people to their cabins, and not have them tampering with the crew. Or, like my master said on the mountain, so that they don't contaminate the rest of the group."

On the flip side, many captains also have Preferred Crew lists, and 13 captains reported sailing with repeat crew members who have sailed with them before, and 11 mentioned crew members that have become lifelong friends. Even one crew member had surreptitiously disobeyed the captain's orders and put more sail up just before a storm hit, resulting in a knockdown with people being thrown from their bunks. She eventually became a lifelong friend of Captain Murray. However, she had to be confined to her cabin for 3 days until he felt he could trust her again and that she had learned a serious lesson.

Dealing with difficult crew members in these tough and often dangerous situations requires a strong sense of command and responsibility toward the rest of the crew, and may be a critical aspect of *in extremis* leadership. It is also an important trait for any leader that they are willing to make the tough decisions and choices in dealing with problem team members in a way that deals directly with the individual and seems fair to the rest of the team so as not to taint them.

9. Managing the stable part of the passage

The captains are scanning the environment, developing situation awareness, and running scenarios as they are sailing under routine conditions enabling them to recognize an extreme situation as early as possible and be prepared for it. As Captain Adam explains,

> *I play that scenario in my head all the time when I'm on another boat, or I have different crew, or it's a different environment, or different weather conditions. And I usually run these worst-case scenarios constantly, day in and day out, 24/7, like running these scenarios through your brain. When bad things do happen, they're not as traumatic, because you've kind of already imagined it, or you're able to assimilate portions of different scenarios into the scenario that you're actually in. ... Or maybe, it's just mentally I'm more prepared. I'm better at being in that situation, so when the life-threatening event is happening, I'm not over reacting. I'm not reacting. I've anticipated it to a certain degree, and I'm able to pull out different skills from past experiences and I'm able to work through it because I've already been through it in my head.*

The transition from normal to extreme means the captain goes into command mode. When things are normal, the captain may be more of a teacher, caretaker, and manager/organizer. They know they are always responsible for the system, but they can be more collegial and participative (8) in managing the team and appear more easy-going. They have the time and inclination to try to help people learn by balancing correcting people constantly with letting small risks go and using them as teachable moments (3). It is a constant assessment of peoples' attitudes and their behaviors to detect anything that could threaten the crew or the boat. The captains have to manage the two together using their emotional intelligence, but also knowing that small things can cascade into big things if not controlled. Just forgetting to tie a knot at the end of a line caused a series of problems for Captain Hank resulting in the line going in the water and getting caught in the propeller and stopping the engine.

The captains always maintain a natural authority and command presence (9), but they react quickly to the unexpected (10) and take charge and command of situations (34).

9.1 Sensemaking during an *In extremis* event

Maitlis and Sonenschein [14] found that sensemaking in extreme events occurs when a new and unexpected variable comes into play in an otherwise steady state, and meaning has to be constructed that integrates it into one's thinking about what is happening [14]. Development of possible meanings requires looking at different aspects of the environment separately, and interpreting those aspects to previously understood frames of reference (mental models or schema). Sensemaking is about connecting new variables to previously understood frames to create a story of what's going on [14], The environmental cues are provided by the situation assessment and resulting situation awareness discussed above. Both sensemaking and situation awareness refer to mental models or frames which must be accessed to provide options for action. Enacted sensemaking is the process of taking actions that construct or change the environment and situation while trying to make sense of it. Commitment, capacity, and expectations are foundational concepts for sensemaking [14]. There is significant synergy between enacted sensemaking and Endsley's situation awareness model.

With the constant scenarios running in their mind, as Captain Adam mentioned above, when the real crisis happens, the captains seem to have an existing frame or schema that they can just insert the real variables into, and start to take actions while continuing their sensemaking. They are primed to make decisions and take action. It is a continuous iterative process in which the captains are characterized as getting control of the situation (mainly the boat and crew) and containing the problem as quickly as possible (17). They then investigate and trouble-shoot (11) to find possible solutions. Of equal importance is to know when doing something could be more dangerous than not doing anything (14), and when to make an initial decision and then evaluate and adjust (9).

Dixon et al. [15] found in their study of leadership *in extremis*, that sensemaking and sensegiving intensify when a leader is "in the zone" or "in the moment" which is a heightened state of mindfulness when the leader is immersed in giving and receiving signals [15]. There are examples of this in other sections of this study, but Captain Patrick sums it up nicely:

> *And it's like, well, you can only deal with one thing at a time, and yeah, you just slow down. You just slow down, and take one thing at a time, no matter what else is going on, because you just can't be side-tracked and get diverted with all these other problems. So, once you solve one problem, you can check that off the list, and now you go to the other one. And, uh, where you have three emergencies at one time, well, you pick the one you want to deal with and ignore the others. And, somehow, the other emergencies just kind of almost, kind of mark time in a way, at least in the situations I've been in. So, yeah, one at a time, and work your way through the list rather than rushing around, and trying to do things too quickly, that just always seemed counterproductive.*

Captain Kelsey describes her signal giving during those zone moments:

> *And, so that's like a coping mechanism, I think, for me to keep everybody else sane. Because they're scared and everything too.... On one hand, I'm very, I can be very serious if we need to do this, "OK you do this, you do this, you do this. We need to get this done. Let's move quickly." At times like that, I can be very serious.*

Captain Andy says, "Yeah, there's not enough time to think about it, so you're just doing. I mean, I've always, I believe that completely, that action always solves anxiety. And, I will say too, the more often we do this, the more comfortable I am with it." Captain Adam believes that the more often you encounter the same or similar problems and handle them successfully, the less you go into the zone and the more you just give commands from your experience more consciously. As incidents become normalized, the anxiety and adrenaline are not as high, so the need for the subconscious to kick in is lessened.

The dual process theory from the psychology literature shows how two decision systems work together allowing the decision maker to think both fast and slow when reasoning to address a problem [16]. What they describe as System 1 is intuitive, efficient, and based on pattern recognition and happens so fast that it may not even be recognized as a distinct cognitive process. This supports the heightened flow state mentioned above, and is very effective when time pressures require immediate action. System 2 is more of a cognitive analytical process that is more intensive and deliberate employing a conscious analytical approach. Which system is activated depends on prior experience and the ability to recognize a similar pattern and activate an existing mental model. The greater the experience and more mental models of patterns available, the more often System 1 will be used. The model oversimplifies the process in real-world practice where the decision maker more likely oscillates between the two systems. When time permits, decisions made with System 1 are often verified with System 2 logic. This dual system reflects how the captains described their decision-making process during extreme events, as getting things under control and contained (17), and then assessing what is next, which may even be to do nothing or wait (14) until conditions become safer if it is not urgent. When there is time, the captains do consciously evaluate and understand risks (12) before deciding on an action. They also store them as additional mental schema.

9.2 Decision-making in the *in extremis* event

Several other models and fields of research around decision-making seem to have relevance to the actions and decision-making of these captains during these extreme events. These areas of research may benefit from studying offshore sailing captains. Each of these models can help us understand what the captains have described as their decision-making and action-taking process when faced with extreme events.

Captain AJ had the most extreme story and discussed the decisions he had to make:

> *... there was like six of us [boats] hove-to, just because we couldn't--it was too rough to sail, too rough to motor, too rough to do anything but just hove-to. And, it just lasted so long. ... Man, that was a nasty trip. And then, we bailed, I ended up just making the decision. My closest land at that point was 700 miles away, which was Charleston. This tropical storm is turning into a hurricane, I'm taking this east wind, and I'm going to the closest land, which was Charleston. ... But, during that heave-to point, one of the crew members, you know, there was so much going on, he flipped. He stressed out, and he got violent. Never hit anybody, but screamed and hollered at me. I wouldn't take his advice. But, I'm the captain, and I'm the one with the experience. And, I'm sorry, you know, your suggestions aren't something I'm going to do. But he took it personally, and he got crazy. He wanted to climb the mast and fix the sail or something like that. This is while we're still hove to and it's blowing way too strong, way too dangerous right now. Yeah, we're losing time, but I wasn't about to haul somebody up in those conditions. So, you know how the boats bounce back and forth, he would have been flung all over the place. ...But, you know, I wouldn't let him go up, and he got pissed.*

Sometimes the captains have to make decisions on behalf of the crew for their own good (4), but they take responsibility for their decisions (10), and they are always willing to make a decision, get moving and then adjust (9), reassess and learn from decisions and mistakes (10), or reevaluate and be more conservative (10). In the moment, they cannot let their ego get involved or become attached to their decisions. They have to adapt and adjust as the dynamics of the situation change or a problem could turn into an *in extremis* event.

To really understand the stress and rapidity with which these captains have to deal, Captain Sara's story of almost sinking in Long Island Sound on a research/educational schooner with professional crew and college students on board, gives us a picture of how she enacted leadership in that moment:

> *Anyway, they [USCG] came out from Montauk, they came out with a helicopter, I think they had pumps on board from the helicopter and the boat, I can't remember, but anyway, they got pumps on board that were able to keep the water from overwhelming us. We still didn't know where it was coming in or what was going on. And at that point, by the time they showed up, I had already made the decision to make for land as quickly as humanly possible. I was just like ... if this ship is going down, I'm going to make sure it goes down in the shallowest water possible. That was all I could think of at that point. And, so we had the engine running full bore, and the sails drawing completely, heading downwind, straight for Greenport. I just wanted to get there as fast as possible. And so, we didn't slow down. And I think at one point the Coast Guard said "Don't you want to, like, take down your sails?" And I'm like, "No, no, I don't." And one of the reasons why I said "no" was that I didn't know what was going on under the waterline, and because of how our main is and how big it is and how heavy it is, to take the main down would have required us to do a 180, head back into the seas that we were running now from, keep punching into them and have every single person on board completely 100% focused on controlling that main boom as soon as the gaff started to come down. I mean, in heavy seas, bringing down that main sail is, it takes really, it takes a lot of people, and it takes, well, I wouldn't say tons of people, but it takes most of the crew and a whole lot of coordination. And you've really gotta know what you're doing. Because that main boom, once it starts, you know, it's no longer being controlled by the sail, it's being controlled by the sheet, and you're trying to take in on the sheet, and meanwhile the boat is going all over the place. So, you have this 65-foot-long huge boom flying back and forth across the deck. I didn't want to do that when the boat was trying to sink. You know, I just, I just thought "no, I don't wanna add that to what we're trying to do right now. It just doesn't make sense to me." So that was a decision I made. And we made it into Greenport with the pumps that the Coast Guard brought we were doing all right. So that, that was exciting.*

Captain Sara was able to make the decision and not be swayed from it, even by the Coast Guard, because she knew her boat, she knew her crew, and she focused on the most immediate important thing--keeping the boat from sinking and getting to shallow water for the boat and crew's safety. She maximized the potential of the boat. She also knew how to keep that focus:

> *There was at one point, when there was enough water in the engine room and we kept running the engine fully, because we were using it to help move us along, that there was so much water in the engine room that it was flying off the belts and hitting the electrical panel and just going everywhere. And so, somebody said, "Do you want to see that?" And, I'm like, "No, no I don't." [laughs] Yeah, I'm back in the aft cabin and I was on the radio constantly. And I wanted to keep the big picture, but, you know, I just made the decision that, no I did not really need to see that, I can picture it in my mind,*

> *and I do not want to get into a place where I look at something and start to get scared. I do not know if that was consciously going through my mind. I would have if I'd had to, but I said "No, I don't need to see that. I trust you to tell me what I need to know."*

9.3 Summary of the dynamic system leadership model

As the model of dynamic system leadership of sailing captains shows, everything that takes place in the more routine and the *in extremis* parts of an ocean passage is processed and added to the captains' self-construct and knowledge base so that it is a continuously learning system giving them new and greater resources for their next passage. Every aspect is connected to every other aspect in a complex system that happens in the minds of the captains. Their sea stories, and the analysis of their content, begin to unpack some of the complexity of *in extremis* leadership and leadership in general. It really is a "Yes, and ...." of what we have learned about leadership to date with significant cognitive and psychological aspects. It truly is complex and messy.

10. Summary and conclusion

The world we live in is a dynamic system. There is no stability, and we cannot afford to let The Blue Threat within lead to denial or complacency, especially people in positions of authority. In *in extremis* environments, the impact on life, and possible death, is much more obvious than in our corporate lives, and so it is taken seriously and provides an inherent motivation to leave nothing to chance (Captains Richard and AJ). These captains passionately love what they do, and that propels them to apply the Third Factor and purposely develop themselves into highly proficient sailors and captain/leaders so they can safely complete their mission to bring everyone home safely, preferably on the boat they left on. They do not look for bailout from the U.S. Coast Guard, except as a very last resort. They do not pass off their responsibilities to others. They are the captain, and know they are the best person for the job because they have made themselves so. They know that danger is always lurking out there, so they prepare and actively scan for it, and deal with it when it happens. They understand the complex system that they function in, and try to keep all the pieces functioning well together to keep their crew safe and give them the best experience possible.

All organizations would benefit from leaders that have a calling and strong sense of personal responsibility for their team, their organization, and their own learning and development toward fulfilling their responsibility safely and effectively protecting human dignity. The way the captains do this is reflected in this model of dynamic system leadership of sailing captains.

As Captain Adam said, someone may be an expert sailor, but it does not mean I would go into battle with them. These captains must be committed and able to be nimble and adaptable, and pay attention all the time, not just in times of crisis, because they know the crisis is coming. Their lives and their crews' lives depend on those qualities. These leaders are aware that crises are lurking out there as a natural part of their world. To keep their crew and their boat safe, offshore captains must pick up on the emergent signals, and constantly scan the horizon and the environment for those subtle changes in patterns that may be the beginning of a new trend or a danger warning. They make decisions without analysis paralysis or allowing fear to take control of themselves or their crew.

The complexity of our world does not allow a single person to know all the variables in play, all their interconnecting relationships, or all of the possible outcomes of a situation. We have to go with the wind, anticipate when the wind will change, and adjust our sails to stay on course while always preparing for and looking for the next storm.

Author details

Lee Ann Avery
Fairwinds Consulting, Seattle, WA, USA

*Address all correspondence to: fairwinds57@gmail.com

References

[1] Kolditz TA. *In Extremis* Leadership: Leading as if your Life Depended on it. Hoboken, NJ: Jossey-Bass; 2007

[2] Hannah ST, Avolio BJ, Uhl-Bien M, Cavaretta FI. A framework for examining leadership in extreme contexts: New York, NY. The Leadership Quarterly. 2009;**20**:897-919

[3] Hannah ST, Campbell DJ, Matthews MD. Advancing a research agenda for leadership in dangerous contexts. Military Psychology. 2010;**22**(1):157-189

[4] Sull D, Sull C, Zweig B. Toxic culture is driving the great resignation. MIT Sloan Management Review. 2022;**63**(2): 1-9. Epub Jan 11, 2022

[5] Aramovitch NP, Blankenship JR. The relative importance of participative versus decisive behavior in predicting stakeholder's perceptions of leader effectiveness. The Leadership Quarterly. 2020;**31**(5):101387. DOI: 10.1016/j.leaqua.2020.101387

[6] Jensen P. The Winning Factor: Inspire Gold-Medal Performance in your Employees. NY, NY: Amacom Publishing; 2012

[7] Daniels TG. The impact life experience has on leadership development [Dissertation]. Gardner-Webb University; 2019

[8] Collins J. Good to Great. New York, NY: Harper Collins; 2001

[9] Hadley CN, Pittinsky TL, Sommer SA, Zhu W. Measuring the efficacy of leaders to assess information and make decisions in a crisis: The C-LEAD scale. The Leadership Quarterly. 2011;**22**:633-648

[10] Bandura A. Social Foundations of Thought and Action: A Social Cognitive Theory. Hoboken, NJ: Prentice Hall; 1986

[11] Cunnliffe A, Coupland C. From hero to villain to hero: Making experience sensible through embodied sensemaking. Human Relations. 2012;**65**(1):63-88

[12] Kern T. Blue Threat: Why to Err Is Inhuman. United States: Pygmy Books; 2009

[13] Salovey P, Mayer JD, Caruso D, Lopes PN. Measuring emotional intelligence as a set of abilities with the Mayer-Salovey-Caruso emotional intelligence test. In: Lopez SJ, Snyder CR, editors. Positive Psychological Assessment: A Handbook of Models and Measures. Washington, DC: American Psychological Association; 2003

[14] Maitlis S, Sonenshein S. Sensemaking in crisis and change: Inspiration and insights from Weick (1988). Journal of Management Studies. 2010;**47**(3):551-580

[15] Dixon D, Boland RJ, Perelli S. Making Sense When it Matters Most: Leadership in Extremis. Academy of Management Annual Meeting; 2012. Boston, MA: AOM; 2012

[16] Manesh R, Connor DM, & Kohlwes J. Dual Process Theory (System 1 and System 2 Clinical Reasoning). docsbay.net

Chapter 11

When Spotting the Glass Cliff Matters for Women: A Qualitative Study Focusing on Gender Inequalities in Corporate South Africa

Winsome Mashele and Imhotep Paul Alagidede

Abstract

Trends of women accessing senior manager roles in corporate South Africa have made considerable gains, and although some women have managed to crack the glass ceiling which has hindered their full participation in economic life, true gender equality is yet to be achieved. Sometimes, what seems like a wonderful opportunity to climb up the corporate ladder is an ascent that leads you to the top and pushes you over the edge. But what happens when women do manage to get to the top? The study investigates the concept of the glass cliff by interrogating its existence and looking further into the implications of the phenomenon. A qualitative research methodology was employed, and data collected through semi-structured interviews from a total of 15 participants. The research suggests that for women managers it is important to understand when, why, and how glass cliff appointments are likely to occur and elaborates on strategies for eliminating the glass cliff. The study goes further to make suggestions to policy makers about the importance of understanding the impact of the choices made by women seeking management positions and provides insights regarding how women feel about taking these precarious manager roles. This chapter aims at contributing to this under-researched area from a South African perspective.

Keywords: social-role theory, corporate, gender, leadership, glass cliff

1. Introduction

Despite evidence that women are breaking through the "glass ceiling" which has hindered their full participation in economic life, true gender equality has not yet been achieved, and it is a puzzle why the entry of women into senior management positions remains restricted. Although the 'glass ceiling' is a metaphor describing an inequitable architectural feature of career paths, its potential impact on individuals is profound [1]. Women around the world who seek managerial positions continue to face systemic barriers and frustrations in the workplace that hinders

IntechOpen

their progress [2]. Having more women entering the workforce, it has become clear that the social environment plays a crucial role in the degree to which they are obstructed in their management aspirations. Therefore, the consequences of the group and organizational contexts have increasingly attracted researchers' attention [2].

Though the gender gap remains wide, apparent advances have been made. The glass cliff phenomenon manifested itself in women being appointed to management positions "associated with the increased risk of failure and criticism because these positions are more likely to involve management of organisational units which are in crisis" [1–3]. Ncube [4] also observed similar findings in the analysis of corporates in South Africa in the last 5–7 years (at the time of the study). Glass cliff appointments in corporate South Africa is quite prevalent. Women were appointed as CEOs in various organisations that were in trouble, namely South African Airways, Prasa, Transnet, Telkom and South African Post Office, noteworthy is that government is a major shareholder in most of the organisations listed above. These women were highly qualified and at the time of their appointments were hailed as being significantly experienced and suitable for the task at hand [4]. Most did not make it in those roles thus potentially reinforcing the harmful idea that women cannot lead and adding to the statistics of women who failed in top positions.

This chapter argues, though, that when organizational decline is excessive, assuming management responsibility can be very risky. Evidence gathered from researchers clearly demonstrates that the contexts in which women and men tend to achieve senior manager roles differ markedly. As compared to men, female managers possess different skills and traits that may increase the probability of successful crisis management [5]. It demonstrates that in comparison to men, women who 'break through' the glass ceiling are often appointed to positions that are more precarious and associated with a higher risk of failure—a phenomenon captured by the metaphor of the glass cliff [6]. Therefore, there is a high probability supported by research that women bring innovative and productive practices to the boardroom [5]. Women's progress in management positions in the public sector have been associated with management positions with higher risks of failure in previous studies [3, 7] referred to as women facing a glass cliff [6, 8]. In such situations, women are perceived as better suited for senior management positions, which is attributed to the association between crisis management and stereotypical female management styles. One of the possible motives for organisations to make glass cliff appointments are based on the need to signal to the market that there is a commitment to innovative strategies, by selecting a woman as a top manager during a crisis [9]. More generally, the appointment of women may serve as a signal of change from the dominant stereotypically male model of management [8]. Mulcahy and Linehan [1] confirmed the glass cliff phenomenon in some studies, which are however rejected in other studies [10] and most studies are situated in private sector contexts [9]. If the organisation's crisis persists or worsens, the huge stakeholder awareness associated with poor performance or crisis status make a female manager highly visible [11]. "It is time for women to accept the challenge—to rightfully claim their space". Women who have challenged the system, and those whose efforts have been hindered. Women and men are encouraged to work together to break down the barriers of gender so that the next generation of female managers can rightfully claim their space [12].

The purpose of this study was to further explore this possibility. Specifically, the focus is on South African corporations.

2. Background

Despite women encountering many issues exacerbating gender inequalities in the workplace, the number of women in the work force has seen a steady increase. According to Statistics South Africa (2015), women make up 51% of the total population of South Africa and account for 45.1% of the working population [13]. However, from the sample reflecting South Africa's mainstream economy, the number of women CEOs in South Africa has doubled from seven in 2015 to fourteen in 2017, but only one state-owned enterprise (SOE) has a women CEO. The interest in doing this study is informed by the claim made [6] that women are overrepresented in senior management positions in organisations during crisis, as stated in the introduction. In joining a new organisation during challenging times for women in the corporate environment, can sometimes present opportunities to display your expertise and be part of the winning team. In other circumstances however, starting in a new management role in stormy times can turn even ordinary work duties into very daunting tasks.

3. Gender bias and management

Wittmann [14] argues that post-apartheid South Africa's transformation process has made significant strides in achieving gender equality through the introduction of legislation such as the Employment Equity Act 55 of 1998 that promotes the inclusion of black people, women and the disabled into the workplace. However, black women continue to be marginalised along racial and gender lines as business is an extension of society, mirroring the complex power relations in South African society that are reminiscent of the discriminatory practices of apartheid South Africa. Gender-responsive, transformative management is not only about achieving gender equality, but about equipping women and men with the tools to change the mindset of society in manner to achieve gender equity at all levels. The intellectual, economic, and social contributions of women are essential to organizations and to economic progress in general, as well as to our communities however gender bias is still rife across the workplace. Women and men, girls and boys are vulnerable in different ways in times of crisis and are often treated differently by perpetrators of violence and by state actors. Gender difference is one of the most significant determinants of an individual's capacity to cope safely during a crisis, and gender profoundly affects whether, how, and when individuals gain access to support in the aftermath [15]. While women and men collectively experience the insecurity of crisis situations and must contend with the economic and social consequences, women – globally the poorest of the poor – bear the additional insecurity of sexual and gender-based violence. Social role theory argues that stereotypes about men and women are based on observations of their behaviours in gender-typical social roles [15]. For example, for men and women to get appointed to senior managerial roles it is plainly based on the applicant's competence [16]. However, gender stereotypes regarding management ability may not uniformly lead to the perception of an individual woman being less competent than a comparable man. Heilman et al. [2] who investigated men's and women's success in a male gender-typed job in a US undergraduate student sample found that in situations of ambiguity about success, women were viewed as less competent and characterized as less achievement oriented than men, whereas in situations in which success was made explicit, there were no gender differences in characterizations. Bosak and Sczesny [15] has suggested that evaluators rely less on gender stereotypical expectations when they can base decisions on actual observations of candidates' performance. Furthermore, in their study of dynamic stereotypes, Bosak and Sczesny [15] found that participants' stereotypes about women, men and managers were malleable.

4. Women and precarious leadership

The perceived proposition that women are suitable in senior manager roles when an organisation is in crisis is likely to increase. In times of crises, female employees are seen as sincerer, emotional and friendly; male employees are more competitive, authoritative and self-confident. Due to these stereotypes, female managers are considered more appropriate than male in the crisis situations in the firm. Since innovation is strategically necessary in organizational change, innovation is perceived as a risk, and in such cases, women employees are appointed as managers. In the women preferences factor, women can be willing to work in risky positions [17].

In a company where exist glass cliff, while male employees do not ascend beyond the glass ceiling, female employees take the tasks beyond the glass ceiling. These tasks are not preferred by male employees as they are perceived as a high risk of failure. On the other hand, female employees thinking that they will turn the crisis into an opportunity, may be more willing to take risky tasks compared to male employees. The reason for the realization of the glass cliff phenomenon is that the failure encountered is attributed to the woman manager appointed to that position [17]. However, if career advancement is available at a precarious organization, it may result in a conflicting state of mind (i.e., there is an opportunity for advancement, however, at a precarious company). Therefore, we believe that the risk status of the job influences the perception of the job as a promotional opportunity. If the job position is perceived as a risky career strategy rather than an opportunity for advancement, the job is less likely to be seen as a promotional opportunity. In turn, a risky job is less likely to be accepted by a job seeker [18].

This speculation is in line with research findings reported by ref. [19] which indicated that the difficulties that men face on their way to the highest echelons in their organisations, are more likely to serve a positive self-developmental purpose than their female counterparts, since they view their challenges more as obstacles to be surmounted. The research findings by Haslam and Ryan [19] suggest that men and women are selected differently for both rewarding and unrewarding jobs, but its correlational nature leaves questions of cause and effect largely unanswered. For example, it may be that in most cases women prefer to select those positions that have challenges or obstacles in the organisation, as compared to others choosing for them.

Clearly, the concept of the glass cliff is relevant when analysing the life of the organisation, as its impact extends beyond just a perception of the suitability of women for management positions that are precarious because they are associated with the coordination of organisational units that are in crisis. Particularly, as these perceptions form the basis for actual organisations, they should have an impact on the kind of duties assigned to women in organisations if they succeed in climbing the corporate ladder. Lyness and Thompson [20], analysed archival and survey data to compare the work experiences of men and women in senior management positions. The results revealed several important differences in male and female positions in the organisation. In particular, the positions women occupy tend to involve risk and less dignity. Women find their positions to be less satisfying or attractive than men, which led the researchers to reach the conclusion that if women are seen breaking into top level positions, they are likely to be confronted with elements of gender discrimination such as glass cliff.

Ryan et al. [8] asked participants to read and respond to a news article summarizing Ryan and Haslam's [6] original archival study. Participants responded to several closed-ended questions assessing the degree to which, they viewed the glass cliff phenomenon as problematic for women, and to an open-ended question asking for comments about factors that prompt glass cliff effects. Several reasons were provided for the effect, ranging from more pernicious explanations that emphasized sexism and women's expendability to relatively more benign explanations that emphasized gender stereotypes and the desire to promote equality. However, without being biased, it is worth noting that women are not easily afforded the opportunity to attain senior roles as corporate executives, oftentimes when the opportunity arises, they do not do the prerequisite research or investigate the risks attached to the position being offered. Women immediately make themselves available to take up the offered position, which highlights the findings that females are over-represented in precarious management positions [6, 8].

Schein's [21] concept of "think manager-think male" demonstrated that mid-level male managers believed that men were more likely than women to possess the characteristics associated with managerial success. This was demonstrated by ref. [6] in their "think crisis-think female" concept, that indicated that women are elevated to positions of power within organisations when things are going poorly and thus face multiple challenges due being appointed in positions of power under these circumstances. Ryan and Haslam's [6] concept outweighs the typical "think manager-think male" viewpoint, in which it is generally assumed that successful managers possess masculine, agentic attributes [22, 23]. Ryan et al.'s [22] concept of "think crisis-think female" proposes that management abilities coincide with stereotypically feminine roles and traits therefore the "think crisis–think female" association may exist [22].

5. Methodology

The current research study employed an interpretivist-constructive paradigm with the focus of the study being the lived experiences of a sample of women managers from corporate South Africa that participated in the study. Based on this, a qualitative research approach was taken to investigate the existence of the glass cliff phenomenon in corporate South Africa. To date limited research has been conducted on the existence of glass cliff appointment and its consequences for women managers in corporate South Africa. Moreover, the qualitative research approach is helpful when investigating traits or trends and helps to understanding individuals' personal and management experiences to extract valuable insights about a specific phenomenon [24]. Phenomenology is effective in studying a small sample size—in this case, 17 participants—to identify the core of their experiences with the phenomenon [25] and to develop patterns and relationships of meaning. Semi structured, open, qualitative interviews were conducted with 17 women in senior management positions (C-suite) in corporate South Africa, who were purposively selected as participants using the snowball method. The interviews were conducted in English and tape-recorded, then transcribed and analysed using ATLAS-ti and thematic analysis was used to review the interviews. All interviews were documented using pseudonyms. This approach allowed the us to recruit the most appropriate sample to answer the research question [26]. For this study, 17 women leaders were purposively sampled, participants ranged from executives (10), senior (5) and Board and non-board members (2).

Confidentiality was maintained by using pseudonyms to protect the identity of participants and their organizations. Each participant was identified by a pseudonym.

6. Results

Previous studies [6, 8] found that it was not that women were bad managers, but that they were appointed as leaders when companies were failing. The study participants were hesitant to confirm the existence of the glass cliff phenomenon in corporate South Africa. Several broad reasons to justify the existence of the glass cliff and why women find themselves in those roles were shared. For example, women regard glass cliff as an opportunity to afforded to occupy the senior management positions. This study found that the reason for accepting these risky positions were based on (1) Challenging traditional views, (2) female career shortage, (3) career benefit and advancement, (4) eagerness to accept challenges. The study also made an interesting finding, that the reasons for women to accept glass cliff appointment were driven by the need for promotional opportunity. To elucidate this notion, we draw on social cognitive career theory and the theory of circumscription and comprise which offer a basis for examining why women must make compromises in career decision-making [18]. We focus on perceptions of the job as a promotional opportunity and individuals' career self-efficacy as key variables in the career decision-making process of men and women to better understand "the road to the glass cliff" [19].

7. Challenging traditional views

The participants in the study indicated that it is through accepting these risky situations that they become committed to proving a point, by dismantling the stereotypes they encounter. And going further to show that women in management have the potential to advance as much as if not better than their male counterparts. Most of the participants recounted numerous stories highlighting how traditional norms and ways of thinking, that have supported recurring behaviour or attributed to maintaining the status quo for decades, and promoting the entrenchment of repeated behaviour, were identified as reasons that the glass cliff exists in corporate South Africa. It is through this process that participants have learned to develop a sense of autonomy, self-respect and the drive that allowed them the opportunity to grow and develop the skills that have enabled them to advance to positions that have given them more power and authority.

Some of the participants noted that women are not expected to perform in senior roles as society has decided that they are incapable of taking on these roles successfully. Chrissie, one of the study participants, further noted that culturally, society does not encourage girls to have an education because they are perceived as an asset due to the dowry paid to their families when they marry. Malawe, another participant shared her view on how women are viewed saying that:

> *Because traditionally, women are perceived to be expert in doing office "housework" like organising office parties. And you just need to prove that you can do it. It is also about our legacy. You want to leave a legacy. You want to say, you know what, I have done it, other women can do it. But also, we are doing it to support other women so that you can bring other women to the level where we are. And even beyond.*

The extract above is indicative that the gender gap as regards to housework seems to be narrowing but women still carry the load. There is no explanation for why women end up doing more housework, it must then be because of societal norms and standards. Several of the study participants acknowledged that the responsibilities for women outside of the office are often more demanding even though they hold senior level positions and are exposed to the same pressures as their male counterparts, they are still responsible for most of the household chores and childcare.

8. Female career shortage

The fact that there is such a shortage of women in management positions adheres to the fact that they are more than willing to accept these managerial positions that are risky. Although this is slowly starting to increase there is still a sense of traditional viewpoints related to women in the workforce as not being worthy of a "man's job". This in return, makes the woman leader more eager to accept these risky managerial positions due to this direct shortage. When Nicci was asked about the issue of women accepting risky managerial positions she responded:

> *I don't know. It is fewer; you know there are very few women in senior management positions. So, there must be an element of truth to the fact that there are very few positions and when you are offered, don't think twice as it might not present itself again.*

Nicci's challenge reflects Mathipa and Tsoka's [27] finding that in South Africa, the problem of very few women in management positions came more to the foreground after the advent of the new political dispensation. It surfaced more and more as the country's political landscape became gradually normalised. As the problem grew and became more and more conspicuous, an attempt to deal with it in the form of a Commission for Gender Equality was undertaken.

9. Career benefit and advancement

Nicola, Vonani Mama and Nicci confirmed their lack of confidence earlier on in their careers. Their confidence was built through hard work and investing in themselves. However, the researcher does not agree that all the other attributes are gender specific, nor does she believe that leaders of whatever gender must be aggressive to succeed. Nicola said:

> *The one is quite aggressive, 'one of the boys' style, and it works quite well in financial services. If you are aggressive and you come across like one of the boys, you go out with them, you drink with them, you swear with them. They keep you in their circles and you end up getting to the top that way.*

In the extract above, the participant is emphasizing that if you cannot beat them join them, it is a good strategy for infiltration so you can be seen to be one of "the boys." The purpose is to learn their weaknesses through being part of the group and beat them at their own game, utilizing the option of joining the boys' club to try and fit in. The potential result being that if women start joining these groups and shaking things up, the traditional boy's club will flat-out not exist. Fitting in should not be about going to work and trying to be like a man, pretending to be someone you are not.

What if instead of trying to fit in, women used a different approach, something that works just for them, perhaps starting a 'girls' only club? The participants also found the workplace to be a "boys' club". Across race, they found that while they could work quite closely and get on well with their male colleagues, they were not quite part of the club. According to Fisher and Kinsey [28] collaboration another dimension that can differ between genders. As a result of old boys' networks and dynamics women face the additional challenge of securing access to key networks that men have access to from the start of their academic careers. This statement also stresses the need for women to turn negative constructions into positive ones by reinterpreting the negative constructions and embracing them as a basis from which they draw their strength. This kind of socializing for the participants was necessary to get ahead. For example, people who skip the pub after work miss out on "office gossip", opportunities for promotions, who has been promoted, etcetera. According to De Klerk [29] networking is not restricted to specific situations and people can network at any time and place, which makes every opportunity a networking opportunity. Networking relationships allow for successful business practices and the development of mutual respect trust and social capital, which contribute to the success of networking efforts in a business [29].

10. Eager to accept challenges

The participants indicated that besides taking risky jobs for career advancement, they agreed that they also accepted risky positions just for the sake of the challenge. The predetermined social mind set of women not being able to face certain challenges are being dismantled from these women's perspectives. Gender inequality is not positioned as a 'woman's problem' and women's management programs need to shift away from a "fix the women" framework, to developmentally examine what women want. Systemic change is required to address power and patriarchy barriers [12].

Rather than accepting stereotypically mediocre jobs or careers, they keep challenging the status quo to prove that they are worthy of greatness and can run a big corporate entity. These women are constantly eager to accept difficult and challenging positions that allow their minds and capabilities to be challenged and would not otherwise be able to function in a job that does not challenge their minds in any way. All the participants in the current study shared how they had become tougher. This had allowed them to deal with challenges without getting emotional. Not only is the struggle to assert power evident in their stories, but male oppression is also re-asserted by dismissing the hurtful impact of the experiences as recounted in the following extract by Iron Lady:

> *For me is that women always think about the bigger picture approach, they think about the joy of winning, they want to be part of creating the better future of the organisation. Even if the organisation is struggling and is made up of people who were appointed for a specific reason, there is a spark, there is something unique seen in them. Since women know that they can inspire and turn that spark into a flame and get the people there, taking the organization out of struggle they can do it.*

11. Discussion

The discussion is based on the findings and is clustered according to themes that have been identified through the literature as well as emanating from the findings.

The study revealed the tools and resources that are critical if you take on a role that is high pressured and requires high performance to avoid falling off the cliff.

12. Adequate support structures

It is important to know what sort of support structures you will require to navigate the glass cliff and to deliver on your responsibilities successfully. Women have different circumstances that require different support systems therefore it is important to put forward the kind of support you will require. This aligns with existing research indicating that one of the ways women bolster belief in their management abilities is through strong support systems [18, 26, 30]. According to Appelbaum et al. [30], encouragement and support are predictors of those who will become leaders (both men and women). Turock [31] spoke of the great importance of support systems for women, stating that, "the advantages that social support structures can supply for mentees should not be minimized". The role mentors can play for mentees in helping them see their potential is crucial. Internal and external structures can serve as buffers against the stress that is inherent in professional women's careers. IronLady emphasised the importance of the board and executive team, stating the importance of their support and the pitfalls of not having it she said that:

> *Also, the board or your EXCO becomes extremely critical, if you don't get the support you quickly look like a lone ranger. You will not be able to handle the situation by yourself.*

13. Importance of proactive research

The study revealed the importance of proactive research to broadening one's knowledge with the purpose of staying relevant and retaining your management position. It also showed that in the process of empowering themselves through the means of knowledge formulation, participants were able to fulfil their job requirements and flourish within their field of expertise, thus highlighting the need for C-suite executives to do more research towards improvement and being innovative. Cheverton [32] noted that C-suite executives have little or no time for further development unless they are developmentally minded and are strongly committed to continuing their own personal development. Many C-suite executives do not feel they have the time for self-reflection, and such developmental activities as executive coaching or further education.

14. Importance of personal development

For women managers to continue growing both personally and professionally, personal development is vital. The study revealed that participants in the study recognise the importance of personal development as a significant survival tool for senior women leaders during crisis. Participants gave examples such as improving self-awareness, knowing, and building your own identity as well as discovering and developing your own talents and knowing your own strengths and weaknesses as part of building personal development.

15. Mentoring and strategic networking

External influences like mentoring and networking were perceived as important to participants, however, mentors are not overwhelmingly positioned as drivers of motivation in this study but were examples highlighted by participants and viewed as necessary to their success and in preventing them from falling off the cliff. Singh et al. [33] found that "individuals with mentors report more positive career outcomes than those lacking a mentor". International women leaders in this study have acknowledged that they have received mentorship support from senior managers to better navigate their leadership skills [33].

A mentor plays the crucial role of a facilitator who encourages the development of the mentee's skills through instructing, coaching, modelling and advising. There were several connections between findings in the current study and the literature reviewed with regards to mentorship and self-efficacy. All participants identified mentors and champions from multiple perspectives of their career progression. Mentors for these female leaders included former CEOs, professional colleagues, university professors, business leaders and their parents as well. This study is consistent with the literature that discusses the impact of mentors as support systems [29, 30]. Strategic networks are coalitions that women form in response to the isolation and social exclusion they face in the corporate world [34].

16. Conclusion

This study uses the glass-cliff phenomenon to investigate when, how and why women who shatter the glass ceiling find themselves into senior management roles that are risky. This study explores the "glass cliff" form of discrimination. From the perspective of the legions of women who have encountered women-specific challenges as they attempted to rise to higher positions, discrimination seemed to be the chief barrier to their leadership. Discrimination became the strongest narrative about the reasons for underrepresentation of women in managerial roles. Researchers, seeking to identify the processes underlying such discrimination, focused on gender stereotypes as the origin of the problem. Gender stereotypes are not easy to erase. Their stickiness is a result not only of the rigidity of people's belief systems but also of the social position of women in society, which has changed, but only gradually [35].

Below we propose the overarching implications that emerge from the gender-based management with regards to main causes of glass cliff in the workplace. First, the lack of support that women receive is also explained by shadow structures, which suggest that women's networks are less resourceful than men's even when they are in similar positions, women also report feeling more excluded than men [36]. Second, of prominence are human capital barriers (lack of education, resources, and experience); differences in communication styles; exclusion from informal networks; lack of mentors and role-models; and organizational biases [37]. Third, the importance for women to feel connected to the goals and objectives of the larger organization and to envision a holistic picture of themselves as integral organisational partners must be of primary emphasis. As organizations structure effective management development systems for women and as women realize management development practices in their organizations, they will likely experience stronger organizational connections that may well lead to increased organizational commitment.

These findings align with existing research indicating that one of the ways women bolster belief in their management abilities is through strong support systems. Furthermore, attention needs to be given to the implications for policy and practice on gender issues, and the importance of understanding women's experiences in the workplace need to be highlighted, rather than treating gender diversity as merely "a numbers game".

Though policy may be in place, there seems to be no obligation, as demonstrated by the results of this study, to translate this into practice. Guided by the capability and involuntary immobility approaches, and applying a qualitative case study, this study found that women leaders in corporate South Africa devised strategies to navigate the challenges they encountered, to avoid falling off. The study has proved that with the necessary support, women leaders can build strong social structures and yield high financial rewards. Through observing high growth in women working in corporate South Africa and occupying high positions, this study is an appeal to women leaders to understand when, why, and how glass cliff appointments are likely to occur. Within this context, the well-being of women leaders' careers should not be taken for granted. The time is now for women to embrace this call and take a stance, and the researcher believes that this research will open more doors for both current and future research.

17. Limitations and future recommendations

This study is not without its limitations. Due to the interpretivist approach adopted in the study, the research purposely consists of a limited number of women leaders in corporate South Africa. What resulted from this was the depth and richness of the qualitative data in the study, which yielded ample fruit in terms of discussions with participants, who were women in C-suite positions within a corporate setting. Furthermore, one social identity category was investigated and that men were excluded from the study as the focus was on the life stories and narratives of the women who participated in the study. The results of the study can, therefore, not be generalised across the population. Future research could include larger samples and incorporate a variety of methods to improve data representativity. If the glass cliff exists, it is important to understand how it impacts the choices of women seeking management positions and explore how women feel about taking these precarious management positions. If advancement to more precarious or risky positions is the only option, women must understand the danger and the potential career impacts. Further in-depth research is recommended in this regard. As mentioned in the preceding paragraphs, there are multiple avenues future research could take regarding the ways in which the shape and direction of the organization and the precariousness of the management position is operationalized.

18. Theoretical and practical implications

This research is important in terms of its theoretical and practical implications to the existing body of research knowledge. It contributes to theory in that there is a substantial body of work that more generally focuses on the way in which males in comparison with female managers are selected [9, 38, 39] but none investigating important factors that help women leaders in leading an organisation during crisis periods more importantly. The glass cliff theory offers a more ambiguous explanation and is considered incomplete without considering the perspective of female managers' attitudes and behaviours towards risk. This chapter contributes to the glass cliff theory by considering the perspective of women rather than focusing on organizational decision makers. In addition, this chapter examines the risk-taking perspective of the glass cliff phenomenon and is one of the first to describe the apparent situation in which women are at a disadvantage when it comes to obtaining support for risk-taking. This chapter sheds new light on the glass cliff phenomenon by examining the factors that lead women to high-risk management positions in organizations.

This study has several theoretical implications. First, because the study is set in a strong diversity policy environment, there is intense pressure on organizations to appoint women to management positions. The pressure to fill managerial positions with women was great. In such circumstances, the term "Think Manager—Think Male" is slowly advancing, so the glass cliff phenomenon may not exist and may explain the inconclusive results. In other words, it can be argued that turbulence can have a positive rather than a negative impact in situations of high political pressure for gender equality and strong diversity policies. Organizations with a lower percentage of women in management positions supported this expectation.

Second, the proportion of women in top management positions is the lowest compared to other roles, so the importance of gender for these positions may be stronger than for lower management positions. Additionally, these positions can be a glass cliff as they ultimately place the blame for the organization's failures on top women managers.

The study has practical implications. From an organisational perspective, this study will advise organisations in adopting practices that foster "debiasing" of decisions regarding promotions to top management. If organizational decision-makers understand that female employees are primarily being appointed only under very specific (and perhaps not ideal) conditions, it is possible that they would make more of an effort to expand the opportunities offered to females. And for human capital departments in providing a series of trainings regarding decision-making that raise awareness about the possibility of biased judgments related to gender and leadership.

From the perspective of women managers, this study provides women aspiring to managerial positions within an organization with the insights behind the positions offered in order to make informed decisions about how to navigate that position. Women managers find themselves in a dangerous position because they are often not exposed to the same social resources as mentors and social networks when offered these risky positions as compared male counterparts.

Therefore, it is worth noting that after understanding how and when the glass cliff effect is likely to occur, it is equally important to discern why females are likely to be offered these positions. Without any insight into the reasons behind these appointments, it is impossible to rectify the issues that the glass cliff effect presents for women and leadership.

Author details

Winsome Mashele[1]* and Imhotep Paul Alagidede[2,3,4]

1 Transnet Soc Ltd, Transnet Freight Rail, Wits Business School, Johannesburg, South Africa

2 Finance at Wits Business School, University of South Africa, Johannesburg, South Africa

3 African Finance and Economics Consult, South Africa

4 Nile Valley Group of Companies, South Africa

*Address all correspondence to: noma04@icloud.com

References

[1] Mulcahy M, Linehan C. Females and precarious board positions. British Journal of Management. 2014;**25**(3):425-438

[2] Heilman M, Wallen A, Fuchs D, Tamkins M. Penalties for success: Reactions to women who succeed at male tasks. Journal of Applied Psychology. 2004;**89**:416-427

[3] Sabharwal M. From glass ceiling to glass cliff: Women in senior executive service. Journal of Public Administration Research and Theory. 2013;**25**(2):399-426

[4] Ncube L. The Intersectionality of Gender, Race and Class: Implications for the Career Progression of Women Leaders in Southern Africa. Unpublished Doctoral Thesis. Pretoria: UNISA; 2018

[5] Eagly A, Carli L. The female leadership advantage: An evaluation of the evidence. The Leadership Quarterly. 2003;**14**:807-834

[6] Ryan M, Haslam S. The glass cliff: Evidence that women are over-represented in precaurious leadership positions. British Journal of Management. 2005;**16**:81-90

[7] Smith A, Monaghan K. Some ceilings have cracks: Representative bureaucracy in Federal Regulatory Agencies. The American Review of Public Administration. 2011;**43**(1):50-71

[8] Ryan M, Haslam S. The glass cliff: Exploring the circumstances surrounding the appointment of women to perilous leadership positions. Academy of Leadership Review. 2007;**32**(2):549-572

[9] Ryan M, Haslam S, Morgenroth T, Rink FF, Stoker J, Peters K. Getting on top of the glass cliff: Reviewing a decade of evidence, explanations and impact. The Leadership Quarterly. 2016;**27**(3):446-455

[10] Bechtoldt M, Bannier C, Rock B. The Glass cliff myth? Evidence from Germany and the UK. The Leadership Quarterly, Advanced Online Publication. 2019

[11] Boin A, Kuipers S, Overdijk W. Leadership in times of crisis: A framework for assessment. International Review of Public Administration. 2013;**18**(1):79-91

[12] Butler-Henderson K, Carbone A, Devlin M, Bull R, Coldwell-Neilson J, Fenton A, et al. Women and leadership in higher education learning and teaching. Journal of University Teaching & Learning Practice. 2022;**19**(1):1-5

[13] BWASA. Women in Leadership Census. South Africa. 2017. Available from: https://bwasa.co.za/wp-content/uploads/2018/04/2017-BWASA-CENSUS-report.pdf

[14] Wittmann V. Gender and empowerment in South Africa. Multicultural Education & Technology Journal. 2012;**6**(4)

[15] Bosak J, Sczesny S. Gender bias in leader selection? Evidence from a hiring simulation study. Sex Roles. 2011;**65**:234-242

[16] Eagly A, Wood W, Diekman A. Social Role Theory of Sex Differences and Similarities: A Current Appraisal. Mahwah, NJ: Lawrence Erlbaum; 2000

[17] Ece S. Youth's view on gender based Glass Ceiling & Glass Cliff Phenomenon. Equinox, Journal of Economics, Business & Political Studies. 2021;**8**(2):134-155

[18] Darouei D, Pluut H. The paradox of being on the glass cliff: Why do women

accept risky leadership positions? Career Development International. 2018;**23**(4):397-426

[19] Haslam S, Ryan M. The road to the glass cliff: Differences in the perceived suitability of men and women for leadership positions in succeeding and failing organizations. Leadership Quarterly. 2008;**19**:530-546

[20] Lyness K, Thompson D. Above the glass ceiling? A comparison of matched samples of female and male leadership. Journal of Applied Psychology. 1997;**82**(3):359-375

[21] Schein E. How "career anchors" hold executives to their career paths. Personnel. 1975;**52**(3):1-24

[22] Powell G, Butterfield D, Parent J. Gender and managerial stereotypes: Have the times changed? Journal of Management. 2002;**28**(2):177-193

[23] Ryan M, Haslam S, Hersby M, Bongiorno R. Think crisis-think female: The glass cliff and contextual variation in the think manager-think male stereotype. Journal of Applied Psychology. 2011;**96**:470-484

[24] Bluhm D, Harman W, Lee TW, Mitchell TR. Qualitative research in management: A decade of Progress. Journal of Management Studies. 2011;**48**(8):1866-1891

[25] Creswell JW. Research Design: Qualitative, Quantitative. Mixed Methods Approaches. 2nd ed. Thousand Oaks, CA: Sage; 2003

[26] Tashakkori A, Teddlie C. Handbook of Mixed Methods in Social & Behavioral Research. Thousand Oaks: Sage; 2003

[27] Mathipa E, Tsoka E. Possible barries to the advancement of women to leadership positions in the education profession. South African Journal of Education. 2001;**21**(4):324-331

[28] Fisher V, Kinsey S. Behind closed doors!Homosocial desire andthe academic boys club. Gender in Management: An International Journal. 2014;**29**

[29] De Klerk S. The importance of networking as a management skill. South African Journal of Business Management. 2010;**14**(1):37-49

[30] Appelbaum S, Audet L, Miller J. Gender and leadership? Leadership and gender? A journey through the landscape of theories. Leadership & Organization Development Journal. 2002;**24**(1):43-51

[31] Turock B. Women and leadership. Journal of Library Administration. 2001;**32**:3-4

[32] Cheverton R. A Leader's guide to protecting mavericks. The Journal for Quality & Participation. 2001:7-9

[33] Nachatar S. Leadership challenges and opportunities experienced by international women academics: A case study in Australia. Journal of University Teaching and Learning Practice. 2022;**19**(1):140-159

[34] Tandrayen-Ragoobur V, Pydayya R. Glass ceiling and sticky floors: Hurdles for Mauritian working women. Eguality, Diversity and Inclusion, An International Journal. 2015;**34**:452-466

[35] Eagly A, Heilman M. Gender and Leadership: Introduction to the Special Issue. 2016

[36] Hopkins M, O'Neil D, Passarelli AM, Bilimoria D. Women's leadership development strategic practices for women and organizations. Consulting

Psychology Journal Practice and Research. 2008;**60**(4):348-365

[37] Riccucci NM. The pursuit of social equity in the federal government: A road less traveled? Public Administration Review. 2009;**69**(3):373-382

[38] Glass C, Cook A. Leading at the top: Understanding women's challenges above the glass ceiling. Leadership Quarterly. 2016;**27**:51-63

[39] Qian Y, Fan W. Men and women at work: Occupational gender composition and affective well-being in the United States. Journal of Happiness Studies. 2019:2077-2099

Chapter 12

Mindfulness in Organizations: The Concept of Mindful Leadership

Aboubacar Garba Konte

Abstract

The main objective of this work is to explore the concept of mindfulness and its growing popularity within organizations with the introduction of the concept of mindful leadership in the management literature. This paper is one of the first in a pair of papers to explore the concept of mindful leadership in organizations. The first section of the paper provides a brief inquiry into the history of mindfulness, the definitions of mindfulness and the neurobiological mechanisms of mindfulness meditation. In the second section, the author considers mindfulness in the organizational research before conducting discussion on the concept of mindful leadership in the third section. The paper claims that while many studies have been conducted on mindfulness in diverse research areas, mindful leadership research is still developing, and the author vows for its adoption by business leaders for positive transformation within their organizations. Putting mindfulness into perspective as an energy resource that can activate a spiral of gains, the paper calls for greater research into the concept of mindful leadership. The paper offers a starting point for researchers and organizational development professionals to consider the possibility that mindfulness can be used as an efficient tool for the benefit of business executives.

Keywords: mindfulness, leadership development, mindful leadership

1. Introduction

As innovative solutions are of crucial importance to the survival of companies, leaders are constantly under the negative effect of stress, and they may find it very hard to step back and use new strategies to effectively manage their teams The twenty-first century leaders operate in a context that has significantly changed; their conditions of work are described as more and more complex and paradoxical, and certainty in the new society is getting increasingly illusory. In order to develop well in this unstable and uncertain environment, companies and leaders are obliged to cultivate new skills, which enable them to handle effectively new challenges for which they cannot control the consequences [1]. As stated by Day and Dragoni, the main purpose of business executives for leadership development in this environment is to reinforce individual and collective capabilities in order to be effective in leadership positions [2]. The skills that must be developed individually are self-awareness, efficacy [2], resilience and cognitive flexibility [3], self-reflection and self-regulation [4]. While King and Nesbit [5] challenged today's leadership development programs and actions in order to develop these leadership skills, Nesbit [4] emphasized on the development of meta-skills that he believes are particularly crucial for leaders who want to develop themselves. Mindfulness can be considered as a kind of meta-skill, which has the potential to develop core functioning like self-awareness and emotion regulation of leaders [6]. Recently, mindfulness training has turned out to be a very popular topic in management publications, which is emerging as a new method of leadership development [7–9]. The concept of mindfulness is employed to describe a state, a trait, and a method of training the mind [10]. A state mindfulness is when one is attentive in a state of full awareness and when one is focused on a clear goal with a non-judgmental attitude [11]. It is induced by clearly focusing on the breath and being aware of thoughts or emotions that arise without making any judgment at that moment. However, mindfulness happens naturally in everyday life whenever a person is aware of his present moment experiences. The majority of mindfulness operationalization measures trait mindfulness as the disposition to be mindful in everyday life differs from person to person.

Nowadays, new leadership theories are emerging. They are suggesting a renewal of leadership theories and practices based on behavioral developments for positive organizational change. These theories preach authenticity, emotions, and humility as core leadership competencies for positive organizational change and sustainable performance [12]. While studies on mindfulness in the workplace are getting more and more popular [6, 13–20], many leaders believe their companies are not equipped enough to face the "highly volatile, increasingly complex business environments" [21]. This work specifically demonstrates that it is possible to overcome this challenge of fostering greater outcomes at workplace by using mindfulness and contribute to leadership development. A growing number of leaders believe that the practice of mindfulness can fundamentally transform management and leadership approaches in organizations. This constitutes the interest of this work as it relates to the application of the ancient practice of mindfulness in organizational setting to not only induce greater work outcomes but also to improve leadership practice.

Therefore, what we are proposing through this work is one of many humble but perhaps useful responses to the issues of inventing an ethical and inspiring leadership, based on mindfulness, that is to say, to lead by consciously paying attention to what is happening in the here and now, in order to face any situation in an innovative way and adapt to it.

To address this purpose, this work aims to review academic literature on investigating the history of mindfulness, the multiple definitions of mindfulness, the mechanisms through which mindfulness operates, and what it purports to do in the context of leadership development.

2. Theoretical framework

2.1 Investigating the history of mindfulness and its definitions

The history of mindfulness as a concept spans over 2500 years, and it takes its roots in the Buddhist tradition. The first written mention of the term mindfulness in ancient Indian comes from a fifth-century Indian philosopher called Asanga [22]. Traditionally, this term is known in Pali as "sati," and it means "bearing something in mind without distraction and without forgetfulness" [22]. Originally, "sati" calls for a voluntary training of the attentional processes allowing constant and sustained attention to be placed on an object of external and internal observation. This training would increase the capacity and quality of attention or presence in the present moment. At the end of nineteenth century, sati was translated from Pali into English by the British Davids under the term mindfulness [23]. As a technique, mindfulness is one of the steps of the Noble Eightfold Path that leads to wisdom and the lack of suffering. The steps of the Noble Eightfold Path are: Right Understanding, Right Thought, Right Speech, Right Action, Right Livelihood, Right Effort, Right Mindfulness, and Right Concentration. The Buddhist Theravada tradition has it that, by increasingly focusing attention on the stream of internal and external experiences without making any judgment or mental comments, the individual can reach a deeper knowledge of himself and the essence of life [24]. In this culture, mindfulness is thought to be one of the five faculties (indriya) among others, which are: confidence, energy, concentration, and wisdom. It is developed in a continuous sequence with stages. The first stage is about developing sustained attention through regular practice. In the second stage, the individual develops the capacity of introspection and a profound understanding of emotions as ephemeral. When the individual goes through all these steps, he will gain in wisdom and will be able to understand the very essence of self and of the factors that lead him to a state of calmness and peace of mind [24].

Until the 1970s, mindfulness was merely considered as a Buddhist culture, and then modern scholars started introducing it into the Western medicine. Hayes [25] encourages scholars to include mindfulness in scientific research by claiming that the concept must not be limited to its religious roots. By liberating mindfulness from its religious origins, it becomes possible to generalize its application and to integrate its practice into clinical treatment thanks to the secularization of the construct. In Western countries, Jon Kabat-Zinn was the first person who standardized mindfulness as an intervention technique that can be utilized in the medicine. In 1979, he created at the Massachusetts Medical Center a stress reduction program, which he called Mindfulness-Based-Stress Reduction [11]. As stated by the MBSR website[1], there are more than 25,000 people who have completed the 8-week mindfulness training program, and it is provided at thousands of hospitals and medical centers around the world. Nowadays, the practice of mindfulness training has surged drastically both in medicine and in psychological practice. In psychotherapy, mindfulness is no more considered as only a means for stress reduction, but also a means to the treatment of diverse psychological problems such as depression, anxiety, attention-deficit disorders, and borderline personality; and the introduction of mindfulness in the organizational settings has recently been debated. A big topic of the debate in the use of mindfulness is the ambiguous nature of the concept; and some scholars have claimed that the operationalization of the term and the standardization of the practice are necessary for its use in research [11, 26, 27]. Different perspectives to defining mindfulness are presented in the next sessions.

3. Definitions of mindfulness

During its recent history, it has been a huge challenge to give a precise definition to mindfulness. Nonjudgmentally paying attention to what happens here and now is an apparently simple notion. However, mindfulness turns out to be a very complex

[1] www.umassmed.edu/cfm/stress

concept, and it gets even more complex when diverse features are taken into account in its definition. Even if mindfulness can be used as an intervention for many psychological disorders, providing an exact operational definition is still an ongoing process [26]. Some scholars have just defined it as from its religious perspectives that stems from ancient Buddhism. Others view it as a skill that can be developed by training, a set of beliefs about how to behave correctly in the daily interactions, a mindset, and a trait of personality. Most of the definitions in the literature take into account all these aspects.

Thich Nhat Hanh [28] a Vietnamese Zen master who is among the first scholars to introduce mindfulness to the Western culture, defines the term as "keeping one's consciousness alive to the present reality." This assumption posits that no matter what one is doing at the present moment that activity must be given the fullest attention possible. Whether it is taking a bath or taking a walk, chatting with friends, or following a course, eating, or reading; whatever one is performing at any given time must be credited with the fullest attention than anything else. Being fully aware of the present moment, no matter what it is, allows individuals to perceive the world more clearly and actively create their own life [28]. Brown et al. [29] advocated for this idea by claiming that mindfulness has existed for a long time in psychology. They recognize that many theoretical approaches suggest the importance of bringing awareness to bear on subjective experience (i.e., thoughts, emotions, external stimuli). By bringing the notions of mindfulness out of darkness, scholars can study its role across diverse psychotherapeutic currents [30]. From Baer' perspectives [31], mindfulness is seen in terms of bringing gently the attention to internal and external experiences that occur here and now. According to him, that skill is cultivated over time if one practices it regularly. Any attitudinal factors related to this definition of mindfulness are viewed as an impact of the skills acquired and not part of the concept itself. Kabat-Zinn [11] defines mindfulness as "paying attention in a particular way: on purpose, in the present moment, and nonjudgmentally." Here Jon Kabat-Zinn depicts mindfulness as a set of skills that includes elements of attitudes, beliefs, and other qualities, such as: acceptance, patience, openness, gratitude, empathy, trust, nonjudging, letting go, gentleness, generosity, nonstriving, and kindness. Among these qualities some are naturally related to the mindfulness practice itself (openness, acceptance, nonjudging), while others tend to be changes in attitudes, which are the resultants of the practice of mindfulness (kindness, generosity, gratitude). Later, Kabat-Zinn [11] made this distinction clearer when he referred to mindfulness as a state of being, in which an individual is nonjudgmentally conscious of his thoughts, emotions, bodily sensations, and external stimuli in the present moment (openness, acceptance, and curiosity). This way of defining mindfulness differentiates what mindfulness actually is (a state of being) from the attitudinal properties that characterize this state. Wallace [22] confirms this difference when he describes mindfulness as a state in which one is open, receptive, and nonresistant to anything that the present moment may provide. The assumption that supports mindfulness practice is the idea that such a state of being enables an individual to efficiently deal with stressors reflectively and responsively, in opposition to a reactive and reflexive way [11]. Bishop et al. [26] argued the outcomes of several meetings, which were held in order to find an established and consensual operational definition of mindfulness for the coming research. They stated that mindfulness is an activity of mental training, which aims to decrease one's reactive thoughts, emotions, and behavior; as opposed to the fact of being relaxed or being able to manage effectively one's mood. This definition of mindfulness incorporates two elements: the self-regulation of attention to experience in the present moment, and the attitude of curiosity, openness, and acceptance. Brown and Ryan [32] distinguished awareness from attention by claiming that awareness is about the ongoing experience of the present moment (thoughts, emotions, bodily sensations, and sensory perceptions); while attention is the fact of focusing awareness on a particular phenomenon. Awareness and attention are interwoven, and they are the main properties of consciousness; and mindfulness is about observing consciousness by having a complete picture of it, which involves both awareness and attention. According to Brown et al. [33], mindfulness is a receptive state of mind when the stream of consciousness unfolding in the present moment (thoughts, images, verbalizations, emotions, impulses, etc.) can be observed without discrimination, categorization, or reaction. This kind of state of mind generates more flexible and informed mental, emotional, and behavioral outcomes. Though mindfulness is considered as a technique of self-detachment from thoughts, it is not a technique of avoidance of thoughts; instead, it allows an individual to utilize thoughts with increased effectiveness and precision [29]. Based on the definition given by Shapiro et al. [34], it has been demonstrated that mindfulness has three elements (attention, intention, and attitude) and a "metamechanism of repercieving" (p. 374). Intention is seen as a personal vision, which is dynamic and which can evolve personal. It changes when mindfulness is increased going from regulation to exploration and ultimately to liberation. According to Shapiro et al. [34], intention is crucial to the process of mindfulness, and it is often neglected in many contemporary definitions. By attitude, Shapiro et al. believe that it is a component that enables an individual to bring to attention a set of qualities that include: compassion, non-striving, patience, curiosity, kindness, and openness. According to them, when an individual has the wrong attitude (e.g., cold, critical, etc.), this may bring about the situation in which he becomes condemning or judgmental of himself. By the concept of reperceiving mechanism, Shapiro et al. see it as the ability to de-identify oneself from the components of consciousness and to view experience with objectivity. This naturally occurs in mindfulness practice. When one is no more attached to own thoughts and emotions as they arise enables one not to be defined, controlled, or conditioned by them inducing objectivity and equanimity [34]. The literature reveals that mindfulness is a complex and multidimensional concept. For Kabat-Zinn [11], mindfulness is "the work of a lifetime and, paradoxically, the work of no time at all" (p. 149). The complex and obscure nature of mindfulness made it difficult to define in operational terms; however, the majority of attempts to define it have common characteristics. For the objectives of this study, mindfulness is defined as intentionally focusing the attention on what happens in the present moment (thoughts, emotions, bodily sensations, and external stimuli) and accept it without judgment. This state of being is characterized by many attitudinal factors (openness, acceptance, equanimity, patience, empathy, calmness, trust, gratitude, kindness, etc.) [32, 34]. According to Dekeyser et al. [35], individual involved in the practice of mindfulness can develop four distinctive competencies: attentively and consciously observe the internal and external phenomena (thoughts, emotions, sounds, smells etc.); consequently act by being fully engaged in an activity with total focus of attention; non-judgmentally accept the unfolding experience; immediately appreciate the unfolding experience. For Salmon et al. [36]: "The focus of attention on the experience of the present moment in an attitude of non-judgment." The literature on mindfulness, both modern and ancient, depicts the practice of mindfulness as a means to quiet the mind, decrease suffering, and improve quality of life.

After reviewing the main definitions of mindfulness, we present next the tools that are used to measure mindfulness.

4. The mechanisms of mindfulness: how does mindfulness operate?

From the historical perspectives, the term meditation is employed in Ref. to the Sanskrit word bhävana and to its Tibetan synonym sgoms. Etymologically, the Sanskrit term means the notion of "cultivation," or "causing to become," and the Tibetan synonym refers to "development of familiarity" [37]. In light of these clarifications, it is clear that, traditionally the meditation practice mostly highlights the process of mental development during which the practitioner cultivates a general sense of well-being and virtue. Along with the development of interventions based on mindfulness, there exist many theories that explain its mechanisms of action. In fact, several mechanisms of action explain the impact of mindfulness meditation on reducing anxiety and depressive symptoms. First, meditation increases metacognitive awareness [38, 39], which means it favors the ability to shift focus from one's thoughts and emotions and realize that they are only transitory mental events rather than identifying oneself with them or believing that they are an exact reflection of reality. This ability predicts a decrease in depressive relapses [40]. Indeed, according to Teasdale et al. [39], metacognitive awareness leads to a reduction in repetitive thoughts such as ruminations [39], which are a risk factor for several psychological disorders [41]. It is worth noting that meditation decreases the tendency to ruminate [42, 43]. Meditation promotes interoceptive exposure [44], which enables the capacity to desensitize oneself to the thoughts, emotions, and physical sensations associated with distress [31]. It promotes experiential acceptance, which results in a reduction in emotional intensity, compared with a non-acceptance attitude [45]. Acceptance is the ability to allow the experience to be as it is at the present moment, to accept pleasant and unpleasant experiences without seeking to hold back the former or push back the latter. According to Choate [46], emotional suffering results more from the non-acceptance of the emotion than from the emotion itself. Furthermore, TDC and ACT consider that change is only possible when the individual has recognized and accepted the emotional distress he feels. For example, studies show that increased experiential acceptance mediates the positive effects of ACT [47, 48]. Meditation improves self-management. In fact, observing emotions, thoughts, and bodily sensations without avoiding them or reacting to them automatically improves their recognition and the possibility of responding to them in different ways, to broaden the behavioral repertoire. For example, mindfulness helps maintain healthy lifestyles: asthma patients detect the emotional states that trigger the attacks, diabetic patients are more diligent in taking insulin, and obese patients can avoid giving in to impulsion when they are hungry [49].

Meditation improves attentional control because mindfulness requires sustained attention to the experience of the present moment and the ability to return to the present moment when the mind wanders [26]. Research shows that mindfulness training improves various aspects of the attentional system: orientation, or the ability to direct attention to a stimulus and maintain attention [50]; conflict monitoring, or the ability to focus the attention on priority tasks when there are several tasks [51]; warning, or the ability to remain alert or receptive to different potential stimuli [50]; sustained attention. Chambers et al. [52] also demonstrate an association between improved sustained attention and a reduction in depressive symptoms. Meditation changes how memory works. It reduces overgeneral autobiographical memory (OGM) [38, 53], which is associated with the severity of depression and suicidality [54]. It minimizes the effect of a decrease in working memory capacity during periods of stress, which is a mediating factor in the reduction of negative affects [55].

It decreases the memory of negative stimuli [56]. Meditation induces relaxation by decreasing oxygen and carbon dioxide uptake, respiratory rate, heart rate, blood pressure, cortisol levels, skin conduction response, and muscle tension [57]. Hölzel et al. [57] have established four mechanisms of action of mindfulness with neurological evidence:

1. Regulation of attention—i.e., sustained attention to an object and, when distracted by an unexpected event, the individual is able to disengage the attention from that stimulus and return it to the object of initial focus (anterior cingulate cortex);

2. Body awareness—the focus of attention on the sensory experiences such as breathing, emotions, and other bodily sensations (insula, temporo-parietal junction);

3. Emotional regulation—that is, the fact that emotional reactivity decreases when the individual does not allow emotional reactions to interfere with his performance in cognitive tasks (modulation of the amygdala by the lateral prefrontal cortex);

4. Change in perspective on the self—that is the capacity to observe mental processes with clarity and allow the development of a meta-awareness that facilitates a detachment from identification with the static sense of self.

From these perspectives, we clearly understand how mindfulness operates through its multiple mechanisms of action by which it impacts on reducing anxiety and depressive symptoms, increasing awareness, developing acceptance and the ability to focus and control attention.

5. Mindfulness in organizations

How to become an ethical and inspiring leader? Perhaps by changing the way we perceive things, by reducing our tendency to interpret and judge them. We can become more ethical leaders by reducing our propensity to put people in tiny boxes and expect them to function exactly as we want them to. We can also become more inspiring leaders by seeing people as a source of unparalleled creativity, not a list of imperfections for improvement. People are easily distracted, they forget important things, and they prefer to act according to their own values rather than according to what is dictated to them. Expecting employees to operate like a machine is a huge mistake. Instead, they must be granted some margins of freedom turning them into a source of innovation by changing the relationship with them and favoring a constructive collaboration, in a climate of trust.

The organizational environment is getting more and more uncertain. Is the competitive strategy of a company built solely based on strategies, technologies, and shareholders? Will the company of tomorrow be merely a financial and technological tool? Assuredly No, the competitive advantage of the company lies above all in the men and women who compose it, and the company of tomorrow will be above all a human community, which will flourish through people's skills and ability to cooperate and adapt. The environmental term VUCA (Volatility, Uncertainty, Complexity, and

Ambiguity) perfectly describes what both managers and employees unanimously depict. This term was introduced by the military in the United States in the 1990s. In recent years, it has been picked up widely in organizations, as it aptly describes what we see in business: the uncertainty and increasing complexity of our environment. However, this concept, if it makes an observation, does not offer any answers.

Today's organizations face impermanence and uncertainty. Everything seems to change much faster, in unexpected ways. People spend most of their time operating in "autopilot" mode. Most of our daily life is managed automatically. Our actions, which we think we control, are often automatic. If we want to change that, which implies to develop the awareness of these automatisms, of the representations which underlie our reactions and of being able to momentarily press "pause" and take the time to reflect. Research on "solution-centered" approaches such as the Appreciative Inquiry has shown that being able to represent "possibilities" opens up the field of innovation, while respecting the needs of each individual. This approach makes it possible to think "broader" and to mobilize the available resources toward a common objective, based on shared values. It is resolutely oriented toward the values of individuals and avoids swimming against the tide and therefore wasting energy unnecessarily trying to cope with "resistance to change." The development of mindfulness appears as a way to promote this new posture in organizations in order to achieve the implementation of processes-oriented change toward innovative solutions.

Because of the uncertainty that characterizes today's society, the high levels of pressure from stakeholders, the "always-on" cultures of the digital era, the complex interpersonal relationships, and the constant changes, paradox, and ambiguity have become part of most managers' everyday working lives. All these factors result in stress, stress-related health problems, sickness, and absenteeism [58], which consequently affect the outcomes of the managers themselves.

Thusly, we are witnessing the disappearance of the Western figure of the manager. In fact, in the past, the manager used to be seen as hero or a visionary thanks to whose extraordinary talents, any difficulty could be easily overcome with the help of a purely rational approach to management [59]. Today's literature theorizes new conceptions of management and leadership, and these conceptions are being relayed by consultants, schools of management, and the management press calling for a new posture of management. The representation of the manager as someone who is responsible for making decisions or someone who only manages by objectives is therefore being questioned. Desmarais and Abord de Chatillon highlighted the role of managers, and they claimed that managers' role consists of interpreting and articulating the concerns of the different stakeholders [60] and inscribing the action of the collaborators in certain coherence, even if this coherence is always local and temporary. As a matter of fact, the contemporary manager is someone who creates meaning, guarantees the coherence of the action, he is the main actor of the co-regulation, and he plays this role by sharing emotions of the stakeholders. During the last decade, in response to the recent problematic of leadership and management, an emerging field of academic research is being focused on the types of leadership, which are centered on ethics, collective, and pro-social behaviors [61]. On the one hand, leadership is viewed as collective or shared behaviors resulting in a set of actions of interdependent individuals from a nonlinear perspective. On the other hand, the new emerging leadership styles emphasize the leaders' ability to foster employees' development through empathy, ethics, altruism, especially through servant leadership [62, 63]. Thusly, this style of leadership has been associated with important effects such as increased job satisfaction and organizational commitment [63], creative behaviors [64], and performance [65]. At the same time, the literature on leadership rehabilitated emotions and their role in managerial performance.

Although there are leadership approaches that have been interested in emotions for a long time, it is only recently that this topic has become the subject of systematic research. In fact, in the research on leadership, the analysis of the impact of emotions and emotional work is omnipresent. There are many approaches and definitions of concept of emotion. A simple and synthetic definition conceptualizes emotions as intense reactions to an event, person, or entity [66, 67]. According to the meta-analysis of Gooty et al. [68], the research unanimously shows the existence of an emotional contagion between leader and followers, i.e., a positive impact of positive emotions of the leaders on the followers and, conversely, for the negative emotions. For example, Avolio et al. [69] demonstrated that the hope and the optimism of the leader had a key influence on the behavior of the followers, while Huy [70] shows that in a situation of change, effective managers build an emotional balance that is characterized by an emotional involvement and an increased attention to the emotions of their employees. Rubin et al. [71] showed the impact of the recognition of emotions by the leader on the exercise of transformational leadership. Hence, the portrait of a new type of manager has emerged: that is a humble manager who is able to integrate the emotional dimension of the work and who is able to control his level commitment in order to respond fairly according to each situation. Many managers find this representation very attractive as it is being promoted by numbers of human resource manager and business executives. This trend is at the heart of some corporate policies, for example, by deploying programs that develop the quality of life at work or training sessions on the notion of mindfulness. So, using mindfulness in management development makes sense as, by enhancing managers' own well-being, it permits not only to provide benefits to the participants, but also to knock-on positive effects for those that these people lead and manage. Since organizations face increased complexity affecting the ways they take actions for change, leadership and management practices have become essential factors of performance and sustainable competitiveness advantages for businesses. That is the reason why inside organizations, we must develop the ability to change management practices. The contemporary approaches to management emphasize the urgency of reinventing human resource management even if organizations are finding it hard to apply concretely these new approaches in their managerial practices. Thusly, mindfulness becomes a useful tool that is likely to help organizations to support the emergence of new managerial practices.

The traditional figure of the manager is associated with a requirement of total dedication to the organization. However the contemporary approaches to management propose to have a more balanced relationship with work. Given the social and organizational evolutions (the feminization of management, the transformations of the family structure, the aspirations of new generations, etc.), balancing professional life and personal or family life is now considered as an essential factor, a factor of attractiveness for organizations and even a source of performance. A balanced attitude at work and performance imply to have the ability to stand back from one's activity, to mentally stay back (psychological detachment) and but also physically observe distance (breaks, weekends, hobbies) from work. Recently, scholars have developed theory with regard to integrative rather than causal relationships between work and family that feature the construct of work-family balance [72–75]. The present moment alertness that characterizes mindfulness should enable individuals to fully immerse themselves with care and attentiveness while engaged in each role. Mindfulness has been associated with increased concentrative capacity and attentional control [29]. For example, FMRI research (functional magnetic resonance imaging or functional MRI (fMRI) measures brain activity by detecting changes associated with blood flow) has demonstrated that self-report of trait mindfulness relates to amygdala activation in ways that suggest more mindful individuals have greater affect regulation ability [76]. As stated previously, mindfulness is a present-centered, clear, non-judging, non-reactive, and receptive form of awareness [11, 29]. Shapiro et al. [34] suggest that by consciously bringing awareness and acceptance to present moment experiences, individuals are enabled to use a wider and more adaptive range of coping skills. Through attending to information contained in the present and creating space between emotions and reactions to them, clarity and self-regulated functioning are improved.

Although the literature of management science perceives commitment as a positive dimension, the pathologies of over commitment are being increasingly studied: workaholism, stress, and their negative impact on the private life [77]. Thus, today's managers are urged to observe a fair and reasonable distance from their work. Also, even if organizations are interested in the new approaches, they find it very hard to put them concretely into their managerial practices. For example, there are many companies that advocate for a radical questioning of the hierarchical structure, as if they fail to change attitudes and behaviors. So, despite the existence of many studies on the new approaches to management, the literature provides little information on the conditions to favor their emergence.

Furthermore, business executives encounter a lot of difficulties in putting into practice the new dimensions of management. The observation of the forms of management in most contemporary organizations shows a weak evolution of the managerial practices. In fact, the contemporary evolutions of many organizations hardly seem to lead to the renewal of management practices but tend to maintain and strengthen the status quo: the Information Systems strengthen centralization and control, the financial goals determine the performance of managers through very short-term considerations; pyramidal and centralized models yield little ground. Managers are busy executing the numerous management processes, and consequently, they have no time to effectively manage and support their teams. This difficulty to integrate new dimensions of leadership into the managerial practice is demonstrated in the analysis of the six reference points of the managerial skills of French big companies carried out by Vernazobres [78]. The posture of traditional leadership, centered on an individual figure, with outstanding qualities, is widely highlighted. Conversely, the spiritual, plural, and collective dimensions of leadership do not appear. Despite the depletion of the model of the rational manager, the universe of management is still refractory to emotional aspects [59]. The model of bureaucracy, focused on rationality, is the model that develops the most the negation and the control of emotions [79]. However, although this model is controversial and questioned, it continues to underpin much of the dynamic of contemporary organizational structures.

Good et al. [6] analyze the current research on mindfulness at work and call for more academic research on this topic. They classify the possible impacts of mindfulness at work into three categories: performance, relationships, and well-being. Without relying on this categorization, we approach these topics by studying mindfulness in the light of the role of manager and leadership, emotional skills, and work relationship. In a context of search for cultural and behavioral changes, it seems to us that the concept of mindfulness, which is focused on awareness and training, will be a promising research avenue. Already two studies have demonstrated that mindfulness trainings generate more positive behaviors than the traditional approach of training. In 2010, Schneider et al. showed that corporate social responsibility training was more effective in inducing behavioral changes when relying on mindfulness [80]. In the same year, a pilot study conducted on primary school teachers who underwent mindfulness training showed a positive and very significant evolution of their ability to accept situations without judgment [81]. The changes operated by the managers involve both their posture and their behavior. The approaches based on mindfulness belong to the field of acceptance and commitment therapies (ACTs). The ACTs aim to help individuals strengthen their psychological flexibility by working on two complementary processes: acceptance and mindfulness processes by allowing not only a change of posture but also the processes of commitment and change behaviors that allow behavioral change.

The first contribution of mindfulness is the awareness that the observed reality is distinct and sometimes profoundly different from the mind that observes it. Throughout the practice, the participant clearly integrates what he perceives as the reality is actually what he decides to see, build, and interpret. This awareness allows a kind of hindsight: the person in a state of mindfulness ceases to identify himself with a situation and is able to observe distance from judgments, which enables him to develop greater clarity and objectivity. By adopting the posture of a witness instead of a subject, the participant becomes part of a more global and relative system. He is able to talk in relative terms and opens himself to others [26]. As Goleman suggests, "The first realization in 'meditation' is that the phenomena contemplated are distinct from the mind contemplating them" [82]. This skill is necessary as it enables the manager to be a translator and have a clear vision of the environment without necessarily identifying himself with it.

At the same time, mindfulness promotes an attitude of curiosity, acceptance of the present situation [26]. Such attitude reduces negative reactions of resistance or avoidance. A person who acts in a state of mindfulness does not seek for self-affirmation, but he advocates for fair actions. By relegating the ego to the background, mindfulness allows the clarification of values and the ability to distinguish the reality from what is dictated by our misrepresentations. In complex situations, managers can therefore question their own vision and renew it by adopting an attitude of non-judgment and acceptance. Finally, mindfulness develops cognitive, emotional, and behavioral flexibility, which is the ability to identify and challenge automatic modes of operation to increase its action [83]. This attentional capacity would allow the manager to better manage the numerous solicitations that he undergoes and the injunctions of the immediacy. Whereas the rationalist approach of contemporary management rejects emotions, the practice of mindfulness suggests managers to welcome their thoughts, their emotions and sensations, as well as those of others [26]. This special attention helps to integrate emotions into interpersonal relationships and to support their leadership on this dimension.

Today, a growing number of companies are making the choice to adopt mindfulness training technique that incorporates mindfulness meditation as its main component. While in the fields of psychology and medicine, the research on mindfulness is well developed, it is still nascent in the organizational literature. However, this trend is changing now as many scholars are confirming the multiple advantages of mindfulness for practitioners [27, 84–90]. Also, attention has always been considered as an important challenge in today's companies, and it is well established that mindfulness provides additional insights on the property and the importance of attention. Organizational scholars and practitioners are showing steady and growing interest in using mindfulness to solve workplace problems. Stahl and Goldstein [91] speak about a "mindfulness revolution" in business as mindfulness is getting more and more popular inside organizations. The world leading organizations have adopted mindfulness (Google, Apple, McKinsey & Company, Deutsche Bank, Procter and Gamble, Astra Zeneca, General Mills, Aetna). Mindfulness practice is being adopted in the world of business as a technique that helps generate the well-being and performance, specifically in high-stress professional contexts [92] and organizational leadership. Mindfulness generates a shift in perspective and provides less identification between the individual and his unfolding experiences [34]. It provides a reduction of automatic mental processes and an awareness of physiological regulatory mechanisms. These three mechanisms would allow the establishment of secondary mechanisms that could be beneficial in the workplace.

As a matter of fact, according to Siegel [93], mindfulness practice develops in a person the ability to take time and think before responding to an environmental stimulus. This time of reflection would allow him to ponder and consider multiple solutions before reacting to an event and avoid acting impulsively or reactively. The person would also take the necessary time to think and act in coherence with his goals, needs, and values. In the professional environment, this would only help improve decision-making but also reduce impulsive or aggressive communication. Ruminations are major bottleneck at workplaces. Nolen-Hoeksema defines it as a mechanism by which the individual who faces difficulties, focuses repetitively and passively on the symptoms, causes, and consequences of these difficulties [93]. Rumination reduces concentration in the workplace, it favors the development of negative moods, and thereby, it decreases the individual's efficiency. Dane [94] stated that mindfulness is positively correlated with performance. According to him, mindfulness practice broadens the individual focus to internal experiences (intuitions) and external experiences: these qualities are very important for making decisions. Karelaia and Reb assess the potential impact of mindfulness on the entire decision-making process [95]. It has been also established that mindfulness enables a better regulation of affect promoting positive emotions and reducing negative ones. This generates many impacts in organizations: resilience to negative experiences; ability to handle stressful situations; better communication with coworkers. Moreover, it has been proven by many empirical studies that the emotions of a leader affect the emotional state of his followers, the general atmosphere of the team, and its effectiveness [96, 97].

Well-being is a fundamental issue that concerns all companies and organizations, at all levels: managers, HR, and all teams. We have discovered that mindfulness reduces stress, burnouts, and it allows better management of psychosocial risks. Therefore, in a business world, which is constantly under pressure and stress, leading mindfully allows leaders and managers to make strategic decisions with serenity and self-control. It is a management method that combines performance and well-being.

6. Discussion

For years, researchers and practitioners have been passionate about how to best describe leadership. Among the touted characteristics they cite: the aspiration for excellence, honesty, emotional intelligence, discipline, self-confidence, open-endedness, adaptability, and truthfulness. So who would be the leader that practices mindfulness? What distinguishes this concept from the previous conceptualizations of leadership? We have already described mindfulness as favoring vigilance and full attention to experiences as they happen, non-reactively and non-judgmentally. Self-awareness, self-regulation, and self-transcendence are presented to anchor the concept of mindfulness in the behavioral dimension. Mindful leadership can be explained from these three perspectives. By developing these skills, leaders are likely to reinforce the skills they need in order to manage not only their own behavior but also to engage with other people and lead them. Below we examine the three foundational elements of mindful leadership (self-awareness, self-regulation, and self-transcendence) and provide a rationale that explains why it is especially important and relevant for leaders to cultivate mindfulness in organizations.

Self-awareness is an important part of effective leadership. It enables people to have a correct understanding of their intentions, emotions, biases, and habits; so that they can more effectively manage their thoughts, feelings, and actions. Three aspects of self-awareness are likely to benefit leaders, their staff, and their organizations: first, the awareness of one's mental, physical, and emotional state; second, the awareness of his automatisms; and third, the awareness of one's experiential or narrative mode of reference. When a leader is aware of himself, all these three aspects can be linked to concrete results that will have effects for employees and the organization as a whole.

When the body and the mind are under stress, part of the brain (the median prefrontal cortex) coordinates the limbic system (sympathetic and parasympathetic nervous systems) in such a way as to balance the bodily systems so that the person can continue to function [93]. If the median prefrontal cortex becomes overwhelmed or overly stressed, the sympathetic system may activate in a way that causes the person to choose a suboptimal response, such as engaging in a struggle while refraining would be more appropriate. For example, a manager experiencing high levels of stress due to a tight deadline who abruptly responds to a coworker asking if anyone wants cream and sugar in their coffee. The manager's reaction is likely to be offensive and fruitless. The states of overload, burnout, and emotional exhaustion that lead to this type of reaction are common in organizations among workers at all levels, and while leaders have responsibility for the well-being of others, they must also make sure to invest in their own well-being. It is indeed important for leaders to take care of themselves, as their mood and decisions are likely to affect a larger population of employees. The Vietnamese Buddhist monk, Thich Nhat Hahn, offers on this subject the analogy with the oxygen mask intended for the passengers of the planes, which illustrates the fact that people must first put on the mask before putting it on someone else [28]. Before managing their workforce, leaders should consider making a conscious effort to take care of their own well-being first. Feeding themselves in this way can generate other resources for themselves and others.

Mindfulness training has been shown to be very successful in coping with burnout, stress, and anxiety and in ensuring overall well-being, both in clinical and non-clinical populations [27]. One study found that mindfulness-trained participants had higher levels of melatonin, an indicator of immune functioning, than untrained participants [31]. In the workplace context, mindfulness-practicing employees have been found to be more committed and satisfied at work and less likely to take time off and quit their jobs. These studies have important implications for executives who are concerned with safeguarding their own well-being at work. Additionally, researchers suggest that leaders who have incorporated mindfulness as a trait have a positive influence on their employees [98]. Reb et al. surveyed 96 managers in various industries and their subordinates. They found that employees whose managers practiced more mindfulness exhibited minor emotional exhaustion, are able to better balance their work and personal life, and were more satisfied at work and performing better. Automaticity is also an integral part of the human life. Automaticity causes narrow habits, prejudices, and perceptions that may become deeply rooted over time. Habitual reactions can happen without our knowing it or being aware of it and can lead to undesirable outcomes, including limitation of innovation, repetition of negative habits, and incapacity to change. Mindfulness helps break the rhythm of automaticity by making it possible to approach the present in a mindful and deliberate way [99]. For example, we may absurdly answer a question when we are not listening with full attention to what other people are actually saying. When we practice mindfulness, we can hear another person's words without having to assume what they are saying. The usual reactions are then interrupted by systematic modes of information processing. Along these lines, mindfulness has been associated with improved decision-making [100], creativity [101], and the ability to counter cognitive biases [102].

The third aspect of self-awareness relates to a person's ability to know when exactly he or she is in the present moment as it is, and when he or she approaches the present moment as a story to tell. The brain uses two processing mode of the present moment [103]: the experiential processing mode and the narrative processing mode. When the narrative processing mode is active, thoughts and emotions are induced by a narrative oriented toward the past or the future, a narrative created by the subject. The experiential processing mode is based primarily on experiencing oneself in the present moment. Psychologists also describe the concept of self as having two dimensions: the subject self ("I") and the object self ("me") [104]. Here, the notion of the subject self, also called the "self as process," is close to the experiential mode, which involves being aware of the activities that are occurring. The notion of self as an object can be understood as a perception of the self that is constructed, in a social perspective, in the narrative mode. This perception of the self inherently activates self-esteem by allowing identification with self-valuing attributes, characteristics, roles, and beliefs [29]. Mindfulness helps develop the experiential mode and combines it with an attitude of unconditional openness [105]. A self-aware leader can be more apt to know when he is caught in this type of constructed self-perception and to leave that mode in order to understand what others are experiencing without feeling threatened. This conscious relief of the ego creates space for self-acceptance, self-compassion, and humility, which makes it possible to be less defensive and have more authentic relationships with others. This suspension of the ego could help bridge the generational gap within organizations by allowing leaders to hear the voices of those they might have difficulties to understand. Integrating self-awareness into mindfulness practice has benefits for both leaders and the organizations they lead. Awareness of one's own thoughts, emotions, and behaviors, when linked to a particular goal, allows for better behavioral control. In the next part, we discuss the second pillar of mindful leadership: self-regulation. While self-awareness offers leaders the ability to know where they are, self-regulation is the way to get them where they are going.

Leonardo da Vinci said: "You will never have a greater or lesser dominion than that over yourself...the height of a man's success is gauged by his self-mastery; the depth of his failure by his self-abandonment.... And this law is the expression of eternal justice. He who cannot establish dominion over himself will have no dominion over others."

Willpower and self-control help people to achieve their goals and make them avoid to take actions that they might regret later. The capacity to control oneself allows people to act in a strategic manner on their thoughts, emotions, and behaviors instead of reacting impulsively to immediate stimuli from their environment. A famous study on delayed gratification and achievement elegantly demonstrated the benefit of willpower: some kids were offered a marshmallow telling them that they were free to eat it if they wanted to, but that, if they could resist the urge to eat it for a short time, they would be offered two marshmallows. Some years afterward, the researchers discovered that kids who had demonstrated the mastery necessary in order to get the benefits from delayed gratification performed better at school with good grades, they were able to better cope with stress, and were more cognitively and socially competent [106]. Recent studies on willpower claim that it is a better predictor than intelligence [107]. This is a particularly interesting conclusion, considering that willpower can be improved with practice; however, it can be very difficult to increase IQ and its effects are minimal [107]. Mindfulness training proves to be an efficacious way to improve self-management skills [101]. Moreover, an additional training could improve the mental health of those who already have a lot of discipline [108].

Mindfulness enhances self-regulation on two levels: attention and emotion Regulation. Attention regulation relates to the capacity to maintain concentration in or out of a particular direction for a specific period of time. This ability has far-reaching implications for leaders. It goes without saying that it is more productive to give sustained attention to the task at hand than having scattered and wandering attention. According to Alan Wallace, one of the first scholars to bring Buddhist mindfulness to the Western countries, all of the most famous artists and scholars in history were endowed with the extraordinary ability to focus their attention, while maintaining a high level of clarity, for long periods of time. During one of his research, Langer, along with his colleagues, recorded an orchestra that played sometimes mindfully and sometimes without attention [109]. Mindful performances have been rated as superior by an audience who ignored the nature of the experience. Working memory may be one of the mechanisms involved in the mindfulness-performance relationship [110]. The notion of working memory relates to the amount of information that an individual can store and handle in the mind at a time, for example, to establish the total cost of an addition before the server brings it. Mrazek [110] conducted a randomized controlled study where students who have gone through 2 weeks of mindfulness training were able to improve their working memory and to perform better on the Graduate Record Examination (GRE) test than the control group.

Mindfulness promotes the development of concentration, enables leaders to see things with more clarity and thus make better decisions. One study found that leaders with more mindfulness as a trait make better decisions under pressure [111]. Sustained focus, along with acceptance and non-judgment, enables leaders to consider the many perspectives that exist beyond a cursory glance at the situation. Steve Jobs, the late CEO of Apple Inc. had his own method of meditation. His biography relates the following: If we sit down and watch, we notice how restless our mind is, but over time it calms down, and by the time it calms down, intuition flourishes, and we begin to see situations more clearly and to be more in the present [112].

Mindfulness could be useful for leaders who cannot stop thinking or, more specifically, thinking at work, in that it can help them cultivate attention regulation to allow them to leave their work in the office and to be more present when they return home. In a study of staff at a Norwegian insurance company, employees who received mindfulness training had a much better perception of their work-life balance at the end of the training [113]. In this vein, Thompson and Bunderson [114] found that work-life balance is determined less by the time a person spends at or outside of work, than by their level of presence in these two contexts. Mindfulness methods rely on deliberately paying attention to the present moment. No matter how much time leaders spend outside of the workplace, mindfulness benefits them by allowing them to be fully present no matter where they are and who they are with.

From a neurological viewpoint, mindfulness is said to strengthen the pathways in the brain that are in charge of emotions regulation [115]. Emotions regulation is the ability to calm down when one is agitated and lift the spirit up when one is depressed. An important aspect of mindfulness training is observing, identifying, and labeling experiences without attaching meaning to what is happening. This process, known as "decentering" [34], allows people to accept thoughts as the interpretations of reality but not necessarily as the reality. When we practice mindfulness, we recognize our emotions in the present moment and decenter ourselves in order to create enough space and take a break before reacting to what we are feeling. For Siegel [93], this possibility of taking a break gives flexibility to react. It allows to take time for reflection and to examine the situation from a non-automatic perspective and choose the action best suited to the person's goal [29, 93]. This decentering technique and flexibility can facilitate the regulation of emotions in leaders who practice mindfulness. Managing emotions effectively provides many benefits to leaders. Three of these benefits are discussed below, namely resistance to stress, improved positive affect, and improved interpersonal communications.

One of the most developed domains of study on mindfulness is to determine the effectiveness of mindfulness in reducing stress, depression, and anxiety [27]. The medical literature has established that the practice of mindfulness promotes psychological well-being, particularly in very stressful situations [11]. Similar results were found in a recent study on employees of The Dow Jones Chemical Company, showing that increased mindfulness practice resulted in increased resistance, engagement and general well-being, and lower stress levels [116]. Mindfulness also ends usual negative thought patterns by decreasing self-centered reflective and introspective attention [29] and amplifying negative thoughts [117] in such a way that that people can better deal with painful and emotional experiences. When the self shifts away from negative emotions, the person thinks less and develops a greater tolerance for negative thoughts and feelings and, as a result, he learns to cope better with stress [118]. In short, mindfulness permits to see what is negative less negatively and to remember what is positive more easily.

Mindfulness has been related to increased positive emotions in a number of studies. Barbara Fredrickson [119], a researcher in the field of positive psychology who has proposed a theory of positive emotions called "Broaden-and-build" (extension and construction of positive emotions), maintains that the more people have positive daily experiences the more they develop other lasting physical, cognitive, and psychological resources. In 2008, Fredrickson and his colleagues conducted an experiment in which adult employees were randomly assigned to an experimental meditation group or a control group. People in the experimental group began to notice and experience more positive emotions, less depressive symptoms, and greater life satisfaction as well as giving more meaning to life [120]. Another research confirms the link between noticing positive experiences and engaging in their experiences [121].

The regulation of emotions arguably benefits leaders with increased emotional intelligence, decreased impulsiveness and improved communication, interpersonal relationships, and social experience [122]. The ego can be managed more effectively through mindfulness training, allowing leaders to intelligently listen to others and articulate the message they want to deliver. Since mindfulness enables people to endure more negative emotions and to overcome them effectively when they occur [29], those who practice more mindfulness may be less defensive and turn out to be more open. In addition to the advantages in terms of communication, there are positive chain effects on the behavior of subordinates whose leaders are less negative

[97] and practice more mindfulness. While conducting their study, Reb et al. [123] recruited leaders and their followers to take part in a web survey. They discovered that leaders who had better integrated mindfulness as a character trait built better connections with their subordinates and were more responsive to and supportive of their needs and that, for their part, their subordinates declared that they are more satisfied at work and were judged to be more efficient.

Mindfulness training technique can be used to modify the way the brain directs and processes thoughts and emotions [124, 125]. This opens up exciting possibilities for organizations with regard to mental illness as well as employee well-being. Self-regulation of thoughts and emotions is an important skill that leaders must possess, not only in order for them to carry out their tasks optimally, but for them to learn how to stay optimally in an environment weighed heavily by pressure, high stakes, and relentless stress. We have tried to introduce two of the three pillars of mindful leadership, self-awareness and self-regulation, to explain the notion of mindful leadership and the advantages associated with these two modes of functioning. Leaders with higher self-awareness and self-control may find themselves better equipped to care for themselves and to lead others more effectively. The final pillar, self-transcendence, examines how leaders can push themselves through mindfulness and why this concept can be valuable in the nowadays workplace.

Self-transcendence is the ability to put aside one's special needs to pay attention to the needs of others. In the Buddhist philosophy, it is said that there are four immeasurable moral qualities: benevolence, compassion, selfless joy, and equanimity [126]. The practice of mindfulness seeks the incarnation and development of these qualities; however, the ability to put the needs of others ahead of one's own needs requires that one first develops enough personal resources to take care of oneself. Mindfulness develops the mind to pay nonjudgmental attention to the present moment. Decentering and pauses for reflection allow people to distance themselves from painful thoughts and emotions so that their negative impacts do not hurt their self-esteem. Once the resources formerly used to defend and provide for themselves are freed, mindful leaders are able to give more and could benefit from doing so. Does not the parent who deprives himself of a pleasure so that his child can enjoy the fruits of his deprivation still experience joy? Self-transcendence in mindful leaders can be conceptualized as actions done for others with genuine empathy and compassion. The inclination toward pro-social behavior has attractive implications for the well-being of individuals and the best interests of the companies that employ them. Empathy involves seeing life from another person's perspective. It allows you to bond with others by understanding their experience and being compassionate. Leaders who can understand the feelings of others have the ability to consider the needs of others and choose a course of action that reflects the interests of a larger group of people [93]. One can read, in a study of the behavior of leaders, that people underwent the following four measures of empathy to establish a profile of dispositional empathy: empathic concern, perspective taking, personal distress, and empathic association [127]. Those with the highest empathy profile were the most likely to exhibit transformational leadership behaviors, a style of leadership that is described as inspiring followers to accomplish more than expected. Empathetic leaders are more promising in resolving conflict, engaging their employees, and effectively motivating them.

A growing body of organizational research suggests that healthy social bonds at work are very important. Some even go so far as to argue that a leader who wants to add value to his team must form strong emotional relationships with and within his team and then manage them [128]. Compassion might even be a necessary leadership trait to engage followers. Tom Rath and Barry Conchie, authors of the popular Find Your Strengths collection, have published Strengths-Based Leadership [129]. They list four needs that make people follow a leader: confidence, hope, stability, and compassion (characterized by caring, friendship, happiness, and love). In fact, the lack of compassion in relationships makes it difficult to build trust [130]. Given that lack of trust is considered to be the main cause of team dysfunction [131], learning to express compassion is far from secondary.

Essentially, we see two great benefits to self-transcendence. First, it fosters positive and fulfilling relationships in this our chaotic and fragmented world of work. Then, it creates lasting happiness and a raison d'être for the leader as a person. In today's workplace, employees have less job security but more responsibilities and a longer schedule that impinges on their personal lives. In many ways, they themselves have integrated the pressure to accomplish and produce. Recently, the fastest growing segment of the workforce, Generation Y, has added a new dimension to the world of work. This generation has higher expectations of employers and aspires to have them committed to these expectations and fulfill them. At the same time, however, it has conflicting priorities in personal life that are more important than career, which makes them difficult to manage [132]. Leaders who can engage their employees through mindfulness, nurturing genuine relationships with them based on compassion and empathy, may be better able to effectively manage their organizations in the workplace today.

The second benefit of self-transcendence for leaders is a personal advantage. To achieve lasting happiness and fulfillment, you have to be committed to something bigger than yourself. Martin Seligman, often referred to as the father of positive psychology in mass media, distinguished between lasting pleasure and fleeting pleasure in his book Authentic Happiness [133]. In it, he describes three methods that people can use to continue their quest for happiness. The first is about the pursuit of positive emotional experiences in oneself: good food, beautiful things, happy experiences. The second is about discovering personal strengths and applying them to positive experiences. The third method, a journey he calls "meaningful life" focuses on the distinctive strengths and virtues that one puts at the service of something greater than oneself [133]. It is important to note that it has recently been established that compassion meditation leads to important improvements in altruistic behavior [134]. Buddhist compassion meditations have been shown to produce the highest level of activation of the left prefrontal cortex, the so-called region of happiness [135], suggesting that cultivating happiness through mindfulness can create opportunities to be kinder to others. Mindful leadership has remarkable potential to generate a positive upward spiral of self-fulfillment.

The performance of business executives and the development of their behavioral skills and leadership capabilities are huge challenges for companies that are looking for new ways for training and coaching. The methods based on mindfulness training could be interesting to address two major themes:

1. The improvement of the emotional intelligence of the leaders is at the heart of the debate on the performance. Earlier we mentioned the impact of MBSR training on the regulation of positive emotion. Bondolfi et al. introduce a dynamic view of emotion management thanks to Mindfulness training [136]. Sobolewski et al. demonstrate that meditators are able to regulate the action of their brain by minimizing the effect of negative emotions, without altering the effect of positive emotions [137]. Studies on another type of meditation, such as the meditation of loving-kindness meditation, reveal that it generates an improvement in positive social emotions that might result in the reduction of isolation [138].

2. The strengthening of the capacity of attention: Meditation improves attention and cognitive abilities (flexibility) [139] even in case of brief mental training [140]. It also increases positive emotions and associated benefits (purpose in life, sociability...) [120].

In conclusion, we can say that in today's new organizational context, the role of manager is increasingly that of an agent of change who is capable of developing the involvement of complex individuals within turbulent projects with uncertain outlines. The manager is thus confronted with a first organizational paradox: the injunction to immediacy and the injunction to action in a hyper complex environment, which also requires greater hindsight and a distance that requires time. He must also find solution to a second paradox, which is of an individual nature: the injunction to be fully involved in the organization and the aspiration for self-realization and quest for meaning. This places him in a permanent tension between contradictory aspirations: well-being and professional performance, authenticity, and adaptation to one's workstation [141]. The manager's posture therefore becomes fundamentally dual, forcing him to learn to reconcile what may seem irreconcilable:

- Goal achievement/self-realization
- Effectiveness of immediate and punctual action/global and complex reflection
- Segmentation/integration between private and professional life
- Maximum involvement/well-being
- Rationality/emotional intelligence and creativity
- Implementation of strategic decisions taken by others/participation and co-decision of the teams

These oppositions force the manager to make a permanent gap and, in the absence of finding the right balance, to love his work but to suffer from it [142]. In this work, we propose avenues that explore how transcend these oppositions and overcome personal and organizational paradoxes. Leadership research follows changes in society and tries to support mutations linked to hypermodernity and individual globalism. Two directions coexist:

- On the one hand, the notions of creativity, authenticity, exemplarity, ethics, values, and even spirituality are found in the positive forms of leadership, and they offer advanced or high-end constructs.
- On the other hand, operational necessities ask for a return to the leadership of structure and consideration. These different works underline from a theoretical point of view the duality between the principle of reality and the aspiration to certain transcendence, as if the operational necessity were irremediably opposed to a "spiritual" perspective, which nevertheless takes a growing place in managerial literature [143].

To overcome these oppositions, Quatro et al. [144] suggest a "holistic" model, which emphasizes the need to reconcile analytical, conceptual, emotional, and spiritual leadership. Fry and Kriger [145] offer a new interpretation of the leadership theories that are based on various levels of relation to reality and converge toward a non-dual leadership, capable of overcoming apparent oppositions. Quatro et al., like Fry and Krieger, support the need to explore new avenues to overcome the paradoxes imposed by modernity. They do not, however, provide operational response on the nature of this new leadership and its learning. This is what we propose to explore by mobilizing the psychological concept of mindfulness along with the theory U [146]. In our opinion, mindfulness is a concept that is both interesting and operational to change perspective, and theory U is an interesting tool to illustrate what could be this renewed leadership.

Theory U, although not explicitly referring to mindfulness, seems to be an excellent illustration of what mindful leadership could be. The proposition is the same: to change perspective by opening up and going beyond traditional patterns by mobilizing the concept of presencing, which is very close to that of mindfulness.

Theory U proposes to respond to the current challenges of our society by favoring the development of collective intelligence, the letter U symbolizing three movements in a process of creativity. It is based on the observation according to which any living system operates from several "interior places," which results in different qualities in the way of giving birth to acts. In order to change the way individuals and groups approach situations and then react to them, it is necessary to develop a state of attention, a particular way of listening, a way that enables individuals to "Slowdown in order to understand." This state of attention and heightened awareness is known to high-level athletes, and this is particularly from their experiences, but also by drawing inspiration in oriental philosophies and in the works of Senge [147, 148] and de Varela that Scharmer developed the U theory.

Leadership is one of the particular fields of application of Theory U, because its success depends, according to Scharmer, on the quality of attention and intention that the manager brings to the various situations he deals with.

7. Research limitations and contributions

The question of representations and factors of adoption of mindfulness in business is a crucial avenue of research. These factors are indeed essential in the dissemination of this managerial innovation. Today, the representations surrounding meditation are unknowns and their effects on adoption processes can be significant. Likewise, diffusion in organizations seems slow and may be a hindrance to the operationalization of mindfulness-based intervention programs (MBIs) in companies.

Throughout this research work, mindfulness has been depicted as a psychological construct that can be beneficial to business executives, and that can be mobilized in organizations and deserves scientific interest.

This research contributes to the reflection on the training of managers and the means to support them personally and collectively toward more efficient leadership styles. It therefore provides a new response to the managerial challenge of developing transformative leadership programs allowing leaders to develop themselves personally and morally. We hope that this research will contribute to the development of a neutral and constructive scientific debate on this subject, particularly in Africa where the concept is still not well known.

8. Conclusion

Introducing mindful leadership to the culture of organizations is not only a useful strategy for managers, but also an overall organizational strategy of utmost importance. It is for this reason that it is present in companies such as Google, LinkedIn, and SAP. A large number of high-level leaders have already included it in their daily agenda. They are mindful leaders.

Mindfulness enables managers to live more authentically and to be proactive partners who have a significant influence on the mental health and performance of their team.

This review paper has shown that this field of research is rich in potential, but it is only at the very beginning of its exploration. Some topics are still the subject of a very limited number of publications. If a notable growth in publications has been measured in recent years, and if the study of mindfulness in a professional context is no longer limited to the medical environment and stress at work, the population of leaders remains a population that is very little studied, and the question of the influence of mindfulness on leadership is still in its very early stages. Other themes highlighted show just as much potential and should not be overlooked in order to understand the role that mindfulness can play in organizations.

Author details

Aboubacar Garba Konte
University of Segou, Mali

*Address all correspondence to: konteaboubacar14@gmail.com

References

[1] Lavine M. Paradoxical Leadership and the competing values framework. The Journal of Applied Behavioral Science. 2014;**50**(2):189-205. DOI: 10.1177/0021886314522510

[2] Day DV, Dragoni L. Leadership development: An outcome-oriented review based on time and levels of analyses. Annual Review of Organizational Psychology and Organizational Behavior. 2015;**2**(1):133-156. DOI: 10.1146/annurev-orgpsych-032414-111328

[3] Abbatiello I, Knight A, Philpot M, Roy S. "Leadership disrupted", rewriting the rules for the digital age. In: Deloitte Global Human Capital Trends. London: Deloite University Press; 2017. p. 2017

[4] Nesbit PL. The role of self-reflection, emotional management of feedback, and self-regulation processes in self-directed leadership development. Human Resource Development Review. 2012;**11**(2):203-226. DOI: 10.1177/1534484312439196

[5] King E, Nesbit P. Collusion with denial: Leadership development and its evaluation. Journal of Management Development. 2015;**34**(2):134-152. DOI: 10.1108/JMD-02-2013-0023

[6] Good DJ et al. Contemplating mindfulness at work: An integrative review. Journal of Management. 2016;**46**(1):114-142. DOI: 10.1177/0149206315617003

[7] Boyatzis A, McKee RE. Resonant Leadership: Renewing Yourself and Connecting with Others through Mindfulness, Hope, and Compassion. Boston: Harvard Business School Press, Boston; 2005

[8] Chaskalson M. How to bring Mindfulness to your company's Leadership. Harvard Business Review. 2016;**1**:1-7

[9] Hougaard J, Carter R. The Mind of the Leader: How to Lead Yourself, Your People, and Your Organization for Extraordinary Results. Boston, Massachusetts: Harvard Business Review Press; 2018

[10] Baer ELB, Lykins RA. Mindfulness and positive psychological functioning, In: Sheldon D, Kashdan T, Steger M, editors. Designing the Future of Positive Psychol-Ogy: Taking Stock and Moving Forward. New York, NY: Oxford UniversityPress, 2011, pp. 335-348.

[11] Kabat-Zinn J. Mindfulness-based interventions in context: Past, present, and future. Clinical Psychology: Science and Practice. 2003;**10**(2):144-156. DOI: 10.1093/clipsy/bpg016

[12] Avolio BJ, Gardner WL. Authentic leadership development: Getting to the root of positive forms of leadership. The Leadership Quarterly. 2005;**16**(3):315-338. DOI: 10.1016/j.leaqua.2005.03.001

[13] Kristensen ML. Mindfulness and resonance in an era of acceleration: A critical inquiry. Journal of Management, Spirituality & Religion. 2018;**15**(2):178-195. DOI: 10.1080/14766086.2017.1418413

[14] Purser RE. Critical perspectives on corporate mindfulness. Journal of Management, Spirituality & Religion. 2018;**15**(2):105-108. DOI: 10.1080/14766086.2018.1438038

[15] Hülsheger UR, Walkowiak A, Thommes MS. How can mindfulness be promoted? Workload and recovery

experiences as antecedents of daily fluctuations in mindfulness. Journal of Occupational and Organizational Psychology. 2018;**91**(2):261-284. DOI: 10.1111/joop.12206

[16] Levett KM, Coughlan S, Longridge S, Roumeliotis V, Adams J. Be well: A systems-based wellness intervention using mindfulness in the workplace—A case study. Journal of Management & Organization. 2017:1-22. DOI: 10.1017/jmo.2017.41

[17] Lomas T, Medina JC, Ivtzan I, Rupprecht S, Hart R, Eiroa-Orosa FJ. The impact of mindfulness on well-being and performance in the workplace: An inclusive systematic review of the empirical literature. European Journal of Work and Organizational Psychology. 2017;**26**(4):492-513. DOI: 10.1080/1359432X.2017.1308924

[18] Vu MC, Gill R. Is there corporate mindfulness? An exploratory study of Buddhist-enacted spiritual leaders' perspectives and practices. Journal of Management, Spirituality & Religion. 2018;**15**(2):155-177. DOI: 10.1080/14766086.2017.1410491

[19] Yu L, Zellmer-Bruhn M. Introducing team mindfulness and considering its safeguard role against conflict transformation and social undermining. The Academy of Management Journal. 2018;**61**(1):324-347

[20] Walsh Z. Mindfulness under neoliberal governmentality: Critiquing the operation of biopower in corporate mindfulness and constructing queer alternatives. Journal of Management, Spirituality & Religion. 2018;**15**(2):109-122

[21] IBM. IBM2010Global CEOStudy: Creativity selected asmostcrutial factorfor future success. News Release. 2010. Available from: www-03.ibm.com/press/us/en/pressrelease/31670.wss

[22] Wallace BA. Minding Closely: The Four Applications of Mindfulness. Ithaca, NY: Snow Lion Publications; 2011

[23] Wallace BA. The Attention Revolution: Unlocking the Power of the Focused Mind. New York: Wisdom Publications Inc; 2006

[24] Gilpin R. The use of Theravā da Buddhist practices and perspectives in mindfulness-based cognitive therapy. Contemporary Buddhism. 2008;**9**(2):37-41. DOI: 10.1080/14639940802556560

[25] Hayes SC. Acceptance, mindfulness, and science. Clinical Psychology: Science and Practice. 2002;**9**:101-106. DOI: 10.1093/clipsy.9.1.101

[26] Bishop SR et al. Mindfulness: A proposed operational definition. Clinical Psychology: Science and Practice. 2004;**11**(3):230-241. DOI: 10.1093/clipsy/bph077

[27] Brown KW, Ryan RM. The benefits of being present: Mindfulness and its role in psychological well-being. Journal of Personality and Social Psychology. 2003;**84**(4):822-848. DOI: 10.1037/0022-3514.84.4.822

[28] Hanh TN. The Miracle of Mindfulness, Gift Edition: An Introduction to the Practice of Meditation. Boston: Beacon Press; 2016

[29] Brown KW, Ryan RM, Creswell JD. Mindfulness: Theoretical foundations and evidence for its salutary effects. Psychological Inquiry. 2007;**18**(4):211-237. DOI: 10.1080/10478400701598298

[30] Brown KW et al. Mindfulness: Theoretical foundations and evidence

for its salutary effects mindfulness: Theoretical foundations and evidence for its salutary effects. Psychological Inquiry. 2007;**18**(4):211-237. DOI: 10.1080/10478400701598298

[31] Baer RA. Mindfulness training as a clinical intervention. Clinical Psychology: Science and Practice. 2003;**10**:125-143. DOI: 10.1093/clipsy/bpg015

[32] Brown KW, Ryan RM. Perils and promise in defining and measuring mindfulness: Observations from experience. Clinical Psychology: Science and Practice. 2004;**11**:242-248. DOI: 10.1093/clipsy/bph078

[33] Brown KW, Ryan RM, Creswell JD, Brown KW, Ryan RM, Creswell JD. Addressing fundamental questions about mindfulness addressing fundamental questions about mindfulness. Psychological Inquiry. 2007;**18**:272-281. DOI: 10.1080/10478400701703344

[34] Shapiro JA, Carlson SL, Astin LE. Mechanisms of mindfulness. Journal of Clinical Psychology. 2006;**62**:373-386

[35] Dekeyser M, Raes F, Leijssen M, Leysen S, Dewulf D. Mindfulness skills and interpersonal behaviour. Personality and Individual Differences. 2008;**44**(5):1235-1245. DOI: 10.1016/j.paid.2007.11.018

[36] Salmon P, Sephton MS, Weissbecker MI, Hoovm K, Ulmer C, Studts UJL. Mindfulness meditation in clinical practice. Cognitive and Behavioral Practice. 2004;**4**(11): 434-446

[37] Jinpa T, Is Meditation a Means of Knowing our Mental World? [Online]. 2009. Available from: http://contemplativemind.word press.com/what-is-mindfulness

[38] Hargus E, Crane C, Barnhofer T, Williams JMG. Effects of mindfulness on meta-awareness and specificity of describing prodromal symptoms in suicidal depression. Emotion. 2010;**10**(1):34-42. DOI: 10.1037/a0016825

[39] Teasdale JD, Moore RG, Hayhurst H, Pope M, Williams S. Metacognitive awareness and prevention of relapse in depression: Empirical evidence. Journal of Consulting and Clinical Psychology. 2002;**70**(2):275-287. DOI: 10.1037//0022-006X.70.2.275

[40] Fresco DM, Segal ZV, Buis T, Kennedy S. Relationship of posttreatment decentering and cognitive reactivity to relapse in major depression. Journal of Consulting and Clinical Psychology. 2007;**75**(3):447-455. DOI: 10.1037/0022-006X.75.3.447

[41] Ehring T, Watkins ER. Repetitive negative thinking as a transdiagnostic process. International Journal of Cognitive Therapy. 2008;**1**(3):192-205. DOI: 10.1521/ijct.2008.1.3.192

[42] Jain S. A randomized controlled trial of mindfulness meditation versus relaxation training: Effects on distress, positive states of mind, rumination, and distraction. Annals of Behavioral Medicine. 2007;**33**(1):11-21. DOI: 10.1207/s15324796abm3301_2

[43] Ramel W, Goldin PR, Carmona PE, Mcquaid JR. The effects of mindfulness meditation on cognitive processes and affect in patients with past depression. Cognitive Therapy and Research. 2004;**28**(4):433-455. DOI: 10.1023/B:COTR.0000045557.15923.96

[44] Carmody J, Baer RA, Lykins ELB, Olendzki N. An empirical study of the mechanisms of mindfulness in a mindfulness-based stress reduction program. Journal of Clinical Psychology. 2009;**65**(6):613-626. DOI: 10.1002/jclp

[45] Campbell-sills L, Barlow DH, Brown TA, Hofmann SG. Acceptability and suppression of negative emotion in anxiety and mood disorders. Emotion. 2006;**6**(4):587-595. DOI: 10.1037/1528-3542.6.4.587

[46] Choate DHBLBAML. Toward a unified treatment for emotional disorders. Behavior Therapy. 2004;**35**:205-230. DOI: 10.1016/S0005-7894(04)80036-4

[47] Bond FW, Bunce D. Mediators of change in emotion-focused and problem-focused worksite stress management interventions. Journal of Occupational Health Psychology. 2000;**20**(1):156-163. DOI: 10.1037/1076-8998.5.1.156

[48] Forman EM et al. Behavior modification effectiveness trial of and depression. Behavior Modification. 2007;**31**(6):772-799. DOI: 10.1177/0145445507302202

[49] Bowen GA, Chawla S, Marlatt N. Mindfulness-Based Relapse Prevention for Addictive Behaviors: A clinician's Guide. 1st edition. New York: The Guilford Press; 2011

[50] Amishi AMJB, Jha P, Krompinger J. Mindfulness training modifies subsystems of attention mindfulness training modifies subsystems of attention. Cognitive, Affective, & Behavioral Neuroscience. 2007;**7**(2):109-119. DOI: 10.3758/CABN.7.2.109

[51] Tang Y et al. Short-term meditation training improves attention and self-regulation. Proceedings of the National Academy of Sciences. 2007;**104**:17152-17156. DOI: 10.1073/pnas.0707678104

[52] Chambers R, Lo BCY, Allen NB. The impact of intensive mindfulness training on attentional control, cognitive style, and affect. Cognitive Therapy and Research. 2008;**32**(3):303-322. DOI: 10.1007/s10608-007-9119-0

[53] Teasdale JD, Williams JMG, Ridgeway VA, Soulsby JM, Lau MA. Prevention of relapse/recurrence in major depression by mindfulness-based cognitive therapy. Journal of Consulting and Clinical Psychology. 2000;**68**(4):615-623. DOI: 10.1037//0022-006X.68.4.615

[54] Teasdale JD, Segal ZV, Williams JMG. Mindfulness training and problem formulation. Clinical Psychology: Science and Practice. 2003;**10**(2):157-160. DOI: 10.1093/clipsy/bpg017

[55] Jha AP, Stanley EA, Kiyonaga A. Examining the protective effects of mindfulness training on working memory capacity and affective experience. Emotion. 2010;**10**:54-64

[56] Alberts HJEM, Thewissen R. The effect of a brief mindfulness intervention on memory for positively and negatively valenced stimuli. Mindfulness (N. Y.). 2011;**2**:73-77. DOI: 10.1007/s12671-011-0044-7

[57] Hölzel BK et al. Mindfulness practice leads to increases in regional brain gray matter density. Psychiatry Research: Neuroimaging. 2011;**191**(1):36-43. DOI: 10.1016/j.pscychresns.2010.08.006

[58] Nielsen K, Daniels K. The relationship between transformational leadership and follower sickness absence: The role of presenteeism. Work and Stress. 2016;**30**:193-208

[59] Chanlat J-F. Émotions, organisation et management: Une réflexion critique sur la notion d'intelligence émotionnelle. Travailler. 2003;**9**(1):113. DOI: 10.3917/trav.009.0113

[60] Desmarais C, Abord de Chatillon E. Le rôle de traduction

du manager. Entre allégeance et résistance. Revue Française de Gestion. 2010;**36**(205):71-88. DOI: 10.3166/rfg.205.71-88

[61] Chiniara M, Bentein K. Linking servant leadership to individual performance: Differentiating the mediating role of autonomy, competence and relatedness need satisfaction. The Leadership Quarterly. 2016;**27**(1):124-141. DOI: 10.1016/j.leaqua.2015.08.004

[62] Van Dierendonck D, Nuijten I. The servant Leadership survey: Development and validation of a multidimensional measure. Journal of Business and Psychology. 2011;**26**:249-267. DOI: 10.1007/s10869-010-9194-1

[63] Liden RC, Wayne SJ, Zhao H, Henderson D. Servant leadership: Development of a multidimensional measure and multi-level assessment. The Leadership Quarterly. 2008;**19**(November):161-177. DOI: 10.1016/j.leaqua.2008.01.006

[64] Neubert MJ, Kacmar KM, Carlson DS, Chonko LB, Roberts JA. Regulatory focus as a mediator of the influence of initiating structure and servant leadership on employee behavior regulatory focus as a mediator of the influence of initiating structure and servant leadership on employee behavior. Journal on Applied Psychology. 2008;**96**(December):1220-1233. DOI: 10.1037/a0012695

[65] Hu J, Liden RC. Antecedents of team potency and team effectiveness: An examination of goal and process clarity and servant Leadership. The Journal of Applied Psychology. 2011;**96**(4):851-862. DOI: 10.1037/a0022465

[66] Beal DJ, Weiss HM, Barros E, Macdermid SM. An episodic process model of affective influences on performance. The Journal of Applied Psychology. 2005;**90**(6):1054-1068. DOI: 10.1037/0021-9010.90.6.1054

[67] Fisher CD. Mood and emotions while working: Missing pieces of job satisfaction? Journal of Organizational Behavior. 2000;**202**:185-202

[68] Gooty J, Connelly S, Griffith J, Gupta A. Leadership, affect and emotions: A state of the science review. The Leadership Quarterly. 2010;**21**(6):979-1004. DOI: 10.1016/j.leaqua.2010.10.005

[69] Avolio BJ, Gardner WL, Walumbwa FO, Luthans F, May DR. Unlocking the mask: A look at the process by which authentic leaders impact follower attitudes and behaviors. The Leadership Quarterly. 2004;**15, 15**:801-823. DOI: 10.1016/j.leaqua.2004.09.003

[70] Huy QN. Of emotional balancing organizational and radical continuity the change: Contribution of middle managers. Administrative Science Quarterly. 2002;**47**(1):31-69

[71] Rubin RS. Leading from within: The effects of emotion recognition and personality on transformational leadership behavior. Academy of Management Journal. 2005;**48**(5):845-858. DOI: 10.5465/AMJ.2005.18803926

[72] Greenhaus TD, Allen JH. Work–family balance: A review and extension of the literature. In: Quick IJC, Tetrick LE, editors. Handbook of Occupational Health Psychology. Washington DC: American Psychological Association; 2011. pp. 165-183

[73] Greenhaus JH, Collins KM, Shaw JD. The relation between work-family balance and quality of life. Journal of Vocational Behavior. 2003;**63**(3):510-531. DOI: 10.1016/S0001-8791(02)00042-8

[74] Grzywacz JG, Carlson DS. Conceptualizing work—Family balance: Implications for practice and research. Advances in Developing Human Resources. 2007;**9**(4):455-471. DOI: 10.1177/1523422307305487

[75] Valcour M. Work-based resources as moderators of the relationship between work hours and satisfaction with work-family balance. The Journal of Applied Psychology. 2007;**92**(6):1512-1523. DOI: 10.1037/0021-9010.92.6.1512

[76] Creswell JD, Way BM, Eisenberger NI, Lieberman MD. Neural correlates of dispositional mindfulness during affect labeling. Psychosomatic Medicine. 2007;**69**(6):560-565. DOI: 10.1097/PSY.0b013e3180f6171f

[77] Vernhet AC et al. Organizational commitment: In sickness and in health? The results of a qualitative study organizational commitment: In sickness and in health? Revue de Gestion des Ressources Humaines. 2014;**4**(January):3-25. DOI: 10.3917/grhu.094.0003

[78] VERNAZOBRES. Tous leaders? Quels leaders? Évolution des théories du leadership et pratiques des grandes entreprises. Paris: Dunod; 2016

[79] Eggrickx M-CA. Bureaucracy and the management of emotions: What kind of paradoxical demands? Bureaucratie et management des émotions: Des injonctions paradoxales. Revue Française de Gestion. 2012;**4**:59

[80] Schneider SC, Zollo M, Manocha R. Developing socially responsible behaviour in managers. Journal of Corporate Citizenship. 2010;**39**:21-40

[81] Gold E, Smith A, Hopper I, Herne D, Tansey G, Hulland C. Mindfulness-based stress reduction (MBSR) for primary school teachers. Journal of Child and Family Studies. 2010;**19**(2):184-189. DOI: 10.1007/s10826-009-9344-0

[82] Goleman D. Focus: The Hidden Driver of Excellence. New York: HarperCollins Publishers; 2013

[83] Walsh R, Shapiro SL. The meeting of meditative disciplines and Western. Psychology. 2006;**61**(3):227-239. DOI: 10.1037/0003-066X.61.3.227

[84] Arch JJ, Craske MG. Mechanisms of mindfulness: Emotion regulation following a focused breathing induction. Behaviour Research and Therapy. 2006;**44**(12):1849-1858. DOI: 10.1016/j.brat.2005.12.007

[85] Chiesa A, Serretti A. Mindfulness-based stress reduction for stress management in healthy people: A review and meta-analysis. Journal of Alternative and Complementary Medicine. 2009;**15**(5):593-600. DOI: 10.1089/acm.2008.0495

[86] Grossman P, Niemann L, Schmidt S, Walach H. Mindfulness-based stress reduction and health benefits A meta-analysis. Journal of Psychosomatic Research. 2004;**57**:35-43. DOI: 10.1016/S0022-3999(03)00573-7

[87] Laxmisan A, Hakimzada F, Sayan OR, Green RA, Zhang J, Patel VL. The multitasking clinician: Decision-making and cognitive demand during and after team handoffs in emergency care. International Journal of Medical Informatics. 2007;**76**(11-12):801-811. DOI: 10.1016/j.ijmedinf.2006.09.019

[88] Oman D, Shapiro SL, Thoresen CE, Plante TG, Flinders T. Meditation lowers stress and supports forgiveness among college students: A randomized controlled trial. Journal of American

College Health. 2008;**56**(5):569-578. DOI: 10.3200/JACH.56.5.569-578

[89] Shapiro SL, Brown KW, Biegel GM. Teaching self-care to caregivers: Effects of mindfulness-based stress reduction on the mental health of therapists in training. Training and Education in Professional Psychology. 2007;**1**(2):105-115

[90] Walach H, Nord H, Zier E, Dietz-Waschkowski C, Kersig B, Schubach S. Mindfulness-based stress reduction as a method for personnel development: A pilot evaluation. International Journal of Stress Management. 2007;**14**:188-198

[91] Stahl E, Goldstein B. A Mindfulness-Based Stress Reduction Workbook. Oakland, CA: New Harbinger Productions; 2010

[92] Davidson RJ et al. Alterations in brain and immune function produced by mindfulness meditation. Psychosomatic Medicine. 2003;**65**(4):564-570. DOI: 10.1097/01.PSY.0000077505.67574.E3

[93] Siegel DJ. The mindful brain: Reflection and attunement in the cultivation of well-being (Norton series on interpersonal neurobiology). New York: WW Norton & Company; 2007. pp. 1-21

[94] Dane E. Paying attention to mindfulness and its effects on task performance in the workplace. Journal of Management. 2011;**37**(4):997-1018. DOI: 10.1177/0149206310367948

[95] Karelaia N, Jochen REB. Improving Decision Making through Mindfulness. Cambridge, England: Cambridge University Press; 2015. pp. 163-189. DOI: 10.1017/CBO9781107587793.009

[96] Bono JE, Ilies R. Charisma, positive emotions and mood contagion. The Leadership Quarterly. 2006;**17**(4):317-334. DOI: 10.1016/j.leaqua.2006.04.008

[97] Sy T, Côté S, Saavedra R. The contagious leader: Impact of the leader's mood on the mood of group members, group affective tone, and group processes. The Journal of Applied Psychology. 2005;**90**(2):295-305. DOI: 10.1037/0021-9010.90.2.295

[98] Reb CS, Narayanan J. Leading mindfully: Two studies on the influence of supervisor trait mindfulness on employee well-being and performance. Mindfulness. 2014;**5**(1):36-45

[99] Glomb TM, Duffy MK, Bono JE, Yang T. Mindfulness at Work. Vol. 30. Bingley: Emerald Group Publishing Ltd; 2011

[100] Weber EU, Johnson EJ. Mindful judgment and decision making. Annual Review of Psychology. 2009;**60**:53-85. DOI: 10.1146/annurev.psych.60.110707.163633

[101] Langer EJ. The construct of mindfulness. Journal of Social Issues. 2000;**56**(1):1-9

[102] Hafenbrack AC, Kinias Z, Barsade SG. Debiasing the mind through meditation: Mindfulness and the Sunk-Cost Bias. Psychological Science. 2014;**25**(2):369-376. DOI: 10.1177/0956797613503853

[103] Farb NAS et al. Attending to the present: Mindfulness meditation reveals distinct neural modes of self-reference. Social Cognitive and Affective Neuroscience. 2007;**2**:313-322. DOI: 10.1093/scan/nsm030

[104] Ryan RM, Deci EL. Self-determination theory and the facilitation of intrinsic motivation, social development, and

well-being. The American Psychologist. 2000;**55**(1):68-78

[105] Welwood J. Perfect Love, Imperfect Relationships: Healing the wound of the heart. Shambhala Publications; 2005

[106] Watts TW, Duncan GJ, Quan H. Revisiting the marshmallow test: A conceptual replication investigating links between early delay of gratification and later outcomes. Psychological Science. 2018;**29**(7):1159-1177. DOI: 10.1177/0956797618761661

[107] Baumeister RFEJT. Willpower: Rediscovering the Greatest Human Strength. New York (NY): Penguin; 2011

[108] Bowlin SL, Baer RA. Relationships between mindfulness, self-control, and psychological functioning. Personality and Individual Differences. 2012;**52**(3):411-415. DOI: 10.1016/j.paid.2011.10.050

[109] Langer TRENE. Orchestral performance and the footprint of mindfulness. Psychology of Music. 2009;**37**(2):125-136. DOI: 10.1177/0305735607086053

[110] Mrazek MD et al. Mindfulness training improves working memory capacity and GRE performance while reducing mind wandering. Psychological Science. 2013;**24**(5):776-781. DOI: 10.1177/0956797612459659

[111] Noonan C, Pittinsky TL, Sommer SA, Zhu W. Measuring the efficacy of leaders to assess information and make decisions in a crisis: The C-LEAD scale ☆. The Leadership Quarterly. 2011;**22**(4):633-648. DOI: 10.1016/j.leaqua.2011.05.005

[112] Isaacson W. Steve Jobs. New York: Simon & Schuster (U.S.).; 2012

[113] Reb J, Choi E. Mindfulness in organizations. The Psychology of Meditation. Seattle, USA. 2014

[114] Thompson JA, Bunderson JS. Work-nonwork conflict and the phenomenology of time. Work and Occupations. 2001;**28**(1):17-39. DOI: 10.1177/0730888401028001003

[115] Davidson RJ. Conceptual and methodological considerations in the study of affective style statistical manual of mental disorders. The American Psychologist. 2000;**55**:535-545. DOI: 10.1037/0003-066X.55.11.1196

[116] Aikens KA et al. Mindfulness goes to work: Impact of an online workplace intervention. Journal of Occupational and Environmental Medicine. 2014;**56**(7):721-731. DOI: 10.1097/JOM.0000000000000209

[117] Weick KE, Sutcliffe KM. Mindfulness and the quality of organizational attention. Organization Science. 2006;**17**(4):514-524. DOI: 10.1287/orsc.1060.0196

[118] Broderick PC. Mindfulness and coping with dysphoric mood: Contrasts with rumination and distraction. Cognitive Therapy and Research. 2005;**29**(5):501-510. DOI: 10.1007/s10608-005-3888-0

[119] Fredrickson BL. The role of positive emotions in positive psychology: The broaden-and-build theory of positive emotions. The American Psychologist. 2001;**56**(3):218-226. DOI: 10.1037/0003-066X.56.3.218

[120] Fredrickson BL, Cohn MA, Coffey KA, Pek J, Finkel SM. Open hearts build lives: Positive emotions, induced through loving-kindness meditation,

build consequential personal resources. Journal of Personality and Social Psychology. 2008;**95**(5):1045-1062. DOI: 10.1037/a0013262

[121] Erisman SM, Roemer L. A preliminary investigation of the effects of experimentally induced mindfulness on emotional responding to film clips. Emotion. 2010;**10**(1):72-82. DOI: 10.1037/a0017162

[122] Gross JJ, Thompson RA. Emotion regulation conceptual foundations. In: Handbook of Emotion Regulation. 2007. pp. 3-24

[123] Reb J, Narayanan J, Chaturvedi S. Leading mindfully: Two studies on the influence of supervisor trait mindfulness on employee well-being and performance. Mindfulness (N. Y). 2012;**5**(1):36-45. DOI: 10.1007/s12671-012-0144-z

[124] Lutz A. Neurophenomenology and the study of self-consciousness. Consciousness and Cognition. 2007;**16**(3):765-767. DOI: 10.1016/j.concog.2007.08.007

[125] Friese M, Messner C, Schaffner Y. Mindfulness meditation counteracts self-control depletion. Consciousness and Cognition. 2012;**21**(2):1016-1022. DOI: 10.1016/j.concog.2012.01.008

[126] Wallace B. The Four Immeasurables: Practices to Open the Heart. New York: Snow Lion Publications; 2010

[127] Skinner C, Spurgeon P. Health services management research valuing empathy and emotional a study of empathy, leadership. Health Services Management Research. 2005;**18**:1-12. DOI: 10.1258/0951484053051924

[128] Goleman D, Boyatzis R, McKee A. The hidden driver of great performance by Daniel Goleman, Richard Boyatzis, and Annie McKee. Harvard Business Review. 2001

[129] Rath T, Conchie B. Strengths based Leadership. NHRD Network Journal. 2009;**2**(5):146-147. DOI: 10.1177/0974173920090531

[130] M. Boverie, P., & Kroth, Transforming Work: The Five Keys to Achieving Trust, Commitment, and Passion in the Workplace. Cambridge, MA: Perseus, 2001.

[131] Lencioni P. The Five Dysfunctions of a Team. New York: John Wiley & Sons; 2006

[132] Sheahan P. Generation Y: Thriving and Surviving with Generation Y at Work. San Francisco: Hardie Grant Books; 2005

[133] M. E. Seligman, Authentic Happiness: Using the New Positive Psychology to Realize your Potential for Lasting Fulfillment. New York (NY): Free Press Simon and Schuster, 2002.

[134] Weng HY et al. Compassion training alters altruism and neural responses to suffering. Psychological Science. 2013;**24**(7):1171-1118. DOI: 10.1177/0956797612469537

[135] Klimecki OM, Leiberg S, Ricard M, Singer T. Differential pattern of functional brain plasticity after compassion and empathy training. Social Cognitive and Affective Neuroscience. 2013;**9**(6):873-879. DOI: 10.1093/scan/nst060

[136] Bondolfi G, Jermann F, Zermatten A. Les approches psychothérapeutiques basées sur la pleine conscience (mindfulness): Entre vogue médiatique et applications cliniques fondées sur des preuves. Psychothérapies. 2011;**31**(3):167-174. DOI: 10.3917/psys.113.0167

[137] Sobolewski A, Holt E, Kublik E, Wróbel A. Impact of meditation on emotional processing—A visual ERP study. Neuroscience Research. 2011;**71**(1):44-48. DOI: 10.1016/j.neures.2011.06.002

[138] Hutcherson CA, Seppala EM, Gross JJ. Loving-kindness meditation increases social connectedness. Emotion. 2008;**8**(5):720-724. DOI: 10.1037/a0013237

[139] Moore A, Malinowski P. Meditation, mindfulness and cognitive flexibility. Consciousness and Cognition. 2009;**18**(1):176-186. DOI: 10.1016/j.concog.2008.12.008

[140] Zeidan F, Johnson SK, Diamond BJ, David Z, Goolkasian P. Mindfulness meditation improves cognition: Evidence of brief mental training. Consciousness and Cognition. 2010;**19**(2):597-605. DOI: 10.1016/j.concog.2010.03.014

[141] Brunel V. Les Managers De L'âme. Entreprise & Société. Paris, France: La Découverte; 2004

[142] Abord de Chatillon E, Carrier Vernhet A. Pas Si Près ! Une Analyse Du Lien Entre Distance, Souffrance Et Bien-être Au Travail Des Cadres. Paris, France: AGRH; 2012

[143] Thévenet M. Management Et Religion. Revue internationale de psychosociologie. 2011;**XVII**(41):27-43

[144] Quatro SA, Waldman DA, Galvin BM. Developing holistic leaders: Four domains for leadership development and practice. Human Resource Management Review. 2007;**17**:427-441. DOI: 10.1016/j.hrmr.2007.08.003

[145] Fry L, Kriger M. Towards a theory of being-centered leadership: Multiple levels of being as context for effective leadership. Human Relations. 2009;**62**(11):1667-1696. DOI: 10.1177/0018726709346380

[146] Otto Scharmer C. The Theory U: Leading from the Future as it Emerges. San Francisco: Berrett-Koehler; 2009

[147] Senge MW, Peter M. Changing how we work together. Reflections: The SoL Journal. 2002;**3**(3):63-67

[148] Senge OL, Peter M. Presence: Human Purpose and the Field of the Future. Cambridge, MA: SoL; 2004

Section 5

Leadership Context

Chapter 13

Leveraging Leader Relations to Cultivate Brain-Friendly Workplaces

Kumars Ahmadi

Abstract

Regarded as the future of management, leadership is becoming increasingly important, but one of the most serious challenges facing leaders today is the declining trend in job satisfaction, commitment, and work motivation in HR, making the current working environment less effective. Today, neuroscience provides a more precise definition and description of the human being, so many different sciences use neuroscience findings more effectively, and leadership is linked to neuroscience in the form of organizational neuroscience. New understandings of human concepts regarding human brain-directed thoughts, feelings, actions, and behaviors consider that almost all human activities are the result of interactions between the brain and chemistry. Founded upon the brain–directed man, the theory of brain-friendly workplace aims to introduce processes and activities, which can lead to a pleasant experience for employees' brains, and it can help HR to experience favorable thoughts, feelings, and behaviors. Conducted on the basis of qualitative research and implication research, the two contributions of brain structure and chemistry are considered as the source for calculating the effects of neuroscience on workplace design. Sampling and validity are also theoretically considered by examining valid sources and implications. This research is first about cognition and finally considers the conceptual extension of the brain-friendly workplace. Based on the theoretical framework and implications, seven processes and dimensions were counted: Communication, happiness and mobility, ability by self-awareness, respect, purposefulness & focus, security & relaxation, and sleep & rest. This brain-friendly workplace model was called CHARPSS, which is intended to help leaders create different and effective workplaces.

Keywords: leadership, organizational neurosciences (ON), brain–friendly workplace, CHARPSS model, implication study

1. Introduction

First of all, we want to consider the state of the existing workplaces, worrying levels of motivation, commitment, and human resource (HR) satisfaction. Organizational leaders need to know new human perceptions to become more effective because leadership is the future of management. A leader's mission is to motivate his subordinates. Human resources (HR), which is the most vital element in the field of organizational management, have always received special attention in various eras by researchers in the field of leadership. However, the quality of employees' performance have been found to be influenced by their motivation within and toward the organization. Leadership in an organization requires new but practical ideas. Creating an ideal work environment is an important investment for the company. Today, with the help of neuroscience, a more suitable workplace must be designed. There is an increasing trend of using neuroscience research results in different fields [1].

According to the prestigious journal of science in 2018, almost 24% of different sciences use neuroscience findings. Neuroscience may be able to make extremely important contributions to management sciences in terms of interdisciplinary studies [2]. In 2018, LinkedIn reported that 93% of employees want to stay longer with their organization, as long as their organization invests more in their workplace [3]. One of the most important responsibilities of a manager is to create a happy and positive environment in which employees feel safe and valued [4]. Leaders need to know that today the ability to create a motivating workplace and have motivated employees is a competitive advantage for an organization as it leads to developing organizational commitment and motivation [5]. The declining trend of commitment, motivation, and satisfaction in the workplace is a matter of serious concern. According to the Gallup Institute, about 20 percent of American employees are not committed and 50 percent are not very committed to their organizations. The annual cost of employee commitment reduction in the United States of America is approximately 300$ billion. This cost is greater than the GDP of countries like Portugal and Singapore and a quarter of the GDP of Iran. In some countries, fully committed employees account for about 3% of their total workforce [6]. Committed employees are 20% more productive and 87% less likely to leave the organization [7]. In a 2013 report by the Business Monitor Institute, about 90% of Iranian employees rated their organization's incentive system as ineffective. On the other hand, about 75% of managers feel that their employees lack the necessary commitment and loyalty [8].

According to Gallup's global study, approximately 13% of employees are completely satisfied with their jobs [9]. The Gallup Institute recently announced that by 2022, employee engagement and workplace belonging will be 21% globally and 15% in the Middle East. In another survey of 20,000 employees, only 36% said they felt positive and energized at work [10]. In another study of 20,000 employees, only 36% said they received positive feelings and energy in their workplace. It is estimated that many workplaces today reinforce the tendency of employees to quit because in today's workplaces up to 30% of employees suffer from mild to severe anxiety disorders.

Another study by the Gallup Institute found that about 88% of employees tended to do their best, but workplace barriers did not allow it, and 55% of employees said they did not do their best in those workplaces. They should strive only to the extent that they will not be dismissed, and they should fulfill their common duties [11]. These examples are important signals and warnings for managers. They point to rethinking and revision at workplace. Leaders need to know that sticking to and insisting on the current workplace is a mistake and that a better and more accurate solution is to rethink and reshape the workplace based on neuroscience findings. This introduction explains the problem and clarifies the concerns.

2. Literature review

Neuroscience is helping improve leadership behaviors while making it easier for employees and, in turn, for organizations. In the light of contemporary research, the leadership training can be a personal, brain-based approach that helps individuals identify their problems and realize their true potential. While there are still many gaps in how the brain makes us better leaders, clear evidence now shows that the brain is the foundation for building effective leadership [12]. Science is just beginning to study the neurological mechanisms underlying these effects [13]. As I said at the beginning, there are many similar examples. This is evidence of the inefficiencies we see in the workplace.

Leaders need to know that existing workplaces are inefficient and boring. Unfortunately, the workplace plays a significant and undeniable role in altering the brain chemistry of employees within the organization. Thus, the quality of employees' thoughts, feelings, and behaviors deteriorates. We need to create a new framework for the workplace design. This chapter introduces a brain-friendly workplace that is also highly efficient. Since our brains function under certain conditions, methods can be used to provide brain-compatible functionality. These are called brain-friendly strategies. You can transform your workplace to boost brain function for your employees, managers, and customers, which means the brain consumes less energy and imposes less tension on the brain. Knowing that the workplace alone cannot provide a brain-friendly environment, it must be provided [14]. According to Franklin Becker, a workspace is like body language, and every part of that environment conveys messages to the brains of employees, managers, and customers. When you talk about improving employee performance and satisfaction, the workplace needs to support it too [15]. When it comes to the evolution of organizational man, we adopt Taylor's economic human theory and witness a new view of man as brain-driven human (**Figure 1**).

Understanding this change in the concept of organizational humans is resourceful and vital for leaders. Brain-directed man is a new conception of man that considers the brain as the basis of all human thoughts, feelings, wills, and behavior and the basis of all actions and reactions of the individual as the brain interacts with the environment. It is the chemical change in our brain that create our emotions and logic and guide our behavioral function. Simply put, hormones and neurotransmitters are quite effective in shaping our performance. This view may be a reinterpretation of the complex concept of man but with its own logic. This view is for the black box to explain the complexities of human thought, emotion, and behavior. Neuroscience translates and explains the black box of the complexity of human behavior. Neuroscience is giving a renewed and serious interest to the accuracy and depth of analysis of human behavior in personal, professional, and social life [16, 17]. Everything we do is a reflection of our brain. Even man, his death is completely under the control of the biological changes of his body, which underline the same concept of man as directed by the brain [18].

The purpose of the new perspective and knowledge resulting from the combination of management and neuroscience is to examine human reality to enhance managers' perception of themselves and their employees [19]. The brain is one of the organs that fully involved in our temperament, character, consciousness, and every

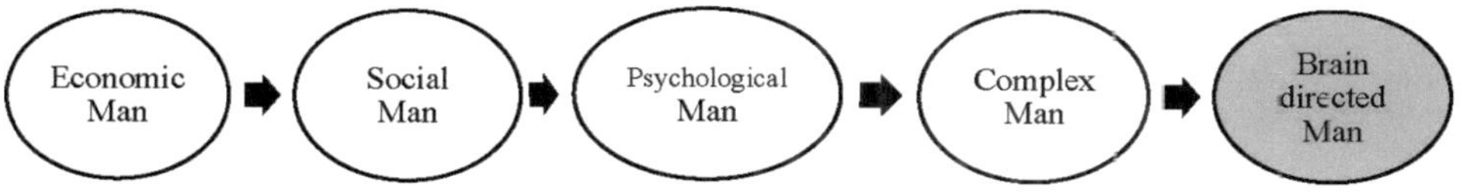

Figure 1.
The evolution of the concept of organizational man [15].

decision. The brain tells us to be cautious or reckless, to try or be indifferent, and considerate [20]. Neuroscience helps us gain valuable insights that are considered unknown and unanalyzable in the dark basements of behavioral science [21].

A brain-friendly workplace seeks to create satisfaction in HR and to create satisfaction within them. An important and guiding fact from neuroscience is that anything that is good for the brain is good for business [22], and this is good news for organizational leaders. The brain-friendly approach is a scientific and practical approach that provides the best working conditions for brain functioning in an organization. It seeks to provide things like convenience, happiness, and many other rewards from the employee's brain's point of view. The condition in which brain energy is consumed the least. Diligence and hard work are kept to a minimum degree. Leaders are advised to improve employee decisions and actions by establishing brain-friendly approaches in their organizations [23]. A brain-friendly workplace that strives to provide a maximum reward experience for the brains of employees, managers, and even customers or consumers, and the conditions under which they experience maximum and minimal threat to create inner satisfaction. Remember that for the brain, rewards and threats may be different from our previous perceptions. The brain needs very subtle stimuli to function properly. Brain-friendly workplaces seek to provide processes to provide a positive emotional experience during the workday for employees so that their brain awareness is one of the maximum rewards and minimum threats. We want to tell organizational leaders that a brain-friendly workplace is where employees' brains are more rewarded and less threatened (**Figure 2**).

The whole point of organizational neuroscience (ON) is that the workplace should be designed to provide the maximum reward experience from the brain's point of view for employees and managers and even customers or clients during the business day to further govern the trend-based approach to thoughts, feelings, and behaviors, and this is an important point that leaders need to keep in mind. Because it will make the workplace more satisfying and attractive. The biased approach in the brain is influenced by the release of hormones and neurotransmitters including serotonin, oxytocin, dopamine, and endorphins, and the avoidance approach in the brain is influenced by the hormones cortisol and even adrenaline or epinephrine, as well as sometimes testosterone. For example, an increase in testosterone is inversely

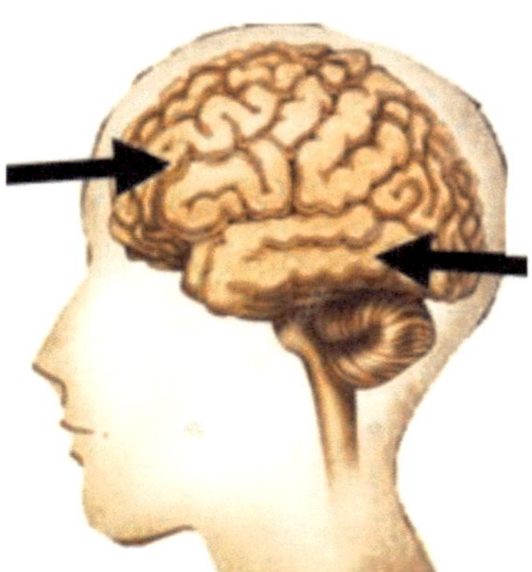

Figure 2.
The tendency-avoidance approach of the brain [24].

associated with development of the prefrontal cortex (PFC). The PFC is one of the brain's upstream systems. This lobe prevents immediate, impulsive, and even hostile actions. Cortisol plays an important role in the amygdala hyperactivity in our brain. The amygdala is one of the downstream systems in the brain that increase our anxious and negligent behaviors. HR brain chemicals, although highly impactful, can be influenced by changes in behavioral and structural conditions in the environment. This golden tip is the window into designing a brain-friendly workplace. ON helps leaders look at the factors that drive employee behavior and performance from a new angle.

3. Methodology

Methodology can determine how an idea and a theory form for us. To present a new point of view and theory, it is necessary to look at this Suddody matrix to see from what angle we are discussing (**Table 1**).

The lower right quadrant of **Table 1** characterizes a theoretical approach that focuses on clear structures and incorporates some literary content. Oswick and colleagues suggest that mixing explicit structures from multiple knowledge domains can produce creative output, depending on the characteristics of the input domains. The higher the similarity between the input domains, the less likely the resulting theory is to be considered entirely new. In the model presented in this chapter, neuroscience was used to combine leadership topics and workplace design to make organizational leadership more effective. For theorizing, a new method of implication study has been used, and the steps of this method are presented in this methodology section. Oswick, Fleming and Hanlon make this observation most clearly, convincingly demonstrating that most (i.e., roughly two-thirds) of the research conducted in management is rooted in theories borrowed from other disciplines [25]. This research also seeks to combine the topics of leadership and workplace with neuroscience. This research is strategic, qualitative, and method-based participatory discovery study. The two contributions of brain structure and chemistry are considered to be the source for calculating the effects of neuroscience on workplace design.

Sampling and validity are also theoretically cited and reliable with valid sources and implications. In this study, the concept of a brain-friendly workplace is first defined and finally will be explained. Implied research is one of the popular strategies for adapting and borrowing knowledge from one field to extend knowledge in another. This approach introduces a new methodology and we can use the findings of

	Theorizing within one literature	**Theorizing across multiple bodies of literature**
Theorizing with implicit assumptions of the literature	• Problematization	• Combining epistemologies • Metaphorical bricolage
Theorizing with explicit constructs of the literature	• Contrasting • Practical rationality • Inductive top-down theorizing	• Blending

Table 1.
Map of different theorizing approaches.

one science in another. However, borrowing the sciences from each other was used and led to the creation of interdisciplinary. In fact, much of human progress is due to studies of this implication. In this study, the researcher extracts important implications that are consistent with the underlying theoretical framework.

In this study, the researcher extracts important implications that are consistent with the underlying theoretical framework. In this study, we identified and calculated significant implications in two areas of brain chemistry and brain structure to demonstrate the dimensions of the theoretical framework. The steps to conducting the research based on the implied research method are as follows:

1. Feasibility of the implied research method for the research topic based on the opinion of the researcher.

2. Introduce the contributions that brain chemistry and structure will make to this research.

3. Identify the basic conceptual framework.

4. Perform theoretical sampling to identify signs.

5. Validate and match meanings with conceptual frameworks.

6. Confirm the main and final implications.

7. Explain the conceptual model obtained [26].

4. Discussion of brain-friendly workplace

A golden tip for leaders to learn is that consider a brain plate that the brain can access during the day to optimize its performance. This study was carried out using the implication research method. Underground research is one of the popular strategies for adapting and borrowing knowledge from one discipline to refine and extend knowledge from another. The two contributions of brain chemistry and brain structure are considered to be the source for calculating the effects of neuroscience on workplace design. In fact, much of human progress owes much to this search for participation. In this approach, the researcher develops a basic conceptual framework in his or her science before borrowing contributions and other scientific implications. For each component of the conceptual framework, it computes the implication. Thus, the researcher derives a meaningful implication that matches the elements of the theoretical framework (**Figure 3**).

A plate for healthy brain human resources can be considered as the processes and conditions for forming a brain-friendly working environment as follows:

- Provide conditions for effective communication in the workplace

- Provide conditions for happiness and mobility in the workplace

- Provide conditions for ability by self-awareness in the workplace

- Provide conditions for respect in the workplace

Figure 3.
Workplace plate for the brain.

- Provide conditions for purposefulness and focus in the workplace
- Provide conditions for security and relaxation in the workplace
- Provide conditions for enough sleep and rest in the workplace

These seven factors can be considered as components of the theoretical framework and are known to be the source for finding implications. In this study, the contribution of neuroscience in the two areas of brain chemistry and brain structure was considered. Two main questions can be asked (**Table 2**):

- what does neuroscience say about the subject of workplace?
- What are the implications for designing or revising workplace?

Based on current implications and evidence, it seems likely that providing the conditions and context for effective workplace communication and interaction as a

Dimension 1 of theoretical framework	Neuroscience implications that confirm effective communication as a brain-friendly process in the workplace
Provide conditions for effective communication in the workplace (C)	• People who are more social have bigger reward parts in their brains [27] • The number of relationships a person has on social media is inversely proportional to their amygdala size [28] • The number and depth of a person's social relationships leading to the development and expansion of the brain's PFC [29] • Good relationships release oxytocin and decrease cortisol providing a feeling of well-being and intimacy [30] • One of the most important brain rewards is effective, intimate, and meaningful communication with others [31] • Effective relationships reduce stress because they lower cortisol [32]

Table 2.
Effective communication as a brain-friendly process in the workplace.

brain-friendly process can be accepted. Therefore, it is an important task for leaders to establish effective communication and interaction in the workplace, as the findings of neuroscience see it as a reward for employees' brains. By providing the right conditions for employee interactions, neuro leaders can truly claim that they have provided a brain-friendly workplace (**Table 3**).

Current evidence and existing findings suggest that coaching-based interactions create relationship emotionalization and provide familiarity in relationships as brain-friendly components in brain-friendly work relationships. Studies have revealed the significance of familiarity and we now know that leaders who profusely used social language in their vision and mission statements are more likely to have greater coherence in the right frontal part (PFC) of the brain than leaders with more self-language [12]. We have learned that effective work interactions and connections are rewarding for the HR brain. Leaders are encouraged to take seriously the impact of some behaviors and preparations that create the conditions for effective workplace communication on institutionalizing brain-friendly interactions.

- Improve communication skills, effective listening, and empathy to increase oxytocin and estrogen

Dimension 1 of theoretical framework	Components	Neuroscience implications for identifying brain-friendly components related to effective communication
Provide conditions for the effective communication in the workplace	Coaching-based relations	• Coaching is a conversation-driven process of mature-mature relationship [33] • Conversation is effective in expanding the PFC of the brain [34] • Effective listening to a person raises his or her self-esteem, and self-esteem is directly related to an increase in brain serotonin [3]
	Emotionalizing work relationships	• Positive emotional words can have a profound effect on brain [35] • Creating emotions during a relationship has a direct effect on remembering that relationship and its details from memory [36] • Positive emotions in the brain have beneficial and lasting effects [37] • Our brain enjoys spending time with those we feel good about [38]
	Familiarity and acquaintance	• Our brains tend to be more confident in making decisions that are familiar or similar to ourselves [39] • Our brain threatens unfamiliarity [39] • Our brains feel more familiar and empathetic with people who feel more familiar with us [40] • Suggestions and solutions that are more familiar with a person's neural circuits are more sustainable [41]

Table 3.
Components related to effective communication.

- Have intimate two-person meetings over hot drinks during work hours to increase oxytocin
- Use our pronouns instead of self-pronouns in business conversations, especially to increase oxytocin and cortisol or modify tissues to lower testosterone
- to increase the hormone serotonin and reduce cortisol, respectfully demanding and even asking questions
- Having a good coffee shop for short intimate meetings, off-duty hours, and during work to increase the oxytocin hormone
- New organizational changes and decisions in the form of small changes to reduce cortisol in addition to previous decisions

In the image below you can see the relationship between the type of hormone and the activity state of the brain system. Some hormones and neurotransmitters cause more activity in the lower and posterior systems of the brain, and some other hormones cause more activity in the upper and front systems of the brain (**Figure 4**).

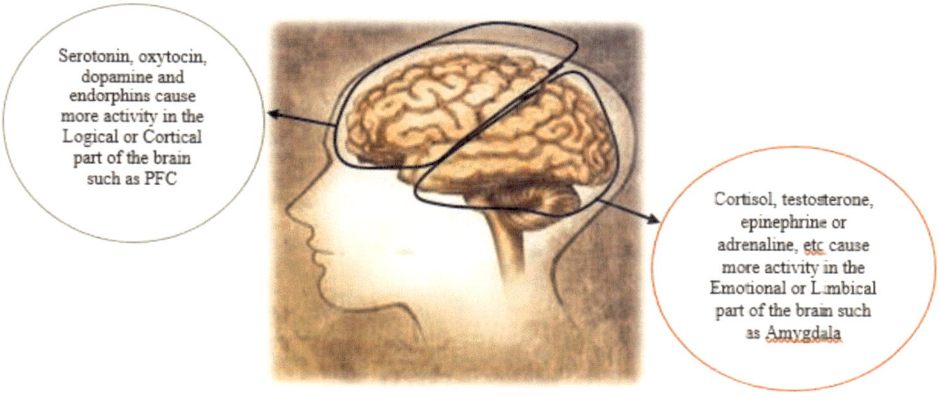

Figure 4.
Brain systems and brain chemistry [24].

Dimension 2 of theoretical framework	Neuroscience implications that confirm happiness and mobility as a brain-friendly process in the workplace
Provide conditions for happiness and mobility in the workplace (H)	• Neuroscience teaches us that happiness in the workplace creates positive mental and emotional experiences [31] • When you are happy, blood flows faster in your arteries, bringing more oxygen and nutrients to your brain [29] • David Rock believes that performing the task with vigor is beneficial for the optimal functioning of the brain [42] • Dopamine, which is hopeful and motivating, is provided through happiness and vitality [43] • Mobility and sports increase brain endorphin [17]

Table 4.
Happiness and mobility as a brain-friendly process in the workplace.

Analyzing the dimensions and components identified, it is important to know that anything that provides maximal activity of the upstream and cortical systems of the brain is considered brain-friendly (**Table 4**).

From the current implications and evidence, it appears that providing conditions and a platform for happiness and mobility in the workplace as a brain-friendly process can be accepted and approved. Maybe before, organizational leaders did not consider happiness in the workplace to be so important, but neuroscience has shown that it is a pleasant reward for the brain, and it has a great effect on improving work performance. Happiness is one of the vital elements for the optimal functioning of the brain, so it will be considered one of the vital elements of brain-friendly workplaces. Creating a happy workplace is one of the characteristics of a neuroleader. A neuroleader is a leader who uses neuroscience as a benchmark to have a deeper and more accurate impact on employees (**Table 5**).

The happiness and mobility of HR, as neuroscience implications have shown, are a reward for the human resource brain. A neuroleader understands the positive effects of happiness in the workplace so he tries to create it. Acts and actions and preparations that provide the conditions for happiness and mobility in the workplace are:

Dimension 2	**Components**	**Neuroscience implications for identifying brain-friendly components related to happiness and mobility**
Provide conditions for happiness and mobility in the workplace	Provide sport conditions	• Exercise and sport improve the state of norepinephrine, increase endorphins in the brain, and make us feel relaxed [44] • Sport with the help of endorphins is released, can separate sad thoughts from the person, and is like food for the brain [45] • Exercise helps keep our brains young [46]
	Encourage laughter	• Laughter is one of the easiest ways to release endorphins in the brain [47] • Laughter, as an internal exercise, releases endorphins, oxytocin, and dopamine in the brain [31] • Laughter can change brain wave patterns from beta waves to alpha waves. Alpha waves are directly related to creative thinking [34] • One minute of laughter can calm our brains for 40 to 45 minutes [48]
	Psychological moments (PM)	• Psychological moments are the moments that bring joy to our minds by reminding us of previous successes and pleasant situations [49]. • Small, persistent joys can be more effective for our brains than great joys [1]
	Physical freshness	• Experience and beautiful perception of the workplace can be considered a powerful source of reward for the HR brain [50] • A stylish and beautiful workplace releases serotonin into employees' brains [34] • A well-groomed and refreshing workplace is a kind of respect for employees [34] • Seeing a beautiful workplace and pleasant pictures can increase beneficial hormones in the brain [51]

Table 5.
Components related to happiness and mobility.

- Enabling employees to exercise to increase endorphins and oxytocin and reduce cortisol
- Promote humor and laughter as an organizational value to increase oxytocin and decrease cortisol
- Review successes and happy memories to motivate colleagues to increase serotonin, dopamine, and oxytocin and decrease cortisol and even testosterone
- Create a happy and positive surprise to increase the hormone dopamine
- Efforts to create order and beautiful decoration of the workplace to increase serotonin hormone
- Using appropriate colors in the environment, such as pink, tends to interact and reduce aggressive behavior in order to increase the hormones oxytocin and dopamine and decrease cortisol and testosterone (**Table 6**).

In a simple and superficial view, it may be thought that these implications are not for organizational issues, but the rewards of the brain are the same for all of us, and this inspiration and borrowing from neuroscience can be the basis of a new approach in leadership. Evidence and current evidence suggest that providing empowerment for self-awareness in the workplace as a brain-friendly process can be acceptable. Organizational leaders should know that the best kind of awareness is self-awareness, so they should try to make their employees self-aware in the workplace (**Table 7**).

The implications, current evidence, and available findings suggest that providing conditions and contexts in the workplace for the emotionalization of memory, flow, independence, and learning are acceptable components of the workplace and activities within the workplace ability by self-awareness process. Any reflection, contemplation, and thinking on oneself or on different topics can cause the creation of new neural circuits in the brains of employees. Self-awareness and HR empowerment are considered a reward for their brains. Suggestion to organizational leaders and activities that provide the conditions to facilitate self-awareness and empowerment in the workplace are:

- Utilizing coaching capabilities for self-awareness and internalizing motivation to increase serotonin and decrease cortisol

Dimension 3	Neuroscience implications that confirm ability by self-awareness as a brain-friendly process in the workplace
Provide conditions for ability by self-awareness in the workplace (A)	• Self-awareness increases neuroplasticity [52] • Self-awareness enables the birth of brain hippocampal neurons [40] • Mental training for Self-awareness rebuilds neural connections and strengthens neuroplasticity [53] • In self-awareness, when we say aha, new circuits are formed in brain [54]

Table 6.
Ability by self-awareness as a brain-friendly process in the workplace.

Dimension 3 of theoretical framework	Components	Neuroscience implications for identifying brain-friendly components related to ability by self-awareness
Provide conditions for Ability by self-awareness in the workplace	Emotional memory	• Information that has an emotional charge is easier to learn and remember in the brain [55] • The emotionalization of learning has a profound effect on the quality of learning [56] • The brain is skilled at learning and remembering emotional events [41]
	Work flow	• When we focus on an activity, that focus can trigger the release of dopamine [29] • Intense and unconscious focus on work reduces activity in the amygdala and cingulate cortex of the brain [57]
	Independence	• Work independence has a strong effect on employees' attitudes and motivations [5] • Environments, where employees feel the independence have a higher rate of dendritic growth of their brain neurons [56] • The thought of not having authority reduces the quality of blood flow to the brain [29]
	Innovation and learning	• New experiences change the structure of the brain [53] • Freshness and variety suitable for the brain can change brain chemistry for the better [56] • Learning new activities is essential for brain efficiency [55]

Table 7.
Components related to ability by self-awareness.

- Identifying the values of employees and linking their values with their job responsibilities in order to increase the hormone serotonin
- Holding friendly and informal job sessions to learn to increase dopamine and oxytocin
- Voluntary and non-compulsory classes to increase dopamine and oxytocin and reduce cortisol and testosterone
- Clarification of career path by observing the inner desire to work in order to increase the hormone serotonin or dopamine
- Allowing employees to choose the time and amount of time allotted to tasks to increase serotonin and lower cortisol
- Make organizational learning gradual and step-by-step to reduce cortisol

Respect is a vital and inseparable part of inner satisfaction. In a work environment where the priority is to respect the employees, in that work environment, the brain function of the employees can be much better and the organizational efficiency can be improved. So that both the employees reach inner satisfaction and the organization achieves efficiency. It has been proven that if we talk to people with behavioral abnormalities with respect, they will behave more reasonably and so, we should have respectful words and behavior with the employees so that their brains feel rewarded (**Table 8**).

Dimension 4	Neuroscience implications that confirm respect as a brain-friendly process in the workplace
Provide conditions for respect in the workplace (R)	• Social acceptance is a kind of social reward that activates the brain stratum [27] • Respected social conditions affect the production of serotonin in our brain [53] • If others approve of you and like you, then the cingulate cortex and the stratum are activated. The stratum is part of the brain's reward processing system [58] • Social rewards such as respect, in addition to releasing serotonin, can also release dopamine in some people [59]

Table 8.
Respect as a brain-friendly process in the workplace.

Dimension 4	Components	Neuroscience implications for identifying brain-friendly components related to respect
Provide conditions for respect in the workplace	Gratitude	• Gratitude can release serotonin in our brains [1] • Gratitude and congratulations can release dopamine in employees [58] • Our brains receive good hormones from respect as a reward [60] • Gratitude to us can be very effective in releasing the hormone serotonin in us [19]
	Compassion and empathy	• Insensitivity and selfishness are harmful to the brain and mental health [52] • Memories with an empathetic emotional burden are more likely to be remembered [61] • Charity activity can be effective in releasing oxytocin in the workplace [30] • In empathy, the activity of the amygdala and the cingulate cortex decreases [62] • PFC of the brain plays an important role in managing emotions and expressing empathy with other people [62]
	Forgiveness	• Forgiveness is a big factor in the quality of our emotions. It increases the hormone oxytocin on both side people [63] • People who were unable to forgive and had high grudges had larger amygdala [17] • The more self-sacrificing we can be in our decisions, the greater the growth of our PFC [64] • Kindness and forgiveness play a role in increasing the volume of the brain insula. Insula is quite effective in cooperation and empathy [65]
	Respect for gender differences	• Organizational neuroscience tells us that imposing male norms is in stark contrast to female talents [66] • Neuroscientists have shown that function and structure of the brain in men and women are more different than in similar people [64 • Women are about 20 percent more likely than men to store unpleasant images in their long-term memory [66] • Cortisol decreases slower in women than in men [58] • Acceptance of premenstrual syndrome (PMS) is a real brainstorming issue in the workplace [58]

Table 9.
Components related to respect.

Current implications and evidence suggest that providing a platform for respect and reverence in the workplace as a brain-friendly process can be accepted and endorsed. Respect has always been important, but leaders now know why and how to increase it. They learned the consequences of disrespect on the brains of employees therefore, conditions for increasing respect for employees should be provided (**Table 9**).

As an important point, we must mention that a neuroleader empathizes with his employees, not with sympathy. Because sympathy aggravates their pain and problems, sympathy strengthens the ability and self-confidence of employees. The neurological reason is that empathy causes the release of serotonin and sympathy causes the release of cortisol. From the implications, current evidence, and findings, it appears that providing conditions in the workplace to appreciate the efforts and actions, compassion and empathy for each other, forgiveness and sacrifice of colleagues toward each other, gender differences in delegating authority can be used as components are brain-friendly. These activities should be considered as part of the process of respect in the workplace. Suggestions to organizational leaders and activities that provide the conditions to facilitate respect in the workplace are:

- To increase the serotonin hormone of the employees, the leaders among the colleagues should thank the employees.
- To reduce harmful cortisol and testosterone hormones, do not criticize the employee among colleagues.
- Congratulating colleagues' successes, however small, to increase serotonin.
- Kind and compassionate words and behavior with colleagues increase the hormone oxytocin and decrease testosterone and cortisol.
- Finding out about the dreams and aspirations of colleagues in order to increase the hormone oxytocin.

Dimension 5	Neuroscience implications that confirm purposefulness and focus as a brain-friendly process in the workplace
Provide conditions for purposefulness and focus in the workplace (P)	• Our brain wants a goal. Our brains are always trying to reduce threats and doubts by making predictions and planning [67] • It is not the details that clutter our brains, it is the fragmented and unfocused energy that bothers our brains [68] • The goal causes the brain RAS* to turn our attention to the goal-related information in the mass of environmental information [45] • One hour of focus on each topic can double the number of neural circuits in the brain associated with the topic [69] • Focusing on a problem can trigger the release of dopamine [29] • Focus is effective in improving the function of the PFC of the brain [20] • According to neuroscience, when we aim, then the random firing of neurons stops and their firing becomes regular [70]

**RAS: Reticular Activation System.*

Table 10.
Purposefulness and focus as a brain-friendly process in the workplace.

- Encouraging sacrificing behaviors in the organization to increase the hormone oxytocin (**Table 10**).

Having a purpose at work helps to build a sense of purpose in employees. The feeling of dignity and satisfaction among employees is increasing day by day. Concentration is important for creating purpose. From the meanings and evidence in the table above, it can be seen that providing the conditions and context to create purpose and focus for personnel in the workplace as a process of the brain-friendly paradigm sets can be accepted and verified. With these discoveries, wise leaders know they must provide the conditions and platforms to increase workplace focus and employee engagement like never before (**Table 11**).

From the implications, current evidence, and available findings, it seems that providing conditions and contexts in the workplace for meaning and hope, mindfulness, lack of multitasking, and appropriateness of workplace conditions as acceptable components and activities within the process of purposefulness and focus can be accepted and approved. Suggestion to organizational leaders, activities that provide the conditions to facilitate purposefulness and focus for HR in the workplace are:

- Translating the organizational mission to the job duties of employees in order to understand the impact of their role to reduce cortisol hormone and increase serotonin

- To increase focus, not allowing the use of mobile phones in business meetings

- Not using partitions in the workplace as focus killers to reduce cortisol

- Using the scents of live flowers in the corridors of the work environment to increase the hormone oxytocin

- Using proper lighting for work rooms to increase serotonin hormone

- Reviewing positive memories of the organization to create hope and increase the hormone serotonin and also dopamine (**Table 12**)

Based on the implications and current evidence, it seems acceptable to provide the conditions and context for safety and relaxation in the workplace as a brain-friendly process. **Table 13** shows the components of the safety and relaxation in the workplace. Therefore, leaders should know that providing a quiet and safe environment can be a good brain reward for their employees.

The implications, current evidence, and available findings suggest that providing conditions and contexts in the workplace to increase similarity, simplicity, support, transparency, and certainty as brain-friendly components and activities within the security and relaxation process are acceptable. It can only be said about the importance of similarity, results showed that in 80 percent of the 43 elections since 1901, the candidates who used the most collective-oriented language (we-or us-referencing) in their official election speech were the victors. Research findings showed that leaders' words are inspiring when they convey a sense of commonality and us. gives some neuroscientific substance to claims that it is only when in-group leaders speak for "us" that followers embrace their pronouncements enthusiastically [13]. Accordingly,

Dimension 5	Components	Neuroscience implications for identifying brain-friendly components related to purposefulness and focus
Provide conditions for purposefulness and focus in the workplace	Meaning and hope	• To increase inner motivation, it is necessary to create a sense of meaning in work [71] • Hope for goals leads to dopamine release and despair for cortisol release and serotonin depletion [59] • The sense of purpose is due to the proper activity of the left PFC of the brain [65] • dopamine is released when you hope to achieve your goals [72] • The less hope we have, the less dopamine and endorphins are released in our brains and the more stress hormones like adrenaline and cortisol are released [72] • Hopeless leads to neuronal damage and apoptosis or suicide of neurons [67]
	Mindfulness	• Mindfulness strengthens the volume of the hippocampus, which is the brain's emotional memory, and shrinks the brain's amygdala [68] • Mindfulness can make PFC 10 to 15 years younger [69] • In mindfulness, there is a pause, which is an opportunity for the brain to consciously react [64]
	Lack of Multitasking	• The brain does not like doing multiple things at the same time, in 97 percent of cases, doing multiple things together reduces employee focus [48] • Multitasking is quite effective in reducing optimal brain performance [42] • People with multitasking have less density in the cingulate cortex of their brains. This area is responsible for empathy and emotional intelligence [17] • Multitasking does not allow the neural connections made in the brain to be established [56]
	The physical environment	• Workplace temperature affects the brain's serotonin and norepinephrin [73] • High temperatures and noise increase testosterone and decrease serotonin [51] • Warm workplace temperatures increase blood cortisol levels and cause anxiety [74] • The aroma of flowers has a complete effect on improving brain performance [45] • Fragrant and aroma scents have antianxiety properties and odors can soothe the limbic system, especially the amygdala [20] • Lack of adequate light, especially natural light, causes a mismatch in the secretion of the hormones serotonin and melatonin in the brain [20] • The more negative ions in the space around us, the more serotonin is released, indoor spaces are harmful to brain performance, even carpets and rugs in the office have a direct effect on reducing brain performance [34] • Managers should increase the dopamine and serotonin levels of their employees in autumn and winter because there is less sunlight [50]

Table 11.
Components related to purposefulness and focus.

Dimension 6	Neuroscience implications that confirm security and relaxation as a brain-friendly process in the workplace
Provide conditions for security and relaxation in the workplace (S)	• Factors that create fear and threat completely weigh on the cognitive abilities and skills of the brain and violate work commitments [75] • "Being safe is better than regretting," says the brain amygdala [76] • Due to the mechanism of mirror neurons, the anxiety of colleagues can be transmitted to us and our worries and anxiety can be transmitted to colleagues [77] • Stress blocks the release of oxytocin by releasing epinephrine [30] • In a workplace where the secretion of epinephrine and cortisol hormones is high and oxytocin is low [66]

Table 12.
Security and relaxation as a brain-friendly process in the workplace.

suggestion to organizational leaders, activities that provide the conditions to facilitate security and relaxation for HR in the workplace are:

- Understand and assign labor to simplify work tasks to reduce cortisol
- Implement SMART techniques in career and organizational goals to reduce cortisol
- Promote empathy as an organizational value to increase oxytocin hormone and decrease cortisol
- Know your subordinates' personal and professional problems to increase endorphins and oxytocin hormones and reduce cortisol
- Interact fairly with subordinates to increase serotonin and oxytocin and reduce cortisol
- Use honesty in words and behavior to increase serotonin and oxytocin hormones and reduce cortisol
- Organizational change plans should be represented by narratives and stories to increase the hormone oxytocin and decrease cortisol (**Table 14**).

Current implications and evidence suggest that providing conditions and contexts to improve the adequate sleep and rest in the workplace as a brain-friendly process can be accepted and approved. With these experimental and important findings, it is necessary for organizational leaders to pay special attention to the quality of sleep and rest of their subordinates (**Table 15**).

Sleep is also an active state that is important for cognitive processes such as memory consolidation, semantic integration, learning, and emotional processing. Sleep is also important for the body, and evidence suggests it may be even more important for the brain. A study of working hours, sleep, and depression of 2643 full-time employed Japanese citizens found that participants worked more than 10 hours a day, slept less than 6 hours a day, and reported inadequate sleep 37 and 43.

Dimension 6	Components	Neuroscience implications for identifying brain-friendly components related to security and relaxation
Provide conditions for security and relaxation in the workplace	Similarity	• We are always dominated by behavior that has a stronger and larger neural circuit, that is, it is older and better known [78] • For the brain, the lack of difference and the similarity is a kind of reward [76] • Our brains release less cortisol and more oxytocin in the face of things like ours [24]
	Simplicity	• By simplifying, you reduce stress and threats to the brain [75] • Our brain is interested in creating a simple and familiar pattern of environmental issues [79] • Simpler explanations are always more acceptable to the brain [80] • Simplicity is a reward for the brain because it reduces energy consumption in the brain [81]
	Support	• The feeling of lack of support, which is a kind of social pain, creates the same patterns of physical pain in the brain and causes suppression of the cingulate cortex and the PFC [82] • For the brain, social pain such as experiencing lack of support and injustice are serious barriers to learning and organizational development [83] • Getting support leads to an increase in the hippocampus of the brain, which is the center of emotional memory [52] • Values such as support, empathy, and altruism cause nervous reconstruction [67]
	Clarity	• Clarity and transparency of managers increase oxytocin in employees' brains [84] • Clarity, transparency, honesty, and justice in the brain activate upstream systems of the brain such as PFC [85] • The satisfaction of mind of employees depends directly on the extent to which they are aware of the transparent process of the current affairs of the organization [10]
	Certainty	• The brain hates ambiguity and uncertainty and considers it a threat [61] • Anything that increases survival and reduces ambiguity, such as a plan and vision, triggers dopamine secretion in the brain [86] • Foresight helps us feel in control of threats, so it lowers cortisol and increases dopamine [34]

Table 13.
Components related to security and relaxation.

respectively, and also 97% were more likely to be depressed than those who worked 6–8 hours a day, slept 6–8 hours a day, and reported getting enough sleep. The study concluded that depression associated with long work hours is primarily a result of sleep deprivation [93]. The implications, current evidence, and available findings suggest that providing workplace conditions to minimize shift work, compensating for sleep deprivation in shift staff, and ultimately providing short restpackages during work are components of sleep and rest and having enough activities. As suggested to organizational leadership, the activities that provide the necessary conditions to facilitate adequate sleep and rest for personnel in the workplace are:

Dimension 7	Neuroscience implications that confirm enough sleep and rest as a brain-friendly process in the workplace
Provide conditions for enough sleep and rest in the workplace (S)	• Insomnia and insufficient sleep impair working memory, mood, and reasoning ability [87] • Insufficient sleep increases cognitive impairments such as stress disorders [75] • Sleep is vital to protecting the brain [52] • We sleep to clear our brains. Sleep can increase the synapse or space between neurons in the brain by up to 60 percent [88] • The quality of sleep facilitates the nervous flexibility of the brain [89]

Table 14.
Enough sleep and rest as a brain-friendly process in the workplace.

Dimension 7	Components	Neuroscience implications for identifying brain-friendly components related to have enough sleep and rest
Provide conditions for enough sleep and rest in the workplace	Minimize shift work	• People who work only at night have better mental performance than those who work shifts day and night [34] • People who did not sleep for about 35 hours had about 60 percent more amygdala activation in response to negative images [76] • Lack of sleep is directly related to creating illusions and suspicious thoughts in people [36]
	Compensate for staff's insomnia on the night shift	• Insomnia damages working memory [76] • Insomnia leads to a decrease in dopamine in the brain [90] • The negative effects of insomnia are more in the brains of male employees than female employees and more in the brains of young employees than employees aged 50 to 65 years [70]
	Prepare short rest packages	• The human brain needs time to rest so that the brain can calm its waves [91] • Do not decide on important issues in fatigue because the brain has low power [92] • The effect of short mental breaks has been scientifically proven [70] • Rest to improve the function of your PFC [52]

Table 15.
Components related to have enough sleep and rest.

- Planning to reduce night shifts of employees to increase serotonin hormone and reduce cortisol
- Using enough light in the workplace for night shifts and increasing serotonin hormone
- Providing rest time to compensate for insomnia

- Allocating a resting place for female employees and reducing the complications of premenstrual syndrome. This means reducing cortisol and improving serotonin status

- Allow employees to set aside time for "doing nothing."

5. Conclusion

The findings and statements in this chapter help leaders execute their strategy more effectively in creating motivation. This model presented a valuable opportunity. A smart organizational leader knows when the current workplace is dysfunctional. This leader should find a way to design a new environment that is more appropriate. Due to the downward trend in job satisfaction, employee engagement, and motivation

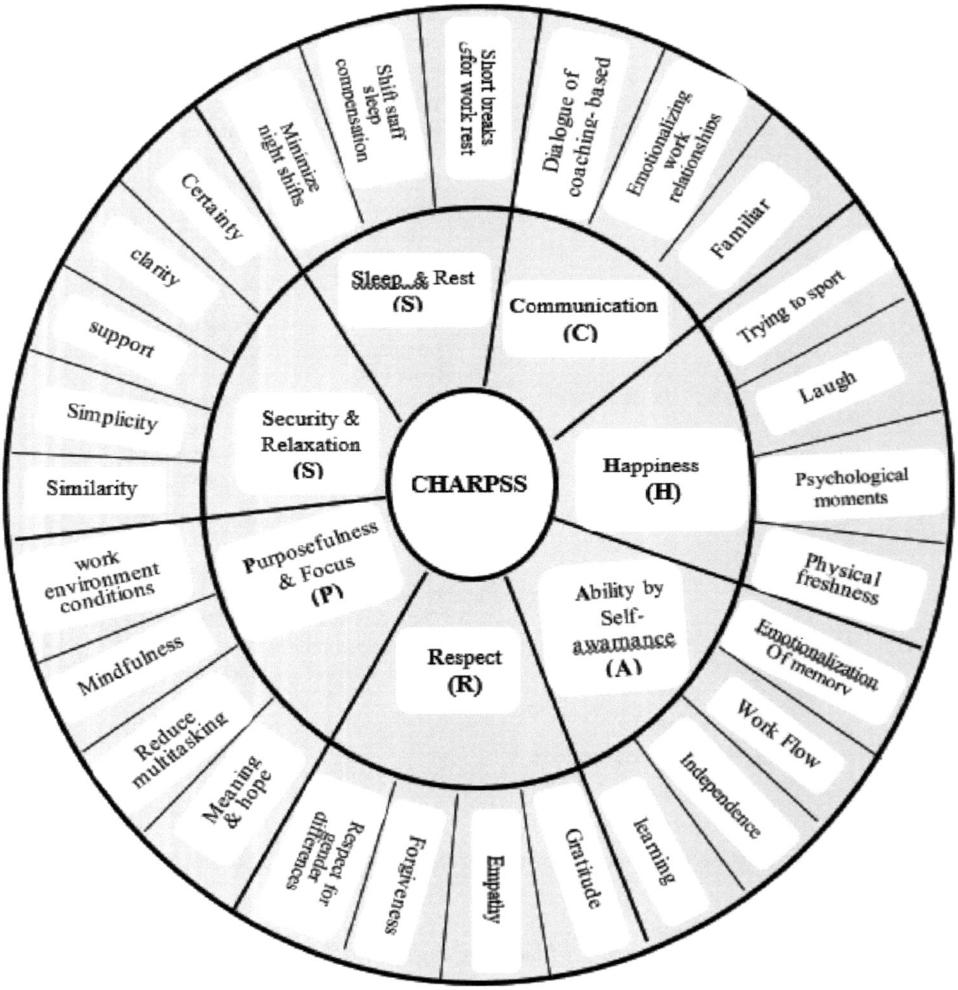

Figure 5.
Brain-friendly workplace of CHARPSS model.

in different organizations, the need to renovate the current workplace is inevitable. Today, neuroscience offers more precise definitions and explanations of human beings, so many different sciences use the findings of neuroscience to have greater effect, and management knowledge is linked to neuroscience in the form of organizational neuroscience. Based on the brain-driven human, brain-friendly workplace theory suggest that workplace implementations bring pleasurable experiences for employees' brains, ultimately introducing favorable processes and activities into employees' thoughts, feelings, and behaviors. This research is first about cognition and finally considers the conceptual extension of the brain-friendly workplace. This is an important message for leaders. Based on the theoretical framework and implications, seven processes and dimensions were counted: Communication, happiness, and mobility, ability by self-awareness, respect, purposefulness and focus, security and relaxation, and sleep and rest. In addition, multiple ingredients are blended for each process, and a total of 27 types of brain-friendly ingredients are blended. This brain-friendly workplace model was called CHARPSS. The quality of employees' thoughts, feelings, and actions is due to brain activity. Therefore, by introducing measures and actions to implement the components of the CHARPSS model, we can create a brain-friendly environment in the HR workplace. The CHARPSS model is able to maximize the satisfaction and rewards that an employee's brain receives from the workplace, while also minimizing frustration and brain threats (**Figure 5**).

This model, derived from the effects of neuroscience on the two contributions of brain chemistry and brain structure, can provide leaders with new insights so they can provide additional motivation and job satisfaction. To create a mind-friendly workplace, a leader must make a list of what to add to the current workplace and a list of what to remove from the current workplace. Most of these changes including changes of values, beliefs, attitudes, and behaviors toward employees must happen within the leader himself. CHARPSS model can create very positive changes in brain chemistry and neural circuits of employees. In our brain, there are neurons called mirror neurons. These neurons are activated when we do something or when we observe or imagine the same thing. These neurons cause emotional transmission and the good feeling of the employees from the workplace, of the brain, will spread to the customers and clients and will have positive effects even in their families.

Author details

Kumars Ahmadi
Department of Management, Islamic Azad University, Sanandaj, Iran

*Address all correspondence to: ahmadi.kumars@gmail.com

References

[1] Friedman R. The Best Place to Work. Publisher of Perigee; 2015

[2] Tracy B. Full Engagement: Inspire, Motivate and Bring Out the Best in Your People. Publisher of American Management Association; 2011

[3] Li L. 17 Surprising Statistics about Employee R. TINYpulse blog; 2020

[4] Mobbs D, Mcfarland W. The neuroscience of motivation. NeuroLeadership Journal. 2010;**3**

[5] Pink D. Published in the Carol Stanford. 2010

[6] Fazli M, Amiran H. The Future and Position of HRM in Iran. Publisher of Amiran; 2011

[7] Valier K, Key HR. Metrics: Measure & leverage employee satisfaction. 2021

[8] Porath C. Creating a More Human Workplace Where Employees and Business Thrive. SHRM Fundation; 2016

[9] Ferreia F, Dacasta R, Pereira.L & Jeroimo. C. The relationship between chemical of stress, leadership, motivation and organizational trust. Journal of International Business and Economics. 2018;**6**(2)

[10] Twyla D. How to Motivate People. Publisher of Kogan; 1989

[11] Montgomery C. Your level of generosity is related to the street you are walking on. Interpreter of Humanities Quarterly. 2018;**8**

[12] Joy M. The Neurosience oF Leadership. Pallikkutam; 2018

[13] Molenberghs P, Prochilo G, Steffens N, Zacher H, Haslam S. The neuroscience of inspirational leadership: The importance of collective-oriented language and shared group membership. Journal of Management. 2017;**43**(7)

[14] Zwaan L, Viljoen R. The role of Neuroleadership in work engagement. Journal of Human Resource Management. 2019

[15] Mundlein K, Zwart T. Business and the Brain. Lund University; 2013

[16] Ghadiri A, Habermacher A, Peters T. Neuroleadership: A Journey through the Brain for Business Leaders. Springer-Verlag Publishing; 2012

[17] Ahmadi K. The basics of Neuroleadership. Publisher of Termeh; 2016

[18] Amodio D. The social neuroscience of intergroup relations. European Review of Social Psyhology. 2008

[19] Karim A, Farid.M & Rafiq.S. NeuroManagement: Key to maintaining performance literature review. The lnternatioal Journal of Business Management and Technology. 2019

[20] Amen D. Use Your Brain to Change Your Age: Secrets to look, Feel and Think Younger Every Day. Publisher of Harmony; 2012

[21] Meacham M. Neuroscience IN corporate training: All hype or practical applications? Journal of L&D Talks. 2011

[22] Lanz K. How to build a brain-friendly work environment after COVID-19. 2020

[23] Affinwala S, Bandy O, Chugh A. How neuroscience transformed business. NHRD Network Journal. 2018;**2018**:4

[24] Ahmadi K. Organizational Neuroscience (ON). Publisher of Termeh; 2020

[25] Suddody R, Hardy C, Huy Q. Introduction to special topic forum where are the new theories of organization? 2011;**36**(2)

[26] Danaeefard H. Methodology of implication studies in social and human sciences. Methodology of Human Sciences. 2016;**36**

[27] Chirico F. Job stress models for burnout syndrome. Journal of Health and social sciences. 2016;**52**(3)

[28] Jaaskelainen I. Introduction to cognitive neuroscience. 2014

[29] Lehmann S. The Science of Happiness. Published by Da Capo Press; 2006

[30] Zak P. The neuroscience of high trust organization consulting. Psychological Journal. 2018;**70**(1)

[31] Ghosh SK. Happy hormones at work. NHRD Network Journal. 2018;**11**(4)

[32] Swart T, Chisholm K, Brown P. Neuroscience for Leadership. Pub Palgrave Macmillan; 2015

[33] Leikomaa T. Coaching as a Tool for Performance Management. Tampere University; 2016

[34] Horne T, Wootton S. Training Your Brain. Hodder Education Group; 2007

[35] Madigan S. Narrative therapy. American Psychological Association; 2011

[36] Crawford J. The Brain-friendly Organization. Cascasdan; 2011

[37] Dispenza J. You Are the Placebo. Hay House Inc; 2014

[38] MacDonald M. Your Brain. O Reily Media Inc; 2008

[39] Garmes E. Big brain friendly workplace ideas for human resource executives. HREC. 2015

[40] Chopra D, Tanzi R. Super Brain. Publisher of Harmony; 2013

[41] PRISM. Coaching and neuroscience: The way ahead. 2018

[42] Dethmer J, Chapman D, Klemp K. *The* 15 Commitments of Conscious Leadership: A New Paradigm for Sustainable Success. Chicago, IL: Conscious Leadership Group; 2014

[43] Hughes D, Baylin J. Brain – Based Parenting. W. W. Norton & Company; 2012

[44] Murphy C, Ozturgut O. Brain–wise leadership. Journal of International Education and Leadership. 2013

[45] Leviton R. Brain Builders: A Life Long Guide to Sharper Thinking. Prentice Hall; 1995

[46] Irimia A, Robles D, Rostowsky K, Maher A, Chowdhury M. Amazon indigenous group's lifestyle may hold a key to slowing down aging. Journals of Gerontology. 2021;**2021**:glab138

[47] Bnadkoki M. Ways to Increase Happiness Hormones: Dopamine, Serotonin, Oxytocin and Endorphins. Profitable Business Site; 2016

[48] Sophie M. Peace in the Workplace. Shamdoni; 2017

[49] Ahola S, Doston C. Psychological momentum. Frontiers in Psychology. 2016

[50] Leon Z. Neuromarketing: Exploring the Brain of Consumer. Springer; 2010

[51] Shams AH. Environmental Psychology. Samt; 2014

[52] Boghosian AJ. Rewire Your Brain: Think Your Way to a Better Life. John Wiley & Sons; 2009

[53] Ratey J. A User Guide to the Brain: Perception, Attention and four Theaters of the Brain. Vintage; 2002

[54] Pageup,People. The Neuroscience of Learning & Development. Pageup People; 2011

[55] Small G. The Memory Bible: An Innovative Strategy FOR Keeping your Brain Young, Hyperion. 2002

[56] Jansen E. Brain and Education, roshd. 2017

[57] Cheruvu R. The Neuroscience of Learning: An Introduction to Mind, Brain, Health and Education. Havard University; 2018

[58] Rippon G. The Gendered Brain. Pantheon; 2019

[59] Breuning LG. Habits of a Happy Brain. Publisher of Adams Media; 2015

[60] Danny R. Motivate to Win. Kogan Page; 2009

[61] Ruyle K. Neuroscience in Performance Management, Inventive Talent Consulting. 2015

[62] Decety J, Bartal I, Uzefovsky D. Empathy as a Driver Prosaically Behavior: Highly Conserved Neurobehavioral Mechanisms across Species. The Royal Society Publishing; 2015

[63] Deblauwe T. Awareness of employee stress response NHRD. Network Journal. 2018

[64] Locas.Marsha. Rewire your Brain for Love. Publisher of Hay House Inc; 2012

[65] Tylor B. My Stroke of Insight. Bloomington Inc; 2006

[66] Brizendine L. Woman Brain. Roshd; 2016

[67] Lombard J. The Mind of God: Neuroscience, Faith and a Search for the Soul. Harmony; 2018

[68] Hicks E. The Astonishing Power of Emotions. Hay House; 2008

[69] Church D. Mind to Matter: The Astonishing Science of How your Brain Material Reality. Publisher Hay House Inc; 2018

[70] Miendlarzewska E, Kometer M, Preuschoff N. Neurofinance. Journal of Organizational Research Methods. 2019

[71] Ariely D. Payoff the Hidden Logic That Shapes our Motivations. Simon & Schuster; 2017

[72] Waldman D, Berka C & Stikic M. Neuroscience and Team Processes, Organizational Neuroscience; 2015. 15

[73] Nori A. Neurological Foundations and Principles of Learning and Education. Samt; 2014

[74] Edrisi M. Heatwaves Dan't Just Give You Sun Burn They Can Harm Your Mental Health Too. Science beta; 2020

[75] Kiran C, Tripathi P. Leadership development through change management. A Neuroscience Prospective. 2020

[76] Pitman C, Karle E. Rewire your anxious brain. New Harbinger Publications. 2015

[77] Elliott V, Horrigan K. Neuroscience: The brains behind behavior based safety. In: Proceedings 19 Triennial Congress of the IEA. Melbourn; 2015

[78] Bagozzi R, Lee N. Philosophical Foundation of Neuroscience in organizational Reaserch. Journal of Organizational Reaserch Methods. 2019

[79] Murphy C, Ozturgut O. Brain–wise leadership. Journal of International Education and Leadership. 2013

[80] Cheruvu R. The Neuroscience of Learning: An Introduction to Mind, Brain, Health and Education,Submission The Neuroscience of Flow. Havard University Extention School Handbook; 2018

[81] Synaptic, potential. Harnessing a brain friendly style of communication. 2015

[82] Hughes D, Baylin J. Brain – Based Parenting. W. W.W. Norton & Company; 2012

[83] Swart T. The role of organizational NeuroScience in human resources. 2019

[84] Ashkanasy N, Becker WJ, Waldman DA. Neuroscience and organizational behavior: Avoiding both neuro-Euphoria and neuro-phobia. Journal of Organizational Behavior. 2014;**35**(7)

[85] Beugre D. Exploring the neural basis of fairness: A model of neuro- organizational justice. Journal of organizational Behavior and Human Decision Proccess. 2009;**110**

[86] Lieberman D. The Molecule of More: How a Single Molecule in Your Brain Drive Love. Ben Bella Books; 2018

[87] Blum F. Opportunities in Neuroscience for Future Army Applications. National Research Council; 2009

[88] Rampton J. The faster your brain moves, the more rest you need. Economic World Newspaper. 2017;**2017**: 4118

[89] Doidge N. The Brain that Change Itself. Penguin; 2007

[90] Dispenza J. You Are the Placebo. Hay House Inc; 2014

[91] Schaufenbuel K. The neuroscience of leadership: Practical Applications. UNC Executive Development; 2014

[92] Alloway T, Parker T. Traning Your Brain for Dummies. Publisher of For Dummies; 2011

[93] Rock D, Siegel D, Poelmans S, Payne J. The healthy mind platter. NeuroLeadership Journal. 2015;**5**

Chapter 14

Impact of Human Resource Management Practice on Organizational Performance: The Case of Food Processing Enterprises in Vietnam

Nguyen Thanh Hung

Abstract

This research aims at exploring relationship among Human resource management practices (HRMP), corporate social responsibility (CSR), Organizational commitment (OC) and food processing enterprise's performance. The sample size of 438 was collected from staffs and managers in 278 food processing enterprises in Viet Nam. Analytical method Structure Equation Model is used to analyze the data. The results of the study showed that HRMP directly positively influences demissions of CSR including CSR to employees, customers and environment. CSR positively relates to organizational commitment. However, there was only directly link between CSR to customers and enterprise's performance. Although HRMP was not directly influence on organizational performance, it was the significant predictors indirectly through CSR and OC. Therefore, it is necessary to improve the functions of HRM practices such as recruitment and training, job evaluation, salary, Compensation, job stability and encourage participation in innovation combined with implementing CSR aspects.

Keywords: human resource management, corporate social responsibility, commitment, business performance

1. Introduction

Entering the twenty-first century, when businesses frequently expand across national borders, not only multinational corporations and international organizations, but even small and medium-sized enterprises (SMEs) are also expanding is working hard to get and maintain a competitive advantage by solving the problem of "people and their potential" with great vitality. In this context, the strategic importance of effective human resource management and development for the future prosperity of organizations can be emphasized.

Although people are the most valuable asset, they can also become a burden if their abilities and attitudes do not match the needs of the organization. Therefore, in a fiercely competitive environment, in the global market and in the local market, finding and nurturing the right human resources to execute the business strategy is an important success factor [1]. Previous transactional leadership methods have failed to attract and retain the best talents by offering better salary, incentives and perquisites [2]. Although these transactional ways provide immediate respite, they are not enough to retain the talented ones for long and solve the talent crunch. Organizations need more than exchange means to engage or involve employees in its growth. They require inspiring leadership, an appealing vision and meaningful engagement of employees to transform organizations into a meaningful, soulful social entity [3]. Leadership is one of the significant driving forces that can radically improve the organizational performance and its fortunes. Leaders are responsible for key organizational decisions.

Effective human resource management is essential, especially for SMEs as international expansion puts additional pressure on their limited resources, especially people. Lado and Wilson [4] defined Human Resource Management (HRM) system as "a set of distinct but interrelated activities, functions, and process that are directed at attracting, developing, and maintaining (or disposing of) a firm's human resources" [4]. In addition to maintaining competitive advantage and sustainable development, organizations should focus not only on human resources but also on other aspects of corporate social responsibility (CSR) such as customers, community community, society, environment, etc. On the other hand, the competition between businesses today is related to quality, price, distribution channels, advertising as well as the implementation of corporate social responsibility.

Carroll [5] argued that CSR operated in an enterprise to have economics, legal, ethical and philanthropic [5]. Taking CSR to make profits and complying with the law is a top priority when it comes to business ethics and corporate social support. Furthermore, Carroll [6] argues that employees are the main factor linking HRM and CSR, and they are also the ones who bring social responsibility to stakeholders [6]. HRM practice plays an important role in achieving the above goal, as it is one of the means of garnering the employee support and commitment necessary for the implementation of CSR policies [7].

The stressors facing organizations throughout call for a focus on the role of the leader. In particular, the organization needs leaders who lead with purpose, values, and integrity; leaders who build enduring organizations, motivate their employees to provide superior customer service, and create long-term value for shareholders [8].

Furthermore, when leaders evaluate the long-term outcomes of making socially and ethically responsible decisions, it is clear that there are significantly positive outcomes [9]. Therefore, in order to evaluate the effectiveness of leaders for the organization, this article analyzes the impacts of human resource management functions on business performance by evaluating the perceptions of employees and managers of Vietnamese seafood processing companies.

However, HRM has different measurement components across studies by Pfeffer [10], Singh [11], Guest [8–10, 12]. In Vietnam, the researches on HRMP mostly focus on small and medium enterprises such as Thang and Quang [13], Dung et al. [12–14]. Therefore, in order to specifically analyze the function of HRM, a path analysis model of the relationship between HRMP and business performance in food processing companies was conducted. Investigate findings as a basis for proposing impacts for enhancing leadership effectiveness to improve organizational performance.

DOI: http://dx.doi.org/10.5772/intechopen.108003

2. Literature review

2.1 Leadership and management

Leadership is a part of management, it is the ability to persuade others to find ways to achieve defined goals, bring cohesion to a group, and motivate the group to achieve its goals. Management activities such as planning, organizing, and decision-making are seeds that do not work until the leader unleashes the motivating power of people and directs them towards certain targets [15, 16]. Leaders are present on the basis of the organization, their essential role being the direct influence of people, in the group's activities.

Managers have activities that derive from the management function: they develop and apply development strategies, they make forecasts and plans; they organize and coordinate work; they provide an environment conducive to performance—this motivates employees; they ensure the effective growth of management action; they promote communication with employees, with customers and with suppliers; they develop strategic relationships [17].

Manager is associated with action verbs: do, develop, intervene, manage, control, fix, etc. Managers do not manage equilibria, but dynamic phenomena; they do not search to maintain an existent situation if it is not profitable. The leader is associated with the inflection of the verb to change [18]. Therefore, within the framework of this article, we will focus on the aspect of human resource management in organizations.

2.2 Human resources management

Schuler and Jackson [18] argued that is HRM practices refer to organizational activities directed at managing the pool of human resources and ensuring that resources are employed towards the fulfillment of organizational goals [19]. Theriou and Chatzoglou [19] stated that all superior practices that lead to performance were given various names as "best HRM practices", "high commitment practices" and finally, "higher productivity and product quality practices" [20]. A significant body of research has suggested specific HRM practices which are expected to promote inimitable attributes in human resources that can help an organization to obtain a competitive advantage and enhance its performance [21].

Tocher and Rutherford [21] defined HRM as "a set of distinct but interrelated activities, functions, and processes that are directed at attracting, developing, and maintaining (or disposing of) a firm's human resources [22]. HRM is as a strategic and coherent approach to the management of an organization's most valued assets—the people (or human talent) working there who individually and collectively contribute to the achievement of its objectives [19, 20]. Human resource management is defined as a very important function in the operation of an organization, including recruitment, compensation, organizational development, safety, employee motivation, health care, effectively share information, train and manage all employee-related activities, and that means employees can carry out activities to achieve goals [23]. The later definitions that more concern on the strategic and humanistic roles of HRM as a trend for sustainable development in the organization [14].

For this study, components of HRM included selection and recruitment; Training and developing; evaluate the work of employees; workplace stability and advancement, compensation and rewards, and encouragement of engagement and innovation.

2.3 Corporate social responsibility

Carroll [5] argued that CSR is the business activity involved economic, legal, ethics, discretionary benefits and social support [5]. The CSR literature suggested that socially responsible companies not only try to be economically sustainable and profitable, but also endeavor to work with their employees, families, local communities and nation–states to improve the quality of life in ways that was both ethical and sustainable in relation to society and the environment [24]. The CSR includes two dimensions: external and internal stakeholder. The external dimension was reflected in the relationship between the organization and the community, the internal dimension as management and employees which is the expectation of employees to seek functional, economic benefits, psychological and ethical from employer organizations [22, 25].

Peterson [26] showed that there was a positive relationship between a civic enterprise and organizational commitment through employee perceptions about corporate social responsibility activities [27]. Crowther and Abreu [28] found five stakeholders of CSR including consumers, suppliers, communities, government and environment [29]. Based on the concepts of Peterson [26], Carroll [6], Mason and Simmons [24] and Vietnam Chamber of Commerce and Industry (VCCI) and CSR's characteristics in Vietnam [6, 23, 25]. The concept of CSR can be understood as activities that meet the expectations of stakeholders and contribute to sustainable development through orientation towards employees, customers and the environment.

Becker [30] recommends a link between CSR and human resources management. This combination can bring many forms of business benefits to a company, such as improved reputation, loyalty, and employee retention within the organization [31]. According to Sarvaiya [27], the interaction between HRM and CSR is mainly due to the factors indicated by CSR: the scope of CSR implementation, the stage of CSR development, and differences between companies [32]. HRM is one of the means to assist employees to enhance their commitment to implementing CSR policies and practices. Hypothesis is proposed:

H1a: There is a positive relationship between HRM practices and CSR to employees.

However, corporate CSR activities are also influenced by external stakeholders [33] such as customers, shareholders, suppliers, competitors, environment, community. HRM practices help foster an environment that provides clients with clear and ambitious production requirements that meet customer satisfaction and organizational performance [34]. Hypothesis:

H1b: There is a positive relationship between HRM practices and CSR to customers.

Clarkson [29] argued that human resource management roles have a significant impact not only on organizational behavior, attitudes, organizational culture, and leadership skills, but also on employee awareness [29, 30]. In addition, Cacioppe and Fox [35] stated that environmental factor is necessary to analyze as referring to CSR [24]. HRM influences employee awareness, behavior, attitudes, organizational culture, and leadership skills development [36].

H1c: There is a positive relationship between HRM practices and CSR to environment.

2.4 Organizational commitment

Presents a spiritual relationship between workers and the organization, reducing the likelihood of leaving the organization [37]. Commitment impacts business goals and results when members perceive the organization and make every effort to help the organization achieve good results [38].

According to social identification theory (SIT—Social Identity Theory). It is often used as the basis for the relationship between CSR perceptions and responses to employee attitudes and behavior [39]. When employees realize that their organization works for the good of society, this contributes to a positive image, making them feel satisfied and wanting to identify with the organization, which enhances employee confidence and pride [24, 34].

Furthermore, De Roeck et al. [37] showed that CSR activities have an impact on improving employees' attitudes towards the organization [40]. Mory et al. [38], Albdour et al. [41] and Thang [39] suggest that her CSR to employees is positively and significantly correlated with organizational commitment [38, 39, 42]. In addition, CSR is viewed as an important tool to influence the emotions, thoughts and purchasing behavior of target customers. However, these activities can not only improve the corporate image, but also affect the perception of employees. At least from the customer's point of view, the employee looks like an agent of the employer. Therefore, if an organization misleads its customers or produces unsafe products, its employees may be ashamed of this behavior as well. On the contrary, if an organization cares about its customers by providing quality products and accurate information about its activities, employees can be proud to be part of that organization [43].

Moreover, in the study of Farooq et al. [40] and Glavas and Kelley [44] said that CSR towards employees, environment and customers are positively related to identification and organizational commitment [43, 45]. It is possible to consider hypotheses:

H2a: CSR to employees has a significant positive effect on organizational commitment.

H2b: CSR to customers has a significant positive effect on organizational commitment.

H2c: CSR to environment has a significant positive effect on organizational commitment.

2.5 Business performance

Is expressed through organizational performance and market performance [46, 47]. According to Richard et al. [48] recommends measuring company performance based on accounting, financial and market factors through company reports and feedback on Likert scales [49].

As employees become more aware of their organization and thereby increase their support to help them improve their performance, the power of organizational performance not only impacts organizational goals, but also job satisfaction and business performance [50].

Commitment is also called the psychological state that shapes the relationship between an employee and the organization and the decision to stay or leave the organization [51, 52]. Committed employees would have effectiveness in terms of high participation and high production leading to relatively low levels of absenteeism and turnover resulting in high levels of operating performance. Engaged employees are effective in terms of high participation rates, high productivity, relatively low absenteeism and low turnover, and therefore more productive operations. An organization's personnel practices should pay attention to employee attitudes and beliefs. Because false beliefs can lead to employees not doing their best, resulting in poor motivation and performance, and poor organizational performance [53].

A high-performance facilitator work system is the relationship between trust, organizational commitment, and perception of organizational performance that positively impacts organizational performance [54].

H3: Organizational commitment relates positively with business performance.

Torgusa et al. [50] found significant positive relationships between CSR measures and employee engagement, CSR, and organizational performance [55]. CSR towards customers had a positive effect on financial performance [50, 52]. If customers are dissatisfied with a product or related service, investors are concerned that negative customer reactions in the form of a shrinking customer base, lawsuits, or both will directly impact revenue [56]. Therefore, companies must pay attention to factors such as ethical advertising standards, the health and safety of their customers while using their products, and a company-wide quality program to offer better products at fair prices. A company's policies and practices for dealing with such issues can signal a positive signal of the company's responsible attitude towards its customers and improve the company's performance [57].

Aragon-Correa et al. [58] examined the impact of the environment on business performance and showed that companies are actively taking steps to minimize their environmental impact [59]. Although the government has introduced many regulations and legal systems to regulate the behavior, implementing CSR that depends on the capacity of the organization [60]. Therefore, we suggest:

H4.a: There is a statistically significant relationship between CSR to employees and business performance.
H4.b: There is a statistically significant relationship between CSR to customers and business performance.
H4.c: There is a statistically significant relationship between CSR to environment and business performance.

Singh [11] have shown that components of HRM practices have a positive effect on performance [9, 61]. Tran Kim Dung et al. [57] have shown that HRM practices not only affect business performance through human resource outcomes, but also have a direct impact on business performance itself [62].

H5: HRM practices effect directly positive on business performance.

3. Method

3.1 Sample

Sample size plays an important role in estimating and interpreting SEM results. Hair and associates. Hair et al. [59] suggested that the sample size for structural equation models with 10–15 indices usually ranges from 200 to 400. This also depends on the number of observed variables and the reliability of each study that can be measured. Can be obtained for different survey samples [63]. According to Hair et al.

[59], the sample size must be at least 4–5 times the number of observations. There are 49 items in the research so the minimum sample size is 49 × 5 = 245. Samples were selected by convenient stratified sampling method for distributing answer sheets in 278 enterprises that allows enough suitable samples to analyze.

The survey was conducted by looking at private businesses/sole proprietorships in 2018. The survey questionnaire was conducted through face-to-face interviews and selected questionnaire responses. Conveniently stratified with 438 observations. The sample structure is made by examining managers and employees working in a company with at least 5 years of professional experience on order.

Based on geographical characteristics and number of food processing enterprises, 7 out of 13 provinces/cities in the Mekong Delta were selected for the survey, ensuring appropriate sampling for analysis in the official study. A total of 452 questionnaires were collected, while 14 of them were rejected as incomplete. Thus, the final usable questionnaires were 438 with a response rate of 75.3%. About half of the respondents were women (41.3%).

3.2 Research methods

Qualitative Research: Through reviewing documents, discussing with survey subjects, collecting expert opinions to establish a preliminary scale, the results of the preliminary scale have 51 observed variables. Quantitative research: Continue to take 51 variables to survey agricultural personnel in 136 companies. Through Cronbach's alpha analysis and exploratory factor analysis (EFA), the remaining 42 variables meet the requirements, they continue to be tested for formal studies with 438 samples at 278 companies, through confirmatory factor analysis (CFA) to test the presence of the observed variables and confirm the conceptual relationship, which aimed to demonstrate the consistency and one-dimensionality of the concept. Using structural equation modeling (SEM), the component relationships in the research model were assessed and calculated [64].

Measure the components of HRM include selection and recruitment; training and improvement; evaluation of employees' tasks; stability and promotion in work, remuneration and reward, and encouragement of participation and innovation. The scale was adapted from Lievens and Chapman [60], Mathis and Jackson [65], Bohlander and Snell [66], Huselid [62], Jiang et al. (2012) [19, 25, 65, 67, 68].

Measurement of "Corporate social responsibility" (CSR) include CSR to staffs, CSR to customers, CSR to environment. The scale is designed to focus [45, 67, 69–71].

Measurement of "Organizational commitment" (OC); The scale was adapted from Meyer et al. [70]; Meyer et al. [71]; Delaney and Huselid [45]; Whitener [72].

The scale for measuring "Business performance" (PER) include Organizational performance (PEP) and Market performance (PEM) was adapted from Huselid [62]; [45, 70, 73].

4. Result

4.1 Descriptive statistics

We made 278 companies, of which 21.6% were Private Enterprises, and 48.6% were Co., Ltd. The Joint Stock Companies accounted for 21.9% of the surveyed Enterprises; and the Household business accounted for 7.9.

Regarding Scale of employees: the total number of enterprises with less than 10 employees is 11.6%, over 100 employees accounted for 41.7%, and 18.3% and 28.4 of the surveyed enterprises had from 10 to 50 employees and from 50 to 100 employees, respectively.

According to the number of years of operation: 16.9% of the surveyed enterprises had the number of years of operation of under 5 years, over 20 years accounted for 19.8%, 32.4% and 30.9% of the surveyed enterprises had operating time from 5 to 10 years and from 11 to 20 year, respectively.

According to the descriptive statistics, it was confirmed that there were no missing values in this study. The remaining 438 responses were then considered for data analysis.

4.2 Analyze reliability of the scales

The results in **Table 1** show that all scales have alpha weight > 0.7 and the variables of each scale have a total variable correlation which can accept the reliability of the analysis. Therefore, the scales ensure the reliability of the analysis.

4.3 Results of CFA analysis for component concepts.

The scale results show the index of df, Chi-square/df; TLI and CFI are both greater than 0.9. The model fits the market data [59]. The normalized weights of the variables are greater than 0.5. The scale reaches one dimension (**Table 2**).

Code	Observed variables	Observed variables	Cronbach's Alpha	Value
Scale of HRM practices				
SET	Recruitment	3	0.859	Qualified
TRA	Training	2	0.733	
APP	Job appraisal	3	0.847	
SAL	Salary	2	0.772	
COM	Compensation	3	0.822	
INN	Participant and Innovation	3	0.789	
Scale of corporate social responsibility				
CSRS	CSR to staffs	3	0.832	Qualified
CSRC	CSR to customers	3	0.812	
CSRE	CSR to environment	3	0.825	
Scale of organizational commitment				
OC	Organizational commitment	4	0.880	Qualified
Scale of Business performance				
PEP	Organizational performance	3	0.824	Qualified
PEM	Market performance	4	0.884	
Source: data calculated by author.				

Table 1.
Testing reliability of the scales.

Concepts	factors	Chi-square	Df	Chi-square /df	P value	TLI	CFI	RMSEA
Human resource management	6	262.936	137	0.000	1.919	0.929	0.943	0.058
Corporate social responsibility	3	53.940	24	2.248	0.000	0.956	0.970	0.067
Organizational commitment	1	3.250	2	2.260	0.040	0.994	0.998	0.048
Business performance	2	77.204	26	2.969	0.000	0.946	0.961	0.062

Source: data calculated by author.

Table 2.
Analysis results of CFA for each component concept.

Concepts	Factors	Variables	Reliability		Cumulative of Variance (%) (ρvc)	Value
			Cronbach's alpha	Composite reliability		
Human resource management	Recruitment	3	0.859	0.860	55%	Qualified
	Training	2	0.733	0.742	61%	
	Job appraisal	3	0.847	0.826	59%	
	Salary	2	0.772	0.776	58%	
	Compensation	3	0.822	0.822	40%	
	Participant and Innovation	3	0.789	0.790	63%	
Corporate social responsibility	CSR to staffs	3	0.814	0.905	61%	Qualified
	CSR to customers	3	0.780	0.783	55%	
	CSR to environment	3	0.811	0.815	60%	
Organizational commitment	Organizational commitment	4	0.880	0.881	65%	Qualified
PER-business performance	Organizational performance	3	0.824	0.833	55%	Qualified
	Market performance	5	0.884	0.885	61%	

Source: data calculated by author.

Table 3.
Summary results of testing the reliability.

Table 3 describes the overall reliability of all scales with composite reliability coefficients greater than Cronbach's alpha value (greater than 0.8). In addition, the scale with total variance was extracted to explain the variability in the data for high scores (all at 55% or greater). Combined with the built-in reliability and reliability values, this scale meets the requirements for reliability and total variance extracted.

4.4 Model results: the standardized estimates

Table 4 shows the results of the model path analysis. As it can be noted from the path analysis of the associated standardized regression weights. However, two of the hypotheses were not confirmed with the required statistical significance. It is not able that the significance threshold for this study was set at the P-value of 0.05. In Tables with the P-values, the P-values given as three asterisks (***) refer to the P-value of less than 0.001 (**Figure 1**).

Relationship			Estimates	Standard error	Critical ratios	P value	Evaluation
HRM practices	→	CSR to employees	0.796	0.114	9.989	***	Accepted
HRM practices	→	CSR to customers	0.758	0.096	9.301	***	Accepted
HRM practices	→	CSR to environment	0.794	0.091	10.028	***	Accepted
CSR to employees	→	Organizational commitment	0.329	0.085	3.731	***	Accepted
CSR to customers	→	Organizational commitment	0.240	0.101	2.804	.005	Accepted
CSR to environment	→	Organizational commitment	0.262	0.105	3.036	.002	Accepted
Organizational commitment	→	Business performance	0.325	0.058	4.047	***	Accepted
CSR to employees	→	Business performance	−0.064	0.078	−.576	.565	Accepted
CSR to customers	→	Business performance	0.366	0.090	3.436	***	Accepted
CSR to environment	→	Business performance	0.243	0.096	2.215	.027	Accepted
HRM practices	→	Business performance	0.174	0.183	0.945	.345	Rejected

****Significant at P ≤ 0.001.*
Source: data surveyed by author.

Table 4.
Results of testing the relationship between concepts in theory model.

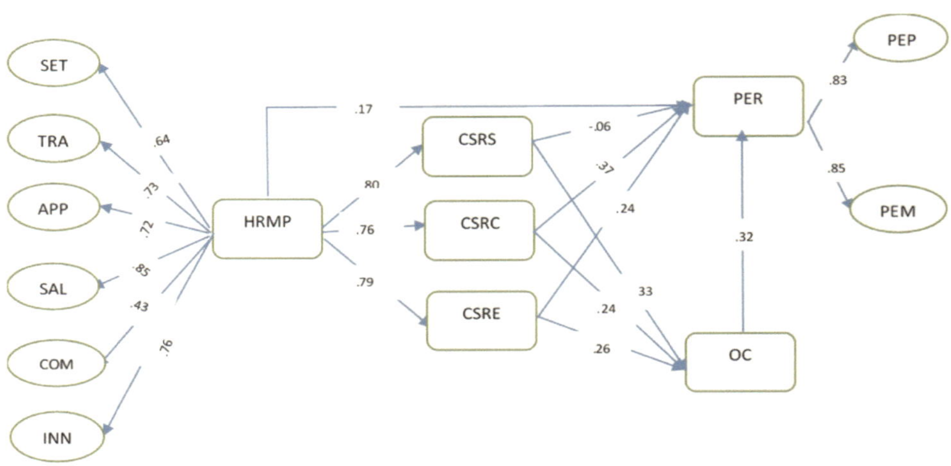

Figure 1.
SEM results for the theoretical model.

The results show that there is a statistical significance of relationship between HRM practices and CSR to stakeholders. This results show that the role of HRM practices in relation to CSR is necessary, especially aspects of environment, employees in the field of food processing. In addition, it is possible to explain the HRM activities that support employees' attitudes positively through organizational commitment. This is similar to studies of Whitener [72], Chew and Chan [74], Gong et al. [75] that states relationship between HRM and business performance through organizational commitment [41, 73–76].

The results show that the implementation of CSR towards customers and the environment directly affects the company's performance, similar to the study by Rettab et al. [76], Murtaza et al. [77] argue that the expansion of CSR improves the image of the organization in the minds of consumers, which has a positive impact on financial performance [78]. Aragón-Correa et al. [58] found that enterprises reduce the positive impact of the environment on financial performance [59].

CSR for employees has no direct impact on company performance. However, if the employee is aware of the level of CSR that the company has for its stakeholders, he will actively promote the attitude to improve productivity. Social Identity Theory (SIT) is often used as a basis to explain the relationship between CSR perception and employee attitudes [39].

5. Conclusion and implications

The research results show that leadership plays an important role in human resource management, it has a positive influence on employee perception and company's performance [2, 3]. It is expressed through HRM practices positively affect CSR in all aspects of employees, customers and the environment. It is consistent with previous studies on the growing practice of HRM organizations contributing to the formulation of social responsibility policies [7, 32]. In particular, the impact of HRM on CSR in terms of human resources and the natural environment is high (weights $\beta = 0.796$ and 0.794), which shows the importance of management and the level of CSR implementation, especially for environmental components, similar to Clarkson's [29] study, highly appreciate environmental factors as important in implementing CSR [78]. This result is completely consistent with the food industry where most companies operating in this field consider the application of management standards such as SA 8000 to ensure a suitable working environment fit. In addition, customer-oriented standards are gradually improved and developed to meet food safety management standards such as GMP, HACCP or ISO 22000.

All three aspects of CSR affect organizational commitment, in which the strongest influence on commitment is CSR for employees ($\beta = 0.329$), which is unavoidable when employment for employees helps increase employee commitment to the organization. This result is consistent with the study of Skudiene and Auruskeviciene [73] on internal CSR (employee orientation), it has a more positive influence on employee motivation than external CSR aspects [77]. Al-bdour et al. [41]; Halim and Rahayu [79] also confirmed that internal CSR strongly influences organizational commitment [80–82].

In addition, organizational commitment has a positive impact on the company's business performance ($\beta = 0.325$), it shows that organizational commitment will promote positive performance, generate business results, high business. Gouldner [78] showed that the benefit that one person receives from another leads to this benefit returning in a process in which organizational commitment positively affects firm performance [81–83]. While CSR for employees and the environment is important, it does not directly affect business performance. However, CSR towards customers positively affects operational efficiency ($\beta = 0.348$). This result motivates companies to take action to strengthen the brand image and reputation in the minds of customers [84].

Although HRM practices do not directly affect performance, HRM activities play an important role in indirectly affecting business performance ($\beta = 0.805$), corresponding to level 82.3% explained. This means that companies carrying out human resource management activities should incorporate an emphasis on performing accountability to stakeholders such as employees, customers and environmental responsibility. It is in the interest of companies to take into account factors such as working conditions, working hours, respect for labor protection and food safety, strengthen the company's role for customers, respect customers, the treatment and rejection of waste in the natural environment are implemented more strictly, as they have a positive effect on the attitudes of employees contributing to improving the performance of the company.

5.1 Implications

In order to improve organizational commitment and business performance among employees in the seafood processing industry through HRM activities, the leaders need to focus on implementing some activities:

Improve management efficiency by maintaining and reforming their ISO management system. It is necessary to approach, maintain and develop a GMP (Good Manufacturing Practice) management system to ensure safe and hygienic conditions for production, including general principles, regulations, and guidelines for basic contents. From production conditions ensuring product quality and safety to the development of the HACCP System and food safety management standards (ISO 22000).

Regarding recruitment and training, the selection should be done publicly, with clear job descriptions for each position. In order to improve the quality of on-the-job training, human resource management needs to focus on two subjects who are employees of the company as follows:

For workers who directly create products, it is necessary to pay special attention to skills and production levels and pay attention to the implementation of regulations and processes, ensuring strict implementation of regulations in occupational safety, hygiene and food safety;

For indirect workers, it is necessary to improve their qualifications in many aspects, including regularly updating standards on quality management and science and technology, accessing and developing products suitable for the market. In addition, encourage employees to be proficient in other areas to increase flexibility in problem solving and easily take on other jobs when there is a change of job. Regularly organize and send employees to participate in professional training and retraining courses. This helps employees update their knowledge in a timely manner to respond to market demands.

Leaders should regularly monitor and evaluate employees through a set of assessment criteria on knowledge, skills, qualifications and work performance in the company, regardless of gender. The criteria should be clear, open and fair in evaluating employees. In addition, it is necessary to build a feedback channel and dialog with the company at least twice a year to answer questions, solve difficulties and complaints of employees.

The salary and bonus policy must be implemented in a timely manner, ensuring the salary suitable to the job position and reasonable compared to other companies of the same type of operation. Today, the demand for human resources for the processing industry in the coming time tends to increase.

DOI: http://dx.doi.org/10.5772/intechopen.108003

Remuneration and bonus policy should be implemented timely to ensure that salary is suitable for the position and reasonably placed in comparison with other enterprises in the same type of business. Today, the demand for human resources for the processing industry in the coming time tends to increase. Therefore, salary and bonus are important factors that must be carefully considered to both increase revenue and ensure organizational commitment. The determination of marginal labor and wages should be reviewed and adjusted every 6 months to suit the actual production and business situation. Regulations on salary, bonus, sick leave, convalescence, maternity, etc.

The leaders should encourage employees to develop rules and procedures within the company to ensure quality improvement and increase employee engagement. At the same time, it will improve operational efficiency through improved management and streamlined and efficient work processes. Therefore, it will improve the quality of the product to meet the needs of the customers, thereby helping to improve the functioning of the market.

Research is limited to analyzing three aspects of social responsibility: employees, customers and the environment. Social responsibility is also expressed in other aspects, such as social responsibility towards the community, suppliers, shareholders, etc. were not analyzed in this study. It therefore underestimates the extent to which social accountability is exercised among stakeholders. This is a necessary research direction from which to analyze the encouraging aspects of corporate social responsibility to stakeholders.

Appendix

Observed variables		Sources	Corrected item-total correlation	Cronbach's Alpha
Scale of HRM practices				
Recruitment				
SET1	Company announce information of recruitment widely	Qualitative research	0.565	0.859
SET3	Provided full information on the work for candidates as admission	[67]	0.676	
SET4	Selection and recruitment based on the capacity of candidates	Qualitative research	0.752	
Training				0.733
TRA1	The company had an apprenticeship and training system for employees	Qualitative research	0.710	
TRA2	Training to solve skills and issues in the enterprise	[25]	0.656	
Job appraisal				
APP1	The enterprise evaluated the work fairly	Qualitative research	0.721	0.347
APP2	The enterprise had a process to evaluate job clearly	Qualitative research	0.717	
APP3	The enterprise evaluated employees that based on their ability and job performance	[19, 65]	0.706	

Observed variables		Sources	Corrected item-total correlation	Cronbach's Alpha
Salary				
SAL1	I was paid full, reasonable for the work I do	[82]	0.631	0.772
SAL2	I was paid on time	Qualitative research	0.631	
Compensation				
COM1	The enterprise had policies that reward appropriate	[85]	0.675	0.822
COM2	Employees received incentives such as promotions, bonuses, etc.	[25]	0.713	
COM3	Rewards and benefits was distributed fairly	[25]	0.644	
Participant and innovation				
INN1	Employees often work to find solutions to meet the difficult problems	[71]	0.585	0.789
INN2	Encouraged employees usually think dynamically	[86]	0.700	
INN3	Employees were encouraged participate to resolve issues	[68, 70]	0.607	
Scale of CSR				
CSR to staffs—CSRS				
CSRS1	Our company provided a wide range of indirect benefits to improve the quality of employees' life	[70, 71]	0.707	0.832
CSRS2	The managers of our company were primarily concerned with employees' needs and wants.	[45]	0.703	
CSRS4	Businesses create flexible conditions to balance the life and work well for employees	[45]	0.666	
CSR to customers—CSRC				
CSRC1	Employees were trained/instructed to provide full information about its products to its customers	[45]	0.583	0.812
CSRC2	Customers satisfaction were highly important for our company	[45]	0.582	
CSRC3	The business always solves customers' complaints satisfactorily	[45]	0.569	
CSR to environment—CSRE				
CSRE1	Our company has the necessary equipment to reduce its negative environmental impact	ISO26000	0.674	0.825
CSRE2	Our company use materials/products which are environmental friendly	ISO26000	0.705	
CSRE3	Environmental factors and surrounding communities was always carefully weighed in business activities	ISO26000, [45]	0.665	

Observed variables		Sources	Corrected item-total correlation	Cronbach's Alpha
Scale of organizational commitment—OC				
OC1	I am proud of my job to tell others that I am part of this organization	[45, 72]	0.674	0.880
OC2	I really feel as if this organization's problems are my own	[45, 72]	0.752	
OC3	I would be very happy to spend the rest of my career with this organization	[84]	0.720	
OC4	For me, this is the best of all possible organizations for which to work	[45, 72]	0.772	
Scale of Business performance—PER				
Organizational performance—PEP				
PEP1	Quality of products services is ensured	[70, 73]	0.682	0.824
PEP2	New products, services is developed		0.761	
PEP3	Number of products production is increased		0.736	
Market performance—PEM				
PEM1	I noticed that customers feedback positively	[70, 73]	0.677	0.884
PEM2	I noticed that the sales of the business increased		0.712	
PEM3	I noticed the profitability of enterprises increases		0.774	
PEM4	I noticed the enterprise market is expanded		0.730	
PEM5	I noticed that the number of customers increased		0.713	

Author details

Nguyen Thanh Hung
Tra Vinh University, Tra Vinh Province, Vietnam

*Address all correspondence to: nthung@tvu.edu.vn

References

[1] Reddy PB, DSC. HRM Practices and its impact on performance—Exploratory literature review in the context of Indian Smes. National Journal of Integrated Research in Medicine. 2011;**1**:73-87

[2] Pradhan S, Pradhan RK. An empirical investigation of relationship among transformational leadership, affective organizational commitment and contextual performance. Vision. 2015;**19**: 227-235

[3] Singh P, Bhandarker A. Winning the Corporate Olympiad: The Renaissance Paradigm. Vikas Publishing House; 2002

[4] Lado AA, Wilson MC. Human resource systems and sustained competitive advantage: A competency-based perspective. The Academy of Management Review. 1994;**19**:699-727

[5] Carroll AB. The pyramid of corporate social responsibiiity: Towards the moral management of organizational stakeholders. Business Horizons. 1991; **34**:39-48

[6] Carroll WR. Organizational Culture, HRM and Firm Performance: Examining Relationships Using the Competing Values Framework in Call Centres. Halifax, Nova Scotia: Saint Mary's University; 2008

[7] Buciuniene I, Kazlauskaite R. The linkage between HRM, CSR and performance outcomes. Baltic Journal of Management. 2012;**7**:5-24

[8] George B. Authentic Leadership: Rediscovering the Secrets to Creating Lasting Value. San Francisco: John Wiley & Sons; 2003

[9] Mahoney LS, Thorne L. Corporate social responsibility and long-term compensation: Evidence from Canada. Journal of Business Ethics. 2005;**57**: 241-253

[10] Pfeffer J. Seven practices of successful organizations. California Management Review. 1998;**40**:96-124

[11] Singh K. Impact of HR practices on perceived firm performance in India. Asia-Pacific Journal of Human Resources. 2004;**42**:301-317

[12] Guest DE. The International Journal of Human Resource Management Human resource management and performance: A review and research agenda. International Journal of Human Resource Management. 2011;**8**(3):37-41

[13] Thang LC, Quang T. Antecedents and consequences of dimensions of human resource management practices in Vietnam. International Journal of Human Resource Management. 2005;**16**: 1830-1846

[14] Dung TK, Thi T, Anh L. A framework of significant human resource management practices in Vietnam. Journal of Economic Development. 2017;**24**:46-63

[15] Răducan R, Răducan R. Leadership and management. Procedia - Social and Behavioral Sciences. 2014;**149**:808-812

[16] Zaccaro SJ, Gulick LMV, Khare VP. Personality and leadership. Leadersh Crossroads. 2008;**1**:13-29

[17] Morrison JL. Management of organizational behavior. The Journal of Education for Business. 2008;**83**:181

[18] Schuler RS, Jackson SE. Linking competitive strategies with human

resource management practices. Management. 1987;**1**:207-219

[19] Theriou GN, Chatzoglou PD. Enhancing performance through best HRM practices, organizational learning and knowledge management. European Business Review. 2008;**20**:185-207

[20] Guest DE, Michie J, Conway N, et al. Human resource management and corporate performance in the UK. British Journal of Industrial Relations. 2003;**41**: 291-314

[21] Tocher N, Rutherford MW. Perceived acute human resource management problems in small and medium firms: An empirical examination. Entrepreneurship Theory and Practice. 2009;**33**:455-479

[22] Armstrong M. A handbook of human resource management practice. 2014. Epub ahead of print 2014. DOI: 10.1007/ s10551-011-1141-1

[23] Freeman RE. The stakeholder approach revisited. Zeitschrift für Wirtschafts-und Unternehmensethik. 2004;**5**:228-241

[24] Mason C, Simmons J. Embedding corporate social responsibility in corporate governance: A stakeholder systems approach. Journal of Business Ethics. 2014;**119**:77-86

[25] Jahanian A, Nawaz N, Yamin R, et al. Human resource management and productivity: A comparative study among banks in Bahawalpur division. European Journal of Business and Management Research. 2012;**4**:253-262

[26] Peterson DK. The relationship between perceptions of corporate citizenship and organizational commitment. Business & Society. 2004; **43**:296-319

[27] Sarvaiya H. The Relationship between CSR and HRM: A Study of Large New Zealand Organizations. Albany New Zealand: Massey University; 2014

[28] Crowther D, Abreu R. Corporate social responsibility in Portugal: Empirical evidence of corporate behaviour. Emerald Gr Publ Ltd. 2005;**5**:3-18

[29] Clarkson ME. A stakeholder framework for analyzing and evaluating corporate social performance. The Academy of Management Review. 1995; **20**:92-117

[30] Becker WS. Are you leading a socially responsible and sustainable human resource function? People and Strategy. 2011;**34**:18-23

[31] Rimanoczy I, Pearson T. Role of HR in the new world of sustainability. Industrial and Commercial Training. 2010;**42**:11-17

[32] Meyer JP, Herscovitch L. Commitment in the workplace: Toward a general model. Human Resource Management Review. 2001;**11**:299-326

[33] Steers RM. Antecedents and outcomes of organizational commitment. Administrative Science Quarterly. 1977;**22**:46-56

[34] Tajfel H. Social psychology of intergroup relations. Annual Review of Psychology. 1982;**26**:1-39

[35] Cacioppe R, Fox M. A survey of managers' perceptions of corporate ethics and social responsibility and actions that may affect companies' success. Journal of Business Ethics. 2008; **82**:681-700

[36] Hogg MA, Terry DI. Social identity and self-categorization processes in

organizational contexts. The Academy of Management Review. 2000;**25**:121-140

[37] de Roeck K, Marique G, Stinglhamber F, et al. Understanding employees' responses to corporate social responsibility: Mediating roles of overall justice and organizational identification. International Journal of Human Resource Management. 2014;**25**: 91-112

[38] Mory L, Wirtz BW, Göttel V. Factors of internal corporate social responsibility and the effect on organizational commitment. International Journal of Human Resource Management. 2016;**27**: 1393-1425

[39] Thang NN. Internal CSR and commitment in Vietnam. International Business Management. 2016:784-792

[40] Farooq O, Payaud M, Merunka D, et al. The impact of corporate social responsibility on organizational commitment: Exploring multiple mediation mechanisms. Journal of Business Ethics. 2013:1-18

[41] Al-bdour A, Nasruddin E, Lin S. The relationship between internal corporate social responsibility and organizational commitment within the banking sector in Jordan. International Journal of Humanities and Social Science. 2010;**5**: 932-951

[42] Turker D. How corporate social responsibility influences organizational commitment. Journal of Business Ethics. 2009a;**89**:189-204

[43] Buzzell RD, Gale BT. The PIMS Principles: Linking Strategy to Performance. New York: Simon and Schuster; 1987

[44] Glavas A, Kelley K. The effects of perceived corporate social responsibility on employee attitudes. Business Ethics Quarterly. 2014;**24**:165-202

[45] Delaney JT, Huselid MA. The impact of human resource management practices on perceptions of organizational performance. The Academy of Management Journal. 1996; **39**:949-969

[46] Welford R. Work life balance in Hong Kong: Survey results.

[47] Sheldon ME. investments and involvements as mechanisms producing commitment to the organization. Administrative Science Quarterly. 2012; **16**:143-150

[48] Richard PJ, Devinney TM, Yip GS, et al. Measuring organizational performance: Towards methodological best practice. Journal of Management. 2009;**35**:718-804

[49] Bakiev E. The influence of interpersonal trust and organizational commitment on perceived organizational performance. Journal of Applied Economics and Business Research. 2013;**3**:166-180

[50] Torugsa NA, O'Donohue W, Hecker R. Capabilities, proactive CSR and financial performance in SMEs: Empirical evidence from an Australian manufacturing industry sector. Journal of Business Ethics. 2012;**109**:483-500

[51] Meyer JP, Alien NJ. A three-component conceptualization of organizational commitment. Human Resource Management Review. 1991;**1**: 61-89

[52] Marcus A. The deterrent to dubious corporate behavior: Profitability, probability and safety recalls. Strategic Management Journal. 1989;**10**: 233-250

[53] Waddock S, Graves S. The corporate social performance- financial performance link. Strategic Management Journal. 1997;**18**:303-319

[54] Berman S. Does stakeholder orientation matter? The relationship between stakeholder management models and firm. The Academy of Management Journal. 1999;**42**:488-506

[55] Mishra S, Suar D. Does corporate social responsibility influence firm performance of Indian companies? 2010. Epub ahead of print 2010. DOI: 10.1007/s10551-010-0441-1

[56] Katou AA. Measuring the impact of HRM on organizational performance. Journal of Industrial Engineering and Management. 2008;**1**:119-142

[57] Tran Kim Dung, Doan Thanh Hai, Le Thi Loan, Bui Thi Thanh, Phan Quoc Tan HVT. The relationship between human resource management practice, human resource management results and business performance in enterprises. Journal of Development Economics. 2010;**3**:37-41

[58] Aragón-Correa JA, Hurtado-Torres N, Sharma S, et al. Environmental strategy and performance in small firms: A resource-based perspective. Journal of Environmental Management. 2008;**86**:88-103

[59] Hair JF, Black WC, Babin BJ, et al. Multivariate Data Analysis. Pearson Prentice Hall, 2010. Epub ahead of print 2010. DOI: 10.1016/j.ijpharm.2011.02.019.

[60] Lievens F, Chapman D. Recruitment and selection. Wilkinson. 2010. Epub ahead of print 2010. DOI: 10.4135/9780857021496.n9

[61] Mellahi K. The effect of regulations on HRM: Private sector firms in Saudi Arabia. International Journal of Human Resource Management. 2007;**18**:85-99

[62] Huselid MA. The impact of human resource management practices on turnover, productivity, and corporate financial performance. The Academy of Management Journal. 1995;**38**:635-672

[63] Jiang J, Wang S, Zhao S. Does HRM facilitate employee creativity and organizational innovation? A study of Chinese firms. International Journal of Human Resource Management. 2012;**23**:4025-4047

[64] Nguyen TH. Impact of leader-member relationship quality on job satisfaction, innovation and operational performance: A case in Vietnam. Journal of Asian Finance, Economics and Business. 2020;**7**:449-456

[65] Mathis RL, Jackson JH. Human Resource Management. 13th ed. Joseph Sabatino; 2011. Epub ahead of print 2011. DOI: 10.1080/09585199200000162

[66] Bohlander G, Snell S. Managing Human Resources. New York: South-Western, Cengage Learning; 2011

[67] Turker D. Measuring corporate social responsibility: A scale development study. Journal of Business Ethics. 2009b;**85**:411-427

[68] Jesús Barrena-Martínez ML-F, PMR-F. Research proposal on the relationship between corporate social responsibility and strategic human resource management. International Journal of Management and Enterprise Development. 2011;**10**:173-187

[69] Maignan I, Ferrell OC. Measuring corporate citizenship in two countries: The case of the United States and France. Journal of Business Ethics. 2000;**23**:283-297

[70] Meyer JP, Allen NJ, Smith CA. Commitment to organizations and occupations: Extension and test of a three-component conceptualization. The Journal of Applied Psychology. 1993;**78**:538

[71] Allen NJ, Meyer JP. Commitment in the workplace: Theory, research and application. SAGE Publications, Inc, 1997. Epub ahead of print 1997. DOI: 10.4135/9781452231556

[72] Whitener EM. Do "high commitment" human resource practices affect employee commitment? Journal of Management. 2001;**27**:515-535

[73] Skudiene V, Auruskeviciene V. The contribution of corporate social responsibility to internal employee motivation. Baltic Journal of Management. 2012;**7**:49-67

[74] Chew J, Chan CCA. Human resource practices, organizational commitment and intention to stay. International Journal of Manpower. 2008;**29**:503-522

[75] Gong Y, Law KS, Chang S, et al. Human resources management and firm performance: The differential role of managerial affective and continuance commitment. The Journal of Applied Psychology. 2009;**94**:263-275

[76] Rettab B, Brik AB, Mellahi K. A study of management perceptions of the impact of corporate social responsibility on organizational performance in emerging economies: The case of Dubai. Journal of Business Ethics. 2009;**89**:371-390

[77] Murtaza IA, Akhtar N, Ijaz A, et al. Impact of corporate social responsibility on firm financial performance: A case study of Pakistan. Journal of Business Ethics. 2014;**1**:1914-1927

[78] Gouldner HP. Dimensions of organizational commitment. Administrative Science Quarterly. 1960; **4**(4):468-490

[79] Halim L, Rahayu M. The effect of employee's perceptions on corporate social responsibility activities on organizational commitment, mediated by organizational trust. International Journal of Business and Management. 2016;**5**:43-49

[80] Mansour N, Gara E, Gaha C. Getting inside the black box: HR practices and firm performance within the Tunisian financial services industry. Personnel Review. 2014;**43**:490-514

[81] Avolio BJ, Gardner WL. Authentic leadership development: Getting to the root of positive forms of leadership. The Leadership Quarterly. 2005;**16**:315-338

[82] Dutra JS. Gestão por competências: um modelo avançado para o gerenciamento de pessoas. 5th ed. São Paulo: Editora Gente; 2001

[83] Omondi G, Magutu P, Onsongo C, et al. The adoption of strategic human resource management practices in commercial banks: The process and challenges in Kenya. Journal of Human Resource Management. 2011;**2011**:1-20

[84] Meyer JP, Stanley DJ, Herscovitch L, et al. Affective, continuance, and normative commitment to the organization: A meta-analysis of antecedents, correlates, and consequences. Journal of Vocational Behavior. 2002;**61**:20-52

[85] Devanna MA, Fombrun CJ, Tichy NM. Strategic Human Resource Management. New York: Wiley; 1984

[86] Amabile TM, Conti R, Coon H, et al. Assessing the work environment for creativity University of Michigan University of Southern California. The Academy of Management Journal. 1996; **39**:1154-1184

Chapter 15

Authentic Leadership: Supporting Employees' Performance, Creativity, Involvement in Decision-Making and Outcomes

Hanan AlMazrouei

Abstract

One of the most important roles in leadership is to support and encourage team members by empowering them and providing them with the opportunity to take greater ownership of their work outcomes. By supporting a culture of innovation, authentic leaders inspire and support individuals, encouraging them to improve performance and develop the confidence to exhibit creativity, demonstrate innovation, and show greater agility when faced with challenges. This enables them to work more independently, helping their organization to better achieve its objectives and increase competitiveness. Authentic leadership enhances an organization's effectiveness by encouraging its employees to approach their tasks with a more optimistic attitude and with creativity. Through the use of emotional sensitivity organizational leaders can tailor their interactions with their employees to elicit their best performance. By drawing on each employee's strengths, erudite leaders can create effective individuals that will enhance performance and foster a positive organizational culture. Authentic leadership also encourages employees to participate in decision-making. This empowers them and offers them a feeling of ownership of their tasks and responsibility for the outcomes. Encouraging such a culture promotes the organization as an employer of choice, further supporting its efforts to gain and maintain competitive advantage.

Keywords: authentic leadership, employees' performance, creativity, participative decision-making, outcomes

1. Introduction

Authentic leadership is a style of leadership that has attracted a significant amount of attention, by both scholars [1, 2] and practitioners [3]. It is characterized by an affirmative psychological attitude that promotes a positive organizational culture with a view to developing increased self-awareness, the objective evaluation of information, the application of supportive moral principles, and transparency on the part of the leader. This then enhances self-development not only for the leader, but also their followers [2]. Academic opinion is that it enhances organizational performance by encouraging positive approaches and behaviors by employees [4]. Authentic leadership enhances an organization's performance by providing employees with the support and motivation to take greater ownership of their work and its outcomes, which benefits the organization as a whole. It also allows employees to participate in discussions regarding their tasks and make decisions that affect their work.

Leaders can reap the benefits of practicing authentic leadership through the enhanced motivation of their employees that it brings. By supporting their employees in this way the employees will, in turn, support their manager and their organization by taking greater ownership of the outcomes derived from their efforts, resulting in mutual benefit.

As the world business environment continues to gather pace, organizational leaders need to adapt in order to benefit from management methodologies that help them to gain and maintain competitive advantage. The purpose of this chapter is to assist managers to better understand the concept of authentic leadership so that they can utilize its practical aspects for the mutual benefit of themselves, their employees, and their organization. The aim is to shed light on the importance of authentic leadership with regard to employee motivation by involving employees in decision-making. This chapter discusses the robust relationship between authentic leaders and followers that could lead to increased employee commitment and job performance. It also seeks to determine the relationship between authentic leaders and their followers and how it supports and encourages employee creativity at both the individual and the team level.

2. Theoretical framework

Uhl-Bien et al. [5] traced the historical study of leadership from its beginnings, where leaders were the focus and followers were considered merely the resources used to achieve the leader's desired goals, through to the concept of a dyadic relationship, where leadership and followership engaged in a symbiotic relationship directed toward the mutual attainment of the organization's goals and objectives. In this, the hierarchical view of the leadership-followership model has developed into more of a social view.

Authenticity has been described as an individual's taking ownership of their experiences, thoughts, feelings, opinions, principles, or longings [6]. This involves an individual possessing a large measure of self-awareness and taking actions commensurate with their beliefs [7]. Erickson [8] advises that authenticity is not either fully present or fully absent in a person but, rather, is on a continuum. Whitehead [9] defined authentic leadership as involving self-awareness, humility, a desire for continuous improvement, an awareness of others' welfare, the ability to create an organizational culture of trust by emphasizing and maintaining strong ethics and morals, and a commitment to the organization's success. Shamir and Eilam [10] based their definition of authentic leadership on the association between leaders' self-concepts and their ensuing actions and behaviors, describing how the leader's organizational role is a part of their concept of self and how, as role models, their actions and behaviors are consistent with this. This, they argue, generates authenticity on the part of their followers, given that the followers are motivated to follow their leaders out of a desire to form genuine working relationships. Zhang et al. [11] and Javed et al. [12] note that the effectiveness of an authentic leader varies between employees, with factors such as employees' political skills and openness to experience affecting how strongly they adopt the behaviors demonstrated by their authentic leader.

Authentic leaders possess transparency in relation to their intentions, linking their actions and behaviors to their values [7]. In rapidly changing business environments, organizations need authentic leaders to engender followers' confidence in the direction they take the organization. Such situations are the basis of leadership of the highest quality [13, 14]. A review of the body of literature by Kernis and Goldman [15] and Kernis [16] found that authenticity involves four aspects relating to both an individual's thoughts and behaviors, these being based on an awareness of themselves and having belief in their emotions, motives and values, objectivity in evaluating their personal qualities, both positive and negative, taking actions based on their values rather than being influenced by others, and the ability and willingness to be both open and genuine in interpersonal relationships.

Given that authentic leadership may be viewed as a function of the dyadic mutual exchange process, research into followership needs to investigate the type of influence that leaders and followers have on each other in their combined pursuit of organizational objectives for their mutual benefit.

3. Method

This chapter is based on a review of the literature concerning authentic leadership and its relationship with employee creativity and participative decision-making. These important associations have not received the attention they deserve, given their importance in developing robust working relationships and, through these, enhanced competitive advantage. This research critically reviews the literature to improve our understanding of authentic leadership based on the theoretical focus of follower participation in decision-making. The focus of this chapter is on creating a clear understanding of how authentic leaders can build a strong relationship with followers. This chapter is centered on theory and its practical application, and although it may be based on existing research, it covers a topic that is only now beginning to receive the attention it deserves. Participative decision-making has enjoyed only limited coverage in the literature to the present time [17, 18], yet it is deserving of increased attention. This chapter aims to examine how the existing theoretical frameworks can be combined with more recent work on authentic leadership to arrive at a better understanding of authentic leadership and how it affects leaders' dynamic relationships with their followers. This stands as one of the most important challenges that leaders face.

4. Discussion

4.1 Leader self-awareness

An authentic leader is one who leverages their own positive characteristics, such as a strong awareness of self and a robust sense of ethical behavior in order to nurture a positive working environment in which employee trust and positive working relationships are developed and employee creativity and innovation are encouraged and rewarded [19]. A leader's self-awareness develops over time as they gain an increased understanding of their strengths and weaknesses and talents, as well as their personal beliefs, values, and desires [1].

Authentic leadership entails a manager possessing well-developed emotional intelligence. With this, leaders can work on building not only their own positive characteristics by recognizing their strengths and weaknesses, but also those of their followers. In so doing, they can develop empathy with their followers and utilize this to develop better and stronger working relationships by enhancing their followers' positive characteristics as well as their own and harnessing them for mutual benefit.

Self-awareness is akin to self-evaluation, in that a better awareness of self is more likely to result in a more accurate self-assessment. How individuals assess their leadership is related to this. Discrepancies between an individual's assessment of themselves and assessments of them by others can indicate a lack of self-awareness regarding their leadership [20]. An individual's awareness of their own leadership may well enhance both their workplace effectiveness and the satisfaction they derive from this [20]. Of course, a leader's self-awareness needs to be truly objective if it is to be an accurate reflection of their capabilities. This is a difficult undertaking for any individual given that the natural human trait is often to view events in a favorable light.

4.2 Follower development

Authentic leadership affects outcomes such as employees' job performance and also their organizational commitment and their demonstration of citizenship behaviors [21, 22]. It develops over time as the leaders become increasingly aware of their values, beliefs, desires, and role within the organization [23]. Followers also develop a greater transparency and a stronger awareness of their values and beliefs within the organizational context as a result of their leader's influence, thereby cultivating their own values, beliefs, and desires. This, then, creates a symbiotic relationship where both leaders and followers can develop. This is not necessarily intentional on the part of the leader, but may occur simply in the act of their being a role model [1].

By building on their awareness of self and of others, authentic leaders increase their ability to evaluate not only their employees' current capabilities, but also their potential capacity for increased responsibility [24]. This, of course, presupposes that followers are resources that exist in a vacuum and need developing by the leader. Followers already have their own views, perceptions, and predispositions. In order for followers to be developed by their leader, they must be willing for this to occur. Good leaders may well be able to develop positive working relationships with most followers, but should recognize that not all followers can be bent to the will of the leader in the way the leader would always prefer.

4.3 Authentic leadership and creativity

By emphasizing the positive aspects of working relationships rather than the negative [21, 25], authentic leaders encourage trust among their followers. This then increases the followers' sense of safety and encourages them to contribute their creative ideas [26]. Followers of authentic leaders obtain increased motivation through their leaders' support [27], thus encouraging creativity [28]. This is achieved by the authentic leaders having a heightened self-awareness, particularly in relation to their strengths and weaknesses, emotions, values, and beliefs. These leaders candidly share these with their followers transparently, engendering trust. In this way, authentic leaders develop trust and encourage creative thinking among their followers by creating a supportive organizational environment that allows reasonable risk-taking. As well as this, these leaders carefully consider all the information available to them, while maintaining a moral standpoint, before deciding on any courses of action.

Authentic leaders encourage constructive exchanges between stakeholders [3] and enhance positive attitudes and emotions among their followers. This encourages their followers to consider creative alternatives [29]. This promotes an organizational culture where employees feel sufficiently safe to seek out alternatives, present and implement creative ideas, and develop their potential [30]. In this context, authentic leaders do not necessarily develop their followers' attitudes directly as their followers will already have their own attitudes but, rather, indirectly in that they, as custodians of the organization's culture, create the conditions and the supportive environment in which followers can feel safe to propose their creative ideas.

4.4 Team leaders' authenticity and team innovation

Innovation is the implementation of creative ideas within a specific context [31] and represents a change to the organization's traditional method of operating. This usually creates resistance to the proposed change and possible conflict, often requiring continuous effort in order to successfully implement the change. This highlights the difference between the leadership needed to encourage employee creativity and that required to support innovation, with each requiring different incentives [32].

Authentic leaders offer empowerment to their followers by instilling in them a common sense of purpose and values and providing encouragement and opportunity to undertake leadership roles in the pursuit of organizational objectives [33]. Authentic leaders do this on an ongoing basis through their presence as a role model, thus providing the conditions in which authentic followership can develop. It is this that sets authentic leadership apart from other styles of leadership. Also, by being transparent, authentic leaders can support their followers by showing their faith and trust in them [32].

As a result of the organizational environment created by the authentic leader, followers will have a greater propensity to perceive their leaders as role models. The leaders, being imbued with increased self-confidence, are themselves encouraged to support the implementation of creative new ideas [34] or generate new ideas themselves. This can, in turn, motivate the followers to devise and implement new ideas [35] as well as becoming role models themselves.

Authentic leaders, indeed, possessing increased levels of self-awareness will have the responsibility to nurture their team members' creative ideas and support their implementation. As leaders, they will use their knowledge of the broader issues and their experience to guide their team members' suggestions into reality by supporting their efforts, rather than taking them over and personally implementing them. This will provide the team members with a greater sense of ownership, not just of the work task itself, but the creative solution to the task's problems and its implementation.

4.5 Affective commitment

Affective commitment relates to the personal and emotional attachment an employee experiences. Those with a high level of affective commitment are less likely to separate from the organization [36] as they believe in the organization's values and goals [37]. Behaviors demonstrated by authentic leaders represent the values that support transparent working relationships. A greater employee perception of leader authenticity is likely to result in an increased emotional connection between employees and authentic leaders [16, 23] leading to an increase in the quality of exchanges between them, thus increasing employees' affective commitment [38]. Based on the author's observation and their experience as an authentic leader, when individuals and teams have a better informal and formal working relationship with their leader, they feel more supported, are more committed to that relationship, their job, and their organization, and are more engaged. This then results in enhanced cohesiveness and a stronger leader-member exchange as well as encouraging employees to demonstrate increased creativity, resulting in mutual benefits for both the leader and the followers.

4.6 Affective commitment and creativity

As creativity involves a process of developing solutions to problems and issues [39], it may assist in increasing employees' commitment to their organization [40] and, as such, may support creative behaviors. Therefore, there is an association between employees' affective commitment and creative behaviors [41, 42]. Employees who are happier in their work display increased creativity [43] and, through this, an affective attachment to their place of employment [44]. Positive emotions enhance cognition and support creative thought [45] so there is a correlation between happiness, affective attachment, and creative thinking [46]. Following this, there is also a correlation between positive affective attachment and workplace creativity as it enhances the chances of employees making associations between seemingly unrelated pieces of information, possibly leading to creative solutions to problems [47].

Employees' affective commitment has been found to be a predictor of creativity [40]. There is also a relationship between employee autonomy, perseverance, achievement, and dedication [48]. These factors create ties between employees and their organizations and define how the creativity exhibited by an employee is influenced by the culture of their workplace [40]. As a result, employees having a strong affective commitment to their workplace are more likely to develop creative solutions and apply them in an effort to enhance their organization's efficiency [49].

4.7 Authentic leadership, employee creativity and performance

Creativity relates to the production of new and useful ideas or solutions to problems [50–52], while performance is concerned with employees' productivity in relation to desired workplace outcomes [53]. Creativity is therefore a predictor for effective workplace performance [54, 55].

Many studies have found that the workplace culture influences a number of employee-related factors, including job satisfaction, job performance, work stress, and organizational commitment [56–58]. An investigation of the literature by Da Costa et al. [59] found that intrinsic motivations, such as interest in the task, job satisfaction, the amount of pleasure derived by undertaking the task, and the challenges presented by the task are greater motivators than extrinsic motivations, such as pressure or rewards and compensation. The positive and supportive environments that authentic leaders create, therefore, lay the foundation for a variety of positive employee behaviors, many of which contribute to many of the others. By contrast, workplace cultures based on sanctions such as pressure can stifle the positivity resulting from supportive environments.

4.8 Authentic leadership is positively related to psychological empowerment

Empowerment, or autonomy, is a psychological concept [22, 60] and is considered to contain four aspects [61]. The first of these is the meaning or value of any work an employee undertakes in the light of their personal values [61]. The second is competence, or self-efficacy, which relates to an employee's belief in their capacity to successfully achieve a required outcome [62]. The third is self-determination, being an employee's perception of their freedom to instigate or alter an action [63]. The fourth is impact, or the amount to which the employee's actions affect their organization's productivity [64]. In combination, these factors encourage proactive behaviors and confidence on the part of the employee [60].

Workplace empowerment is also a function of the relationship between an employee and their manager [65]. The concept of empowerment differs between cultures. In individualistic cultures, empowerment is considered to be a function of the job itself, while in collectivist cultures, it relates more to the amount of trust a manager has in their subordinate [66, 67]. As a function of social exchange, employees gain a sense of empowerment when their supervisor has a working relationship with them. This is particularly so where large amounts of information are present requiring transparency in the sharing and processing of that information [68]. This enhances the development of trust between the supervisor and the subordinate and contributes to the enhancement of the employee's performance [2, 69, 70]. Authentic leaders are able to balance the flow of information while allowing the employee to develop a greater sense of ownership of the work. This develops an increased sense of empowerment on the part of the employee [22, 27].

Empowerment can be considered as having two varieties within the workplace environment, these being structural and psychological. The structural variety relates to the hierarchy within the workplace and the workplace environment [71], while the psychological variety relates purely to the motivation to undertake tasks [60]. Psychological empowerment practiced by authentic leaders has been found to motivate employees [72, 73] by facilitating employee autonomy and provides them with the feeling that they have influence over their tasks [74]. The concept of empowerment in cultures other than those in the west, particularly in the south-east Asian region, is the power distance between the leader and the employee and the degree of trust the leader has in the employee [75]. These theoretical aspects determine employee behaviors. This is of particular importance in organizations where the amount of information is high and where decisions need to be made quickly [76].

Based on the existing body of knowledge in this field, empowerment influenced by authentic leaders is positively related to creativity [55, 77]. This is founded on the principle that authentic leaders cultivate and sustain working relationships with their followers as a result of their personal characteristics [78]. Employees working in organizational cultures oriented toward interpersonal relationships therefore have the perception of empowerment and respond with creative thoughts that may lead to innovative solutions [76].

4.9 Authentic leadership and organizational culture

Based on the adage that the standard you walk past is the standard you accept an organization's authenticity was defined by Novicevic et al. [79] as a manifestation of the authenticity of the organization's leadership. This then creates an authentic organizational culture. The culture of a workplace directly results from the values and beliefs of its leaders. As such the role leaders play in creating and maintaining the workplace culture is vital [80]. Authentic leaders are effectively the role models for their organization. By making decisions and undertaking behaviors in accordance with their values and beliefs, authentic leaders encourage similar behaviors among their followers [81]. Authentic leadership is therefore vital in developing an inclusive workplace culture [82] that develops and maintains an atmosphere of inclusion that encourages creativity. Authentic leaders engage in inclusive behaviors, which involve the use of participative decision-making, encouraging free and open communication from employees, and valuing opinions from a diverse variety of perspectives [81]. Employees will soon detect any incongruence from leaders who make decisions and undertake behaviors that are not aligned with their values and beliefs, undermining the leader's position.

Authentic leaders enhance an organization's culture in several ways. By demonstrating transparency, they create a culture of commitment to the organization, encourage the sharing of knowledge, and increase employee satisfaction, engagement, performance, and productivity [83], as well as increasing employees' feelings of inspiration and passion for their work [84]. By being transparent with their employees, authentic leaders promote an organizational culture that supports employee psychological safety [4], respect, and trust and, through this, encourages creativity [85]. Authentic leaders, therefore, as custodians of their organizational culture, are responsible for nurturing the positive workplace environment that results in their employees feeling sufficient confidence to propose ideas, safe in the knowledge that not only will their leaders support their efforts, but also the other employees, as all workers should share in the positivity created by the leader, having taken on some of the authenticity the leader displays as a role model.

4.10 Authentic leadership and followers' participative decision-making

While there has been much written about authentic leadership and its effect on employee motivation and employee requests for feedback from their leaders [86], less has been written about the effect of authentic leadership and its impact on participative decision-making. The organizational culture created by an authentic leader through their transparency also encourages participative decision-making by providing a safe environment in which employees feel trust and confidence that their creative ideas will be noted and considered. By encouraging employees to participate in the decision-making process, authentic leaders inspire employees at all levels to be a part of the organization's decision-making process.

Authentic leaders can also act as mentors for their employees, providing them with the guidance they need to approach their work and the decisions relating to it, increasing their self-reliance. This builds confidence among employees and helps the organization to innovate, benefitting the employees, their leaders, and the organization as a whole. By taking this path, the organization will be more likely to identify creative solutions to unsolved problems. An added benefit of this is that employees can share some of the responsibilities for managing the completion of tasks, reducing the authentic leader's workload, and providing them with greater time to manage other aspects of their role. Taking part in making workplace decisions helps employees to feel self-actualized, which increases their motivation and, through this, their performance [87]. Employees will also experience feelings of empowerment and affective commitment, thus strengthening the organization's retention of corporate knowledge. The creation of such an environment increases the organization's reputation as an employer of choice and increases its competitive advantage.

DOI: http://dx.doi.org/10.5772/intechopen.108624

5. Conclusions

5.1 Theoretical contribution

To the present time, much of the research in this field has focused on the effectiveness of empowering leadership in improving employee efficiency [55]. There has been relatively little investigation into determining the relationship between authentic leaders and their followers and how this relationship supports and encourages employee participation in decision-making and leads to creativity at both the individual and the team levels.

This chapter has focused on understanding and applying the theory of authentic leadership in order to make use of the practical features it contains as a way for leaders to utilize it for their own benefit as well as for the benefit of their followers and the wider organization. Of necessity, theory regarding authentic leadership will adapt as new research refines it by retaining its fundamentals, while incorporating new concepts. While authentic leadership has been researched [9] and found to be a characteristic of the exchange between leaders and followers, investigation of followership should examine the nature of the mutual influence between leaders and followers as all parties involved in the process seek to gain shared benefit from the pursuit of their organization's goals.

While there has been a significant amount written about the effects of authentic leadership on employee motivation and employee requests for feedback from their leaders [86], there has been less attention paid to how authentic leadership affects participative decision-making. The culture an authentic leader's transparency creates in their organization promotes participative decision-making by generating an environment where employees can feel confident that their creative ideas will receive appropriate consideration. This chapter provides an opportunity for researchers to gain a stronger understanding of how the relationships between leaders and followers develop and continue through employee involvement in making decisions and challenges researchers to investigate how the effectiveness of leaders can better be facilitated. Additionally, this study helps authentic leaders to become increasingly aware of how important it for their leadership to promote a culture based on participative decision-making, such that it increases both employees' performance and organizational commitment, as well as utilizing this awareness to develop and improve training in authentic leadership.

5.2 Practical contribution

Authentic leaders should build an innovative culture in their organization. They should support and inspire their employees to enhance their performance and gain the confidence to demonstrate creativity and agility when confronted with challenges. Doing so will facilitate their ability to do their work with greater independence and help their organization to realize its objectives. Authentic leaders exemplify mutual exchanges between themselves and their followers. Therefore, research relating to followership should examine how leaders and followers influence each other as they work in combination to achieve their organization's goals and, in so doing, achieve mutually beneficial outcomes. Authentic leaders involving their followers in the decision-making process promote an organizational environment that encourages the investigation of creative ideas and innovation in resolving workplace problems, leading to a culture of learning and organizational commitment.

This chapter increases leaders' knowledge of authentic leadership and the effects it has on participative decision-making. The environment an authentic leader creates in their organization as a result of their transparency promotes participative decision-making by building an organizational culture where employees can have sufficient confidence that their creative ideas will gain a fair hearing that they are motivated to suggest them. This chapter assists authentic leaders to increase their awareness of how authentic leadership encourages a creative organizational culture, which then enhances employees' performance as well as their organizational commitment. This awareness can then form the basis of enhancements to leadership training so that both leaders and their organization can benefit. Employees working with an authentic leader who has created a culture that supports them are more likely to not only develop a positive attitude toward their workplace, but also experience elevated levels of job satisfaction and organizational commitment [88].

5.3 Conclusion

In summary, authentic leadership develops the cohesiveness of working relationships, improves both employee and organizational performance, and enhances the likelihood of improved outcomes by increasing employees' affective commitment, thereby motivating them to approach their work more positively and display creative behaviors that support their organization. It also plays an important role in encouraging employees to become more involved in the decision-making process. This gives them a sense of empowerment and ownership of their work and strengthens retention of the organization's knowledge. Authentic leaders can improve their organization's culture by creating an environment of commitment by motivating followers to share their knowledge, experience, and creative ideas, all of which can contribute to improved organizational performance. Authentic leaders can benefit by encouraging their employees to participate in decision-making as a way to enhance their organizational commitment to the extent that their creativity is maintained. Developing an environment such as this enhances the organization's reputation as an employer of choice, which helps to increase its competitive advantage.

Notes/thanks/other declarations

I would like to thank Joseph Crawford for the opportunity he has given me to contribute this chapter of his book.

Author details

Hanan AlMazrouei
UAE University, Al Ain, United Arab Emirates

*Address all correspondence to: h.almazrouei@uaeu.ac.ae

References

[1] Avolio BJ, Gardner WL. Authentic leadership development: Getting to the root of positive forms of leadership. The Leadership Quarterly. 2005;**16**:315-338

[2] Walumbwa FO, Avolio BJ, Gardner WL, Wernsing TS, Peterson SJ. Authentic leadership: Development and validation of a theory-based measure. Journal of Management. 2008;**34**(1):89-126

[3] George B. Authentic Leadership: Rediscovering the Secrets to Creating Lasting Value. San Francisco, CA: Jossey Bass; 2003

[4] Rego R, Sousa F, Marques C, Pina e Cunha M. Authentic leadership promoting employees' psychological capital and creativity. Journal of Business Research. 2012;**65**:429-437

[5] Uhl-Bien M, Riggio RE, Lowe KB, Carsten MK. Followership theory: A review and research agenda. The Leadership Quarterly. 2014;**25**:83-104

[6] Harter S. Authenticity. In: Snyder CS, Lopez SJ, editors. Handbook of Positive Psychology. Oxford: Oxford University Press; 2002. pp. 382-394

[7] Luthans F, Avolio BJ. Authentic leadership development. In: Cameron KS, Dutton JE, Quinn R, editors. Positive Organizational Scholarship: Foundations of a New Discipline. San Francisco: Barrett-Koehler; 2003. pp. 241-261

[8] Erickson RJ. The importance of authenticity for self and society. Symbolic Interaction. 1995;**18**:121-144

[9] Whitehead G. Adolescent leadership development: Building a case for an authenticity framework. Educational Management Administration and Leadership. 2009;**37**:847-872

[10] Shamir B, Eilam G. What's your story?: A life-stories approach to authentic leadership development. The Leadership Quarterly. 2005;**16**:395-417

[11] Zhang J, Song LJ, Wang Y, Liu GJ. How authentic leadership influences employee proactivity: The sequential mediating effects of psychological empowerment and core self-evaluations and the moderating role of employee political skill. Frontiers of Business Research in China. 2018;**12**(5):1-21

[12] Javed B, Rawwas M, Khandai S, Shahid K, Tayyeb H. Ethical leadership, trust in leader and creativity: The mediated mechanism and an interacting effect. Journal of Management & Organization. 2018;**24**(3):388-405

[13] Conger J. The dark side of leadership. Organizational Dynamics. 1990;**19**(2):44-55

[14] Luthans F, Peterson SJ Ibrayeva E. The potential for the "dark side" of leadership in post communist countries. Journal of World Business. 1998;**33(2**:185-201

[15] Kernis MH, Goldman BM. A multicomponent conceptualization of authenticity: Theory and research. In: Zanna MP, editor. Advances in Experimental Social Psychology. Vol. 38. San Diego: Academic Press; 2006. pp. 283-357

[16] Kernis MH. Toward a conceptualization of optimal self-esteem. Psychological Inquiry. 2003;**14**:1-26

[17] Miller KI, Monge PR. Participation, satisfaction and productivity: A

meta-analytic review. Academy of Management Journal. 1988;**29**:727-753

[18] Kayode BK, Mojeed AQ, Fatai IA. Leadership and decision-making: A study on reflexive relationship between leadership style and decision-making approach. British Journal of Education, Society & Behavioural Science. 2014;**4**(4):473-484

[19] Novitosari D, Siswanto E, Purwanto A, Fahmi K. Authentic leadership and innovation: What is the role of psychological capital? International Journal of Social and Management Studies. 2020;**1**(1):1-21

[20] Sims HP Jr, Manz CC. Companies of Heroes: Unleashing the Power of Self-leadership. New York: John Wiley; 1996

[21] Jensen S, Luthans F. Entrepreneurs as authentic leaders: Impact on employees' attitudes. Leadership and Organization Development Journal. 2006;**27**(8):646-666

[22] Walumbwa FO, Wang P, Wang H, Schaubroeck J, Avolio BJ. Psychological processes linking authentic leadership to follower behaviours. The Leadership Quarterly. 2010;**21**(5):901-914

[23] Gardner WL, Avolio BJ, Luthans F, May DR, Walumba FO. Can you see the real me? A self-based model of authentic leader and follower development. The Leadership Quarterly. 2005;**16**(3):343-372

[24] Dvir T, Eden D, Avolio BJ, Shamir B. Impact of transformational leadership on follower development and performance: A field experiment. Academy of Management Journal. 2002;**45**(4):735-744

[25] Peterson S, Luthans F. The positive impact and development of hopeful leaders. Leadership and Organization Development Journal. 2003;**24**(1):26-31

[26] Avolio BJ, Gardner WL, Walumbwa FO, Luthans F, May DR. Unlocking the mask: A look at the process by which authentic leaders impact follower attitudes and behaviors. The Leadership Quarterly. 2004;**15**(6):801-823

[27] Ilies R, Morgeson FP, Nahrgang JD. Authentic leadership and eudaemonic well-being: Understanding leader-follower outcomes. The Leadership Quarterly. 2005;**16**(3):373-394

[28] Zhou J, Ren R. Striving for creativity: Building positive contexts in the workplace. In: Cameron KS, Spreitzer GM, editors. The Oxford Handbook of Positive Organizational Scholarship. New York: Oxford University Press; 2012. pp. 97-109

[29] Wright TA, Cropanzano R. The role of psychological well-being in job performance: A fresh look an age-old quest. Organizational Dynamics. 2004;**33**(4):338-351

[30] Ribiero N, Duarte A, Filipe R, Torres de Oliviera R. How authentic leadership promotes individual creativity: The mediating role of affective commitment. Journal of Leadership and Organizational Studies. 2020;**27**(2):189-202

[31] Crossan MM, Apaydin M. A multi-dimensional framework of organizational innovation: A systematic review of the literature. Journal of Management Studies. 2010;**47**(6): 1154-1191

[32] Černe M, Jaklič M, Škerlavaj M. Authentic leadership, creativity, and innovation: A multilevel perspective. Leadership. 2013;**9**(1):63-85

[33] George B, Sims P, McLean A, Mayer D. Discovering your authentic leadership. Harvard Business Review. 2007;**85**(2):129-138

[34] Mumford M, Scott G, Gaddi B, Strange J. Leading creative people: Orchestrating expertise and relationships. The Leadership Quarterly. 2002;**13**(6):705-750

[35] Tierney P. Leadership and employee creativity. In: Zhou J, Shalley CE, editors. Handbook of Organizational Creativity. New York, NY: Lawrence Erlbaum Associates; 2008. pp. 95-123

[36] Meyer JP, Allen NJ. A three-component conceptualization of organizational commitment. Human Resource Management Review. 1992;**1**:61-89

[37] Allen N, Meyer J. Construct validation in organizational behavior research: The case of organizational commitment. In: Goffin RD, Helmes E, editors. Problems and Solutions in Human Assessment. Norwell, MA: Kluwer; 2000. pp. 285-314

[38] Paillé P. The relationship between support, commitment and intent to leave team: A social exchange perspective. Team Performance Management. 2009;**15**(1/2):49-62

[39] Amabile TM. A model of creativity and innovation in organizations. In: Staw BM, Cummings LL, editors. Research in Organizational Behavior. Greenwich, CT: JAI Press; 1988. p. 10

[40] Semedo AS, Coelho A, Ribiero N. Effects of authentic leadership, affective commitment and job resourcefulness on employees' creativity and individual performance. Leadership and Organization Development Journal. 2016;**37**(8):1038-1055

[41] Binnewies C, Ohly S, Niessen C. Age and creativity at work: The interplay between job resources, age, and idea creativity. Journal of Management Psychology. 2008;**23**(4):438-457

[42] Organ DW, Ryan K. A meta-analytic review of attitudinal and dispositional predictors of organizational citizenship behavior. Personnel Psychology. 1995;**48**(4):775-802

[43] Isen M, Daubman A, Nowicki P. Positive affect facilitates creative problem solving. Journal of Personality and Social Psychology. 1987;**52**:1122-1131

[44] Rego R, Ribiero N, Cunha MP, Jesuino JC. How happiness mediates the organizational virtuousness and affective commitment relationship. Journal of Business Research. 2011;**64**(5):524-532

[45] Fredrickson B. The role of positive emotions in positive psychology: The broaden-and-build theory of positive emotions. The American Psychologist. 2001;**56**(3):218-226

[46] Lyubomirsky S, King L, Diener E. The benefits of frequent positive affect: Does happiness lead to success? Psychological Bulletin. 2005;**131**(6):803-855

[47] Amabile T, Barsade S, Mueller J, Staw B. Affect and creativity at work. Administrative Science Quarterly. 2005;**50**(3):367-403

[48] Rice G. Individual values, organizational context, and self-perceptions of employee creativity: Evidence from Egyptian organizations. Journal of Business Research. 2006;**59**(2):233-241

[49] Montani F, Courcy F, Vandenberghe C. Innovating under stress: The role of commitment and leader-member

exchange. Journal of Business Research. 2017;**77**:1-13

[50] Amabile TM. Motivating creativity in organizations: On doing what you love and loving what you do. California Management Review. 1997;**40**(1):39-58

[51] Oldham GR, Cummings A. Employee creativity: Personal and contextual factors at work. Academy of Management Journal. 1996;**39**(3):607-634

[52] Zhou J, George JM. When job dissatisfaction leads to creativity: Encouraging the expression of voice. Academy of Management Journal. 2001;**44**(4):682-696

[53] Babin BJ, Boles JS. Employee behavior in a service environment: A model and test of potential differences between men and women. Journal of Marketing. 1998;**62**(2):77

[54] Shalley CE, Gilson LL. What leaders need to know: A review of social and contextual factors that can foster or hinder creativity. The Leadership Quarterly. 2004;**15**(1):33-53

[55] Zhang X, Bartol KM. Linking empowering leadership and employee creativity: The influence of psychological empowerment, intrinsic motivation, and creative process engagement. Academy of Management Journal. 2010;**53**(1):107-128

[56] Carr JZ, Schmidt AM, Ford JK, DeShon RP. Climate perceptions matter: A meta-analytic path analysis relating molar climate, cognitive and affective states and individual level work outcomes. Journal of Applied Psychology. 2003;**88**(4):605-619

[57] Ostroff C, Kinicki AJ, Tamkins MM. Organizational Culture and Climate: Handbook of Psychology. Hoboken, NJ: John Wiley and Sons; 2003

[58] Parker CP, Baltes BB, Young SA, Huff JW, Altmann RA, LaCost HA, et al. Relationships between psychological climate perceptions and work outcomes: A meta-analytic review. Journal of Organizational Behavior. 2003;**24**(4):389-416

[59] Da Costa S, Páez D, Sánchez F, Garaigordobil M, Gondim S. Personal factors of creativity: A second order meta-analysis. Revista de Psicologia Del Trabajo y de Las Organizaciones. 2015;**31**(3):165-173

[60] Spreitzer GM. Psychological empowerment in the workplace: Dimensions, measurement, and validation. Academy of Management Journal. 1995;**38**(5):1442-1465

[61] Thomas KW, Velthouse BA. Cognitive elements of empowerment: An "interpretive" model of intrinsic task motivation. Academy of Management Review. 1990;**15**(4):666-681

[62] Gist ME. Self-efficacy: Implications for organizational behavior and human resource management. Academy of Management Review. 1987;**12**(3):472-485

[63] Deci EL, Connell JP, Ryan RM. Self-determination in a work organization. Journal of Applied Psychology. 1989;**74**(4):580-590

[64] Ashforth BE. The experience of powerlessness in organizations. Organizational Behavior and Human Decision Processes. 1989;**43**(2):207-242

[65] Arnold JA, Arad S, Rhoades JA, Drasgow F. The empowering leadership questionnaire: The construction and validation of a new scale for measuring leader behaviours. Journal of Organizational Behavior. 2000;**21**(3):249-269

[66] Ahearne M, Mathieu J, Rapp A. To empower or not to empower your sales force? An empirical examination of the influence of leadership empowerment behavior on customer satisfaction and performance. Journal of Applied Psychology. 2005;**90**(5):945-950

[67] Cheung C, Baum T, Wong A. Relocatingempowermentasamanagement concept for Asia. Journal of Business Research. 2012;**65**(1):36-41

[68] Spreitzer GM. Taking stock: A review of more than twenty years of research on empowerment at work. Handbook of organizational behavior, Vol. 2008;**1**:54-72

[69] Blau P. Exchange and Power in Social Life. Sri Lanka: Transaction Publishers; 1964

[70] Cropanzano R, Mitchell MS. Social exchange theory: An interdisciplinary review. Journal of Management. 2005;**31**(6):874-900

[71] Laschinger HKS, Finegan J, Shamian J, Wilk P. Impact of structural and psychological empowerment on job strain in nursing work settings: Expanding Kanter's model. The Journal of Nursing Administration. 2001;**31**(5):260-272

[72] Block P. The Empowered Manager. San Francisco: Josey-Bass; 1991

[73] Spreitzer GM, De Janasz SC, Quinn RE. Empowered to lead: The role of psychological empowerment in leadership. Journal of Organizational Behavior: The International Journal of Industrial, Occupational and Organizational Psychology and Behavior. 1999;**20**(4):511-526

[74] Ahmad N, Oranye NO. Empowerment, job satisfaction and organizational commitment: A comparative analysis of nurses working in Malaysia and England. Journal of Nursing Management. 2010;**18**(5):582-591

[75] Gupta V, Surie G, Javidan M, Chhokar J. Southern Asia cluster: Where the old meets the new? Journal of World Business. 2002;**37**(1):16-27

[76] Imam H, Naqvi MB, Naqvi SA, Chambel MJ. Authentic leadership unleashing employee creativity through empowerment and commitment to the supervisor. Leadership and Organization Development Journal. 2020;**41**(6):847-864

[77] Fernandez S, Moldogaziev T. Using employee empowerment to encourage innovative behavior in the public sector. Journal of Public Administration Research and Theory. 2012;**23**(1):155-187

[78] Gill C, Caza A. An investigation of authentic leadership's individual and group influences on follower responses. Journal of Management. 2018;**44**(2):530-554

[79] Novicevic MM, Harvey MG, Buckley MR, Brown JA, Evans R. Authentic leadership: A historical perspective. Journal of Leadership and Organizational Studies. 2006;**13**:64-76

[80] Dickson MW, Smith DB, Grojean MW, Ehrhart M. An organizational climate regarding ethics: The outcome of leader values and the practices that reflect them. The Leadership Quarterly. 2001;**12**(2):197-217

[81] Buttner EH, Lowe KB, Billings-Harris L. Diversity climate impact on employees of color outcomes: Does justice matter? Career Development International. 2010;**15**:239-258

[82] Boekhorst JA. The role of authentic leadership in fostering workplace inclusion: A social information processing perspective. Human Resource Management. 2015;**54**(2):241-264

[83] Fusco T, O'Riordan S, Palmer S. Authentic leaders are...conscious, competent, confident and congruent: A grounded theory approach to authentic leadership group coaching. International Coaching Psychology Review. 2015;**10**(2):131-148

[84] Rhine AS. An examination of the perceptions of stakeholders on authentic leadership in strategic planning in non-profit arts organizations. The Journal of Arts Management, Law, and Society. 2015;**45**(1):3-21

[85] Alzghoul A, Elrehail H, Emeagwali OL, AlShboul MK. Knowledge management, workplace climate, creativity and performance: The role of authentic leadership. Journal of Workplace Learning. 2018;**30**(8): 592-612

[86] Qian J, Lin X-S, Chen GZ-X. Authentic leadership and feedback-seeking behaviour: An examination of the cultural context of mediating processes in China. Journal of Management & Organization. 2012;**18**:286-299

[87] Siddique M, Nawaz A. Effects of participative decision making on leadership styles: A student survey at Gomal University, Pakistan. International Transaction Journal of Engineering, Management, & Applied Sciences & Technologies. 2019;**10**(11):1-8

[88] Kim M, Beehr TA, Prewett SM. Employee responses to empowering leadership: A meta-analysis. Journal of Leadership and Organizational Studies. 2018;**2018**:1-20

Chapter 16

Perspective Chapter: Creativity in the Work Environment – Reflections on the Role of Management for Creative Individuals Work

Vânia Bessi, Paula Schmitz and Caren Rinker

Abstract

The paper aims to reflect on creativity at work, broadening the perspective on the influence of the environment and leadership practices and policies for expressing creative individuals. Based on theory, it is argued that the creative abilities of individuals need to be associated with an organization whose leadership allows and encourages creative work. The methodology consists of a theoretical essay, to answer the proposed research question: how do leadership and management practices influence the creative expression of workers in different contexts? It appears that leadership plays a fundamental role in creating and maintaining an organizational culture that allows creativity and innovation on the part of employees. Based on this reflection, a theoretical expansion of the componential model of the invention (cyclic model—systemic approach) is presented, listing elements that must be considered when one intends to analyze creativity in the work environment.

Keywords: creativity, leadership, management, engaging leadership

1. Introduction

Over time and with the advance of capitalist systems, companies were constituted as rigid and hierarchical structures in search of predictability of action and acting in a pyramidal model, where power relations were established rigorously. With the advancement of the twenty-first century, the insertion of technologies and new consumption patterns led to numerous transformations in the organizational environment

These changes have driven the emergence of new organizational models, more organic and flexible, common to segments of the economy whose main asset is employees' cognitive and intellectual capabilities. In this context, the creative skills of workers are considered essential for companies to remain innovative and competitive in the market.

To authors such as Sternberg [1], creativity is a decision, an attitude toward life, and a matter of individual skills. As the author mentions, intellectual conformity is a common point of the rigid structures that condition adults' way of thinking. This conditioning of creativity is very present in companies with management modes, especially people management, focused on standardization and rigid and bureaucratic hierarchical relationships.

Therefore, research indicates that it is not enough for workers to have creative skills, they must be engaged in the organization, so that they can obtain the best result in their work. This will happen as the worker finds, in the organizational environment, conditions that encourage them to try, experiment, create and, therefore, innovate at work.

For the understanding of creativity [1, 2], a systemic approach is important, considering the internal aspects of the individual (intrinsic factors) and their environment (extrinsic factors). When talking about factors related to the environment, creativity at work can find, in the organizational culture, elements that are configured as incentives or as obstacles to its expression.

Culture, seen as the set of assumptions, values, beliefs, policies, and practices of people, configures an organization's way of being [3]. Leadership, as guardian of the organizational culture, plays a fundamental role in creating an environment that is conducive to the expression of creativity by workers.

The leader can play the role of pushing workers to do their best, to mobilize their best skills, in favor of superior results. Engaging leadership can make your team act in an integrated, systemic, flexible, creative and innovative way, fundamental characteristics of contemporary organizations [4].

This study, whose methodology is based on a theoretical essay supported by unsystematic observation, aims to reflect on creativity at work, broadening the perspective on the influence of the environment and management practices and policies for expressing creative individuals. The aim is to answer the following research question: how do leadership and management practices influence the creative expression of workers in different contexts?

The relevance of the text lies in the relationship established between creativity, leadership and engagement. Although there are many studies demonstrating the importance of leadership for the creativity of individuals in the work environment, the association with engagement can bring new elements for reflection on the themes [5].

As an answer to the proposed question, this study presents, in the next sections, a theoretical approach to creativity, followed by the topic of leadership, engaging leadership and organizational culture. Next, the authors' theoretical reflections and observations results are pointed out. It ends with a suggestion to expand the contingency approach to creativity, which may include other elements related to organizations' leadership and management methods.

2. Creativity

Creativity has been associated with people's characteristics and abilities for a long time. To Boden [6], creativity is "the ability to present new, surprising, and valuable ideas and artifacts". To Florida, creativity is selecting and filtering data, information, and perceptions to create something new and useful.

Intrinsic motivation is an important principle for creativity [2]. This intrinsic motivation makes the individual perform the task for pleasure, for their interest, and challenge. Thus, people would be more creative when motivated mainly by the interest, pleasure, satisfaction, and challenge of the work itself.

Through intrinsic motivation, people seek more knowledge, which develops domain skills. The model proposed by Amabile mentions that domain skills and creative processes are important for creative work [7, 8]. As a mastery skill, what the person possesses as skill, talent, or knowledge acquired through formal and informal education and their life experience stands out. As creative processes, the way of working, personality traits, and ways used to stimulate new ideas stand out [9].

Creativity is a decision to "buy low and sell high in the world of ideas", according to the investment theory of creativity proposed by Sternberg in partnership with Todd Lubart. Creative people generate ideas or seek out disadvantaged ideas that have growth potential, persisting in this idea until they get value and move on to the next idea [1, 10].

What is creative is new, and the human mind produces positive changes. However, the new can also seem strange, which can bring fear, which is why creativity is often not wanted to be considered, both in personal life and in companies. Creative people will be able to advance with their original ideas and improve the environment in which they are inserted, bringing benefits to those involved [11].

Different studies on the issue of creativity added new elements to the debate, as the importance of the environment where the individual is inserted was glimpsed so that they can express their creativity. According to this theory, creativity requires the interaction of the following aspects: intellectual ability, knowledge, thinking style, personality, motivation, and environment [1].

To Sternberg, no matter how much the person has all these six creative skills, if there is no favorable environment for accepting and stimulating ideas, all this inner creativity may not be demonstrated. However, in some cases, one force may be so great that it will neutralize the other, as high motivation can neutralize the influences of the environment when it is not conducive to the development of creativity [1, 9, 10].

The same author says that creativity is a decision, so in addition to having the skills proposed by this author, it is necessary to decide to use them. Thus, to be creative, it is necessary to "generate new ideas, analyze them, defend and sell them to other people" [1].

As for intellectual ability, the author highlights the ability to see problems from new perspectives, select the best ideas, and persuade with them until obtaining value [1]. It is important to know to be able to proceed with the idea, but according to this author, high knowledge in the domain area can make it impossible to visualize beyond this [1, 9]. However, creativity requires experience and practice. Ideas in creative people arise from well-developed skills and sufficient knowledge in the area in question [12].

The willingness to overcome obstacles, willingness to take risks and tolerance for ambiguity are important characteristics in the personality of the creative person [1, 11].

Analyzing external factors to the individual, extrinsic motivation such as rewards, evaluations, control, competition, and limited choices can harm creativity. The social environment can intervene in the individual's motivation, significantly influencing the creative process performance [2, 13, 14].

The research by Madjar et al. showed that employees' creative performance was related to encouraging creativity in their work environment, such as by supervisors and co-workers, but also by sources unrelated to this work environment, such as the family and friends [2].

Another important aspect of the creative process is the multicultural experience [15]. Cultural diversity can increase creativity, allowing new relationships to be made by enriching the cultural environment [12]. In this sense, groups and work teams presenting diversity among their members can facilitate creativity. Therefore, encouraging diversity in organizations must be a management decision and a leadership policy.

The creation process is also related to culture, as it serves as a reference for what the individual "is, does, communicates, and elaborates" [15]. Thus, to the author, human creativity is developed in the cultural context due to people being and developing within certain cultures, in which they share and determine their life values. The creative process lies in the interconnection between creativity, as the expression of each individual, and creation, as the realization of their potential within a cultural context. Therefore, this process is related to structuring and forming something, coming out of imagination only [15].

The human motivation to create is in the search for ordering and meanings. Creation processes occur within the scope of intuition. Intuitive, these processes become conscious as they are expressed, given form [15]. The intuitive act is a value choice through relevant and selected processes regarding its importance for each individual. In this intuitive act, the memories and knowledge acquired are renewed and resignified [15].

When thinking about creativity, it is necessary to have a broad vision, considering the individual's intrinsic and extrinsic factors, such as the environment in which they are inserted.

Creativity results from the reciprocal and favorable relationship between the individual and the environment [9, 16]. In creative expression, there is the interaction of personal variables (individuals) and elements of the historical and cultural context. To understand why, when, and how new ideas are produced, we need to consider both internal and external variables to the individual [9].

For the understanding of creativity, a systemic approach is important, considering the internal aspects of the individual (intrinsic factors) and their environment (extrinsic factors) [1, 2, 13].

To promote intrinsic motivation in the workplace, we need to have the freedom to experiment. However, concerning the work context, with technical and administrative work routines, one must reconcile creativity with management and quality in carrying out the work [17].

A study carried out by Schmitz aimed to identify how the work environment is configured as a stimulus to the creativity of the professional and to analyze the relationships between the creativity of the individual (professional) and its use in gastronomic work in food services (work environment) [18]. The research demonstrated that creativity in the work environment has a cyclical relationship; that is, as a factor increases in a category (individual's creativity category and work environment category), there is a small or moderate increase in the other factors addressed in the study. The study also demonstrated that in gastronomy, concerning creativity, there is an interaction between the intrinsic factors of the technologist and the extrinsic ones related to their gastronomic work environment.

So that the worker can exercise their creativity, it is important that they are engaged and committed to the work they perform and that they find, in the environment, the necessary elements for their motivation. In this sense, we explain the ideas about engaging leadership and the importance of this leader profile so that creativity can be manifested and converted into superior results, ultimately leading to organizational innovation.

3. Engaging leadership

One of the fundamental assets of an organization today is people and intellectual capital. Faced with this new scenario and organizational configurations, leaders now have the fundamental role of investing in companies' human capital and seeking superior results, investing in strategy and appropriate policies for people management.

Leaders play a key role in organizations, as they are responsible for defining, implementing, and disseminating strategies with their employees [19]. In addition, they assume enormous importance in the competitive environment of companies since their leadership style directly reflects on their subordinates. Being a leader means being prepared to plan, organize, execute, and analyze but always attentive to the engagement process, working with communication, flexibility, problem-solving ability, and systemic vision. Carrying out people management implies getting involved not only in issues that, sometimes, are directly linked to the goals and objectives of the organization but thinking about the individual and creating a good work environment is also a function of the manager.

Many approaches, perspectives, and definitions are recurrent for leadership in organizational studies [5, 20, 21]. However, there is a consensus among scholars that leadership reveals the influence of the leader on the subordinate, which is essential for managers to be aware that their actions and definitions will reflect on the team and the delivery of expected results. What is needed is leadership that inspires and engages.

One of the new leadership approaches is the one that deals with the engaging leader, which is important to understand the new profile of leaders in the contemporary organization [4, 22–24]. Engaging leadership motivates and believes that employee engagement comes first, regardless of the size or segment of the company [18]. In this sense, leadership plays a fundamental role in creating a work environment that allows the creative expression of all workers.

In the engagement process, it is important to create opportunities for employee contribution through practices such as flexible teamwork, employee involvement policies, and information sharing [25, 26]. This role belongs to the leader, that is, to promote actions to involve their employees.

From this perspective the leader must have some attitudes that enable the improvement in employee performance, which, consequently, can lead to team engagement, such as maintaining a team that can meet job requirements, replacing members when they do not achieve adequate levels of performance after appropriate follow-up, enabling open and internal communication that encourages everyone's active participation, and encouraging trust and respect for the differences of each team member [27]. By creating a suitable work environment, engaging leadership lays the groundwork for creativity to be explored by workers.

Tamara Erickson points out that increasing engagement—finding ways to encourage individuals to invest more psychic energy in their work—is the most powerful lever corporations have to improve productivity [28]. There is, therefore, the understanding that people are the main asset of organizations, and leadership needs to be aware and attentive to its employees, seeking to achieve the company's objectives with them, leading to innovation and competitiveness in the market [5].

Successful organizations realize that they can only grow, prosper, and maintain their continuity if they can optimize the return on employees' investments, that is, invest in their employees and engage them so that they can deliver with more vigor, absorption, and dedication [4, 22–24]. The profile of leadership in organizations has undergone several changes. Recycling was necessary since the leadership role was no longer focused on imposing and controlling tasks.

The latest generation in the job market seeks a challenging environment with the possibility of flexible working hours and formats. It is a propitious space to develop their creative potential [22]. These aspects also shape the new profile of managers. Therefore, it becomes necessary to develop strategies and establish criteria for obtaining results, in addition to disseminating the organization's vision of what is expected of each professional [19, 22].

In this scenario, some aspects common to successful teams are observed, point out: recognition of the need for mutual support in the team, feeling of co-responsibility for the work done and for the company, trust between team members, open and transparent communication, training and recognition of conflicts in a constructive way [27]. Everyday situations are configured as opportunities for emerging new ideas and exploring creativity.

Given the notes by the authors [27, 29], it is noteworthy that the leader must be aware of these points and promote a favorable environment within organizations, as this would possibly promote the process of engagement. To this end, cultivating positive emotions is essential, as it promotes an expansive, tolerant, and creative mental disposition, leaving people open to trying out new ideas, which creates challenges for management, since it needs to be based on positive psychology, aware that promoting well-being in the work environment can attract, retain, and obtain extraordinary results [30].

Therefore, the key piece is in the role of the leader when working with their team, transforming it into a multidisciplinary team focused on results, emphasizing cooperation and not coercion, and bringing about situations that benefit everyone mutually [20]. This becomes a big challenge for managers; being present, assessing risks and opportunities, giving freedom to create and innovate, and obtaining mechanisms to achieve the expected results with team engagement and delivery.

Organizational strategies are fundamental to employee engagement, leading them to full involvement in work, where their creative abilities can be fully exercised. It needs to be an appropriate combination between people and working conditions and that a planned organizational action tends to have more results than those carried out individually by the areas [31].

In addition to performing the traditional "roles", a leader who inspires, strengthens the team, teaches and supports, is participative, and works creatively and flexibly with subordinates [30]. Leadership must foster a trusting environment; it is up to the leader to inspire and trust their team, allowing the employee to have flexibility, be aware of the organization's strategies and have the autonomy to carry out their activities.

The trust allows employees to believe in the organization and leadership, do their best, and exercise their abilities to the fullest [20]. To do so, the leader needs to trust their team and allow them to act so that the organization's objectives are achieved, and employees feel part of the process.

According to research by the Gallup Institute, when employees are inspired, motivated, and supported in their work, they naturally work harder—and that work is significantly less stressful. Therefore, management can directly influence the engagement or disengagement of its employees. According to assumptions defended by this study, the creation of an adequate environment for work can favor the use of creative skills by workers.

The idea is that engaging leadership can stimulate employees to use their cognitive and creative capacities fully. According to the theories of creativity presented, the work environment is fundamental for creativity to be exercised.

4. Reflections on the relations between creativity and leadership

The resources, when appropriately available in the environment, promote initiative, creativity and leadership, creating engagement at work. Therefore, understanding the scenario in which the employee operates, the challenges for their performance, with regard to the structure and organization of work, are factors that can contribute to engaging the teams. A suitable workplace, with psychological and physical conditions, encourages the engagement of the teams [31].

However, creativity is a decision, in addition to having creative skills, the worker must decide to use them. To be creative, it is necessary to generate new ideas, analyze them, defend and "sell" solutions to other people [1]. The leader has the role of stimulating his subordinates, but the employee will have the decision-making power if he wants to use his creativity.

Empowering teams and actively listening is important to promote engagement and requires mutual trust between the manager and his employees. Trust allows employees to believe in the organization and its leadership, to do their best [20].

Trust helps the team to reduce the fear of the new and the strange to that group, allowing creative people to advance with their original ideas and improve the environment in which they are inserted, bringing benefits to all the people involved [11].

It is important to point out that the leader needs to trust his team and allow the workers to act safely. Thus, the organization's objectives will be achieved and workers will feel like subjects of the process. Trust happens when people feel safe to act, have initiative, reinforcing confidence in their work [28].

In the creative process, it is important to highlight the differential of the multicultural experience for workers [15]. Cultural diversity can increase creativity, as it allows new relationships to be made from the enrichment of the cultural environment [12]. The leadership approach, in order to encourage trust and respect for the differences of each team member, helps engagement and expands individual and organizational results [27].

Given the diversity of knowledge and exchange of ideas, the role of the leader is necessary for the progress of activities. In this process of engaging teams, leaders are responsible for defining and implementing strategies with employees [19]. They also have the role of inspiring their teams, being motivators, believing in the potential of their employees, considering that their engagement must come first [28].

The motivating leader can provide the right environment for increasing the employee's intrinsic motivation, which is one of the main aspects for creativity [2]. Thus, people would be more creative when motivated mainly by the interest, pleasure, satisfaction and challenge of the work itself.

Working with greater intensity, focusing on your responsibilities and having an emotional connection to your tasks are some of the positive factors that are observed from encouraging engagement, which can be promoted from actions taken by leadership with the definition of organizational policies [31].

Added to these incentives is the personality of the creative person, who demonstrates the willingness to overcome obstacles, willingness to take risks and tolerance for creative ambiguity [1, 11]. Having a creative personality and being led by engaging leadership can lead workers to develop themselves and make teams more productive.

Authors point out that there must be an appropriate combination between personal skills and working conditions and that a planned organizational action tends to have more results than those carried out individually by the areas [31]. This reciprocal and favorable relationship between the individual and the environment is fundamental for creativity [9, 16].

The importance of the systemic approach in relation to creativity is highlighted, considering the internal aspects of the individual (intrinsic factors) and their environment (extrinsic factors), for the understanding of creativity, according to the analyzed authors [1, 2, 13]. This idea is illustrated in **Figure 1**, where it is identified that creativity in the work environment happens at the intersection between resources, techniques and motivations. The overlapping area is the area of greatest creativity both for individuals and for innovation in organizations.

The Componential Model of Creativity for the individual occurs through the intersection between domain skills, relevant creative processes and intrinsic motivation [7]. For the author, for true creativity to happen and generate innovation, it is necessary to combine these three elements in the environment.

Resources are important for creativity in a given area or domain, both individually and in organizations. In individuals, these are their domain skills, such as talents, technique and knowledge in a certain area. In companies, however, they are the resources in the domain task, such as materials, human resources, specific software for each area, among others. In individuals, techniques are considered the relevant creative processes, such as the style of thinking and working, the way of checking the world, which provide new ideas. In companies, techniques are innovation skills, such

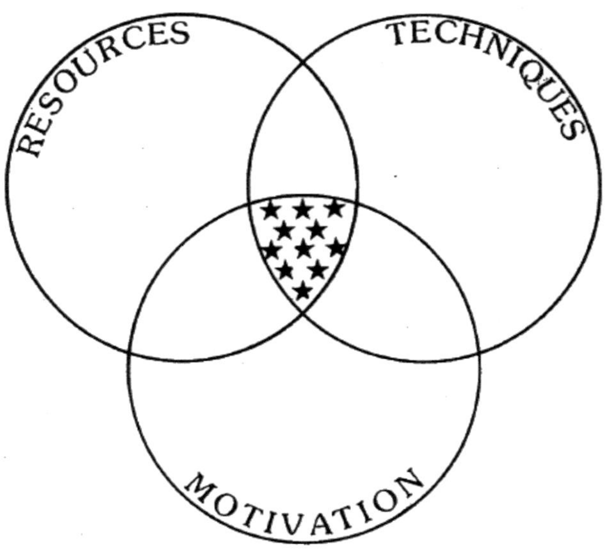

Figure 1.
Creativity intersection, both for the individual and for the organization. Source: [7].

as management for the generation of creativity. Both individually and in organizations, techniques and resources complement each other [7]. Motivation drives actions aimed at creativity and innovation. In the individual there is intrinsic motivation for the task and in companies the motivation for innovation.

Based on studies carried out and the considerations pointed out in this theoretical essay, where the role of engaging leadership was considered fundamental in the creative process of teams, an expansion of the componential model of creativity is proposed [18]. The proposed framework is that of a cyclical model, where both elements related to the individual's characteristics and those related to organizational policies and leadership practices interact with each other, dynamically and in constant interrelationship. **Figure 2** presents this proposed cyclical model.

In this cyclical framework, all factors in the individual's creativity category are correlated with each other, as well as those in the environment's creativity category. It proposes, therefore, an expansion of the role of management policies and practices for the understanding of creativity in everyday work. From this model, it is

Figure 2.
Ciclical framework of this study's creativity. Source: Designed by the authors (2022).

understood that creativity can be dispersed in all activities and people and it is the responsibility of the leader to encourage it for the superior results of the organization and of the workers themselves.

5. Conclusion

The aim of the study was to reflect on creativity at work, broadening the perspective on the influence of the environment and leadership practices and policies for the expression of creative individuals. The study addressed theories about creativity and leadership, focusing on engaging leadership. Theoretical reflection demonstrated the importance of the role of the leader for the construction of a work environment that allows the worker to express himself creatively.

This study addressed team leadership and management, in order to analyze the organizational strategies that encourage the stimulation and appreciation of creativity in the work environment. Thus, aspects related to engaging leadership are pointed out, which, based on team support actions, can result in more engaged workers and with superior results in their work.

It was possible to advance in studies on creativity in the work environment, demonstrating that it occurs in a cyclical relationship between the individual's creativity factors and the creativity factors in the work environment in which the worker is inserted, with emphasis on the role of engaging leadership. The proposed cyclic approach understands that creativity at work occurs in a dynamic relationship between individual creative skills, techniques, intrinsic motivation, available resources, management policies and leadership practices.

Understanding this dynamic relationship raises the importance of leadership related to creating a work environment that encourages innovation. The worker's intrinsic motivation can be increased when he finds in his leader engaging team management practices, adequate organizational support and an environment conducive to the expression of his creative potential. Finally, it is understood that creative teams lead to organizational innovation, closing the virtuous cycle of work, guiding individuals and the organization to superior results.

Author details

Vânia Bessi*, Paula Schmitz and Caren Rinker
Feevale University, Novo Hamburgo, Brazil

*Address all correspondence to: vania@feevale.br

References

[1] Sternberg RJ. The nature of creativity. Creativity Research Journal. 2006;**18**(1):87-98

[2] Hennessey BA, Amabile TM. Creativity. Annual Review of Psychology. 2010;**61**:569-598

[3] Hofstede G, Hoftede GJ, Minkov M. Cultures and Organizations: Software of the Mind. New York: Mcgraw-hill; 2005

[4] Schaufeli WB. Engaging leadership in the job demands-resources model. Career Development International. 2015;**20**:446-463

[5] Hughes DJ, Lee A, Tian AW, Newman A, Legood A. Leadership, creativity, and innovation: A critical review and practical recommendations. The Leadership Quarterly. 2018;**29**(5):549-569

[6] UNCTAD. Relatório de economia criativa 2010: economia criativa uma opção de desenvolvimento [Creative Economy Report 2010: Creative Economy One Development Option]. Brasília: Secretaria da Economia Criativa/Minc [Creative Economy Secretariat/Ministry of Culture]. São Paulo: Itaú Cultural; 2012. p. 424

[7] Amabile TM. A model of creativity and innovation in organizations. Research in Organizational Behavior. 1988;**10**(1):123-167

[8] Amabile TM. Componential Theory of Creativity. In: Kessler EH, editor. Encyclopedia of Management Theory. London: Sage Publications; 2013:134-139. DOI: 10.4135/9781452276090.n42

[9] Alencar EMLS d, Fleith D d S. Contribuições teóricas recentes ao estudo da criatividade [Recent theoretical contributions to the study of creativity]. Psicologia: Teoria e Pesquisa [Psychology: Theory and Research], Brasília. 2003;**19**(1):1-8. Available from: http://www.scielo.br/scielo.php?script=sci_arttext&pid=S0102-37722003000100002&lng=en&nrm=iso. [Accessed: February, 2020]

[10] Sternberg RJ. Psicologia cognitiva [Cognitive Psychology]. 4.ed. Porto Alegre: Artmed; 2008

[11] Sternberg RJ, Lubart TI. Le Creatividad en Una Cultura Conformist: Un Desafio a Las Massas [Creativity in a Conformist Culture: A Challenge for the Crowds]. Buenos Aires: Ediciones Paidós Ibérica S.A; 1997

[12] Simonton, Dean Keith. Creativity—Cognitive, personal, developmental, and social aspects. American Psychologist. Vol. 55, n° 1. 2000. p. 151-158

[13] Sternberg, Robert J. Teoria e Estilos de Pensamento. 2018. Available from: www.robertjsternberg.com/thinking-styles [Accessed: July, 2018]

[14] Ryan R, Deci E. Intrinsic and extrinsic motivations: Classic definitions and new directions. Contemporary Educational Psychology 2000;**25**:54-67. Available from: https://mmrg.pbworks.com/f/Ryan,+Deci+00.pdf. [Accessed: November, 2018]

[15] Ostrower F. Criatividade e processos de criação [Creativity and creation processes]. 30th ed. Petrópolis: edit. Vozes; 2014

[16] Alencar, Eunice M.L Soriano de; Bruno-Faria, Maria de Fátima; Fleith, Denise de Souza. Medidas de

Criatividade [Creativity Measures]. Porto Alegre: Artmed, 2010

[17] Salazar VS, Moraes WFA, Leite ÝVPL. Você tem fome de que? O processo criativo de um chefe de cozinha [Do you have what hunger? The creative process of a chef]. In: XIX SEMEAD-Seminários em Administração [Management Seminar]. 2016

[18] Schmitz PT. A criatividade nas atividades gastronômicas: estudo sobre a criatividade do indivíduo e a sua relação com o ambiente de trabalho [Creativity in gastronomic activities: study on the individual's creativity and its relationship with the work environment], Paula Tarrasconi Schmitz - 2019. Dissertação (Mestrado Em Indústria Criativa [Master in Creative Industry]) – Feevale University. Brasil: Novo Hamburgo. p. 2019

[19] Carvalhal, Felipe. No Ccaminho para uma gestão criativa: a percepção dos gestores da economia criativa sobre suas experiências [On the way to creative management: the perception of creative economy managers about their experiences]. Dissertação Mestrado em Administração [Thesis - Master in Business Administration] – Universidade Federal de Pernambuco, CCSA, 132 folhas, 2016. Available from: https://repositorio.ufpe.br/bitstream/123456789/18949/1/DISSERTA%C3%87%C3%83O%20%282016-02-29%29%20-%20FELIPE%20CARVALHAL.pdf. [Accessed: June, 2022]

[20] Carvalhal F, Muzzio H. Economia criativa e liderança criativa: Uma associação (im) possível? [Creative economy and creative leadership: An (im)possible association?]. Revista Eletrônica de Administração [Electronic Journal of Administration]. 2015;**21**(3):659-688

[21] Inceoglu I, Thomas G, Chu C, Plans D, Gerbasi A. Leadership behavior and employee well-being: An integrated review and a future research agenda. The Leadership Quarterly. 2018;**29**(1):179-202

[22] Van Tuin L, Schaufeli WB, van Rhenen W, Kuiper RM. Business results and well-being: An engaging leadership intervention study. International Journal of Environmental Research and Public Health. 2020;**17**:4515. DOI: 10.3390/ijerph17124515

[23] Rahmadani VG, Schaufeli WB. Engaging leadership and work engagement as moderated by "diuwongke": An Indonesian study. International Journal of Human Resource Management. 2022;**33**(7):1267-1295

[24] Rahmadani VG, Schaufeli WB, Ivanova TY, Osin EN. Basic psychological need satisfaction mediates the relationship between engaging leadership and work engagement: A cross-national study. Human Resource Development Quarterly. 2019;**30**(4):453-471

[25] Jiang K, Lepak DP, Hu J, Baer JC. How does human resource management influence organizational outcomes? A meta-analytic investigation of mediating mechanisms. Academy of Management Journal. 2012a;**55**(6):1264-1294

[26] Lepak DP, Liao H, Chung Y, Harden EE. A conceptual review of human resource management systems in strategic human resource management research. Research in Personnel and Human Resources Management. 2006;**25**(6):217-271

[27] Wiebusch, Andressa. Lima, Valderez Marina do Rosário. Inovação nas práticas pedagógicas no Ensino Superior: possibilidades para promover o engajamento acadêmico [Innovation

in pedagogical practices in Higher Education: possibilities to promote academic engagement]. 2018. Available from: https://repositorio.pucrs.br/dspace/bitstream/10923/14662/2/Inovacao_nas_praticas_pedagogicas_no_Ensino_Superior_possibilidades_para_promover_o_engajamento.pdf. [Accessed: March, 2021]

[28] Macey WH et al. Muito além do comprometimento: como montar equipes que farão sua empresa chegar ao topo [Going Beyond Commitment: How to Build Teams That Will Take Your Company to the Top]. São Paulo, SP: Gente; 2011. p. 207

[29] Florida R. A ascensão da Classe Criativa [The Creative Class]. Porto Alegre: L&PM; 2011

[30] Hansen R, Fabricio A, Rotili LB, Lopes LFD. Inteligência Emocional e Engajamento no Ambiente de Trabalho: Estudo Empírico a Partir de Gestores e Equipes [emotional intelligence and engagement in the workplace: An empirical study based on managers and teams]. Revista Gestão Organizacional [Journal of Organizational Management]. 2018;**11**(1):3-24

[31] Schaufeli W, Dijkstra P, Vazquez AC. O engajamento no trabalho [Work Engagement]. São Paulo: Casa do Psicólogo; 2013